ANNUAL EDITIONS

Assessment and Evaluation 10/11

First Edition

W9-CFK-651

EDITOR

Sandra C. Williamson
Wilmington University

Sandra C. Williamson earned a PhD in educational psychology with an emphasis in instructional technology from Kent State University in 1999. Her research interests focus on cooperative learning/ peer interactions, computer-based instruction, and metacognition.

Boston   Burr Ridge, IL   Dubuque, IA   New York   San Francisco   St. Louis
Bangkok   Bogotá   Caracas   Kuala Lumpur   Lisbon   London   Madrid   Mexico City
Milan   Montreal   New Delhi   Santiago   Seoul   Singapore   Sydney   Taipei   Toronto

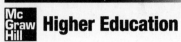

ANNUAL EDITIONS: ASSESSMENT AND EVALUATION 10/11

Published by McGraw-Hill, a business unit of The McGraw-Hill Companies, Inc., 1221 Avenue of the Americas, New York, NY 10020.
Copyright © 2010 by The McGraw-Hill Companies, Inc. All rights reserved. Previous edition(s) 1994–2008. No part of this publication may
be reproduced or distributed in any form or by any means, or stored in a database or retrieval system, without the prior written consent of The
McGraw-Hill Companies, Inc., including, but not limited to, in any network or other electronic storage or transmission, or broadcast for distance
learning.

Some ancillaries, including electronic and print components, may not be available to customers outside the United States.

Annual Editions® is a registered trademark of The McGraw-Hill Companies, Inc.
Annual Editions is published by the **Contemporary Learning Series** group within the McGraw-Hill Higher Education division.

1 2 3 4 5 6 7 8 9 0 QPD/QPD 0 9

ISBN 978–0–07–813589–7
MHID 0–07–813589–3
ISSN 1948–2655

Managing Editor: *Larry Loeppke*
Senior Managing Editor: *Faye Schilling*
Developmental Editor: *David Welsh*
Editorial Coordinator: *Mary Foust*
Editorial Assistant: *Cindy Hedley*
Production Service Assistant: *Rita Hingtgen*
Permissions Coordinator: *DeAnna Dausener*
Senior Marketing Manager: *Julie Keck*
Marketing Communications Specialist: *Mary Klein*
Marketing Coordinator: *Alice Link*
Project Manager: *Joyce Watters*
Design Specialist: *Tara McDermott*
Senior Production Supervisor: *Laura Fuller*
Cover Graphics: *Kristine Jubeck*

Compositor: Laserwords Private Limited
Cover Image: © Image source/Alamay/RF (inset); © Comstock/PictureQuest/RF (background)

Library in Congress Cataloging-in-Publication Data
Main entry under title: Annual Editions: Assessment and Evaluation 10/11
   1. State and Local Government—Periodicals. I. Williamson, Sandra C., *comp*. II. Title: Assessment and Evaluation.
658'.05

www.mhhe.com

Editors/Advisory Board

Members of the Advisory Board are instrumental in the final selection of articles for each edition of ANNUAL EDITIONS. Their review of articles for content, level, currentness, and appropriateness provides critical direction to the editor and staff. We think that you will find their careful consideration well reflected in this volume.

Dana Rothlisberger
Towson University Music Department

Jason E. Rybinski
Indiana University Northwest

Jerome Shaw
University of California Santa Cruz

Judy Sherwood
Brown Mackie College South Bend

Bradley Sidle
Antioch University McGregor

Howard R. Smith
Pittsburg State University

Louise M. Soares
University of New Haven

R. William Sowders
Johns Hopkins University

Marsha Speck
Arizona State University at West Campus

Cathleen Spinelli
Saint Joseph's University

Jerald Thomas
Aurora University

Rachel Turniansky
Center for Jewish Education

Marilyn Verna
St. Francis College

Molly Vitale
Misericordia University

Justin J. Wageman
North Dakota State University

Rhea Walker
Winona State University

Catheryn J. Weitman
Barry University

Amelia Wenk
Michigan State University

Judith Yoho
Lock Haven University of PA

Ming Zhang
Central Michigan University

Preface

In publishing ANNUAL EDITIONS we recognize the enormous role played by the magazines, newspapers, and journals of the public press in providing current, first-rate educational information in a broad spectrum of interest areas. Many of these articles are appropriate for students, researchers, and professionals seeking accurate, current material to help bridge the gap between principles and theories and the real world. These articles, however, become more useful for study when those of lasting value are carefully collected, organized, indexed, and reproduced in a low-cost format, which provides easy and permanent access when the material is needed. That is the role played by ANNUAL EDITIONS.

Educational assessment and evaluation are extremely important components of the learning and teaching process. Assessment attempts to determine how well students are learning, and to provide information about the effectiveness of schooling and the educational system. To that end, educators seek to be skilled in knowing how to create or select assessment activities in order to collect evidence or information about student learning (assessment), make judgments about student performance (evaluation), and assign some numerical or symbolic value that represents a quantitative description (measurement). These three processes ideally supplement and complement the teaching and learning process along with a number of other activities and decisions teachers do and make.

The articles in the volume support the premise that assessment and evaluation have the potential to be vital components of the education process and that the practices of assessment and evaluation may yield information for improving student learning. Instruction and assessment are discussed as being closely related and evaluation is embedded within the relationship. The editor chose articles that emphasize the importance of planning instruction and assessment simultaneously.

Current assessment practices influence classroom interactions; shaping people's understanding about what is important to learn, and what learning is. Articles in the book support the idea that educators are continuous learners as they seek ways to support student learning. Many of the articles have case studies and examples of instructional and assessment strategies that can lead to discussions about teaching and learning. In other articles, the content may provide a basis for an activity that can possibly help pre-candidate teachers and professional educators to understand an assessment technique more thoroughly, or to learn a new assessment method. Current topics and controversial issues are included to stimulate conversation, while challenging present day practices and assumptions. The editor encourages readers to include in their discussion topics of equity, technology-based assessments, and ways to bridge research and practice so that transformations in assessment will occur in a timely manner. At the beginning of each unit, activities across the cognitive domain are recommended. No prior knowledge of measurement or statistics is required to understand the material. The articles are intended to provide ideas, suggestions, methods, and techniques that can be used to make decisions that enhance student learning.

Annual Editions: Assessment and Evaluation 10/11 is divided into seven units. Each unit has an overview that provides information about the topic and an explanation of how the unit articles are related. In addition, there are thought-provoking questions and Internet sites that provide useful and current information for extending discussions. The first unit, *Standards, Accountability, and Issues,* presents a short historical context for the test-based reform movement and issues that are central to the topic of assessment and evaluation. The first section encourages readers to consider the implications associated with the adoption of a nation-wide, standards-based curriculum for teaching and professional development. Readers may be interested in conducting a self-assessment using the *Standards for Teacher Competence in Educational Assessment.* These standards can serve as a foundation for strengthening one's knowledge and skills about the assessment of students.

The second unit, entitled *Instruction and Assessment,* includes articles that discuss the relationship between an assessment system and instruction. The articles address ways to align instruction with assessment activities. Tips are given on two topics: how to design instruction to collect information for continual evaluation of instructional choices and ways to engage students in learning.

Monitor Student Learning is the third unit that addresses the continual assessment and evaluation process. Choosing an appropriate assessment strategy depends upon the purpose for evaluating a student and its location in the instructional process. The articles in this unit discuss two types of assessments: formative and summative assessments. Homework as an assessment strategy is also suggested.

The topic for the fourth unit is *Performance Assessments.* Often standards emphasize an actual performance of a complex task that has many components. Performance assessments are one method of measuring multifaceted and complex-problem solving learning outcomes. The articles in this collection describe methods currently used to integrate performance assessment activities into a teaching practice, the limitations associated with these types of assessments, and different types of scoring guides.

The topic *Data Driven Decisions* in unit five is a relatively new term in the education setting. Seeking to determine how well students are learning and their academic changes over time, administrators, teachers, and state department personnel are collecting and analyzing various types of data to guide a range of decisions. The articles present ways educators are attempting to interpret and use data results to make instructional decisions.

The sixth unit, *Communication, Grading, and Reporting*, addresses issues and concerns about grading. Communication is the common link between grading, reporting systems, and feedback. The topic, feedback, addresses response statements teachers can use to inform students about their learning strengths and needs, as well as the cognitive and motivational aspects associated with effective comments.

The articles in the seventh unit address the topics, *Self-Assessment and Motivation.* These two components are vital for guiding students to become independent, autonomous learners. High-stakes testing is discussed as a potential factor that may hinder motivation.

The collection of articles presents information about the process of assessing and evaluating student learning along with posing stimulating questions or issues concerned with existing practices. The articles were selected based on current ideas and usefulness to the education community. Your responses to the selection and organization of materials are appreciated. Please complete and return the postage-paid article rating form on the last page of the book.

Sandal. Williamson

Sandra C. Williamson
Editor

Contents

UNIT 1
Standards, Accountability, and Issues

UNIT 2
Instruction and Assessment

The concepts in bold italics are developed in the article. For further expansion, please refer to the Topic Guide.

UNIT 3
Monitor Student Learning

The concepts in bold italics are developed in the article. For further expansion, please refer to the Topic Guide.

UNIT 4
Performance Assessments

The concepts in bold italics are developed in the article. For further expansion, please refer to the Topic Guide.

UNIT 5
Data Driven Decisions

The concepts in bold italics are developed in the article. For further expansion, please refer to the Topic Guide.

UNIT 6
Communication, Grading, and Reporting

The concepts in bold italics are developed in the article. For further expansion, please refer to the Topic Guide.

UNIT 7
Self-Assessment and Motivation

The concepts in bold italics are developed in the article. For further expansion, please refer to the Topic Guide.

Correlation Guide

The *Annual Editions* series provides students with convenient, inexpensive access to current, carefully selected articles from the public press. **Annual Editions: Assessment and Evaluation 10/11** is an easy-to-use reader that presents articles on important topics such as *poverty and achievement, curriculum mapping, data use,* and many more. For more information on *Annual Editions* and other *McGraw-Hill Contemporary Learning Series* titles, visit www.mhcls.com.

This convenient guide matches the units in **Annual Editions: Assessment and Evaluation 10/11** with the corresponding chapters in three of our best-selling McGraw-Hill Education textbooks by Airasian/Russell, Green/Johnson, and Musial et al.

Annual Editions: Assessment and Evaluation 10/11	Classroom Assessment, 6/e by Airasian/Russell	Assessment is Essential by Green/Johnson	Foundations of Meaningful Educational Assessment by Musial et al.
Unit 1: Standards, Accountability, and Issues	**Chapter 1:** The Breadth of Classroom Assessment	**Chapter 1:** Why Is Assessment Essential? **Chapter 11:** Large-Scale Standardized Tests and the Classroom	**Chapter 1:** The Nature of Assessment **Chapter 3:** The Social Foundations of Assessment **Chapter 4:** Assessment **Chapter 12:** Using Standardized Achievement Tests as Assessments
Unit 2: Instruction and Assessment	**Chapter 4:** Assessment During Instruction **Chapter 11:** Computer-Based Technology and Classroom Assessment	**Chapter 12:** Tying it All Together **Chapter 5:** Progress Monitoring **Chapter 11:** Large-Scale Standardized Tests and the Classroom	**Chapter 2:** The Psychological Foundations of Assessment **Chapter 7:** Assessment through Observation and Interview **Chapter 14:** Exceptionality and Assessment
Unit 3: Monitor Student Learning	**Chapter 4:** Assessment During Instruction **Chapter 9:** Grading	**Chapter 5:** Progress Monitoring **Chapter 10:** Grading and Communicating about Student Achievement	**Chapter 4:** Assessment **Chapter 10:** Developing Grading Procedures
Unit 4: Performance Assessments	**Chapter 8:** Performance Assessments	**Chapter 9:** Teacher-Made Assessments	**Chapter 8:** Performance-Based Assessment **Chapter 15:** Technology and Assessment
Unit 5: Data Driven Decisions	**Chapter 1:** The Breadth of Classroom Assessment	**Chapter 5:** Progress Monitoring **Chapter 11:** Large-Scale Standardized Tests and the Classroom	**Chapter 10:** Developing Grading Procedures **Chapter 15:** Technology and Assessment
Unit 6: Communication, Grading, and Reporting	**Chapter 7:** Improving Achievement Tests **Chapter 9:** Grading	**Chapter 2:** Learning Goals **Chapter 10:** Grading and Communicating about Student Achievement	**Chapter 10:** Developing Grading Procedures
Unit 7: Self-Assessment and Motivation	**Chapter 4:** Assessment During Instruction	**Chapter 5:** Progress Monitoring **Chapter 4:** Formative Assessment **Chapter 12:** Tying it All Together	**Chapter 2:** The Psychological Foundations of Assessment **Chapter 16:** Reflective Self-Assessment

Topic Guide

This topic guide suggests how the selections in this book relate to the subjects covered in your course. You may want to use the topics listed on these pages to search the Web more easily.

On the following pages a number of websites have been gathered specifically for this book. They are arranged to reflect the units of this Annual Editions reader. You can link to these sites by going to *http://www.mhcls.com*.

All the articles that relate to each topic are listed below the bold-faced term.

Accountability
1. Assessments and Accountability (Condensed version)
3. Assessment around the World
27. Testing and Assessment 101

Achievement
5. Schools, Poverty, and the Achievement Gap
17. Homework: A Few Practice Arrows
25. First Things First: Demystifying Data Analysis
34. Grades as Valid Measures of Academic Achievement of Classroom Learning

Alignment
6. Making Benchmark Testing Work

Alternative assessments
22. A Teacher's Guide to Alternative Assessment: Taking the First Steps

Attitudes
38. Self-Assessment through Rubrics
39. Launching Self-Directed Learners

Child development
32. Partnerships for Learning: Conferencing with Families

Collaboration/Communication
8. Curriculum Mapping: Building Collaboration and Communication
35. Grading to Communicate

Conferences
31. Developing Teacher-Parent Partnerships across Cultures: Effective Parent Conferences
32. Partnerships for Learning: Conferencing with Families
33. Student-Led Parent-Teacher Conferences

Cultural awareness
8. Curriculum Mapping: Building Collaboration and Communication
9. Developing Standards-Based Curricula and Assessments: Lessons from the Field
12. Engineering Successful Inclusion in Standards-Based Urban Classrooms
18. Using Curriculum-Based Measurement to Improve Achievement
31. Developing Teacher-Parent Partnerships across Cultures: Effective Parent Conferences

Data
18. Using Curriculum-Based Measurement to Improve Achievement
24. Using Data to Differentiate Instruction
25. First Things First: Demystifying Data Analysis

Decision-making
19. Research Matters/How Student Progress Monitoring Improves Instruction

Differentiated instruction
24. Using Data to Differentiate Instruction

Electronic portfolios
23. Digital-Age Assessment: E-Portfolios Are the Wave of the Future

Evaluation
15. Classroom Assessment: Minute by Minute, Day by Day
19. Research Matters/How Student Progress Monitoring Improves Instruction
27. Testing and Assessment 101
37. Helping Students Understand Assessment

Family conferences
31. Developing Teacher-Parent Partnerships across Cultures: Effective Parent Conferences
32. Partnerships for Learning: Conferencing with Families
33. Student-Led Parent-Teacher Conferences

Feedback
30. Feedback That Fits

Formative assessments
13. The Best Value in Formative Assessment
17. Homework: A Few Practice Arrows
25. First Things First: Demystifying Data Analysis
30. Feedback That Fits
37. Helping Students Understand Assessment

Grading
16. Seven Practices for Effective Learning
20. Teaching with Rubrics: The Good, the Bad, and the Ugly
34. Grades as Valid Measures of Academic Achievement of Classroom Learning
35. Grading to Communicate
36. Making the Grade in Middle School

High-stakes tests
2. Why Has High-Stakes Testing So Easily Slipped into Contemporary American Life?
3. Assessment around the World
4. Are Standards Preventing Good Teaching?

Homework
17. Homework: A Few Practice Arrows

Inclusion
12. Engineering Successful Inclusion in Standards-Based Urban Classrooms

International trends
3. Assessment around the World

Instruction
10. Assessing Problem-Solving Thought

Internet References

The following Internet sites have been selected to support the articles found in this reader. These sites were available at the time of publication. However, because websites often change their structure and content, the information listed may no longer be available. We invite you to visit *http://www.mhcls.com* for easy access to these sites.

Annual Editions: Assessment and Evaluation 10/11

General Sources

U. S. Department of Education
http://www.ed.gov/nclb/landing.jhtml

The government website has information about the No Child Left Behind Act of 2001 and the reauthorization of the Elementary and Secondary Education Act (ESEA) signed into law on January 8, 2002 by President Bush. The website has information about the four principles which form the basic premise of the law: accountability for results; more choices for parents; greater local control and flexibility; and an emphasis on doing what works based on scientific research.

American Council on Education
http://www.acenet.edu/resources/policy-research/

The American Council on Education is a major coordinating body for all the nation's higher education institutions. It seeks to provide leadership and a unifying voice on key higher education issues and to influence public policy through advocacy, research, and program initiatives.

Education Commission of the States (ECS)
http://www.ecs.org/

ECS is the only nation-wide interstate compact devoted to education. The website is the nation's most extensive on-line resource for education policy.

ERIC—Education Resources Information Center
http://www.eric.ed.gov/

ERIC provides free access to more than 1.2 million bibliographic records of journal articles and other education-related materials and, if available, includes links to full text. ERIC is sponsored by the U.S. Department of Education, Institute of Education Sciences (IES).

Clearinghouse on Assessment and Evaluation
http://ericae.net/

The Clearinghouse provides information concerning educational assessment, evaluation, and research methodology.

Phi Delta Kappan
http://www.pdkintl.org/kappan/kappan.htm

Phi Delta Kappan, the professional journal for education, addresses issues of policy and practice for educators at all levels. Advocating research-based school reform, the *Kappan* provides a forum for debate on controversial subjects. Published since 1915, the journal appears monthly September through June.

Northwest Regional Educational Library: Center for Research, Evaluation, and Assessment
http://www.nwrel.org/assessment/

Since 1966, the Northwest Regional Educational Laboratory (NWREL) has been working with schools and communities to improve education for children, youth, and adults. NWREL's Center for Research, Evaluation, and Assessment serves anyone who needs data-based information to make decisions, improve effectiveness, or document work—from principals, teachers, and superintendents to decision-makers in state, federal, corporate, and nonprofit organizations.

National Middle School Association
http://www.nmsa.org/

The National Middle School Association was founded in 1973. The organization is comprised of educators in secondary and higher education, parents, and community leaders who are interested in the educational and developmental needs of young adolescents. NMSA provides professional development, journals, books, research, and other valuable information to assist educators on an ongoing basis. The organization publishes the highly acclaimed *Middle School Journal* and *Middle Ground* magazine to support members throughout the year. The website offers information for professional development and conferences.

National Association for the Education of Young Children
http://www.naeyc.org/

The National Association for the Education of Young Children (NAEYC) was founded in 1926 and remains one of the largest, most prestigious organizations dedicated to improving the well-being of all young children, with particular focus on the quality of educational and developmental services for all children from birth through age 8. NAEYC is committed to becoming an increasingly high performing and inclusive organization.

National Education Association
http://www.nea.org/index.html

The National Education Association (NEA), the nation's largest professional employee organization, is committed to advancing the cause of public education. The organization has 3.2 million members working at every level of education—from pre-school to university graduate programs. NEA has affiliate organizations in every state and in more than 14,000 communities across the United States. The NEA is a volunteer-based organization supported by a network of staff at the local, state, and national levels.

http://www.nea.org/aboutnea/code.html

Code of Ethics of the Education Profession

International Society for Technology in Education
http://www.iste.org/

The International Society for Technology in Education (ISTE) organization provides leadership and service to improve teaching, learning, and school leadership by advancing the effective use of technology in PK–12 and teacher education. The organization home of the National Educational Technology Standards (NETS), the Center for Applied Research in Educational Technology (CARET), and the National Educational Computing Conference (NECC), ISTE represents more than 85,000 professionals worldwide. It supports its members with information, networking opportunities, and guidance as they face the challenge of transforming education.

The Council of Chief State School Officers
http://www.ccsso.org/

The Council of Chief State School Officers (CCSSO) is a nonpartisan, nation-wide, nonprofit organization of public officials who head departments of elementary and secondary education in the states, the District of Columbia, the Department of Defense Education Activity, and five U.S. extra-state jurisdictions. CCSSO

Internet References

provides leadership, advocacy, and technical assistance on major educational issues. The Council seeks member consensus on major educational issues and expresses its views to civic and professional organizations.

The Joint Committee on Standards for Educational Evaluation
http://www.wmich.edu/evalctr/jc/

Created in 1975, the Joint Committee is a coalition of major professional associations concerned with the quality of evaluation. The Joint Committee is housed at The Evaluation Center, Western Michigan University. The Joint Committee has published three sets of standards for evaluations that are now widely recognized. The Personnel Evaluation Standards was published in 1988.

Project Zero Research Projects: Assessment
http://pzweb.harvard.edu/Research/ResearchAssess.htm

The on-line organization has posted information about Project Zero's assessment projects. The website has multiple links that provide manuscripts about assessment research.

Practical Assessment, Research, and Evaluation (PARE)
http://pareonline.net/

Practical Assessment, Research, and Evaluation (PARE) is a scholarly on-line journal website that features refereed articles that have implications for practice in education, certification, or licensure.

UNIT 1: Standards, Accountability, and Issues

Standards for Teacher Competence in Educational Assessment of Students
http://www.unl.edu/buros/bimm/html/article3.html

Seven *standards* provide the professional community with a set of guidelines for the purpose of designing professional development and teacher preparation programs. Educators and precandidate teachers can use the standards as a self-assessment instrument to evaluate their knowledge and skills about student assessment.

Code of Fair Testing Practices in Education
http://www.apa.org/science/fairtestcode.html

The document is a set of standards for educational test developers and users in four areas: developing/selecting tests, interpreting scores, striving for fairness, and informing test takers. The Code is a guide for professionals in fulfilling their obligation to provide and use tests that are fair to all test takers regardless of age, gender, disability, race, ethnicity, national origin, religion, sexual orientation, linguistic background, or other personal characteristics.

Fair Test: The National Center for Fair and Open Testing: Principles and Indicators for Student Assessment Systems
http://www.fairtest.org/principles-and-indicators-student-assessment-syste

Fair Test is funded by grants from the Bay and Paul Foundation, Ford Foundation, Polk Brothers Foundation, Schott Foundation, United Church of Christ, Wiener Educational Foundation, Woods Fund of Chicago, and many individual donors. The National

Center for Fair & Open Testing (FairTest) advances quality education and equal opportunity by promoting fair, open, valid, and educationally beneficial evaluations of students, teachers, and schools.

Center for the Study of Testing, Evaluation, and Educational Policy (CEEP)
http://www.bc.edu/research/csteep/
http://www.bc.edu/research/intasc/library/toolsforteaching.shtml

Center for the Study of Testing, Evaluation, and Educational Policy (CSTEEP) is an educational research organization located at Boston College in the School of Education. Since its inception in 1980, CSTEEP has conducted research on: testing, evaluation, and public policy; studies to improve school assessment practices, and international comparative research.

Next Generation Accountability Models: Principles from Interviews
http://www.ecs.org/clearinghouse/40/29/4029.htm

Principles for accountability emerged from interviews conducted by policy researchers from the Education Commission of the States (ECS) with 15 members of the National Forum on Accountability and 15 other national experts.

National Center for Research on Evaluation, Standards, and Student Testing
http://www.cse.ucla.edu/

The Center for the Study of Evaluation (CSE) and the National Center for Research on Evaluation, Standards, and Student Testing (CRESST) located at the University of California, Los Angeles, contributes to the development of scientifically-based evaluation and testing techniques.

Teaching to Academic Standards
http://www.thirteen.org/edonline/concept2class/standards/index.html

Concept to Classroom is an online series of FREE, award-winning professional development workshops covering important and timely topics in education. The workshops are intended for teachers, administrators, librarians, or anyone interested in education.

Goals 2000 Legislation and Related Items
http://www.ed.gov/G2K/index.html

Visit the site to access archived information about legislation concerning Goals 2000.

The National Education Goals Panel
http://govinfo.library.unt.edu/negp/

The National Education Goals Panel is an independent executive branch agency of the federal government charged with monitoring national and state progress toward the National Education Goals.

Organisation for Economic Co-operation and Development/The Programme for International Student Assessment (PISA)
http://www.pisa.oecd.org/

The Programme for International Student Assessment (PISA) is an internationally standardized assessment that was jointly developed by participating countries and administered to 15-year-olds in schools. The website has information about countries who participate, what topics/content are assessed, and assessment results.

Internet References

UNIT 2: Instruction and Assessment

Critical Issues: Using Technology to Improve Student Achievement
http://www.ncrel.org/sdrs/areas/issues/methods/technlgy/te800.htm#context

The North Central Educational Laboratory (NCREL), now known as the Regional Educational Laboratory Midwest (REL Midwest), is associated with Learning Point Associates. The regional laboratory supports educational endeavors.

Center for Comprehensive Reform and Improvement
http://www.centerforcsri.org/

The Center for Comprehensive School Reform and Improvement is funded by the U.S. Department of Education and administered by Learning Point Associates. Learning Point Associates is a nonprofit education research and consulting organization that helps clients to achieve breakthroughs that improve teaching and learning.

Practical Assessment, Research, and Evaluation (PARE)
http://pareonline.net/

Practical Assessment, Research, and Evaluation (PARE) is a scholarly on-line journal website that features refereed articles that have implications for practice in education, assessment, research, and certification/licensure.

teAchnology
http://www.teach-nology.com/currenttrends/alternative_assessment/

The website is supported by Technology, Inc. Their mission is to provide services designed to support educators in effectively incorporating technology in teaching and learning.

Awesome Library for Teachers
http://www.awesomelibrary.org/Office/Teacher/Assessment_Information/Assessment_Information.html

This url is a weblink to a variety of assessment strategies for teachers. The Evaluation and Development Institute (EDI) offers the database through the Web portal "Awesome Library."

inTASC (Tools for Teaching)
http://www.bc.edu/research/intasc/library/toolsforteaching.shtml

The website has interactive tools that allow students to explore basic statistics by building data sets. The website was developed to teach concepts visually.

National Center for Educational Achievement
http://www.just4kids.org/en/

The National Center for Educational Achievement (NCEA) is a non-profit, non-partisan organization and the national sponsor of Just for the Kids (JFTK). Our goal is to support efforts to reach excellence in education—to raise academic expectations and to promote the practices that will help more

Framework for 21st Century Learning
http://www.21stcenturyskills.org/index.php?option=com_content&task = view&id=254&Itemid=120

The framework presents a holistic view of 21st century teaching and learning that combines a discrete focus on 21st century student outcomes (a blending of specific skills, content knowledge, expertise, and literacies) with innovative support systems to help students master the multi-dimensional abilities required of them in the 21st century.

UNIT 3: Monitor Student Learning

National Center for Postsecondary Improvement
http://www.stanford.edu/group/ncpi/unspecified/assessment_states/stateReports.html

The National Center for Postsecondary Improvement (NCPI) strives to provide leadership for the transformation and improvement of postsecondary education—including research universities and comprehensive colleges to community colleges and vocational-technical schools.

Improving America's Schools: A Newsletter on Issues in School Reform
http://www.ed.gov/pubs/IASA/newsletters/assess/index.html

This website has newsletters for educators and families that provide information on key topics in educational reform. Issues focus on critical reform elements and describe current perspectives on assessment and accountability.

Organisation for Economic Co-operation and Development/The Programme for International Student Assessment (PISA)
http://www.pisa.oecd.org/pages/0,3417,en_32252351_32235907_1_1_1_1_1,00.html

The Programme for International Student Assessment (PISA) is an internationally standardized assessment that was jointly developed by participating countries and administered to 15-year-olds in schools. The website has information about countries who participate, topics assessed, and assessment results.

Teacher Vision
http://www.teachervision.fen.com/special-education/resource/5350.html

The website is part of the Family Education Network supported by Pearson—the international media company that owns several of the world's leading education and financial publishing companies.

School Improvement in Maryland
http://mdk12.org/index.html

The School Improvement website is designed to provide access to information about standards, assessment, instruction, and data analysis. The Maryland State Department of Education maintains the site.

Delaware Science Comprehensive Assessment Program
http://www.scienceassessment.org/

The website is part of the Delaware Department of Education. The Delaware Comprehensive Assessment Program is supported by grants.

Kathy Schrock's Guide for Educators
http://school.discoveryeducation.com/schrockguide/assess.html

Sponsored by Discovery Education, Kathy Schrock has compiled assessment and rubric information for teachers.

4 Teachers Family of Tools
http://www.4teachers.org/tools/

Website is a collection of resources dedicated to providing educational materials that use technology to improve instruction.

Looking at Student Work
http://www.lasw.org/

The website represents an association of individuals and educational organizations that focus on looking at student work to strengthen connections between instruction, curriculum, and other aspects of school life to students' learning.

Internet References

UNIT 4: Performance Assessments

Trends in Assessment Research
http://pareonline.net/

Practical Assessment, Research, and Evaluation (PARE) is a scholarly on-line journal website that features refereed articles that have implications for practice in education, certification, or licensure.

Performance Assessment
http://performanceassessment.org/consortium/index.html

The Performance Assessment website is a coalition of high schools across New York State which have pioneered the creation of educational communities synonymous with active student learning, exemplary professional development, and innovative curriculum and teaching strategies for 21st century students.

Alternative Assessments
North Central Regional Educational Laboratory
http://www.ncrel.org/sdrs/areas/issues/methods/assment/as8lk30.htm

Rubistar
http://rubistar.4teachers.org/index.php

Rubistar is a web-based generated rubric generator. The website is supported by The Advanced Learning Technologies project at the University of Kansas Center for Research on Learning.

Authentic Assessment Tool Box
http://jonathan.mueller.faculty.noctrl.edu/toolbox/standards.htm

Jon Mueller is Professor of Psychology at North Central College in Naperville, IL. For more than ten years he has taught a graduate course entitled "Authentic Assessment Strategies for the Classroom" as part of North Central's Master of Education program.

New Horizons for Learning
http://www.newhorizons.org/strategies/assess/front_assess.htm

A website that offers information about alternative assessments and instruction. New Horizons for Learning has often been a "launching pad" for new educational organizations and projects.

UNIT 5: Data Driven Decisions

PDA for Learning
http://www.ed.gov/about/offices/list/os/technology/plan/2004/site/stories/edlite-Chicago2.html

The website discusses the collaborative partnership between the Chicago Public Schools' Office of Technology Services eLearning (OTS eLearning) and the Office of Literacy to use personal digital assistants (PDAs) and a Web-based data management tool. The project goal is to streamline assessments so teachers can make data-driven decisions to improve instruction and enhance student achievement.

Assessment and Accountability Comprehensive Center
http://www.aacompcenter.org/cs/aacc/print/htdocs/aacc/home.htm

WestEd and the National Center for Research on Evaluation, Standards, and Student Testing (CRESST) joined together to form the Assessment and Accountability Comprehensive Center (AACC) to help states and districts.

WestEd
http://www.wested.org/cs/we/print/docs/we/home.htm

A nonprofit research, development, and service agency that works with education and other service communities.

United States Department of Education: My Child's Academic Success, No Child Left Behind: A Parent's Guide
http://www.ed.gov/parents/academic/involve/nclbguide/parentsguide.html

The website provides facts and terms every parent should know about the NCLB Act.

UNIT 6: Communication, Grading, and Reporting

GradeConnect
http://www.gradeconnect.com/front/index.php

GradeConnect is an on-line course management system that streamlines and enhances communication between teachers, students, and parents.

Engrade
http://www.engrade.com/

Explore the free web-based reporting system, Engrade. The website has web-based tools that allow teachers to set up grade books and produce progress reports, and parents and students can access personal information.

Scholastic: Communicating with Parents and Families
http://www2.scholastic.com/browse/parentsHome.jsp

Scholastic Magazine provides a website dedicated to family involvement.

Education World
http://www.education-world.com/a_curr/strategy/strategy046.shtm

This site contains web-based teacher resources dedicated to assisting educators interested in integrating web-based programs into the classroom.

National Parent-Teacher Association
http://www.pta.org/

Parent Teacher Association (PTA) website provides support, information, and resources to families focused on the health and education of children.

UNIT 7: Self-Assessment and Motivation

ALPS, Active Learning Practice for Schools
http://learnweb.harvard.edu/alps/tfu/info3f.cfm

Active Learning Practice for Schools is an electronic community dedicated to the improvement and advancement of educational instruction and practice. The mission of the organization is to create an on-line collaborative environment between teachers and administrators from around the world with educational researchers, professors, and curriculum designers at Harvard's Graduate School of Education and Project Zero.

Looking at Student Work
http://www.lasw.org/

The website is supported by an association of individuals and educational organizations that focus on looking at student work to strengthen connections between instruction, curriculum, and other aspects of school life to students' learning. This association grew out of a meeting on "Examining Student Work and School Change" held in Chicago in October 1998, hosted by the Chicago Learning Collaborative and the Annenberg Institute for School Reform.

Self-Assessment in Portfolios
http://www.ncrel.org/sdrs/areas/issues/students/learning/lr2port.htm

North Central Regional Educational Laboratory

UNIT 1

Standards, Accountability, and Issues

Unit Selections

1. **Assessments and Accountability** (Condensed version), Robert L. Linn
2. **Why Has High-Stakes Testing So Easily Slipped into Contemporary American Life?,** Sharon L. Nichols and David C. Berliner
3. **Assessment around the World,** Iris C. Rotberg
4. **Are Standards Preventing Good Teaching?,** Clair T. Berube
5. **Schools, Poverty, and the Achievement Gap,** Ben Levin

Key Points to Consider

- Can adopting an assessment system affect change in the educational system?
- Can educators implement an educational system that will achieve national quality or maintain levels of quality?
- Can a standardized education system be implemented globally? Is a standards-based education system important in a global society or is the philosophy over-rated?
- What are the salient points between equity in income, education, and economic performance?
- Discuss ways that schools can reduce the effects of poverty, or if this philosophy is possible.
- Define the term assessment and describe effective and ineffective assessment practices.
- Define the following terms: Title I, Test-Based Educational Reform, Competency Testing, Standards-Based Reform
- Compare Content and Performance Standards from different states and discuss the terminology each state uses.
- Review Rotberg's assumptions on global accountability and discuss if her arguments are valid.
- Conduct a self-assessment using the Standards for Teacher Competence in Educational Assessment of Students to develop a professional development plan. Standards are located at this website: http://www.unl.edu/buros/bimm/html/article3.html
- Conduct an analysis of a standardized test using the **Code of Fair Testing Practices in Education to determine the test developers have followed the code.** Standards are located at this website http://www.apa.org/science/fairtestcode.html

Student Website
www.mhcls.com

Internet References

Standards for Teacher Competence in Educational Assessment of Students
   http://www.unl.edu/buros/bimm/html/article3.html

Code of Fair Testing Practices in Education
   http://www.apa.org/science/fairtestcode.html

Fair Test: The National Center for Fair and Open Testing: Principles and Indicators for Student Assessment Systems
   http://www.fairtest.org/principles-and-indicators-student-assessment-syste

Center for the Study of Testing, Evaluation, and Educational Policy (CEEP)
   http://www.bc.edu/research/csteep/
   http://www.bc.edu/research/intasc/library/toolsforteaching.shtml

Next Generation Accountability Models: Principles from Interviews
   http://www.ecs.org/clearinghouse/40/29/4029.htm

National Center for Research on Evaluation, Standards, and Student Testing
   http://www.cse.ucla.edu/

Teaching to Academic Standards
   http://www.thirteen.org/edonline/concept2class/standards/index.html

Goals 2000 Legislation and Related Items
   http://www.ed.gov/G2K/index.html

The National Education Goals Panel
   http://govinfo.library.unt.edu/negp/

Organisation for Economic Co-operation and Development/ The Programme for International Student Assessment (PISA)
   http://www.pisa.oecd.org/

History and Context

The mention of standards-based curricula and accountability systems often stimulates debates and lively conversations among educators. Questions that may be discussed include: "What should be learned?", "Do current monitoring practices stifle innovative thinking and creativity?", "What are fair testing policies?", "Is the test biased?", and "How are assessment results being used?" Standards-based curriculum is a fairly new topic, only being about twenty-years old. In contrast, educational testing and accountability have been around for a while. Policymakers have long required students and teachers to be accountable. Let's examine how test-based reform movements have evolved since the middle of the 19th century.

As early as 1914, spelling and mathematics tests were administered at public schools in Massachusetts holding the schools accountable. Testing gained momentum following both World Wars and accelerated during the 1960s. The Elementary and Secondary Education Act of 1965, known as Title I, is probably the first federally supported act that sought to recognize **disparities in educational opportunities and student performances** while demanding some type of accountability to policymakers. Then in the 1970s and 1980s, **minimum competency testing** requirements were implemented due to the widespread perception that students lacked basic skills. A huge wave of reform followed the 1983 report, *A Nation at Risk: The Imperative for Education Reform,* issued by the National Commission on Excellence in Education. The report concentrated on the shortcomings of student achievement and recommended reforms. Testing became the central method of accountability and there was tremendous pressure on the education community to "increase test scores."

Standards and accountability systems became an integral part of the education reform movement with the *Goals 2000: Educate America Act.* Focused on establishing high academic standards for all children, the act transformed education as professional experts concentrated on the development of **content** and **performance standards** and assessment systems aligned to these guidelines. Coinciding with the standards-based movement was a shift in thinking about ways to evaluate student achievement and performance. New approaches such as **authentic assessments, alternative assessments,** and **performance assessments** focused on problem solving tasks and the thinking skills aspect of learning while attempting to emphasize that traditional testing methods and accountability should be viewed differently.

Federal involvement, accountability issues, statewide testing, and standards-based curriculum continue to be the focus with educators, policymakers, and families. The *No Child Left Behind Act of 2001* accentuates that all children have a fair, equal, and significant opportunity to obtain a high-quality education and reach proficiency on challenging statewide achievement standards. The act mandates a stronger accountability system, annual improvement reports, rewards and sanctions, and highly qualified teachers in every classroom. In terms of accountability,

© Comstock/PictureQuest

states are now required to administer tests yearly and biennially and to develop a plan for holding schools responsible for student achievement.

The public and policymakers concerned with the welfare of our society have created the demand for more testing. Yet, whether to test or not to test is a narrowly focused controversial issue when one begins to examine major concerns associated with the aspect of testing, assessment, and evaluation. Topics that can stimulate discussion might include: (a) assessment formats, (b) interpretation and appropriate use of data results, (c) biases for minorities and gender fairness, (d) reliability and validity issues, (e) the effects of testing on students, and (f) teaching to the test.

Standards

Standards, goals, and objectives are all descriptive statements of learning expectations for students. There are two types of standards: **content standards** and **performance standards.** Content standards specify the knowledge and skills. **Performance standards** align with content standards by providing 'evidence of' and the 'quality of the performance' (Linn, 2001).

Since the development of a national set of standards, nearly every state has adopted or designed a set of state-wide standards that served as the basis for developing assessments: that are intended to be aligned with instruction. State-wide standards vary in terminology and format because state departments have the flexibility and freedom to establish their own set of academic standards. Questions such as, "Where do I find state standards?", "Does a particular state have an assessment system?", and "What should I know about a particular set of content standards for my discipline?" can be topics of discussions. Whether you are a precandidate teacher or a professional educator, it would be beneficial for you to become knowledgeable about the standards in the state in which you plan to teach or are currently teaching. Often state-wide standards are posted on state department of education websites. In many states, the content standards serve as a basis for developing state-wide tests.

Assessing students will become an integral part of your instructional activity. Naturally, you will want to be competent in all aspects of planning, choosing or designing, administering, and reporting assessment activities. To help you become knowledgeable, or to assess your current level of assessment competence, the American Federation of Teachers, the National Council on Measurement in Education, and the National Education Association (1990) published *Standards for Teacher Competence in Educational Assessment of Students.* These standards are located at the Buros Institute of Mental Measures website: http://www.unl.edu/buros/bimm/html/article3.html.

Accountability Systems

Standards-based curricula is currently providing the foundation for an accountability system and assessment activities. Steeped in this policy is the belief that schools have the capacity to measure the standards, and testing is the best way to evaluate a student and school performance. Embedded in this system of evaluation are conditions of rewards or sanction, commonly referred to as **high-stakes accountability** (Linn, 2001).

The *No Child Left Behind Act of 2001* focuses on 'every child' getting a similar education and 'everyone' involved in the schooling of children being accountable. Administrators, teachers, students, and families all together are accountable and known as **stakeholders** in a child's education. For example, administrators must promote high standards while supporting the work of teachers, students, and families. Teachers must have high expectations for all students while providing instruction that will enable all students to succeed. All students are included in the testing process and are being held accountable to learn. Families are being encouraged to be involved in their children's education by participating in school functions and assisting with homework. For each group of stakeholders, there are accountability measures. For example, schools are responsible for how well students perform. In many states, children who perform well might receive a certificate of acknowledgment or be eligible for a specific type of graduation diploma. Conversely, for schools and children who perform poorly, there will be sanctions and consequences.

Standards, accountability, and testing are activities having an impact on curricular changes, instructional approaches, and assessment practices. Choices about planning, designing, administering, and reporting assessment activities are decisions currently being made by many groups of individuals. The federal government, state department personnel, and families have active roles in establishing policies and assessment programs for schools.

The articles for the first unit present a variety of topics associated with achievement issues. The first article provides the reader with an overview of the reform efforts. The following articles address concerns educators have associated with testing, data results, and educational trends. After becoming familiar with characteristics of the reform movement, the reader might be interested in delving into the following issues: (a) high-stakes complacency, (b) comparison of international test scores, (c) standards-based testing, and (d) socioeconomic status and achievement. These issues are worthy of discussion in your classes or study groups. The articles provide interesting information that can be crafted into surveys, debates, or presentations.

Assessments and Accountability
(Condensed version)

Robert L. Linn

A ssessment and accountability have played prominent roles in many of the education reform efforts during the past 50 years. In the 1950s, under the influence of James B. Conant's work on comprehensive high schools, testing was used to select students for higher education and to identify students for gifted programs. By the mid-1960s test results were used as one measure to evaluate the effectiveness of Title I and other federal programs. In the 1970s and early 1980s, the minimum competency testing movement spread rapidly; 34 states instituted some sort of testing of basic skills as a graduation requirement. Overlapping the minimum competency testing movement and continuing into the late 1980s and early 1990s was the expansion of the use of standardized test results for accountability purposes.

Assessment is appealing to policymakers for several reasons: it is relatively inexpensive compared to making program changes, it can be externally mandated, it can be implemented rapidly, and it offers visible results. This Digest discusses significant features of present-day assessment programs and offers recommendations to increase positive effects and minimize negative ones.

What Are the Characteristics of Current Reform Efforts?

Although a number of other important features might be considered in any discussion of assessment and education reform (e.g., the emphasis on performance-based approaches to assessment, the concept of tests worth teaching to, and the politically controversial and technically challenging issue of opportunity to learn), I focus on the following three:

- An emphasis on the development and use of ambitious content standards as the basis of assessment and accountability.
- The dual emphasis on setting demanding performance standards and on the inclusion of all students.
- The attachment of high-stakes accountability mechanisms for schools, teachers, and sometimes, students.

Content standards. The federal government has encouraged states to develop content and performance standards that are demanding. Standards-based reform is also a central part of many of the state reform efforts, including ones such as Kentucky and Maryland that have been using standards-based assessments for several years and ones such as Colorado and Missouri that have more recently introduced standards-based assessment systems. A great deal has been written about the strengths and weaknesses of content standards (e.g., *Education Week,* 1997; Lerner, 1998; Olson, 1998; Raimi & Braden, 1998).

It is worth acknowledging that content standards vary a good deal in specificity and in emphasis. Content standards can, and should, if they are to be more than window dressing, influence both the choice of constructs to be measured and the ways in which they are eventually measured.

Performance standards. Performance standards are supposed to specify how good is good enough. There are at least four critical characteristics of performance standards. First, they are intended to be absolute rather than normative. Second, they are expected to be set at high, world-class levels. Third, a relatively small number of levels (e.g., advanced, proficient) are typically identified. Finally, they are expected to apply to all, or essentially all, students, rather than a selected subset such as college-bound students seeking advanced placement.

Should the intent be to aspire not just to high standards for all students, but to the same high standards for all students and on the same time schedule for all students (e.g., meet reading standards in English at the end of Grade 4)? Coffman (1993) sums up the problems of holding common high standards for all students as follows: "Holding common standards for all pupils can only encourage a narrowing of educational experiences for most pupils, doom many to failure, and limit the development of many worthy talents" (p. 8). Although this statement runs counter to the current zeitgeist and may not even be considered politically correct, it seems to me a sensible conclusion that is consistent with both evidence and common sense. Having high standards is not the same as having common standards for all, especially when they are tied to a lock step of age or grade level.

High-stakes accountability. The use of student performance on tests in accountability systems is not new. Examples of payment for results such as the flurry of performance contracting in the 1960s can be found cropping up and fading away over many decades. What is somewhat different about the current emphasis on performance-based accountability is its pervasiveness. As Elmore, Abelmann, and Fuhrman note, "What is new is an increasing emphasis on student performance as the touchstone for state governance" (1996, p. 65). Student achievement is being used not only to single out schools that require special assistance, but also to provide cash incentives for imrovements in performance. Yet several fundamental questions remain about the student assessments, the accountability model, and the validity, impact, and credibility of the system.

As noted earlier, for example, the choice of constructs matters. Content areas (and subareas within those content areas) that are assessed for a high-stakes accountability receive emphasis while those that are left out languish. Meyer (1996) has argued that "in a high-stakes accountability system, teachers and administrators are likely to exploit all avenues to improve measured performance. For example, teachers may 'teach narrowly to the test.' For tests that are relatively immune to this type of corruption, teaching to the test could induce teachers and administrators to adopt new curriculums and teaching techniques much more rapidly than they otherwise would" (p. 140).

It is unclear, however, that there is either the know-how or the will to develop assessments that are sufficiently "immune to this type of corruption." It is expensive to introduce a new, albeit well-equated, form of a test on each new administration. And if ambitious performance-based tasks are added to the mix, still greater increases in costs will result.

A second area of concern regarding high-stakes assessments relates to what data the basic model should employ. Some possibilities include current status, comparisons of cross-sectional cohorts of students at different grades in the same year, comparisons of cross-sectional cohorts in a fixed grade from one year to the next, longitudinal comparisons of school aggregate scores without requiring matched individual data, and longitudinal comparisons based only on matched student records. Should simple change scores be used or some form of regression-based adjustment? And, if regression-based adjustments are used, what variables should be included as predictors? In particular, should measures of socioeconomic status be used in the adjustments?

Elmore, Abelmann, and Furhman (1996) present both sides of this issue, noting that on the one hand, schools can fairly be held accountable only for those factors they can control, but on the other, controlling for student background or prior achievement institutionalizes low expectations for poor, minority, low-achieving students (pp. 93–94). Kentucky's interesting approach to this dilemma has been to set a common goal for all schools by the end of 20 years, thus establishing faster biennial growth targets for initially low-scoring schools than initially high-scoring schools (Guskey, 1994).

The biggest question of all is whether the assessment-based accountability models that are now being used or being considered by states and districts have been shown to improve education. Unfortunately, it is difficult to get a clear-cut answer to this simple question. Certainly, there is evidence that performance on the measures used in accountability systems increases over time, but that can also be linked to the use of old norms, the repeated use of test forms year after year, the exclusion of students from participating in accountability testing programs, and the narrow focusing of instruction on the skills and question types used on the test (see Koretz, 1988; Linn et al., 1990; Shepard, 1990). Comparative data are needed to evaluate the apparent gains. The National Assessment of Educational Progress provides one source of such data. Comparisons of state NAEP and state assessment results sometimes suggest similar trends; for example, increases in numbers of students scoring at or above basic or proficient levels on NAEP may track with improved state test scores over time. In other cases, the trends for a state's own assessment and NAEP will suggest contradictory conclusions about the changes in student achievement. Divergence of trends does not prove that NAEP is right and the state assessment is misleading, but it does raise important questions about the generalizability of gains reported on a state's own assessment, and hence, about the validity of claims regarding student achievement.

How Can Assessments Be Used More Wisely?

Assessment systems that are useful monitors lose much of their dependability and credibility for that purpose when high stakes are attached to them. The unintended negative effects of the high-stakes accountability uses often outweigh the intended positive effects. It is worth arguing for more modest claims about uses that can validly be made of our best assessments and warning against the over-reliance on them that is so prevalent and popular. To enhance the validity, credibility, and positive impact of assessment and accountability systems while minimizing their negative effects, policymakers should:

1. Provide safeguards against selective exclusion of students from assessments.

2. Make the case that high-stakes accountability requires new high-quality assessments each year that are equated to those of previous years.

3. Don't put all of the weight on a single test. Instead, seek multiple indicators. The choice of construct matters and the use of multiple indicators increases the validity of inferences based upon observed gains in achievement.

4. Place more emphasis on comparisons of performance from year to year than from school to school. This allows for differences in starting points while maintaining an expectation of improvement for all.

5. Consider both value added and status in the system. Value added provides schools that start out far from the mark a reasonable chance to show improvement while status guards against institutionalizing low expectations for those same students and schools.

6. Recognize, evaluate, and report the degree of uncertainty in the reported results.
7. Put in place a system for evaluating both the intended positive effects and the more likely unintended negative effects of the system.

References

Coffman, W. E. (1993). A king over Egypt, which knew not Joseph. *Educational Measurement: Issues and Practice 12*(2), 5–8.

Education Week (1997, January 22). Quality counts: A report card on the condition of public education in the 50 states. *A Supplement to Education Week,* vol. 16.

Elmore, R. F., Abelmann, C. H., & Fuhrman, S. H. (1996). The new accountability in state education reform: From process to performance. In H. F. Ladd (Ed.), *Holding schools accountable: Performance-based reform in education* (pp. 65–98). Washington, DC: The Brookings Institution.

Guskey, T. R. (Ed.) (1994). *High stakes performance assessment: Perspectives on Kentucky's reform.* Thousand Oaks, CA: Corwin Press.

Koretz, D. (1988). Arriving at Lake Wobegon: Are standardized tests exaggerating achievement and distorting instruction? *American Educator 12*(2), 8–15, 46–52.

Lerner, L. S. (1998). *State science standards: An appraisal of science standards in 36 states.* Washington, DC: Thomas B. Fordham Foundation.

Linn, R. L., Graue, M. E., & Sanders, N. M. (1990). Comparing state and district results to national norms: The validity of the claims that "everyone is above average." *Educational Measurement: Issues and Practice 9*(3), 5–14.

Meyer, R. H. (1996). Comments on chapters two, three, and four. In H. F. Ladd (Ed.), *Holding schools accountable: Performance based reform in education* (pp. 137–145). Washington, DC: The Brookings Institution.

Olson, L. (1998, April 15). An "A" or a "D": State rankings differ widely. *Education Week 17,* 1, 18.

Raimi, R. A., & Braden, L. S. (1998). *State mathematics standards: An appraisal of science standards in 46 states, the District of Columbia, and Japan.* Washington, DC: The Thomas B. Fordham Foundation.

Shepard, L. A. (1990). Inflated test score gains: Is the problem old norms or teaching the test? *Educational Measurement: Issues and Practice 9*(3), 15–22.

From *Practical Assessment, Research & Evaluation,* January 2001, pp. 1–3. Copyright © 2001 by Robert L. Linn. Reprinted by permission of the author.

Why Has High-Stakes Testing So Easily Slipped into Contemporary American Life?

Ms. Nichols and Mr. Berliner suggest five reasons that high-stakes testing has become such a popular approach to "fixing" schools. What is interesting is that none of the reasons has to do with evidence that this approach will actually work in its intended ways.

SHARON L. NICHOLS AND DAVID C. BERLINER

High-stakes testing is the practice of attaching important consequences to standardized test scores, and it is the engine that drives the No Child Left Behind (NCLB) Act. The rationale for high-stakes testing is that the promise of rewards and the threat of punishments will cause teachers to work more effectively, students to be more motivated, and schools to run more smoothly—all of which will result in greater academic achievement for all students, but especially those from poverty and minority backgrounds. Although it is certainly arguable, we believe that, to date, there is no convincing evidence that high-stakes testing has the intended effect of increasing learning.[1] By contrast, there is a growing literature suggesting that the unintended consequences are damaging to the education of students.[2]

Collateral Damage of High-Stakes Testing

In our recent book, we use Donald Campbell's law to illustrate how the high-stakes testing provision of NCLB has wreaked havoc with our education system, causing irreversible harm to many of our nation's youths and educators. Campbell's law states: "The more any quantitative social indicator is used for social decision-making, the more subject it will be to corruption pressures, and the more apt it will be to distort and corrupt the social processes it is intended to monitor."[3] Under the current system of high-stakes testing, this is exactly what is happening. The pressure to score well on a single test is so intense that it leads to nefarious practices (cheating on the test, data manipulation), distorts education (narrowing the curriculum, teaching to the test), and ends up demoralizing our educators.

Perhaps the most visible and noticeable of the areas in which Campbell's law operates is the business world, where economists have long recognized the possibility for corruption when stakes are high. Despite the research, some businesses are structured such that incentives are especially weighty and salient. Such incentives as big bonuses for increased sales or for spending less time with patients increase the likelihood of corruption. Salespeople or physicians in such situations often take short cuts to obtain the incentives available. Of course, it is not surprising that many examples exist of how incentives in business can corrupt individuals. The pursuit of money, prestige, and power, as we all know, often leads to behavior that is unseemly, if not immoral or even illegal. Enron, sadly, is not an anomaly.

But it isn't only the business world where Campbell's law plays out so predictably. Corruption, cheating, gaming the system, taking short cuts, and so forth—all exist in the fields of medicine, athletics, academe, politics, government agencies, and the military. Given the widespread applicability of this social science law regarding corruption in the presence of a single highly valued indicator, we asked ourselves, Why has high-stakes testing so easily become a part of contemporary American life? We offer five reasons—and our thoughts on each—for why high-stakes testing has been so easily embraced by a culture looking for a way to judge and monitor the progress of the public schools.

The 'Business' of Education

First, and the most popular explanation, is one that notes the co-evolution of the prominence of business and accountability in our daily lives. In recent decades business has come to dominate a great deal of American cultural life through its influence on the media and on a broad range of policy at all levels of government. Tax policy, government spending, health care, employment training, and education policy have all been strongly influenced by business through the efforts of lobbyists and highly visible CEOs. As the influence of business on government has risen over the last few decades, so have business' interest in the skill set possessed by graduates of our schools and its concern for how tax dollars are used to support education. So basic business 101 models were applied to our schools: namely, ways were found first to monitor productivity, then to increase it, and finally to do so without spending any more money.

Tests were chosen as the means of measuring productivity. It was believed by the business community that productivity could be increased without spending more money simply by holding schools and educators accountable through the practice of high-stakes testing. Lazy teachers and students would be discovered and made to work harder. The models of accountability used in business could be applied to the inefficient school systems of America and, voilà, the schools would improve. Or they could be closed down or turned over to private entrepreneurs. For many Americans, these policies seemed sensible and worth pursuing, so it was easy to buy into the high-stakes accountability movement.

But the analogy doesn't really fit, because it is easier to judge the number and quality of widgets coming off an assembly line than to determine the knowledge and skill possessed by students. A widget is a widget, but a well-educated student is both a good citizen and a caring person, as well as someone with aesthetic sensibilities, good habits of health, and so forth. These are outcomes our citizens demand that we produce through our schools, but they are never assessed by tests.

Thus productivity for our teachers and our schools has a vastly different meaning than does productivity in a manufacturing plant or in the delivery of routine services. Furthermore, when inputs cannot be controlled, it is hard to assess a process by its outputs. Measuring the production of widgets assumes control over the quality of the raw materials needed to produce widgets. But in education we have little control over the input side. A class that contains two emotionally disturbed children or two English-language learners or many more boys than girls will inevitably affect its teacher's productivity, as measured by test scores. In addition, mobility rates of 40% or 50% at the school level, and much higher rates in particular classrooms, mean we are holding schools and teachers accountable for students they never had much chance to teach. So while ordinary ways of measuring productivity appear to be sensible, they do not work as well in educational settings. The high-stakes tests, with their threats and incentives to boost productivity, are not well matched to the ways our schools operate. Thus scores on tests will mislead us about genuine productivity. But it all sounds quite sensible and so appeals to many citizens who end up supporting the use of high-stakes testing programs for our schools.

The World Is Flat . . . Isn't It?

A second and related reason high-stakes testing has slipped into the routines of our culture is the emerging belief on the part of both business and government that the future economy depends on a highly educated work force. This belief took on new urgency after Thomas Friedman's book *The World Is Flat* became a best seller.[4] Large numbers of Americans now believe that we need to push all our children to the highest levels of education, moving most students to high school graduation with a degree that guarantees mastery of a rigorous curriculum. After that, the story goes, most graduates need to move into degree-granting two- and four-year colleges. Obviously, the demand for a rigorous curriculum and college-level preparation means a seriousness about testing in our public schools never before required. High-stakes testing is compatible with these national ambitions. High-stakes testing fits neatly into the American mindset that to be competitive in the global economy we need high rates of college graduation, especially in the STEM (science, technology, engineering, and math) fields.

In fact, this whole theory may be wrongheaded. As Dennis Redovich has reported in article after article, the employment profile of the future does not support the need for a big increase in the mathematical and scientific knowledge of our youths.[5] We may well be demanding more than we will need in these areas and already producing enough scientists and enough college graduates for the needs of the economy. Certainly a scientifically sophisticated citizenry is in our national interest, but making advanced mathematics and science a major goal of U.S. education may be counterproductive. Creating a rigorous, high-quality science and math curriculum for those who will not be majoring in one of the STEM fields may be a better goal than putting all high school students through courses designed for the future college majors in these fields. The current system contributes to both student anomie and the already too high dropout rate.

But earnings are also an issue. Decades ago, those who failed to graduate from high school experienced a drop in real wages. That drop was followed only a short time later by a drop in real wages for those who had only a high school education. Now, even those with college degrees are suffering the same fate. Earnings for workers with four-year degrees fell 5.2% from 2000 to 2004, when adjusted for inflation, according to White House economists.[6] Apparently, large percentages of recent college graduates are taking jobs for which no college degrees are necessary, and the trend may be accelerating. Nevertheless, we continue to demand that the education system produce ever-increasing numbers of high school and college graduates, though we may actually now be near record levels of high school graduation rates.[7]

Despite the fact that our national productivity is much more dependent on our tax structures, relative lack of corruption, and remarkable entrepreneurship, the citizenry believes that we need better schools to be competitive in the world economy. And although the goal of better schools should be a national priority, bringing them into conformity with what our colleges and universities demand should not. Yet high-stakes testing virtually ensures that schools will force students into submitting to these uniform goals. Unknowingly, high-stakes testing has easily slipped into our everyday life as the solution for the misguided goals of advanced achievement for all students in a narrowed curriculum.

Old, White, and Self-Serving

The third reason for the ease with which high-stakes tests have become commonplace in our culture is changing demographics. We can now see clearly the shape of an emerging gerontocracy. An older citizenry, much whiter than the youths of the nation and relatively well off financially, is now likely to outlive its resources and is beginning to act politically in its own best interests.[8] As a powerful political and economic force, these folks will want income and services. They will demand medical, pharmaceutical, and social services; full payment of social security; and some form of housing support as their income stays relatively fixed. They will not want to spend much on youths—especially youths of color—whom they perceive as lazy and unappreciative. For many people in this category, high-stakes testing separates the deserving poor from the undeserving poor. It becomes, in effect, a policy mechanism to preserve social status more than to improve our schools. High-stakes testing subtly fits the mindset of this growing demographic group and thus makes it easier for this policy to gain purchase in our contemporary society.

Power Elite

A fourth reason is related to a new and larger power elite among the citizenry, along with the vast middle and upper-middle class whose children now attend good public schools and who see high-stakes testing working to their own children's advantage. While they bristle that their own children must suffer through these tests (e.g., the Scarsdale, Westchester County, mothers' rebellion[9]), the schools their children attend are not much bothered by the tests, and the pass rates for their children are very high. Thus on a day-to-day basis, many of these citizens are largely unconcerned about the impact of high-stakes tests.

But we think that the unnoticed slipping of high-stakes testing into our culture has taken place partly because it hits our poorest and most racially diverse student body hardest and thereby forces the kind of education on the children of the poor that ensures that they cannot compete successfully with the children of the wealthy. The drill-and-test-prep education we see in schools for the poor does not prepare them for knowledge workers' jobs or for the best universities in the nation. This makes room for the children of the more privileged. Since the status of children from advantaged families is preserved though high-stakes testing, it is easy for these folks to defend their use.

Middle- and upper-class Americans largely saw no reason to oppose high-stakes testing for accountability when it was first proposed because they knew that their children would do well. But even if their children were in danger of not succeeding on such tests, middle-class families always had the intellectual and

financial resources needed to ensure their children's success. Thus high-stakes tests slipped easily into the culture because, by and large, the power elite didn't foresee a problem for themselves.

Middle- and upper-class Americans saw no reason to oppose high-stakes testing for accountability when it was first proposed because they knew that their children would do well.

Five years later, many middle-class parents and students are speaking out against high-stakes tests. Some do it because of how it affects them, but, thankfully, others argue that the system is unfair and unjust for others. For example, high school student John Wood refused to take his high school exit exam on grounds that the test is biased and unjust. Even though he would certainly pass, the decision cost him his diploma. In spite of these impassioned voices, relatively wealthy, higher-social-status politicians on both sides of the aisle continue to defend high-stakes tests as the solution to all our educational problems.

Sports Enthusiasts

Fifth—and least noted by any commentators we have read on the subject—is the fit between high-stakes testing and other spectacles that the public enjoys, such as baseball, football, basketball, or hockey. We are a game-playing, competition-seeking nation, and high-stakes testing fits easily into such a culture.

As is true of many sports, high-stakes testing has a tournament-like quality to it, bringing seasonal excitement to fans who now can follow the heavily publicized "winning" and "losing" streaks of their local schools, as they have often followed their local teams. Every summer when spring test results are released, there is a flood of publicity and great fanfare about how well (or poorly) our nation's teachers and students performed in the previous year. And like rabid fans who delight in watching rivals have a losing season, the American media feed on whatever bad news exists.[10] Those who follow the news ponder endlessly about why certain schools/teams fail. How many times has this school/team failed in the past? What is its track record? What schools/teams might need to be reconstituted or even closed down or moved? What will we do to get rid of the bad teachers/ players, and precisely which ones are they? Is it the science teacher or the first baseman, the English teachers or the defensive line, the coach or the principal? Exactly whom can we pin this failure on?

Numerous similarities between sports and testing explain the country's fascination with testing. After all, a match in the sport of cricket is called a test. Professional athletes in cricket and in most other sports practice hours and hours, repeating the same activities endlessly so that their responses at "test" time will be automatic. In the high-stakes-testing game, teachers also engage their students in endless repetitive activities to better ensure that students' responses are accurate and automatic come test time. In professional sports, teams with the highest-paid athletes are more likely to have winning seasons. Similarly, schools with more resources and those that serve the most affluent students tend to perform better academically.[11] In professional sports, fans are immersed in statistics that highlight the successes and failures of their favorite teams and players; in the testing game, parents, politicians, and other community members are immersed in media coverage of academic data showing who is winning and who is losing.

Of course, we know stats say little about a player's many other contributions to the team, such as level of dedication, commitment, morale, and leadership. Similarly, when teachers and administrators are judged by their students' scores, we don't take any account of teachers' many other contributions, such as their nurturance of a love for learning, individual counseling of students in times of need, extra time spent meeting with students' families, provision of money from their own pockets for classroom items, and so forth.

High-Stakes Testing: We Are against It

High-stakes testing is now a part of our culture, and we are against it. It has come to prominence, we think, because it fits easily into contemporary ways of thinking about our nation and ourselves. We are a political and an economic system dominated by the interests of big business, and so business models of accountability for our schools naturally follow. High-stakes testing seems to be a hard-headed business practice brought to bear on the schools, despite the fact that no one uses such a system in knowledge-oriented businesses. And unless we are greatly mistaken, schools still fall into that category.

High-stakes testing also seems to help with preparing us for the vicissitudes of a competitive world economy, and so it is easily embraced. The argument that the new American economy may be vastly more service oriented than previously believed and that it may not require nearly as many college graduates as is now thought necessary is a point of view that is ignored.

The needs of the emerging gerontocracy and those who already have some status in society are also served by high-stakes testing. And high-stakes testing fits neatly into the gaming and spectacle seeking that so permeate the U.S. cultural scene.

For all these reasons high-stakes testing has grown to be an acceptable part of the culture. Those who oppose the spread of high-stakes testing are seen as status-quo oriented, against quality in education, against school improvement, obstructionist, anti-efficiency, anti-George W. Bush, and so forth.

But we are actually against high-stakes testing for none of these reasons. We oppose it for the same reason we are against forcing everyone to participate in extreme sports. If any person voluntarily chooses to jump the Grand Canyon on a motorcycle, scale Everest, or BASE jump, we wish them luck. We just don't think everyone should be required to engage in the same high-stakes sports because, if everyone did, lots of people would be

hurt. We are against high-stakes testing for the same reason. If a person volunteers to take exams for the medical boards, the bar, or a pilot's license, that individual should be encouraged to follow a dream. But not all of us should be forced to take and fail such exams. In the current high-stakes environment, teachers, students, parents, and American education are being hurt by required high-stakes testing. This policy is corrupting our education system and needs to be stopped.

References

1. See, for example, Sharon L. Nichols, Gene V. Glass, and David C. Berliner, "High-Stakes Testing and Student Achievement: Does Accountability Pressure Increase Student Learning?," *Education Policy Analysis Archives,* vol. 14, 2006, http://epaa .asu.edu./epaa/v14n1; and Sharon L. Nichols, "High-Stakes Testing: Does It Increase Achievement?," *Journal of Applied School Psychology* (in press). By contrast, a more recent study suggests that high-stakes testing under NCLB is associated with increases in student achievement. See *Answering the Question That Matters Most: Has Student Achievement Increased Since No Child Left Behind?* (Washington, D.C.: Center on Education Policy, June 2007). Available at www.cep.org, or readers may google the title.

2. Monty Neill et al., *Failing Our Children: How No Child Left Behind Undermines Quality and Equity in Education and an Accountability Model That Supports School Improvement* (Cambridge, Mass.: FairTest, 2004); Gary Orfield et al., *Losing Our Future: How Minority Youth Are Being Left Behind by the Graduation Rate Crisis* (Cambridge, Mass.: Civil Rights Project at Harvard University, 2004); Jaekyung Lee, *Tracking Achievement Gaps and Assessing the Impact of NCLB on the Gaps: An In-Depth Look into National and State Reading and Math Outcome Trends* (Cambridge, Mass.: Civil Rights Project at Harvard University, 2006); and M. Gail Jones, Brett Jones, and Tracy Hargrove, *The Unintended Consequences of High-Stakes Testing* (Lanham, Md.: Rowman & Littlefield, 2003).

3. Donald Campbell, "Assessing the Impact of Planned Social Change," in Gene Lyons, ed., *Social Research and Public Policies: The Dartmouth/OECD Conference* (Hanover, N.H.: Public Affairs Center, Dartmouth College, 1975).

4. Thomas L. Friedman, *The World Is Flat: A Brief History of the Twenty-First Century* (New York: Farrar, Straus & Giroux, 2006).

5. Dennis W. Redovich, *The Big Con in Education: Why Must "All" High School Graduates Be Prepared for College?* (New York: Universe, 2005).

6. Molly Hennessy-Fiske, "That Raise Might Take 4 Years to Earn as Well: Those with Bachelor's Degrees Are Finding Their Incomes Stagnate Despite a Growing Economy," *Los Angeles Times,* 24 July 2006.

7. Lawrence Mishel and Joydeep Roy, *Rethinking Graduation Rates and Trends* (Washington, D.C.: Economic Policy Institute, 2006); and idem, "Accurately Assessing High School Graduation Rates," *Phi Delta Kappan,* December 2006, pp. 287–92.

8. Gene V. Glass, "Fertilizers, Pills, and Robots: The Fate of Public Education in America," lecture presented at the annual meeting of the American Educational Research Association, San Francisco, 2006.

9. "Scarsdale Parents Call Test Boycott a Success," *New York Times,* 4 May 2001, p. B-1; and Michael Powell, "In NY, Putting Down Their Pencils: Parent Rebellion Against Standardized Testing Strikes at Heart of Bush Plan," *Washington Post,* 18 May 2001, A-1.

10. See Sharon Nichols and Tom Good, *American Teenagers— Myths and Realities: Media Images, Schooling, and the Social Costs of Careless Indifference* (Mahwah, N.J.: Erlbaum, 2004), for a discussion on how the media exaggerate, distort, and overrepresent the bad news about American youths. See also Michael Males, *Kids and Guns: How Politicians, Experts, and the Press Fabricate Fear of Youth* (Philadelphia: Common Courage Press, 2000); and idem, *The Scapegoat Generation: America's War on Adolescents* (Philadelphia: Common Courage Press, 1996). See also David C. Berliner and Bruce J. Biddle, "The Lamentable Alliance Between the Media and School Critics," in Gene Maeroff, ed., *Imaging Education: The Media and Schools in America* (New York: Teachers College Press, 1998).

11. David C. Berliner, "Our Impoverished View of Educational Research," *Teachers College Record,* vol. 108, 2006, pp. 949–95; and Bruce J. Biddle, ed., *Social Class, Poverty, and Education* (New York: Routledge Falmer, 2001).

Sharon L. Nichols is an assistant professor in the Department of Counseling, Educational Psychology, and Adult and Higher Education at the University of Texas, San Antonio. **David C. Berliner** is a Regents' Professor of Education in the Department of Educational Leadership and Policy Studies at Arizona State University, Tempe. They are the authors of *Collateral Damage: How High-Stakes Testing Corrupts America's Schools* (Harvard Education Press, 2007). © 2008, Sharon L. Nichols.

From *Phi Delta Kappan*, May 2008, pp. 672–676. Copyright © 2008 by Sharon Nichols. Reprinted by permission of the author.

Assessment around the World

How does NCLB fit in an international context? Here's what's happening in the rest of the world.

IRIS C. ROTBERG

S tandardized testing is controversial everywhere, regardless of its purpose. Most countries use testing for tracking and for selecting students for admission into academic secondary schools or universities, but generally not for holding educators accountable. Many countries don't even administer standardized tests until the later grades. In fact, most Canadian universities don't require the Scholastic Aptitude Test (SAT) or other standardized admissions tests—except for students applying with a U.S. high school diploma! (Ghosh, 2004)

In a recent collection of studies of education systems worldwide, which I edited,[1] numerous experts discussed current education policies in their countries, including the role that standardized testing plays in their public schools (Rotberg, 2004). I draw on these overviews here to set No Child Left Behind (NCLB) in the context of testing across the globe.

The current preoccupation with test-based accountability in the United States is founded on several misperceptions about other countries' practices as well as about international test score comparisons and the extent to which test scores are valid indicators of the quality of education or the state of the economy. These assumptions have dominated U.S. public policy dialogue for decades.

Assumption: The Rest of the Developed World Is One (High-Achieving) Country

Much of the rhetoric about international test score comparisons treats the rest of the developed world as though it were one mythical country that does a better job of educating students than the United States does. However, the rhetoric does not recognize the significant differences in student academic achievement among developed countries; the level and distribution of education funding; the extent to which schools track students by academic ability; secondary school and university enrollment rates; and perhaps most important, the quality of education that each country offers low-income students, minority students, students with disabilities, language-minority students, and recent immigrants.

Assumption: Other Countries Have Found the "Right" Way to Improve Student Achievement

Many people in the United States assume that other countries have centralized education systems and that the resulting standardization is the magic bullet for improving student achievement. This assumption ignores the fact that many countries question that policy. France, for example, is reassessing its highly centralized education system because it doesn't meet the needs of an increasingly diverse immigrant population. Many other countries, such as China, Israel, and Sweden, are moving from a centralized to a decentralized system of governance. Australia, Canada, and Germany—countries with long-standing decentralized systems—envision little change. In addition, no evidence supports the contention that organizational structure, whether centralized or decentralized, bears any relationship to academic achievement or the ability to compete in the global economy.

Assumption: International Test Score Rankings Are Valid Measures of the Quality of Education

Data do not support the causal relationships that many people establish on the basis of international rankings. If a country ranks high on a given international comparison, people assume that its schools must be "good"; if the country ranks low, its schools must be "bad." The problem is, international test score comparisons are virtually impossible to interpret, not only because of enormous differences among nations in poverty rates and in societal values and objectives, but also because of major sampling problems, which make it difficult to ensure that comparable samples of students, schools, and regions are being tested across countries.

Assumption: A Country's Ranking on Test Score Comparisons Predicts Its Ability to Compete in the Global Economy

This assumption has been repeated in various guises for the past 40 years, with little evidence to support it. The fact is, many countries typically perceived as high-scoring on international test score comparisons—such as Austria, France, Sweden, Switzerland, and the United Kingdom—are not the United States' main economic competitors. The United States outsources technical jobs because U.S. consumers are unwilling to accept higher prices and U.S. workers are unwilling to accept lower wages to compete with computer programmers in India or with computer manufacturers in China. These two countries enroll only about one-third of a given age group by the final years of secondary school. Moreover, the education systems of Western European countries and Japan have not immunized their economies against competition from less developed countries with significantly lower rates of literacy and lower enrollment in secondary and higher education.

Assumption: Testing Can Help the United States Address the Problems That Poverty Has Created

The rhetoric about NCLB ignores the overwhelming impact of poverty, the primary correlate of low academic achievement in every country (Grissmer, Kirby, Berends, & Williamson, 1994). Although the size of the achievement gap among students from different socioeconomic backgrounds may vary among countries, the existence of this gap is universal.

The link between poverty and achievement is higher in the United States than in many other industrialized countries. This is not surprising, given the fact that the United States has both larger income gaps between rich and poor (Blackburn, 1997) and fewer social support systems than most industrialized countries do. But high-stakes testing, accountability requirements, and centralization cannot cure the problems associated with poverty. As one educator put it,

> We believe that schools solve the problem of poverty, and now this program [NCLB] assumes that tests solve the problem of schools. By implication, that means tests are supposed to solve the problem of poverty. (Rotberg, Bernstein, & Ritter, 2001, p. 14)

Assumption: Countries That Score High on International Test Score Comparisons Hold Their Educators Accountable for Students' Scores on Standardized Tests

In reality, few countries hold educators accountable for students' test scores. Many of the countries that the United States most admires for their rankings on international comparisons—for example, Canada, Finland, France, Japan, and Sweden—do not use tests to hold educators accountable. Some do not even administer standardized tests until secondary school.

Many of the countries that the United States most admires for their rankings on international comparisons do *not* use tests to hold educators accountable.

It is ironic that many countries throughout the world are attempting to reduce their emphasis on rote learning, whereas current testing pressures in the United States promote just that kind of learning. NCLB supporters believe that because the legislation makes schools' "failures" public, it encourages educators to try harder to focus on important academic subject matter and pay more attention to marginalized students. Those opposed to NCLB are concerned that the pressure to raise test scores will encourage educators to narrow the curriculum and make questionable decisions about student assignments and grade retention. For example, schools may be reluctant to recommend their highest-achieving students to gifted programs in other schools because they would lose the advantage of these students' test scores. Schools may also focus on students who are close to meeting proficiency goals rather than on the lowest-achieving students. Moreover, NCLB may further increase attrition rates of the most qualified teachers and principals, especially in high-poverty schools, because these educators may not wish to be publicly associated with schools designated as "needing improvement."

Testing Practices in Other Countries

Do other countries use tests to evaluate educators' performance? What role does testing play internationally in tracking students and providing access to universities? How strong is the link in other countries between testing and classroom practice? The following examples from England, Turkey, Germany, Singapore, Japan, and China illustrate how these countries manage these issues.

England

Like the United States, England holds educators accountable for students' scores on standardized tests, although major differences exist between the two countries' accountability systems. England has a national curriculum, which serves as the basis for its tests and avoids the problem so prevalent in many U.S. school districts where, in the absence of a clear curriculum, the tests *become* the curriculum. England's national curriculum is one of Europe's most prescriptive. Tests are administered at several points throughout the students' schooling, beginning in early elementary school, with the scores used to rank primary and secondary schools.

The initial versions of the tests were designed to be "authentic," to give a fuller picture of a student's learning and avoid the problems inherent in paper-and-pencil standardized tests. But these tests took up so much time and left so many students unsupervised as the teacher tested students individually that paper-and-pencil tests eventually replaced them.

The test-based accountability policy remains highly controversial and raises issues similar to those currently discussed in the United States. A major question is the validity of using test scores, which are strongly influenced by students' socioeconomic status, to evaluate the quality of education. This problem is endemic in national and international test score comparisons.

England has continued its tradition of administering examinations at age 16 to determine which students will move on to A-level (advanced level) upper secondary schools. Examination results at the end of upper secondary school then determine the universities that a student can attend and the students area of specialty. Students used to be tested at age 11 to determine admission to highly selective "grammar schools," which served as a pipeline to selective universities. In an attempt to make the education system more egalitarian, England replaced the grammar schools with comprehensive schools. However, this move may have had the opposite effect by encouraging affluent families, particularly in center cities, to move out of the state system into private schools.

Turkey

Turkey's heavily bureaucratic and centralized education system is modeled after the French system. It has been called "more French than the French system" (Simsek & Yildirim, 2004, p. 155) because French schools have undergone changes in the past 20 years that have not taken place in Turkish schools. However, Turkey's attempts to reduce the emphasis on rote learning have had limited success.

Turkey is a developing country with limited resources, high poverty rates, and relatively low access to secondary and higher education. It also has one of the highest birthrates in the world, which stretches the country's scarce education resources thin. These factors affect how national examinations play out in the country.

Examinations in Turkey are first administered at the end of basic education, although they influence what schools teach long before that. These exams determine admission into the prestigious Anatolian and science high schools, which accept approximately one-quarter of the students who take the exam. Students who wish to enter a university must take another nationwide exam at the end of high school; but because demand outweighs available spaces, acceptance rates are low (around 20 percent). Because of these conditions, Turkish students experience "some of the world's worst exam anxiety" (Simsek & Yildirim, 2004, p. 165).

Germany

Germany has a highly stratified education system that tracks students, generally beginning in grade 5, into three types of schools: the *Gymnasium,* which provides an academic, university-track education; the *Realschule,* which provides a general and vocational/technical education and occasionally permits transfer to a Gymnasium; and the *Hauptschule,* which provides a lower-level general and vocational education that often leads to unemployment. Teachers and parents—not an examination—determine a child's placement.

Because socioeconomic status highly correlates with academic achievement, affluent students are disproportionately represented in the Gymnasium, whereas the children of migrant workers are often tracked into the Hauptschule. The 2003 Program for International Assessment (PISA) study showed that the performance of German students correlates more highly with socioeconomic status than does the performance of students from almost any other country, suggesting that Germany's trucking system magnifies the effects of socioeconomic status (Organisation for economic Cooperation and Development, 2004).

Students attending the Gymnasium through grade 13 receive a school-leaving certificate called the *Abitur,* which fewer than one-quarter of German students receive. The Abitur provides access to universities after students pass a final examination.

School rankings in Singapore include a measure of how students in each school performed on a physical fitness test, combined with the percentage of overweight students in the school.

Singapore

In Singapore, educators are only held accountable for their students' test scores in the sense that secondary schools and junior colleges are ranked in publicly reported "league tables"; the 40 highest-ranked secondary schools receive cash awards. But this "accountability" system bears little resemblance to NCLB. In addition to test scores and a "value-added" measure, the rankings include a measure of how students in each school performed on a physical fitness test, combined with the percentage of overweight students in the school.

The main purpose of testing in Singapore is to determine student placement in the education system and access to elite academic programs—not to evaluate teachers. The system is heavily tracked; in a 10-year span, students are "streamed" three times. The goal is to make the system as efficient as possible in training students to contribute to the national economy.

The Singaporean system places enormous pressure on students to score well in the national examinations, which play a major role in determining students' Futures. At the same time, Singapore is attempting to reduce its emphasis on rote learning and pay greater attention to critical thinking, problem solving, and creativity. Singapore's traditional classroom practices, however, have been difficult to change because many believe that a flexible learning environment is inconsistent with the demands of an examination system that requires students to memorize large amounts of material.

Japan

Japan has a highly competitive examination system, but it doesn't hold educators accountable for students' scores on standardized tests. Indeed, Japan specifically excludes student achievement on these tests as a criterion for the self-evaluations that Japanese schools conduct.

In Japanese public schools, elementary and lower secondary students do not take high-stakes tests nor are they assigned to schools by achievement. The examination pressures begin between lower and upper secondary school, when examination results determine the upper secondary school that students will enter. The pressures that students applying to universities face have been well publicized, as have the supplementary schools (*juku*) that many Japanese students attend to study for the examinations. In recent years, because of a dramatically declining population, Japanese students have not had a problem gaining admission into higher education institutions. However, competition for admission to the most prestigious universities remains severe because graduates of these universities usually fill the top jobs in government and industry.

Japan, like Singapore, is attempting to increase the flexibility of the learning environment to cultivate "Japanese people with 'rich humanity' and 'rich creativity' by letting individual abilities grow" (Watanabe, 2004, p. 237). One component of this reform has been to reduce the school week from six to five days to give students more time to explore nature and participate in community-based activities. However, many families appear to be using this "free" time to increase their children's participation in juku.

Although the response to Japan's reforms has generally been positive, conservative politicians and some parents are concerned about changing an education system that they believe played a major role in the country's rapid economic growth after World War II, about encouraging individualism at the expense of Japans traditional values of cooperation and consensus,

about weakening nationalism, and—perhaps most important to parents—about making any changes that might decrease their children's test scores and chances of gaining admission into prestigious universities.

China

For many centuries, the Chinese have viewed their country's examination system, which dates back to the Shui dynasty in 603 CE, as the main route out of poverty for a child from a low-income family. However, like Singapore and Japan, China is attempting to reduce its reliance on rote learning. Realizing that examinations inevitably drive classroom practice, China has revised its highly competitive university entrance exams by requiring students to integrate knowledge from a wide range of fields. For example, a recent exam question on the increased number of private cars in China required students to draw on the diverse fields of statistics, comparative analysis, supply and production, urban traffic, pollution, and social studies.

China's reforms in classroom and examination practices have occurred in an exceptionally short period of time. China's practice of building on traditional culture—or "holding new wine with the old bottle" (Cheng, 2004, p. 16)—appears to have contributed to its unusual success in implementing change. China's reforms, however, are not without controversy. The new teaching approaches have not reached the majority of schools in China's decentralized education system, with its increasing gaps in school quality between the country's rich and poor areas. Some Chinese are concerned that if examinations reduce their emphasis on memorization, children from poor families will be at an even greater disadvantage than before because they will be tested on skills that their schools have not taught them.

Chinese students face a highly competitive and stressful examination system. Yet China, like many other countries, has concluded that national exams are the best way to ensure objectivity and avoid the favoritism that might occur if the system permitted greater subjectivity in university admissions decisions.

Another Assumption—Dispelled

People generally assume that the education policies most visible today will continue unabated into the future. However, evidence shows that many policies are cyclical or gradually weaken until they have little influence, Well before NCLB, some states' test-based accountability programs began with great fanfare only to become largely irrelevant to school policies. It was simply considered educationally unwise—and politically incorrect—to acknowledge large failure rates, with the burden falling disproportionately on students in high-poverty schools.

Despite its current dominance in U.S. education policy, NCLB may well suffer the same fate. Opinions differ, of course, on whether weakening test-based accountability would be a positive or negative outcome. If test-based accountability does lose its centrality to U.S. policy, however, we would move closer to education practices in other countries, few of which assess educators' performance on the basis of their students' standardized test scores.

Note

1. This article draws on *Balancing Change and Tradition in Global Education Reform*. Alison Wolf of King's College, University of London contributed the chapter on England; Hasan Simsek and All Yildirim from Middle East Technical University, Ankara, contributed the chapter on Turkey; Barbara Kehm from the University of Kassel contributed the chapter on Germany; Batia P. Horsky from Nanyang Technological University in Singapore and Phyllis Ghim-Lian Chew from the National Institute of Education contributed the chapter on Singapore; Ryo Watanabe from Japan's National Institute for Educational Policy Research contributed the chapter on Japan; and Kai-ming Cheng from the University of Hong Kong contributed the chapter on China.

References

Blackburn, M. L. (1997). *Comparing poverty: The United States and other industrial nations.* Washington, DC: AEI Studies on Understanding Economic Inequality, American Enterprise Institute.

Cheng, K. (2004). China: Turning the bad master into a good servant. In I. C. Rotberg (Ed.), *Balancing change and tradition in global education reform* (pp. 3–19). Lanham, MD: ScarecrowEducation.

Ghosh, R. (2004). Canada: A multicultural policy. In I. C. Rotberg (Ed.), *Balancing change and tradition in global education reform* (pp. 261–282). Lanham, MD: ScarecrowEducation.

Grissmer, D. W., Kirby, S. N., Berends, M., & Williamson, S., (1994), *Student achievement and the changing American family.* Washington, DC; RAND Institute on Education and Training.

Organisation for Economic Co-operation and Development. (2004). *Learning for tomorrow's, world: First results from PISA 2003.* Paris: Author.

Rotberg, I. C. (Ed.). (2004). *Balancing change and tradition in global education reform.* Lanham, MD: ScarecrowEducation.

Rotberg, I. C., Bernstein, K. J., & Ritter, S. B. (2001, July). *No Child Left Behind: Views about the potential impact of the Bush Administration's education proposals.* Washington, DC: Graduate School of Education and Human Development, The George Washington University.

Simsek, H., & Yildirim, A. (2004). Turkey: Innovation and tradition. In I. C. Rotberg (Ed.), *Balancing change and tradition in global education reform* (pp. 153–185). Lanham, MD: ScarecrowEducation.

Watanabe, R. (2004). Japan: Encouraging individualism, maintaining community values. In I. C. Rotberg (Ed.), *Balancing change and tradition in global education reform* (pp. 229–242). Lanham, MD; ScarecrowEducation.

IRIS C. ROTBERG is Research Professor of Education Policy in the Department of Educational Leadership, Graduate School of Education and Human Development, The George Washington University, Washington, DC.

Are Standards Preventing Good Teaching?

CLAIR T. BERUBE

The National Standards movement seeks to raise the quality of the American educational system. According to one of its chief architects, Diane Ravitch (2000), national standards give clear expectations for students, teachers, parents, colleges, and employers that will result in improved student achievement. Forty-nine of the fifty states (save Iowa) have implemented such standards. In many cases, they have raised scores. In Virginia, for example, scores are going up on standardized tests (Virginia Department of Education 2001). But what, ultimately, does this mean? Is it possible for scores to go up without teacher creativity and student comprehension suffering?

For instance, I love the game show "Jeopardy." The game is on a higher level than other game shows, and the contestants are all intelligent, well-read individuals. Although these contestants could perform at much higher levels, all they are asked to do on the show is to recall facts, the lowest level of thinking (Bloom 1956). Problem-solving activities, checks for comprehension, and evidence of analysis, synthesis, or evaluation are absent. But we view these contestants as the smartest of the smart just because they can recall facts at blazing speed. However, very intelligent people possessing this talent also can comprehend, analyze, synthesize, and evaluate.

In the same way, has the American educational system chosen an incomplete set of tools to measure the progress of the standards movement? Unlike the SAT, where a combination of multiple-choice and essay questions offer an understanding of a college-bound student's abilities, some states only use one type of test to measure student comprehension. In Virginia, it is the Virginia Standards of Learning (SOL). This particular test is used because (1) it is cheap, (2) it is easy to read, and (3) it is simple to grade. The test is also extremely objective, leaving no room for graders' opinions and differences of viewpoints. Although multiple-choice standardized tests claim to measure every level of learning, they really only test knowledge recall. And as educators, we use these multiple-choice "bubble" tests to convince ourselves that our students truly "understand" what we teach them, as evidenced by a passing test score.

But picture this scenario in any middle-school science classroom in America: A science teacher proudly explains to her principal how she has successfully taught Einstein's theory of relativity to her students (a very lofty concept indeed for middle schoolers). Her assessment of student discussions, projects, and papers has proven that they have "gotten" it. However, the principal looks over her bifocals in a disapproving manner and scolds, "Well that's fine, but can they pass *the test*?" Not understanding, the teacher reiterates that they have passed her assessments. But the principal is speaking of "The Test," the high-stakes, multiple-choice standardized test that is given at the end of each year. This really happened to me; I was that sixth grade science teacher.

The problem is not the standards but, rather, how the standards are assessed. I would have been unable to teach without the Virginia Standards of Learning. They gave me a wonderful roadmap that I coordinated with my curriculum guide and the district's guidelines. But something went terribly wrong when my former state (Virginia) began measuring the standards with multiple-choice, high-stakes tests. These tests hold teachers' and administrators' creativity hostage and threaten job security and professional contentment. In addition, the tests hardly prove that students have learned anything other than rote memorization of facts. And although there are multiple-choice tests that try to focus on higher-order thinking skills (the SAT, for example), they also employ other forms of assessment, such as qualitative essays.

Toward the end of every school year, Virginia eighth graders are required to take the Standards of Learning (SOL) test, which is supposed to assess what they learned in eighth grade physical science class but also covers sixth and seventh grade science material as well. I wondered if the grades on this test were good indicators of the students' comprehension of the subject matter. So, I conducted a large study with middle-school science classes in Norfolk, Virginia. I hypothesized that teacher style affected SOL scores, such that the more constructivism-oriented teachers' classes would receive higher scores over those taught by lecture-oriented teachers, especially on the comprehension test.

Table 1 Comparison of Students Who Passed the SOL but Failed the Comprehensive Exam

Teacher	Students Passing SOL	Same Students Failing Comprehensive Exam	Percentage
A (mixed)	17	3	17
B (constructivist)	18	15	83
C (mixed)	6	5	83
D (constructivist)	12	12	100
E (constructivist)	8	8	100
F (mixed)	19	14	73

Note. Mixed = teachers exhibiting mixture of constructivist and traditional teaching traits. Constructivist = teachers exhibiting constructivist teaching traits (as defined by Taylor and Fraser's CLES: The Revised Constructivist Learning Environment Survey).

Constructivism has been implemented in classrooms all across America and is recognized as a student-centered, discovery learning process where the teacher—while still teaching strong content and skill development—assists the students in problem-based learning. Given that children build knowledge from their own experience and beliefs, this epistemology emphasizes the construction of concepts rather than transmission and recording of information given by others (Applefield, Huber, and Moallem 2000/2001; Gatlin 1998).

I constructed my own version of the eighth grade SOL test that I called the "Comprehension Measurement." It was the same SOL test they had taken one week earlier with one adjustment: After answering the multiple-choice question, I asked them to explain or defend their answers in short-answer/essay format. I created this instrument to find out if students taught by the more constructivist teachers also had higher comprehension scores, meaning that the students could adequately explain and defend their answers and, therefore, were not just memorizing answers supplied by their teachers.

I first had to find out what kind of teachers I had in my sample. I sent out a self-scoring Lickert scale taken from CLES: The Revised Constructivist Learning Environment Survey (Taylor, Fraser, and White 1994). The CLES measures teacher perception of constructivist attributes in the learning environment, namely their own classroom, and could determine if the teachers were constructivist, traditional, or a mix between the two styles. After returning and scoring the questionnaires, I visited each classroom to ensure that the teachers were indeed what they said they were. To do this, I used the subscales of the CLES, which detail behaviors to observe in constructivist classrooms. I coded the behaviors and developed cut-off points with which to categorize the teachers into either constructivist, traditional, or mixed. Then the students took the SOL test, and one week later, the same students took my comprehension test. I analyzed the SOL scores and compared them to my comprehension assessment scores. What I found was astonishing. Some students passed,

some failed, which was to be expected, but I found that 71 percent of the students who passed the state mandated, multiple-choice test failed my comprehension test. They either could not explain their answers or gave bogus explanations. It seemed they could pass the SOL but did not understand the subject matter.

In teacher A's class, seventeen out of eighteen students passed the SOL test. Only three of those passing students failed the comprehension measurement test. Not bad. But still three students who passed the SOL test could not explain their answers. Teacher A was one of my mixed style teachers, teaching with some lecture and some discovery and student-centered instruction. But teacher A was the exception. Teacher B had eighteen students who passed the SOL. Fifteen of those failed my comprehension test. Only four students in her class passed both. Teacher C had six students out of nine pass the SOL. Five of those that passed failed the second test. And teacher D had twelve students out of eighteen pass the SOL. Every one of those students who passed the SOL failed the comprehension exam. Teacher E also had every one of her eight SOL-passing students fail my exam. Finally, teacher F had nineteen students pass the SOL, but fourteen of them failed the comprehension test (see Table 1).

One of the constructs that I measured during this study was teacher style. I hypothesized that the constructivist teachers would generate more student understanding because they employ more hands-on experiences, group work, and discovery learning. Some evidence supports this idea that constructivist teaching strategies that employ conceptual learning, those which do not isolate basic skills but incorporate them into skills required for completion of problemsolving tasks, does increase student comprehension (Applefield, Huber, and Moallem 2001). However, results from a multivariate analysis of variance (MANOVA) showed that scores were not higher for constructivist teachers; the more mixed and traditional, "drill and grill" teachers produced the students with the higher SOL scores. But many of those students still failed my comprehension test in high numbers. Surprisingly, the constructivist teachers, whom I thought would produce the highest scores all-around, produced high pass rates on the SOL but the *lowest* pass rates on the comprehension test. Students could answer the simpler multiple-choice questions but could neither defend nor explain their answers, which requires higher-level skills than memorization. The constructivist teaching style (high-level teaching, according to Bloom's taxonomy) that some teachers employed during most of the year was essentially useless in preparing students for the high-stakes test.

The National Board on Educational Testing and Public Policy at Boston College conducted an extensive study to determine the effects of high-stakes testing on teacher practices. The study found that the influence of the test is greater as the stakes increase, with 40 percent of teachers in high-stakes states, such as Virginia, reporting that the tests influence their teaching on a daily basis (Lewis 2003). Teachers in high-stakes testing situations felt more pressure to have their students perform well, and therefore, more closely aligned their teaching to the test. These findings suggest that tests often affect instruction in ways that directly contradict the state educational reform policies' intent to raise standards (Schroeder 2003).

The most recent push for high-stakes testing grew out of the standards-based reform movement in the 1990s. This type of testing gave rise to accountability systems that are characterized by four components (Abrams and Madaus 2003):

- Content standards
- Tests designed to measure achievement of the content standards
- Performance targets
- Incentives, such as awarding diplomas upon passing the test

We rely on such systems for several reasons. First, public perceptions view test scores as conclusive proof that achievement is attained. Tests are seen as symbols of order, control, and attainment. However, if important decisions—jobs and governmental funding—rely on the outcome of high-stakes tests, then teachers will only teach to the test, allowing test content to define the curriculum (Abrams and Madaus 2003). School systems have gone as far as to "bribe" students to perform well. In Florida, Governor Jeb Bush implemented an educational accountability system called the "A+ plan," where financial rewards of $100 per student were offered to schools that receive an A on the basis of FCAT (Florida Comprehensive Assessment Test) scores (Myers and Curtiss 2003). In this case, it was not a reward but more like a bribe since the students were told before the test what they would receive if they passed.

Then there is the problem of high-stakes testing penalizing economically disadvantaged children. Gary Orfield, the co-director of the Civil Rights Project at Harvard University, found that high-stakes testing penalized low-income and ethnic minority students and is linked to high dropout rates in these groups. He warns that high-stakes tests are not standards but "punishment of innocent victims of unequal education" (Myers and Curtiss 2003).

Stuart S. Yeh (2001) argues that we should construct state-mandated tests that emphasize critical thinking. Conceptualizing critical thinking, beginning by looking at the term's meaning in the workplace, would be the first step. According to Yeh, critical thinking is frequently conceptualized as argumentation, a skill that the students failing the comprehension test could not display. By kindergarten, children know how to argue their side in a debate, and critical thinking could be introduced in that context very early. Yeh also argues that the current trove of critical-thinking tests consist of multiple-choice items that call for responses to artificial questions that have no bearing on real life. This, in his view, forces the tests to lack content validity. His solution is to construct standardized tests that emphasize argumentation, where students would have to use facts to defend their opinions instead of simply recalling them. Significant issues would be implemented that would tie real life problems into content.

Again, the problem is not standards or the standards movement. We, as a nation, should hold our teachers and students to high standards. But do high-stakes tests cancel out any form of higher-level teaching and learning? Do teachers who previously taught at high levels resort to "teaching to the test" during assessment crunch time at the end of the year?

As educators, we have to look closely at what material we assess and how we measure achievement. Low costs and ease in grading are hardly valid reasons to use high-stakes tests as indications of student achievement. Achievement should not be measured by how well we train our students to take multiple-choice tests. If we are not careful, we could become a nation of people who score high on standardized tests but who cannot understand, analyze, synthesize, and evaluate what we have truly learned.

References

Abrams, L. M., and G. F. Madaus. 2003. The lessons of high-stakes testing. *Educational Leadership* 61, no. 3 (November): 31–35.

Applefield, J. M., R. Huber, and M. Moallem. 2000/2001. Constructivism in theory and practice: Toward a better understanding. *The High School Journal* (December/January): 35–53.

Bloom, B., ed. 1956. *Taxonomy of educational objectives: The classification of educational goals handbook 1: Cognitive domain.* New York: David McKay.

Gatlin, L. S. 1998. The effect of pedagogy informed by constructivism: A comparison of student achievement across constructivist and traditional classroom environments. PhD diss. Univ. of New Orleans.

Lewis. A. C. 2003. Beyond testing. *Education Digest* 69, no. 1 (September): 70–71.

Myers, M. A., and D. Curtiss. 2003. Failing the equity test. *Principal Leadership.* 3, no. 2 (October): 70–73.

Ravitch, D. 2000. Personal communication with author. December 4: New York.

Schroeder, K. 2003. High-stakes horrors. *Education Digest* 68, no. 9 (May): 54–55.

Taylor, P. C., B. H. Fraser, and L. R. White. 1994. CLES: An instrument for monitoring the development of constructivist learning environment. Paper presented at the annual meeting of the American Educational Research Association, New Orleans, LA.

Virginia Department of Education. 2001. Statewide spring passing rates. http://www.pen.k12.va.us/VDOE/Assessment/StatePassRates01.html (accessed April 23, 2004).

Yeh, S. S. 2001. Tests worth teaching to: Constructing state mandated tests that emphasize critical thinking. *Educational Researcher* 30, no. 9 (December): 12–17.

CLAIR T. BERUBE is an assistant professor of education at Wagner College on Staten Island, New York.

Schools, Poverty, and the Achievement Gap

BEN LEVIN

Last June, representatives from more than 20 countries and several international agencies came together under the midnight sun in Trondheim, Norway, to discuss the challenge of creating greater equity in the outcomes of education. This meeting, sponsored by the Organisation for Economic Co-operation and Development (OECD) and the Norwegian Ministry of Education, was the culmination of several years of work on the theme of "equity in education." The OECD will shortly issue a report titled *No More Failures,* replete with analysis and recommendations on how to improve equity in educational outcomes.

The concern for "raising the bar and closing the gap" in educational outcomes is now widespread around the world. *Kappan* readers will be familiar with the debate on the achievement gap, especially in the context of No Child Left Behind. In Europe, the results of PISA (Programme for International Student Assessment—www.pisa.oecd.org) brought the issue into stark relief as well. PISA, a large, carefully designed study now involving more than 40 countries, tests 15-year-olds in reading, science, and mathematics. There have been two rounds of results so far, in 2000 and 2003, with a third due to be released this December.

The findings of PISA have been striking and consistent. Some countries that thought they were doing well educationally found that they had not only poor overall results but also very large gaps between their highest- and lowest-achieving students. In Germany, the phrase "PISA Schock" has come into the language as a sign of how serious the problem is. In contrast, some other countries, such as Finland, Korea, and—yes—Canada, showed very high overall results and much smaller gaps in their achievement distribution.

The reality, in PISA and in every other assessment of student outcomes, is that socioeconomic status remains the most powerful single influence on students' educational and other life outcomes. This is true in Finland and Canada as well as in the U.S. and everywhere else. Where you are born and grow up matters enormously to what you are able to be and do. A recent study in my home town of Winnipeg, using a database of all children born in the city in 1984, showed that, whereas 89% of

all students writing the grade-12 language exam passed, only 12% of students whose families had received social assistance in the previous two years passed the exam.[1] Indeed, a large proportion of this group was either a year or more behind or out of school entirely.

Although the achievement gap in Canada is smaller than in the United States, it is far from trivial. UNICEF's Innocenti Research Centre recently released a report with the fascinating title of *Child Poverty in Perspective: An Overview of Child Well-Being in Rich Countries* (www.unicef-irc.org/publications). Using a rich array of data, it compares the situation of children in Canada, the U.S., the United Kingdom, and 18 other European countries on six dimensions, including material well-being, health and safety, education, peer and family relationships, behaviors and risks, and young people's subjective sense of well-being.

No country ranks high on all six dimensions. The Netherlands gets the best overall score. Canada's average ranking across the six areas is 12th, while the U.S. and the U.K. are at the bottom. And the kicker is that the report concludes: "Variation in government policy appears to account for most of the variation in child poverty levels between OECD countries. No OECD country devoting 10% or more of GDP to social transfers has a child poverty rate higher than 10%. No country devoting less than 5% of GDP to social transfers has a child poverty rate of less than 15%."[2]

About 15% of Canadian children live in poverty, defined as living in a household with income less than 50% of the national median. What makes the Canadian situation galling is that in 1989 the Parliament of Canada passed a unanimous motion to end child poverty in the country by the year 2000. Surprise! When 2000 rolled around, the child poverty rate was higher than in 1989. In Canadian schools students in special education, recent immigrants, some visible minority groups, and Aboriginal youths lag behind national averages of educational achievement.

All of this makes one skeptical of new pronouncements by governments on their commitment to greater equity. Yet equity in educational outcomes is high on the international policy agenda for powerful reasons. First, it is widely claimed that better educational outcomes are essential for national economic and social success, though as Gerald Bracey has pointed out in these pages, the claim is not necessarily well supported by the empirical evidence. In public policy and politics, though, evidence matters only if it affects beliefs, and this does not happen so quickly.

We should not lose faith in evidence entirely, though, because another factor driving the current interest in narrowing the achievement gap is research showing that reduced inequities in income and education are connected to better economic performance. Countries with less inequality in income and education actually show better economic performance, calling into question the long-standing belief that countries face an inevitable choice between equity and efficiency.[3]

Governments and international agencies are all considering what steps they can take. Some take the view that schools could do much more to reduce, if not eliminate, the effects of poverty. This has led to some very dubious strategies, such as various kinds of takeovers or reconstitution of so-called failing schools, as if the problem were simply one of working a little harder.

Others argue that socioeconomic status is too powerful and that schools alone will not be able to mitigate its impact. Richard Rothstein, another *Kappan* contributor, has made this argument particularly well, including pointing to alternative policy measures that might have more impact on outcomes than some school programs.[4]

For educators working in high-poverty communities, finding an appropriate stance toward poverty and the achievement gap can be difficult. Educators see the daily challenges in the lives of their students, including poor housing, inadequate income, and the effects of discrimination. Schools did not create these problems, and on their own they cannot solve them.

But folks in schools are not always clear on what they can or should do about the problems of poverty and inequality, and the steps we take are not always the best ones.[5] We know that poor children often get teachers who are less qualified and instruction that is less challenging, when they need the best we can give them. The OECD report *No More Failures* lists such sensible steps as reducing retention in grade, stressing early intervention to address reading problems, reducing early tracking in secondary schools, directing additional resources to the highest-need schools, reaching out more to parents, and managing school choice to make sure it does not exacerbate inequities.

There are some good practices in Canada that address equity issues. First Nations are slowly increasing their high school graduation rates. British Columbia is working hard to improve outcomes for Aboriginal students in provincial schools, while Alberta has its Initiative for School Improvement, and Quebec has a strategy for student success. Ontario has developed ambitious strategies that are yielding improved literacy and numeracy skills in elementary schools and higher high school graduation rates. Most of these efforts rightly stress working with teachers to improve their ability to support success in diverse student populations.

A Personal Introduction

I am delighted to be able to write the In Canada column for the *Kappan,* a magazine I have read and admired for many years. Heather-Jane Robertson's knowledge, intelligence, and writing skills make her a tough act to follow! I thought it would be useful to introduce myself briefly to readers.

Though I now live in Toronto, I was born and have spent most of my life in Winnipeg. My career in education has moved back and forth between government and academe. I have been a civil servant in a department/ministry of education four times, including serving as deputy minister (chief civil servant) in Manitoba from 1999 to 2002 and in Ontario from 2004 to early 2007. In academe, I have been a researcher and professor and currently occupy a Canada Research Chair in Education Leadership and Policy at the Ontario Institute for Studies in Education, which is part of the University of Toronto. I have been a member of PDK since 1984. My three daughters are all graduates of Manitoba public schools.

I hope to write about a broad array of issues from a Canadian perspective while connecting them to the experience of *Kappan* readers in the U.S. and elsewhere. I welcome comments from readers or ideas for content for future columns. I can be reached at blevin@oise.utoronto.ca.

References

1. Noralou P. Roos et al., "The Complete Story: A Population-Based Perspective on School Performance and Educational Testing," *Canadian Journal of Education,* vol. 29, 2006, pp. 684–705.
2. UNICEF, *Child Poverty in Perspective: An Overview of Child Well-Being in Rich Countries* (Florence: Innocenti Research Centre, Report Card 7, 2007), p. 7.
3. *World Development Report 2006: Equity and Development* (Washington, D.C.: World Bank, 2005).
4. Richard Rothstein, *Class and Schools: Using Social, Economic, and Educational Reform to Close the Black-White Achievement Gap* (New York: Teachers College Press, 2004).
5. Benjamin Levin and J. Anthony Riffel, "Current and Potential School System Responses to Poverty," *Canadian Public Policy,* vol. 26, 2000, pp. 183–96.

BEN LEVIN is Canada Research Chair in Education Leadership and Policy at the Ontario Institute for the Study of Education, University of Toronto (blevin@oise.utoronto.ca).

UNIT 2

Instruction and Assessment

Unit Selections

6. **Making Benchmark Testing Work,** Joan L. Herman and Eva L. Baker
7. **Mapping the Road to Proficiency,** Thomas R. Guskey
8. **Curriculum Mapping: Building Collaboration and Communication,** Angela Koppang
9. **Developing Standards-Based Curricula and Assessments: Lessons from the Field,** Nancy A. Clarke et al.
10. **Assessing Problem-Solving Thought,** Annette Ricks Leitze and Sue Tinsley Mau
11. **Looking at How Students Reason,** Marilyn Burns
12. **Engineering Successful Inclusion in Standards-Based Urban Classrooms,** Deborah L. Votz et al.

Key Points to Consider

- Why are assessment activities and instruction linked?
- Why is effective instruction the most important factor for student achievement?
- How do you gather evidence that the student understands? Is a question posed in the article, *Assessing Problem-Solving Thought,* by Annette Ricks Leitze and Sue Tinsley Mau?
- What are the advantages and disadvantages of incorporating assessment into classroom discussions?
- Define the terms assessment, corrective instruction, reliability, validity, fairness, appropriateness, and bias.
- Identify six different assessment strategies.
- Identify advantages and disadvantages of constructing a Table of Specifications and Curriculum Maps.
- Choose a standard and create a table of specification using Webb's four cognitive levels (*Making Benchmark Testing Work,* Joan L. Herman and Eva L. Baker).
- Consider the following statement and question: Valid assessments are necessary for (a) measuring the intended learning outcomes (content validity), (b) interpreting the data results, and (c) identifying instructional targets. Question: "How do educators ensure that all criteria are met when choosing the appropriate assessment?"
- Examine the Framework for 21st Century Learning and write standards that would be appropriate for potential jobs and careers that have yet to be created or identified.
- Compare the Framework for 21st Century Learning to a set of current standards for alignment. The framework is located at the website: http://www.21stcenturyskills.org/index.php?option=com_content&task=view&id=254&Itemid=120.
- Analyze a lesson using the M^{2}ECCA framework, from *Engineering Successful Inclusion in Standards-Based Urban Classrooms,* Deborah L. Voltz et al.

Student Website
www.mhcls.com

Internet References

Critical Issues: Using Technology to Improve Student Achievement
http://www.ncrel.org/sdrs/areas/issues/methods/technlgy/te800.htm#context

Center for Comprehensive Reform and Improvement
http://www.centerforcsri.org/

Practical Assessment, Research, and Evaluation (PARE)
http://pareonline.net/

teAchnology
http://www.teach-nology.com/currenttrends/alternative_assessment/

Awesome Library for Teachers
http://www.awesomelibrary.org/Office/Teacher/Assessment_Information/Assessment_Information.html

inTASC (Tools for Teaching)
http://www.bc.edu/research/intasc/library/toolsforteaching.shtml

National Center for Educational Achievement
http://www.just4kids.org/en/

Framework for 21st Century Learning
http://www.21stcenturyskills.org/index.php?option=com_content&task=view&id=254&Itemid=120

Planning instruction and creating good assessments are at the heart of teaching. Today, teaching requires educators to examine the curriculum to ensure that the instruction, learning experiences, and assessment activities are aligned with the standards. Two important instructional tasks are identifying the content to teach and determining the performances expected from students. What is taught in the classrooms plays a primary role in determining student achievement.

Effective instruction and assessment practices involve identifying (a) what the students know (student prior knowledge); (b) deciding what content and skills needs to be learned, and (c) determining what was learned. It is evident that instruction and assessment are connected, as assessment practices dominate the first and last steps of the process and instruction is the middle component. Designing instruction involves making decisions about which topics are important, how much time to allocate to a particular subject, what is acceptable evidence of learning and the level of mastery, and to which students (Porter, 2002). Collectively these decisions and the implementation define the context of instruction and assessment.

Developing an Assessment Strategy

Because the instructional unit, learning experiences, and assessments need to replicate learning outcomes stated in the standard, you may be asking, "How does a teacher translate the standard into an instructional-assessment activity?" Remembering that the purpose of the learning outcome is the basis for the assessment strategy, there are three important questions you can ask yourself: (1) What is the nature of the learning task?, (2) What is the level of thinking?, and (3) What is the appropriate context for the assessment?

The first step is to identify the nature of the learning task. Determining the learning task means examining the standard statement for content and skills. Content is commonly referred to as verbal information. When students use terms, facts, and principles, they are using their verbal information. Skills are ways of doing specific tasks to become competent, so students learn how to apply their verbal information to specific situations. Another mental activity is knowing "when and how" to use the content and skills together. Knowledge and skills are the fundamental building blocks of the standard statements. Teachers examine the standards for these components to determine the best way to create an activity that allows students to show what they know and can do. This can be a complex task and often a difficult process to explain. Wiggins and McTighe (2005, p. 62) coined the term "unpacking the standard" to explain the practice of analyzing standard statements. Unpacking the standard means identifying the content and skills stated in the standard.

The second step is determining the level of cognitive processing. This question is closely related to the first question, yet different. The second question involves determining the mental

© Getty Images

skills of an activity. There are different levels of thinking (cognition) or mental skills. Bloom's taxonomy is the most commonly known hierarchy of cognition used to classify thinking and write learning outcomes. Using Bloom's model helps teachers identify various levels of thinking performances.

The third step is choosing the assessment strategy. The closer the assessment strategy can be designed to resemble an authentic activity, the better. Assessment strategies that require students to use paper and pencils are commonly known as: (a) supply types (i.e, fill-in the blank); (b) selection types (i.e, matching, multiple-choice, true-false, interpretative exercises, and alternative responses); and (c) constructed-responses (i.e., extended-response, restricted-response, and brief-constructed response). Another set of assessment strategies are associated with observations. Comments and explanations can be recorded via anecdotal records, running records, and rating scales. In addition to these traditional assessment strategies, performance-based assessment strategies for interviews, projects, portfolios, contracts, technology-based activities, and games might be rated using a rubric or checklist. Documentation is a key consideration in determining the assessment strategy, as the collection of evidence is an important component of accountability. Additionally, other factors to consider are the classroom environment, the number of students, and whether to design a group or individual assessment activity. Before making a final decision, educators may take into account the amount of time it takes for students to complete the assessment, the amount of time available for scoring, and the criteria for evaluating the assessment.

To ensure suitability and fairness for all students, check the assessment strategy for its appropriateness and if there are racial and gender biases. All students should have an opportunity to demonstrate what they know and can do. Assessments should be culturally and linguistically appropriate, recognizing that most assessment activities measure language. Useful information depends upon valid and reliable assessments. Appropriate, fair, and bias-free assessments have clearly stated directions, instructionally relevant content, and have an adequate number of assessment items to judge the performance.

Two articles were included in the unit to introduce ways to assess and evaluate student thoughts using a rubric (assessment strategy was a brief constructed response) and assess student thinking via questioning techniques. Both assessment methods provide teachers with a wealth of information about ways students organize their information cognitively, along with information about students' perspectives and misconceptions.

As teachers design or choose assessment strategies, there are helpful things that they can do as they plan the assessment activity. For example, a table of specifications guides the preparation of assessments and a curriculum map documents what is actually being taught and assessed in the classroom.

Creating Matrices

A table of specifications is a two-way chart that provides a holistic overview of the relationship between the type of the learning task and the level of cognitive processing. The purpose of the chart is to ensure that a sufficient number and variety of items appear on the assessment activity for each level of cognitive processing. Constructing a table of specifications enables the educator to crosscheck for important and essential details. The teacher can verify the alignment of the instruction and assessment strategy, detect trivial items that are unrelated to the standard, and clarify what students need to learn and be able to do.

Two articles in the unit examine the application of Tables of Specifications to help align instruction and assessment strategies. In the first article, six criteria for determining the validity of benchmark tests: alignment, diagnostic value, fairness, technical quality, utility, and feasibility (Linn, Baker, & Dunnbar, 1991, p. 49) are addressed. Examples of assessment items are presented that are useful prompts for discussion. The second article focuses on translating standards into instruction and assessments. Often teachers design assessment activities. This is a good article that explains how the process of constructing a table of specifications is embedded in designing instruction. Both articles discuss validity and reliability issues. The difference between the articles is that one is curriculum-based, the other focuses on instructional units and lessons.

Another important activity to help teachers align standards, instruction, and assessment activities is curriculum mapping. Curriculum mapping is a procedure for documenting the actual facilitation of instruction-assessment activities. Content, skills, assessment activities, and resources are often the basic information included in the matrix. It is a productive way for multiple teachers to ensure horizontal and vertical alignment of instruction and assessment activities among grades and across grades. The chart shows pacing, sequence, and when data are collected. According to the authors, creating curriculum maps guarantees consistency and thoroughness. Furthermore, maps created digitally and shared with others enhance collaboration and communication about assessment and teaching practices. By mapping "what is" actually taught and "when" it is taught, teachers have curriculum information that can be used with assessment data to make modifications in the instruction.

Curriculum development is the primary focus of two articles in the unit. A model for developing curriculum, *Process Leads to Product* (Clarke, Stow, Ruebling, & Kayonna, 2006) is applicable across all disciplines and beneficial for a K–12 population learning about curricula. Curriculum mapping and the planning process are explained with examples provided. Included in the article is information about the adaptation of the process for special education teachers. Candidates can learn that collaboration and communication are two powerful outcomes when communities of teachers work together.

Student achievement and success depend upon the content taught and the assessment activities used to measure student performance. Instruction and assessment work in tandem because assessment is an outgrowth of instruction, revealing the effectiveness of the learning experiences. However, the classroom represents a diverse population. Inclusive education is a concern for many educators. An article that addresses ways to meet the curriculum needs of a diverse population was included to stimulate discussion about this ever-increasing phenomenon. With the passage of the *No Child Left Behind Act of 2001,* there is an emphasis on serving the instructional needs of all students.

Making Benchmark Testing Work

Six criteria can help educators use benchmark tests to judge student skills and to target areas for improvement.

JOAN L. HERMAN AND EVA L. BAKER

Many schools are developing assessment systems to monitor their students' progress toward state standards throughout the academic year. Educators in these schools wisely recognize that information from annual state tests is often too little, too late. State tests can be powerful motivators, communicating expectations and focusing curriculum and instruction. But they rarely provide the ongoing information that schools need to guide instructional programs and address the learning problems of students who might otherwise be left behind.

Vendors and service providers have jumped in to fill this gap with a variety of products and services, known by such names as *benchmark tests, progress monitoring systems, and formative assessments.* These vendor-developed products and locally developed testing systems are designed to coordinate with state standards and assessments and are administered regularly—often quarterly—to gauge student progress. Available options include customized testing programs, off-the-shelf products aligned with existing state tests, and CDs and Web portals containing item banks from which educators can construct their own tests. Services include rapid, automated scoring and elaborate reporting systems for multiple audiences and purposes. Not uncommon, for example, are separate reports for administrators, teachers, parents, and students, providing information on class, group, and individual performance on specific grade-level standards and for overall grade-level proficiency.

Despite the glitz and gee-whiz appeal of such products, information about their effectiveness in improving student learning is generally hard to come by. Yet the quality of the assessment is essential: There is little sense in spending the time and money for elaborate testing systems if the tests do not yield accurate, useful information. If the information is flawed or erroneous, it is unlikely to provide good guidance for instruction or to support better decision making. The whole rationale for conducting the assessment falls apart; it merely creates the illusion that something is being done and people are paying attention.

The *validity,* or quality, of an assessment is derived from an array of evidence showing the extent to which that assessment provides sound information for particular purposes. The purpose of benchmark testing is to provide both accurate information about how well students are progressing toward mastery of standards and useful diagnostic feedback to guide instruction and improve learning. Here we discuss six criteria that determine the validity of benchmark tests: alignment, diagnostic value, fairness, technical quality, utility, and feasibility (Linn, Baker, & Dunbar, 1991). "Recommendations for Benchmark Tests" summarizes the implications of these criteria for educators.

Alignment

Alignment is the linchpin of standards-based reform. Unless benchmark tests reflect state standards and assessments, their results tell us little about whether students are making adequate progress toward achieving the standards and performing well on the assessment. The term *alignment,* however, has many potential meanings.

Aligning benchmark tests with state standards does *not* mean creating formative tests that mimic the content and format of annual state tests as specifically as possible. Although a strategy of strict test preparation may boost state test scores in the short term, available evidence suggests that early gains achieved in this way are not sustained in the long run (Herman, 2005; Hoff, 2000; Linn, 2000).

Aligning benchmark tests with state standards does *not* mean mimicking the content and format of annual state tests.

Further, aligning benchmark tests too closely with a state's tests gives short shrift to the state's standards. Annual tests of an hour or two's duration cannot address all the curriculum standards that a state has deemed essential knowledge for students. Because educators and students tend to focus on what will be tested, benchmark testing that covers only what appears on the state tests may accelerate curriculum narrowing. In contrast,

Recommendations for Benchmark Tests

1. *Align standards and benchmark assessments from the beginning of test development.* Decide what specific content to assess and at what level of intellectual demand. Include the application of complex learning. To create benchmark tests that enrich student learning opportunities, focus on the big ideas of a content area and counteract curriculum narrowing by designing benchmark tests that allow students to apply their knowledge and skills in a variety of contexts and formats.

2. *Enhance the diagnostic value of assessment results through initial item and test structure design.* Use extended-response items to reveal student thinking and potential misconceptions. Build distracters into multiple-choice items that reveal common student misunderstandings.

3. *Ensure the fairness of benchmark assessments for all students, including English language learners and students with disabilities.* Avoid unnecessarily complex language or specific contexts that could unfairly confound some students' ability to show what they know.

4. *Insist on data showing tests' technical quality.* Study psychometric indices to determine the reliability of assessments.

5. *Build in utility.* Design reports of test results to be user-friendly and to provide guidance on how to appropriately interpret and use the results.

6. *Hold benchmark testing accountable for meeting its purposes.* Crafting good benchmark tests and ensuring their wise use for improving student learning requires systematic design and continual evaluation.

good benchmark testing can encourage instruction on the full depth and breadth of the standards and give students opportunities to apply their knowledge and skills in a variety of contexts and formats.

Good benchmark testing can encourage instruction on the full depth and breadth of the standards.

For example, knowledge of Newton's laws is included in most states' physics standards. The typical state test may address this knowledge with one or two multiple-choice items or perhaps a short-answer item. In contrast, well-developed benchmark tests use not only multiple-choice and open-ended items but also performance tasks and laboratory experiments to delve deeper into students' understanding of Newton's laws. A test might ask students to explain the underlying principles of force and motion at work in a car crash, for instance, or to design a roller coaster that makes optimal use of physics principles.

Mapping Content

The alternative to aligning benchmark tests with the specific content and format of state assessments is to align them with priority content and performance expectations *implicit* in state standards. Alignment researchers and learning theorists have suggested that in establishing such priorities, educators must define both the major knowledge and skills to be addressed and the expected intellectual level of the performance (Porter, 2002).

The matrix in Figure 1 shows how a school might map expectations for a state's grade 6 mathematics standards. This matrix lays out the substance of standards in terms of the specific content knowledge that students need to acquire and includes four cognitive levels suggested by Norman Webb (1997): *recall* (knowledge of specific facts, definitions, simple procedures, formulas, and so on); *conceptual understanding* (knowledge of principles and the ability to apply them in relatively routine situations); *problem solving* (the ability to reason, plan, use evidence, and apply abstract thinking in novel situations); and *extended and strategic thinking* (the ability to apply significant conceptual understanding to extended, novel tasks requiring complex reasoning; to make connections among different content areas; and to devise creative solutions).

Figure 1 provides a starting place for identifying what content the school should teach and assess. But even when educators develop such a matrix, they have not yet resolved an important tension: Like the annual state tests, benchmark tests cannot possibly address all of a state's standards. Imagine a test that included items for every cell in Figure 1, with every standard implying a myriad of important objectives and topics that could be assessed at every cognitive level. Testing time would be endless. Instead, educators need to decide in advance what content is most important to assess, and at what levels.

Focusing on Big Ideas

By incorporating the key principles that underlie state or district standards into benchmark assessments, educators have a reasonable strategy for addressing the breadth of these standards. Cognitive research across many different subject areas suggests the power of focusing on the key principles underlying a content domain rather than on the specific topics within the domain (Ball & Bass, 2001; Carpenter & Franke, 2001; diSessa & Minstrell, 1998; Ericsson, 2002). Encompassing specific topics, the principles help students to organize and use their knowledge. For example, understanding the principle of *equivalence* can help students balance mathematical equations.

Research also demonstrates the power of engaging students in applying and explaining key principles (see, for example, Chi, 2000; VanLehn, 1996). Incorporating this idea into assessments can help increase their learning value. Therefore, despite the ease of scoring multiple-choice items, benchmark tests should

Assessment Plan——6th Grade Math Standards
Carver School District

Standard: *Number Sense*

Side tabs (top to bottom): Math Reasoning · Statistics & Analysis · Measurement & Geometry · Algebra & Functions · Number Sense

		Recall	Understanding	Problem Solving	Extended Thinking
1.0 Students compare and order positive and negative fractions and decimals. Students solve problems involving fractions, proportions, ratios, and percentages.	1.1 Compare and order positive and negative fractions and decimals and place them on a number line.		✔		
	1.2 Interpret and use ratios in different contexts (e.g., batting averages) to show the relative sizes of two quantities.	✔	✔		
	1.3 Use proportions and cross-multiplication to solve problems.			✔	
	1.4 Calculate given percentages of quantities and solve problems involving discounts at sales, interest earned, and tips.	✔			✔
2.0 Students calculate and solve problems involving addition, subtraction, multiplication, and division.	2.1 Solve problems involving addition, subtraction, multiplication, and division of positive fractions and explain why a particular operation was used for a given situation.			✔	
	2.2 Explain the meaning of multiplication and division of positive fractions and perform the calculations.	✔			
	2.3 Solve addition, subtraction, multiplication, and division problems in concrete situations that use positive and negative integers.			✔	
	2.4 Determine the least common multiple and the greatest common divisor of whole numbers; use them to solve problems with fractions.		✔		

Figure 1 A sample matrix to map expectations.

employ many different formats to enable students to reveal the depth of their understanding.

For example, the following two test items call for students to give short answers, choose multiple-choice options, offer extended explanations, and draw pictures to demonstrate their understanding of fractions:

> Six people are going to share five chocolate bars. Write the fraction that shows how much chocolate each person gets: _____
>
> Then, explain what you did to find this answer. You can draw a picture of the chocolate bars to help explain your answer.
>
> Which of the following fractions is between 2½ and 2¾?
>
> A. 2¼
>
> B. 2⅚
>
> C. 2⅔
>
> D. 2⅓
>
> Explain how you found the answer to this problem. Draw a picture that shows your answer is correct.

Diagnostic Value

A test has diagnostic value to the extent that it provides useful feedback for instructional planning for individuals and groups. A test with high diagnostic value will tell us not only whether students are performing well but also why students are performing at certain levels and what to do about it.

Open-ended test items that ask students to explain their answers increase the diagnostic value of benchmark tests. Students' responses reveal their thinking, helping teachers to refine their instructional strategies and design targeted instruction for individual students.

Circle the circuit that has the highest current. Assume that the circuits are properly connected, all bulbs are identical, and wiring does not contribute a significant amount of resistance to the circuit.

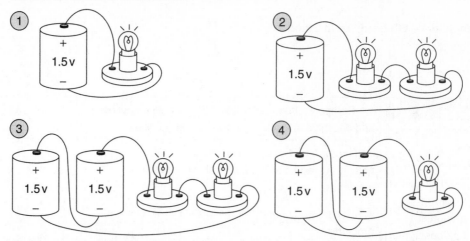

Figure 2   Sample Test Item, Electricity Principles.   This test item is intentionally designed so that each incorrect answer suggests a different misconception or common student error.

Multiple-choice items can also yield important diagnostic information, particularly when they are purposely designed so that distracters—the incorrect answer options—reflect common student misunderstandings. Consider the science test item shown in Figure 2, which is designed to assess students' understanding of electricity principles. Number 4 is the correct choice; it has the highest current because the voltage is the largest and the resistance is the smallest of all the circuits. Students who incorrectly choose number 2 show the weakest understanding of current because the voltage is the smallest and the resistance is the largest of all four circuits. We may infer that students who circle number 1 realize that smaller resistance is often associated with larger current but do not understand the role of voltage; conversely, students who circle number 3 may understand that larger voltage is often associated with larger current but do not understand the importance of resistance. Our inferences would be stronger, of course, if the assessment also asked students to explain their reasoning for their choices.

To provide good diagnostic information on where and how students are experiencing difficulties, benchmark tests must include enough items on each potential topic to render a reliable diagnosis. Drawing inferences from performance on only one or two items or from unreliable subscales may result in faulty conclusions.

Fairness

Fair benchmark tests provide an accurate assessment of diverse subgroups. Biased test items, in contrast, introduce unnecessary complexities that systematically hamper access for particular subgroups. For example, when test items use complex language to assess students' science knowledge, English language learners or poor readers may suffer an unfair disadvantage because they are unable to demonstrate their actual skill in science. Similarly, setting problems in contexts that are less familiar to some subgroups can impede those groups' ability to apply their knowledge and skill. A mathematics problem that asks students to compute the best route for a subway trip may be clear to students from New York City but may confuse students who have never been on a subway, even if they know what it is.

Fairness also is a prime issue in testing students with disabilities. For example, students with specific reading disabilities may need more time to process text. Although details on accommodations are beyond our scope here, two points are worth underscoring: (1) Accommodations offered to students in benchmark testing should mirror those documented in their individualized education plans and offered to them on annual state tests, and (2) the design of benchmark tests should make these tests accessible for as many students as possible. As with any standardized assessment, benchmark test items should be thoroughly reviewed for possible bias by representatives of diverse communities, as well as tested empirically to identify any items that have aberrant results for particular subgroups.

Technical Quality

Tests with high technical quality provide accurate and reliable information about student performance. Those of us who are not psychometricians tend to zone out when talk turns to technical indices of test quality. But item and test quality provide important information about whether we can trust the scores. If a test is weak on this characteristic, plans and decisions made on the basis of test data are likely to be faulty.

For example, *reliability*—determined by internal consistency, item response theory, inter-rater agreement, and a number of other indices—stands for the consistency of a measure and the extent to which scores on that measure represent some stable and coherent core. When a measure is highly reliable, the items within it operate similarly. Reliability problems arise if a student's performance varies significantly across items, within a short period of time, or under a whole host of other conditions (during the stress of an exam, when the student is tired, when the testing room is uncomfortable, and so on).

Reliability problems arise if a student's performance varies significantly across test items.

Imagine, for instance, a test of archery skill in which hitting the bull's-eye represents high levels of performance. One individual shoots five arrows that all hit the bull's-eye or very close to it. A second individual also shoots five arrows, but they all land in the outer ring of the target. Although the first archer's performance is more accurate, both performances are *reliable*. Looking at the results, we can be confident that we have an accurate measure of each individual's archery skills—at least on that particular day, under those conditions. A third archer's performance, however, is inconsistent, or unreliable: One arrow hits the bull's-eye; one lands near it; another hits the outermost ring; and two miss the target altogether. Assessing that performance, we would find it difficult to judge the archer's skill level, predict performance on the next shot, or devise corrective action—all inferences we want to draw from benchmark testing.

Inter-rater reliability enters the picture for open-ended and performance items—for example, a district writing assessment—which must be scored by human judges. Low inter-rater reliability often means that raters have not been trained well enough to agree on the meaning of high-quality performance. Districts should carefully monitor inter-rater reliability and take action to improve it if needed.

For benchmark tests to have diagnostic value, we must ensure the reliability of the diagnosis. We can easily create subscales that look useful—for example, aggregating the results from four items that appear to measure students' understanding of rational numbers. But if those items do not result in a reliable scale—if a student's performance on them varies widely—then the results do not provide good information for our instructional decisions.

Reliability and accuracy are necessary but not sufficient prerequisites to *validity* (that is, the extent to which a test accomplishes its intended purposes). A prime purpose of benchmark testing is to show whether students are progressing toward achieving proficiency on state tests; therefore, if the benchmark tests are doing their job, there should be a strong predictive relationship between students' performance on the benchmark tests and students' performance on the state assessments.

Educators should plan to document the reliability and validity of their benchmark tests on an ongoing basis. Good tests aren't magically created by simply assembling test items that seem reasonable—even if the tests are aligned with priority standards and teachers and psychometricians developed them collaboratively. Schools need to pilot-test and revise their items and their test forms on the basis of the technical data, ideally before a test becomes operational. Devoting sufficient time for development will yield better information from a benchmark test in the long run.

Utility

Utility represents the extent to which intended users find the test results meaningful and are able to use them to improve teaching and learning. Benchmark tests with high utility provide information that administrators, teachers, and students can use to monitor student progress and take appropriate action. District administrators, for example, may use the data to identify schools that need immediate help in particular subjects. School principals may use the data to identify students for special after-school tutoring. And teachers may use the information to modify their teaching and to regroup students for supplementary instruction.

To make benchmark tests useful, schools must put the results in intended users' hands quickly and train them to interpret the information correctly. In addition, schools must administer assessments and provide feedback when such guidance can be most useful—that is, around the time when teachers address the test content in classroom instruction. If teachers in different classrooms or schools use different curriculum materials or take more or less time teaching the topic, then finding common testing times may be an issue. For example, if one school covers Newton's laws in the fall and another covers this topic in the spring, a fall benchmark test on the topic will be of little use to the second school. To address the problem, some school districts give teachers flexibility in determining what content to assess during each testing period.

Schools can also increase the effectiveness of benchmark tests by helping teachers use the results. Teachers who lack such support may not know what to do when assessment results show that students are struggling; they may hesitate to go back and reteach because they feel pressure to move on and "cover" the curriculum. Even if they do go back, they may replicate the same strategies that were unsuccessful in the first place.

Schools can increase the effectiveness of benchmark tests by helping teachers use the results.

In addition to giving teachers the data, schools must ensure that they have the pedagogical knowledge and access to alternative materials that they need to bridge identified learning gaps. Some districts and schools help teachers by establishing grade-level or subject-matter teams, including content and curriculum experts, to meet regularly to analyze student work, discuss strengths and weaknesses in learning, and formulate next steps for individual students and subgroups representing various learning needs.

Some of the benchmark testing products available address this need by producing test score reports that explicitly identify student strengths and weaknesses, make suggestions for teaching, and direct teachers to useful materials. However, the value of such approaches depends on the validity of score interpretations and the actual learning benefits of the suggested next steps. Educators considering the purchase of such products should look for evidence to support both of these components.

Feasibility

Benchmark testing should be worth the time and money that schools invest in it. Well-designed benchmark tests can contribute to, as well as measure, student learning. But if such tests are not well designed, they can waste students' and teachers' valuable time and energy, ultimately detracting from good teaching and meaningful learning.

Of course, to determine whether benchmark testing is worth the effort, educators ultimately need to look at the results. Are benchmark tests focusing attention on student performance and providing solid information on which to base improvement efforts? Are they actually improving student learning? The history of testing is fraught with good intentions that have gone awry. Like state assessments, benchmark tests will fulfill their promise only if we monitor their consequences and continually improve their quality.

References

Ball, D. L., & Bass, H. (2001). What mathematical knowledge is entailed in teaching children to reason mathematically? In *National Research Council, Knowing and learning mathematics for teaching: Proceedings of a workshop* (pp. 26–34). Washington, DC: National Academy Press.

Carpenter, T., & Franke, M. (2001). Developing algebraic reasoning in the elementary school. In H. Chick, K. Stacey, J. Vincent, & J. Vincent (Eds.), *Proceedings of the 12th ICMI Study Conference* (Vol. 1, pp. 155–162). Melbourne, Australia: University of Melbourne.

Chi, M. T. H. (2000). Self-explaining: The dual processes of generating inference and repairing mental models. In R. Glaser (Ed.), *Advances in instruction psychology* (Vol. 5, pp. 161–238). Mahwah, NJ: Erlbaum.

diSessa, A., & Minstrell, J. (1998). Cultivating conceptual change with benchmark lessons. In J. G. Greeno & S. Goldman (Eds.), *Thinking practices in learning and teaching science and mathematics* (pp. 155–187). Mahwah, NJ: Erlbaum.

Ericsson, K. A. (2002). Attaining excellence through deliberate practice: Insights from the study of expert performance. In M. Ferrari (Ed.), *The pursuit of excellence in education* (pp. 21–55). Hillsdale, NJ: Erlbaum.

Herman, J. (2005). *Making accountability work to improve student learning.* (CSE Technical Report #649). Los Angeles: National Center for Research on Evaluation, Standards, and Student Testing.

Hoff, D. (2000, Jan. 26). Testing ups and downs predictable. *Education Week,* pp. 1, 12–13.

Linn, R. (2000). Assessment and accountability. *Educational Research,* 29, 2.

Linn, R. L., Baker, E. L., & Dunbar, S. B. (1991). Complex, performance-based assessment: Expectations and validation criteria. *Educational Researcher,* 20(8), 15–21. (ERIC Document Reproduction Service No. EJ 436 999)

Porter, A. (2002). Measuring the content of instruction: Uses in research and practice. *Educational Researcher,* 31, 3–14.

VanLehn, K. (1996). Cognitive skill acquisition. In J. Spence, J. Darly, & D. J. Foss (Eds.), *Annual review of psychology* (Vol. 42, pp. 513–539). Palo Alto, CA: Annual Reviews.

Webb, N. L. (1997). *Criteria for alignment of expectations and assessments in mathematics and science education.* Madison, WI: University of Wisconsin, National Institute for Science Education.

JOAN L. HERMAN (herman@cse.ucla.edu) and EVA L. BAKER (eva@ucla.edu) are Codirectors of the National Center for Research on Evaluation, Standards, and Student Testing (CRESST), University of California–Los Angeles, 300 Charles Young Dr. North, Los Angeles, CA 90095.

Mapping the Road to Proficiency

A table of specifications provides a travel guide to help teachers move students toward mastery of standards.

THOMAS R. GUSKEY

When the standards movement began in the United States more than 15 years ago, most educators welcomed the idea. The enthusiasm that greeted the first set of clearly articulated student learning goals, published by the National Council of Teachers of Mathematics in 1989, led other professional organizations to follow suit. During the next decade, the National Council for the Social Studies, the National Academy of Sciences, and the National Council of Teachers of English all developed standards in their respective disciplines. States also took up the task, with Kentucky leading the way in 1990. Today, 49 of the 50 states have established standards for student learning.

Thoughtfully constructed standards guide education reform initiatives by providing consensus about what students should learn and what skills they should acquire. Standards also bring much-needed focus to curriculum development efforts and provide the impetus for fashioning new forms of student assessment.

To bring about significant improvement in education, we must link standards to what takes place in classrooms.

But to bring about significant improvement in education, we must link standards to what takes place in classrooms. For that to happen, teachers need to do two important things: (1) translate the standards into specific classroom experiences that facilitate student learning and (2) ensure that classroom assessments effectively measure that learning (Guskey, 1999).

Teachers need to translate standards into experiences that facilitate student learning.

Some states, school districts, and commercial publishers have developed teaching guides that identify instructional materials and classroom activities to help teachers meet the first challenge. Rarely, however, do teachers get help in meeting the second challenge—developing classroom assessments that not only address standards accurately, but also help identify instructional weaknesses and diagnose individual student learning problems.

Translating Standards into Instruction and Assessments

Large-scale assessments provide evidence of students' proficiency with regard to the standards developed by states and professional organizations. These assessments are well suited to measure the final results of instruction and, thus, to serve the purposes of summative evaluation and accountability.

But teachers cannot be concerned only with final results. Their primary concern lies in the process of helping students reach proficiency. Large-scale assessments just don't offer teachers much help in that respect. They tend to be too broad and are administered too infrequently. In addition, teachers often don't receive their results until several weeks or months after students take the assessment.

To understand the difference between assessing the final product and supporting progress toward that product, we might consider a youngster learning to play tennis. If you were concerned only with summative evaluation and accountability, you would need to have a clear mental picture of a "proficient" tennis player—the standard that you wanted the student to attain at the end of the learning process. Your mental picture might include approaching the ball, positioning the racket correctly, swinging smoothly, returning the ball to the other side of the court, and following the rules of the game. You would then need to identify specific criteria for judging the student's performance and finally develop a rubric describing various levels of proficiency on each of these steps.

If you were a tennis coach, forming a clear mental picture of a "proficient" tennis player would be only your starting point.

If you were a tennis coach, however, that mental picture would be only your starting point. From there, you would go on to divide the aspects of your desired final performance into various components. You would probably think about matching the racket to the student's size and strength; adjusting the student's grip for backhand and forehand returns; explaining the importance of watching the ball; and demonstrating the backswing, return, and follow-through. You would introduce important terms, such as *service line, backcourt,* and *volley.* You would also need to explain the rules and describe how to keep score.

Building on this analysis, you would consider an appropriate sequence of learning steps, perhaps ordered in terms of difficulty or complexity. You would present basic elements, such as watching the ball, before such advanced elements as achieving appropriate follow-through and recovery. As you taught, you would check for any special problems the student may experience and correct them when they appeared. You would also need to become aware of individual differences among players and adapt your teaching to those differences. For instance, some players do well using a traditional closed stance; others do better with a more open stance. In addition, you would probably make a point of complimenting the student whenever progress was evident and providing reassurance during challenging times. And, of course, you would emphasize the enjoyable aspects of the game and give the student opportunities to experience these.

This example illustrates the complex process that takes place in effective standards-based teaching and learning. To organize instructional units and plan appropriate classroom activities, teachers must *unpack* the standards—that is, determine the various components of each standard that students must learn and then organize and arrange these components in a meaningful sequence of learning steps. Teachers must make adaptations for individual learning differences to ensure that all students understand, practice, and master each component as they progress toward the final goal. As part of this process, teachers need to develop procedures to formatively assess learning progress, identify learning problems, and determine the effectiveness of their instructional activities.

A Tool to Link Assessments to Standards

One tool to analyze standards for instruction and assessments is a *table of specifications*: a simple table that describes the various kinds of knowledge and abilities that students must master to meet a particular standard. Growing numbers of teachers are discovering how this strategy, described years ago in the work of Ralph Tyler (1949) and Benjamin Bloom (Bloom, Hastings,

& Madaus, 1971), can help them align their classroom instruction and assessments with curriculum standards.

As a planning tool, a table of specifications serves two important functions. First, it adds precision and clarity to teaching. The information in the table helps teachers break down standards into meaningful components that exactly convey the purpose of the instruction. It also clarifies for students the learning goals of a course or unit so that students understand what they are expected to learn. In fact, many teachers use tables of specifications as teaching guides, sharing their tables with students to reinforce students' understanding and learning progress.

Second, a table of specifications serves as a guide for consistency among standards, the steps needed to help students attain them, and procedures for checking on students' learning progress. Although this alignment is essential in standards-based teaching and learning, teachers often neglect it in their planning (Guskey, 1997). For example, many teachers stress that they want their students to develop higher-level cognitive skills—such as the ability to apply knowledge to new situations—but administer quizzes and classroom assessments that tap mainly the skills that are easiest to assess, particularly knowledge of facts and definitions of terms.

Developing Tables of Specifications

To develop tables of specifications, teachers must address two essential questions regarding the standard or set of standards in question. The first question is, *What must students learn to be proficient at this standard?* In other words, what new concepts, content, or material are students expected to learn? Teachers often use textbooks and other learning resources as guides in addressing this question. But textbooks should not be the only guide. Teachers should feel free to add to or delete from what the textbook and other learning materials provide to better match the standards and better fit students' learning needs.

The second essential question is, *What must students he able to do with what they learn?* In answering this question, teachers must determine what particular skills, abilities, or capacities must pair up with the new concepts and material. For example, will students simply be required to know the steps of the scientific method of investigation, or should they be able to apply those steps in a classroom scientific experiment?

Teachers generally find it helpful to outline their answers to these two questions using some of the categories in the *Taxonomy of Educational Objectives* (Bloom, Englehart, Furst, Hill, & Krathwohl, 1956), These categories represent a hierarchy of levels, moving from the simplest kinds of learning to more advanced cognitive skills. Figure 1 shows the categories that teachers in a wide variety of subject areas find most useful:

- *Knowledge of terms.* Terms include new vocabulary, such as names, expressions, and symbols. Students may be expected to know the definitions of these terms, recognize illustrations of them, determine when they are used correctly, or recognize synonyms. Examples

TABLE OF SPECIFICATIONS						
Knowledge of						
Terms	**Facts**	**Rules & Principles**	**Processes & Procedures**	**Translation**	**Application**	**Analysis & Synthesis**
New Vocabulary: Words Names Phrases Symbols	Specific Information: Persons Events Data Operations	Relations Guidelines Organizational cues	Patterns Sequences Order of events or operations Steps	Identify Describe Recognize Distinguish Compute	Use Illustrate Solve Demonstrate	Compare Contrast Explain Infer Combine Construct Integrate

Figure 1 General format for table of specifications.

include the terms *factor* and *product* for a mathematics standard dealing with multiplication and *photosynthesis* for a science standard related to plant life.

- *Knowledge of facts.* Facts include details that are important in their own right and those that are essential for other kinds of learning. Examples of facts are "The U.S. Senate has 100 members, two elected from each of the 50 states," and "Wealthy families or church officials commissioned many well-known works of art and music produced during the Renaissance."

- *Knowledge of rules and principles.* These generally bring together or describe the relationships among a number of facts. Typically, they concern patterns or schemas used to organize major concepts. Other terms for rules and principles include *organizers, scaffolds, guidelines,* and *organizational cues.* Examples include the commutative principle related to a mathematics standard and the rules for subject/verb agreement incorporated in a language arts standard.

- *Knowledge of processes and procedures.* To demonstrate their proficiency on some standards, students must know the steps involved in a certain process or procedure. Frequently, they must recall these steps in a specific sequence. For example, students may be expected to know the specific patterns of character development used in a novel, the appropriate order of steps in a mathematics problem, or the sequence of events necessary to enact legislation.

- *Ability to make translations.* Translation requires students to express particular ideas or concepts in a new way or to take phenomena or events in one form and represent them in another, equivalent form. It implies the ability to identify, distinguish, describe, or compute. In general, students employ translation when they put an idea in their own words or recognize new examples of general principles they have learned. Examples include having students identify the grammatical errors in sentences or convert temperatures from Fahrenheit to Celsius.

- *Ability to make applications.* Making applications means using terms, facts, principles, or procedures to solve problems in new or unfamiliar situations. To make applications, students first must determine what facts, rules, and procedures are relevant and essential to the problem and then use these to solve the problem. The ability to make applications involves fairly complex behavior and often represents the highest level of learning needed to be proficient on a particular standard. For example, writing a persuasive letter using appropriate elements of argument and correct grammatical forms requires the student to make applications.

- *Skill in analyzing and synthesizing.* Because of the complexity of analyses and syntheses, these skills typically are involved in standards for more advanced grade levels. Some teachers, however, believe that students at all levels should engage in tasks involving analysis and synthesis. Analyses typically require students to break down concepts into their constituent parts and detect the relationships among those parts by explaining, inferring, or comparing/contrasting. Examples of analyses include distinguishing facts from opinions in editorials published in the newspaper or comparing and contrasting George Washington and Ho Chi Minh, each considered the "father" of his country. Syntheses, on the other hand, involve putting together elements or concepts to develop a meaningful pattern or structure. Syntheses often call for students to develop creative solutions within the limits of a particular problem or methodological framework. They may require students to combine, construct, or integrate what they have learned. The assignment "Write a paragraph explaining how knowledge of mathematics and science helped Napoleon's armies improve the accuracy of their cannons" would require synthesis.

Once they become familiar with the format of a table of specifications, most teachers have little difficulty breaking down standards in terms of these categories. Those who use textbooks or other learning materials in developing tables usually find these resources to be helpful in answering the first essential question (What must students learn to show their proficiency with regard to this standard?) but less helpful in addressing the second question (What must students be able to do with what they learn?). And because tables clarify the learning structures that underlie standards, many teachers use them both as teaching guides to help plan lessons and as study guides for students.

Advantages of Tables of Specifications

Although developing tables of specifications can be challenging at first, teachers generally find that doing so offers several advantages. First, analyzing standards in this way helps teachers link instructional activities more meaningfully to standards. If faced with several narrowly prescribed standards, for example, teachers can use the table as a framework for combining those standards and developing relationships among them in effective instructional units. On the other hand, if confronted with a very broad or general standard, developing a table can help teachers clarify the individual components that students must master to demonstrate their proficiency.

Tables of specifications also bring precision to teaching. By analyzing standards according to the categories in the table, teachers identify the different subskills that students may be required to learn and bring attention to the relationships among those subskills. Students may need to know the definition of a term, for example, to understand a fact pertaining to that term. Knowing two or three facts may be essential to understanding a particular procedure. Similarly, knowing a procedure will probably be a prerequisite to being able to apply that procedure in solving a complex problem. Clarifying these relationships makes instructional tasks more obvious and improves the diagnostic properties of classroom assessments.

Although this kind of analysis may guide teachers in choosing classroom activities, it does not dictate specific instructional practices. Teachers may address the "what" questions in developing a table of specifications in exactly the same way, and yet teach to that standard very differently. One teacher, for example, may use a discovery approach by introducing a complex problem or application to students and then helping students determine the facts, rules, or processes needed to solve the problem. Another teacher may use an advanced organizer approach by first explaining important rules or procedures to students and then posing complex problems to which students must apply those rules and procedures. In other words, precision does not prescribe method. Clarifying our goals does not dictate how we will reach them.

Tables of specifications bring added validity and utility to classroom assessments.

Finally, and perhaps most important, tables of specifications bring added validity and utility to classroom assessments. They help teachers ensure that their assessments provide honest evidence of students' learning progress, accurately identify learning problems, and provide useful information about the effectiveness of instructional activities.

Linking Classroom Assessments to Tables of Specifications

To serve formative evaluation and instructional purposes well, classroom assessments must include items or prompts for each important concept or subskill related to the standard being measured. By matching assessment items or prompts to the elements outlined in the table of specifications, teachers can ensure that their assessments measure all these important skills and abilities.

Consider, for example, the table of specifications shown in Figure 2, developed for an elementary school social studies standard related to the use and interpretation of maps. Although a large-scale assessment may include only one or two problems asking students to use or interpret maps, a classroom assessment designed for formative evaluation purposes would look very different. It would include items that assess students' knowledge of relevant terms, facts, principles, and procedures related to maps, as well as other items that measure their skill in translating that information into new forms. It would also include constructed or extended-response items that require students to apply their knowledge in using or interpreting maps. (Note that this particular elementary standard does not require analysis and synthesis skills.)

Incorporating items that draw on this wide range of cognitive skills enhances an assessment's diagnostic properties and makes it more useful as a learning tool. Suppose students are unable to answer a complex, high-level assessment item that asks them to look at a map showing various geographic features (two major rivers and their intersection, mountain ranges, flat and steeply sloped areas); to identify the location on the map where a major settlement is likely to develop; and then to explain their reasons for selecting that location.

A closer look may reveal that some students correctly answered earlier items in the formative assessment demonstrating their knowledge of the necessary facts and principles, but could not apply that knowledge in this practical, problem-solving situation. Such students clearly need additional guidance and practice in making applications. Other students may answer this high-level item incorrectly because they did not know the requisite facts and principles, as evidenced by their incorrect answers to those items appearing earlier on in the assessment. These students need to return to activities that help them gain this basic knowledge. Although such a distinction in students' learning needs matters little to those concerned only with summative evaluations of students' proficiency, it matters greatly to teachers concerned with helping students attain proficiency.

Linking classroom assessments to tables of specifications also guarantees consistency and thoroughness. In analyzing their formative classroom assessments, teachers often find

TABLE OF SPECIFICATIONS

Knowledge of					
Terms	**Facts**	**Rules & Principles**	**Processes & Procedures**	**Translation**	**Application**
Geography Geographer Map Scale Legend Topography Topographic features Longitude Latitude Coordinates	The skill of map-making is very old. Early people based maps on inaccurate information. Inaccurate maps affected early explorations. Rivers determined the location of many early settlements.	Earth features influence many human activities: • The routes traveled • The location of towns and cities • Occupations • The things eaten	Travel routes came first. Settlements, towns, and cities were established along major travel routes and intersections, especially rivers. Occupations were based on the needs of travelers.	Describe how geography affected early travel routes. Describe why accurate maps were important to early explorers. Identify lines of longitude and latitude on a map. Describe how longitude and latirude help locate points on maps.	Explain why major cities developed in their current locations. Identify specific points or locations on a new and unfamiliar map. Use a map in planning a travel route.

Figure 2   Table of specifications for a social studies unit on maps.

items they cannot locate on the table of specifications. Such items usually tap trivial aspects of learning that are unrelated to the standard, and they can be revised or eliminated from the assessment. At other times, teachers find essential learning elements included in the table that are not tapped in their classroom assessment. In such instances, teachers must expand the assessment to include measures of these vital aspects of learning. As a result, classroom assessments become more thorough, complete, and effective at serving their formative purposes.

Destination: High Achievement for All

In developing tables of specifications, teachers identify the signposts that students must reach on the way to demonstrating their proficiency on standards. Although some teachers initially find the process challenging, most soon discover that it not only improves the quality of their classroom assessments but also enhances the quality of their teaching. Analyzing standards in this way clarifies what students need to learn and be able to do. With that focus established, teachers can concentrate more fully on how best to present new concepts and engage students in valuable learning experiences.

A table of specifications is much like a travel guide. Although it never limits the pathways available, it enhances traveling efficiency, enjoyment of the journey, and the likelihood of successfully reaching the intended destination.

References

Bloom, B. S., Englehart, M. D., Furst, E. J., Hill, W. H., & Krathwohl, D. R. (1956). *Taxonomy of educational objectives, handbook 1: Cognitive domain.* New York: McKay.

Bloom, B. S., Hastings, J. T., & Madaus, G. F. (1971). *Handbook on formative and summative evaluation of student learning.* New York; McGraw-Hill.

Guskey, T. R. (1997). *Implementing mastery learning* (2nd ed.). Belmont, CA: Wadsworth.

Guskey, T. R. (1999). Making standards work. *The School Administrator, 56*(9), 44.

Tyler, R. W. (1949). *Basic principles of curriculum and instruction.* Chicago: University of Chicago Press.

THOMAS R. GUSKEY is Professor of Education Policy Studies and Evaluation, College of Education, University of Kentucky, Taylor Education Building, Lexington, KY 40506; 859-257-8666; guskey@uky.edu. He is author of the upcoming book *Benjamin S. Bloom: Portraits of an Educator* (Rowman & Littlefield Education, 2006).

Curriculum Mapping
Building Collaboration and Communication

This article explores the application and use of curriculum mapping as a tool to assist teachers in communicating the content, skills, and assessments used in their classrooms. The process of curriculum mapping is explained, and the adaptation of the process for special education teachers is detailed. Finally, examples are given of how curriculum mapping can assist both special and general education teachers in meeting the needs of students in the classroom. Although this article will apply the use of curriculum mapping data at the middle school level, the process of mapping is equally effective at the elementary and high school levels.

ANGELA KOPPANG

Mrs. Anderson, a seventh-grade life science teacher, has 24 students in her class, 4 of whom are students with disabilities. Jesse has a mild learning disability and needs little assistance in the class, although he has some difficulties with organization. Jenny and Brian have mild cognitive disabilities and have some modified expectations for vocabulary and lengthier written assignments. John has multiple disabilities, including moderate cognitive impairment and physical disabilities. He is responsible only for a small part of the vocabulary and content, and his work is primarily designed to parallel the classroom content. In addition to these students, Mrs. Anderson has Marina, an English language learner, and 19 other students of differing abilities. Twice each week, Mr. Jones, a special education teacher, joins Mrs. Anderson, and they share teaching responsibilities and group students for instruction in a variety of ways. On the remaining days, Mrs. Smith, a teaching assistant, is available to assist Mrs. Anderson and individual students in the classroom. How do these teachers effectively communicate about the content and skills that will be used in the classroom? They base all instructional planning—as well as decisions about curriculum adaptations and modifications—on the content, skills, and assessments found in curriculum maps developed by the teachers in the school.

What Is Curriculum Mapping?

Curriculum mapping is a method of collecting data about what is really being taught in schools. It has been advocated as a method of aligning the written and taught curriculum

since the early 1970s. More recent advances in technology have expanded the use of curriculum mapping as a tool for improving communication among teachers about the content, skills, and assessments that are a part of the instructional process. This new application of curriculum mapping holds great promise for enhancing the collaboration between general and special education teachers to benefit all learners.

Curriculum mapping is a process used to gather a database of the operational curriculum of a school (Hayes-Jacobs, 1997). Although most schools have well-developed curriculum guides, information is often limited about how the standards set forth in those guides directly relate to what is actually happening in the classroom. Most curriculum guides identify what students should know and be able to do but give little insight into how students accomplish this learning or what assessment methods are used by teachers. In combination with traditional curriculum guides, curriculum maps can provide information about content and skills used for instruction, as well as the length of time devoted to various aspects of the curriculum. Including assessment methods on the maps provides a link to the expectations for the manner in which students will be expected to demonstrate their knowledge. The details included in the curriculum maps give a clearer picture of what actually occurs in each classroom.

In the curriculum mapping process, teachers use a calendar-based system (see Table 1) to map the skills, content, and assessments used in their classrooms (Hayes-Jacobs, 1997). Because each teacher takes an individual approach to meeting the curriculum standards, the individual

Table 1 Life Science Curriculum Map

Life Science	Content	Skills	Assessment
January	• Characteristics of plants • Seedless plants • Seed plants • Complex plants • Plant reproduction • Rain forest	• List characteristics of plants • Compare vascular & nonvascular plants • Describe & illustrate structures of roots, leaves, & stems • List characteristics of seed plants & find seeds in plant lab • Describe & label the functions of the flower in flower dissection lab • Describe methods of seed dispersal • Understand the environmental impact of the rain forest	• Plant worksheet • Vascular plant art • Plant drawings • Oral presentation of group work in plant lab • Flower lab report & labels • Rain forest essay

maps will reflect the differences in approaches for achieving curricular goals. The completed maps may be used for many purposes, including

- aligning instruction to the written standards;
- developing integrated curriculum units;
- providing a baseline for the curriculum review and renewal process;
- identifying staff development needs; and
- most important, providing communication among teachers.

One of the most powerful outcomes of the curriculum mapping process is using the maps as a communication tool among teachers within a school.

Hayes-Jacobs (1997) said, "Curriculum mapping amplifies the possibilities for long-range planning, short-term preparation, and clear communication" (p. 5). This focus on planning, preparation, and communication facilitates a higher level of collaboration between general education teachers and special education staff. This process can involve general and special educators on many different levels to enhance effective collaboration within a school.

Curriculum Mapping Process

While mapping is most effective when the entire school staff is involved, many school staff members have started this process by mapping one or two grade levels at an elementary school or one interdisciplinary team or department in middle or secondary schools. The process is easily accomplished by both novice and veteran teachers. The key to the success of the process is staff discussions and how data are used after the maps are completed.

Each teacher begins the process of mapping by recording his or her content, skills, and assessments. Using a computer program enhances the process of mapping by allowing for revision of the maps, as well as the ability to share the maps

throughout a school by posting them on a server or school Web site. Several excellent software programs are specifically designed for curriculum mapping; however, it is not necessary to purchase software to complete the mapping process. Many schools have started the process with a simple computer template created in a word-processing program resembling the one found in Table 1. This enables teachers to benefit from the use of technology in the mapping process, even if they do not have access to curriculum mapping software.

Mapping Content, Skills, and Assessment

Teachers begin by recording the content for the course or subject area. A curriculum map does not represent a daily lesson plan but reflects the major concepts and content that will be covered during that period. In facilitating the process with teachers in a variety of settings, I have found that on average, a teacher can map the content for one course or subject for the entire school year in 30 to 45 minutes.

After completing the content, the teacher identifies the key skills that will be used. The list of skills is often significantly longer than the list of content, and as a result, the skills portion of the map takes the greatest amount of time for teachers. I have found that it takes most teachers 1 to 1½ hours to complete the skills portion of the map for one course or subject area for the school year.

It is critical to identify the new skills that will be used and to be specific enough in that description and identification that it is clear to other readers. For example, instead of indicating that the students will be identifying the animals found in the rain forest, you would indicate that they would classify the animals by kingdom, phylum, and genus. When mapping skills, it is important to identify the new skill or the new context in which the skill will be applied. The more clearly the skill is identified, the more useful the map will be to other teachers. Clarity regarding skills will enable special education teachers to prepare a learner for the skills that will be used and help the learner compensate for deficits in the skills so he or she can fully participate in the classroom.

The final element of the curriculum map is assessment—both formal and informal. Assessment strategies should be identified for all content and skills on the map. These could include informal assessments, such as teacher observation and student self-assessments, as well as formal assessments, such as student projects, presentations, quizzes, and traditional tests. The process of mapping assessments takes about 30 to 45 minutes to complete for one course or subject area for the year.

Mapping Time Frame

Mapping one course or subject area for the year will take about 2 to 3 hours and can be accomplished in several ways. Mapping can be completed in advance of teaching by projecting ahead for a month, a semester, or an entire year. Mapping can be done at the completion of a school year in preparation for the next year, or it can be completed month-by-month as you progress through the school year. Many teachers find it easiest to map as they go through the course of the school year and generally find that it takes only about 15 to 20 minutes a month to complete the map in this manner. Using a software program or computer template for mapping allows teachers to refine and realign their maps in an ongoing process and facilitates sharing the maps with other teachers in the building.

After all teachers complete their maps, copies of all the maps are given to all teachers in the building. Everyone reads the maps to gain an understanding of the content, skills, and assessments that will be covered in each grade level or course. Sharing maps allows teachers to gain information and identify repetitions, gaps, and potential areas for integration. Teachers then come together in mixed groups to discuss the maps and compare their findings. They determine any immediate revision points and identify any areas that require research and planning. Subcommittees are then formed to research these issues and make recommendations to the staff regarding curriculum alignment. The powerful impact of this process is that it puts decisions about curriculum alignment in the hands of the teachers who deliver the instruction.

Increased collaboration and communication among teachers ultimately benefits the students. As the curriculum alignment is achieved, students' educational experiences are enhanced. The curriculum is more coherent and clear for building knowledge and skills. In addition, instruction becomes more closely aligned to the state and district standards on which students will be tested. Finally, as teachers share information about what they teach, they begin to

dialogue and share effective instructional strategies. General and special education teachers learn from each other and build strong partnerships that provide instruction to best meet the needs of their students.

Curriculum Mapping for Special Education Teachers

Special education teachers use curriculum maps to get a clear picture of the content, skills, and assessments used in the general education classroom so they can assist students with disabilities in inclusive classroom settings. The information the map provides is critical in helping special education teachers understand the instructional processes students will experience in the general education classroom. For those students with more severe disabilities, instruction is often so highly individualized that maps would have to be specific for each student to give a clear picture of the instruction. To truly communicate the appropriate information, traditional maps as completed by general education teachers would need to be created for each individual student. Because this is already done as a part of Individualized Education Programs (IEPs) the process would only increase the paperwork load for special education teachers. A different process must be used to develop communication among special education staff members.

In working in schools with special education teachers involved in curriculum mapping, I adapted a process that has been used by library media specialists for special education staff. The special education staff began to compile a list of curriculum-based resources that supported the content, skills, and assessments outlined in general education teachers' curriculum maps. These resources were entered into a searchable database that was accessible by all staff in the building (see Table 2). The database included information about the content and skills contained in the materials, along with information such as an approximation of reading level and/or the grade-level equivalency of the materials. It included any other specialized adaptive information that would assist anyone searching the database in understanding how the material might support classroom instruction. The database indicated where in the building these materials were located and the contact staff person in charge of these materials.

Thus began a process of sharing curriculum materials and other supportive resources among special education staff members, as well as between special and general education teachers. Any staff member can access these materials to support the learning needs of students who are not identified for any type of special service programs, but who may have specialized learning needs.

Table 2 Teacher Curriculum Resource List

Materials	Publisher	Features	Map Correlation	Location
Trees and Plants in the Rain Forest	Steck Vaughn	Reading Level 3 Includes photos, stories, & activities about conservation and environment	7th January Life Science	Mental retardation classroom
Flower parts	Teacher made	Includes digital photos of parts of flowers with terms— can be matched to actual flower dissection	7th January Life Science	English as a second language classroom
Johnny Tremain	Recorded books	Tape recording of full book text	7th February Language Arts	Learning disabilities classroom
The Call of the Wild	Steck Vaughn	Reading Level 4	8th December Language Arts	Library

Curriculum materials that parallel the classroom content to a lower grade-level equivalency reading level could be used to support English language learners (ELL) or students with other learning delays. Teachers searching for materials to assist students in their classrooms can determine if materials that may fit their purposes are available. In addition, they know whom to contact about these materials. This often began a dialogue about strategies and materials that support learning needs of students and created a situation in which the special education teachers were able to share their specialized skills in teaching strategies with general education teachers. As teachers borrow and adapt these materials for students in the classroom, they gain more knowledge and skills in working with specialized learning needs of students with disabilities. They are better prepared to serve not only students with disabilities in their classrooms but all students in their classrooms.

After general education teachers complete their maps, special education staff code the resource database to the classroom teachers' maps, indicating those resources that specifically support the content, skills, and assessments used by the general education teachers. Not only does this facilitate the sharing of resources, it also clearly identifies those areas in which the school does not currently have many resources to support the classroom curriculum. Available budget moneys can then be directed toward the purchase or development of materials in those areas. Rather than having each special education staff member create his or her own adapted materials, educators can pool resources and expertise to find or develop appropriate materials.

Sharing this information helps all educators better direct limited budget resources and gives educators time to acquire and develop materials that best support the actual general education classroom curriculum and curriculum standards. Sharing is facilitated not only between general education teachers and special education teachers but also among program areas within and outside of special education.

Benefits of Curriculum Mapping

Although curriculum maps facilitate communication among teachers, the key benefit is improving the learning needs of all students, especially individuals with disabilities. Special education teachers are able to develop a clearer understanding of the general education classroom curriculum, along with knowledge of the skills and assessments that will be used. This information is vital for general and special education teachers who collaborate to support learning in the general education classroom. The maps also provide a strong basis for making decisions about inclusion and acquiring knowledge about the necessary level of classroom adaptation and modification to assist students with disabilities to participate in the general education classroom and curriculum. Beneficial information gained from mapping includes preteaching skills, correlating community-based outings with upcoming curriculum-based content, and using alternative assessments.

Maps give more detail about the skills and processes that will be used in the general education classroom than do traditional content-based lesson plans. Knowing the skills that will be used in upcoming lessons, special education teachers can begin to preteach skills to students before the skills are introduced in the general education classroom. This gives students more time and repetition to learn skills. When the skill is introduced in the general education classroom, these students will be able to participate at a level more comparable to their peers and will gain confidence in the ability to more fully participate in the general classroom.

Students in Mrs. Anderson's science class will be working on a rain forest project that will culminate in an essay about the rain forest. Mr. Jones, the special education teacher, works with Mrs. Anderson's curriculum map to identify the key concepts of the lesson. He prepares a graphic organizer or concept map for the students to use in class. This concept map is organized in a manner that reflects the structure and relationship of the concepts that will be highlighted in Mrs. Anderson's instruction about the rain forest. This is a type of content-enhancement routine that improves the organization of the instruction by presenting it in a learner-friendly format that emphasizes the "big picture" ideas (Boudah, Lenz, Bulgren, Schu-maker, & Deshler, 2000).

Mrs. Anderson and Mr. Jones model using the concept map for organizing instruction while students take notes or create their own concept maps. Students with disabilities receive a partially completed concept map that contains the key ideas and issues from the instruction (see Figure 1). The students add details to the concept map in each of the identified key categories during the instruction. Mr. Jones and Mrs. Anderson model how to appropriately use the concept map by adding information to a template of the map on an overhead projector. Having students fill in the information on this concept map not only helps them stay organized but provides them the multisensory approach of seeing the key concepts on the graphic organizer, hearing concepts from the teacher, and writing concepts on the map. All of this helps them retain information while focusing on the most important concepts (Friend & Bursuck, 2001).

At the end of the lesson, students review the concepts on the map and prepare questions for review, which they can then use in class or at home to review and prepare for a test. Students can use another template of the map as an organizer to outline the key ideas from their reading assignment. Finally, concept maps can become the framework for the information students will use to write their essays on the rain forest.

To assist students in writing these essays, Mr. Jones proposes to Mrs. Anderson that he teach a composition strategy called DEFENDS (Ellis & Lenz, 1987) to the science class. Mrs. Anderson is not familiar with this strategy but recognizes that the DEFENDS strategy will assist students as they write a paper defending their position on the destruction of the rain forest (see Figure 1). The strategy uses the following steps:

D   Decide on an exact position
E   Examine the reasons for the positions
F   Form a list of points that explain each reason
E   Expose the position in the first sentence
N   Note each reason and supporting points
D   Drive home the point in the last sentence
S   Search for errors and correct

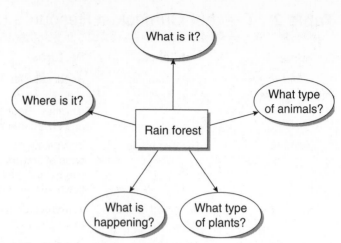

Figure 1   Rain forest concept map.

After Mr. Jones teaches the strategy to the class, he works with a small group of students who need additional assistance in the use of the strategy. When students have completed their essays, all students are asked to use the steps of the strategy to self-assess and refine them.

Curriculum maps also give special education teachers more time to develop appropriate classroom activities that parallel the classroom content for those students who may need significant modifications to participate in the general education classroom. Knowledge of the content, skills, and assessments used in the classroom will help special education teachers identify activities that will parallel general education activities and reinforce the same skills at a different level. Teachers can analyze the skills involved and determine if the student can perform the same task as other students, perform the same task with an easier step, perform the same task with different materials, or perform a different task with the same theme (Lowell-York, Doyle, & Kronberg, 1995).

In Mrs. Anderson's science class, students are classifying types of animals by kingdom, phylum, and genus. A student who is able to do the same task with an easier step may be classifying an animal only by kingdom. A student who needs to undertake the same task with different materials may be using picture cards with the name and pictures of animals. A student who needs to tackle a different task with the same theme may be naming animals or determining if they live on land or water.

Knowledge of the content, skills, and assessments that are part of the general education curriculum assists special education teachers in planning community-based learning experiences that support the content being taught in inclusive settings. Using the community-based experiences to support inclusive classroom learning can also provide opportunities for special education students to share what they have gained with the general education students. If

Table 3 Defends Strategy

D	Decide on an exact position	The student decides on his or her personal position about the destruction of the rain forest
E	Examine the reasons for the positions	The student determines & explains why he or she holds these beliefs
F	Form a list of points that explain each reason	The student makes a list of points about the rain forest that supports his or her beliefs
E	Expose the position in the first sentence	The student composes a topic sentence that supports his or her position
N	Note each reason & supporting points	The student creates short paragraphs that elaborate on the points identified earlier
D	Drive home the point in the last sentence	The student restates his or her position & reasons in the summary statement
S	Search for errors and correct	The student self-edits the essay

the science class is studying reptiles, a community-based learning experience might include a trip to a local pet store or zoo. Students may take along an instant picture or digital camera to record the reptiles they see on the outing, or they may gather information about the reptiles to share with their classmates when they return to school. The photos and information gathered can become a part of the curriculum materials for the special education students as well as supporting materials for the general education teachers and students.

One particularly successful community-based outing involved having students purchase and prepare lab kits for use in the science classroom. The science teacher prepared a list of materials needed for an upcoming lab in which students would dissect and label parts of a flower. On a community-based outing, students purchased the materials for the lab activity. They also visited a greenhouse to learn about plants and to purchase the flowers to be used in the lab. Students then worked with a teaching assistant to learn how to assemble the materials into lab kits to be used in the science lab. This collaboration supported the learning needs of the special education students and assisted the general education teacher in preparing lab materials. The greatest benefit was the pride students had later that day when they participated in the lab activity that they had prepared. The science teacher recognized their efforts, and they were able to share materials and photos they had gathered in their trip to the greenhouse for the benefit of all students.

Finally, assessment information included on the curriculum maps will help special education teachers understand how general education teachers will be assessing students' accomplishment in terms of the knowledge, skills, and processes in the curriculum.

Special education teachers can assist students in developing study guides and equip students with test-taking strategies that fit the assessments used by general education teachers.

Special education teachers can use samples of classroom projects and assessments to build a portfolio that will demonstrate the attainment of IEP goals. In addition, information on the curriculum map offers general and special educators the opportunity to collaborate on alternative methods of assessing student knowledge. Because of the needs of their students, many special education teachers have a great deal to offer general education teachers in the development of assessment methods that do not rely solely on traditional tests and quizzes. As general education teachers collaborate on designing these alternate assessments, they improve their own skills in using multiple assessment methods.

The greatest benefit of using curriculum maps is the improved communication among all teachers in the school. As special and general education teachers have a better level of understanding of the content, skills, and assessments used in classrooms, they can build stronger collaborations to assist all students with special learning needs. General education teachers can gain a wealth of knowledge about strategies and structures that support learning from special education teachers. Special education teachers benefit from curriculum mapping by gaining a deeper understanding of the general classroom curriculum and how they can create meaningful curricular connections for students. Improved communication among all teachers in the school provides professional educators with another tool for effectively enhancing the learning of all students in the classroom, especially students with disabilities.

References

Boudah, D. J., Lenz, B. K., Bulgren, J. A., Schumaker, J. B., & Deshler, D. D. (2000). Don't water down! Enhance content learning through the unit organizer routine. *Teaching Exceptional Children, 32*(3), 48–56.

Ellis, E., & Lenz, K. (1987). A component analysis of effective learning strategies for LD students. *Learning Disabilities Focus, 2,* 94–107.

Friend, M., & Bursuck, W. D. (2001). *Including students with special needs: A practical guide for classroom teachers* (3rd ed.). Needham Heights, MA: Allyn & Bacon.

Hayes-Jacobs, H. (1997). *Mapping the big picture: Integrating curriculum & assessment K–12*. Alexandria, VA: Association for Supervision and Curriculum Development.

Lowell-York, J., Doyle, M. E., & Kronberg, R. (1995). *Curriculum as everything students learn in school: Individualizing learning opportunities*. Baltimore: Brookes.

ANGELA KOPPANG, PhD, is an assistant professor in the Educational Leadership Department at the University of North Dakota and specializes in the areas of curriculum, instruction, assessment, and school leadership. She is a former elementary and middle school teacher and administrator and serves as a consultant in the areas of curriculum development and alignment. Address: Angela Koppang, Department of Educational Leadership, Box 7189, Grand Forks, ND 58201; e-mail: angela_koppang@und.nodak.edu.

Developing Standards-Based Curricula and Assessments
Lessons from the Field

NANCY A. CLARKE ET AL.

Changes in thinking and behavior on the part of all instructional leaders who work to improve academic success for all students must occur if there is to be increased student achievement. In *Lessons from a Comprehensive Appraisal Project*, Manatt (1987), reported that student achievement is influenced by (a) entry-level ability (51 percent), (b) how teachers teach (8 percent), (c) what teachers teach (38 percent), and (d) all other factors (3 percent). Because what is taught has greater importance for improving student achievement than how teachers teach, in the late 1980s the School Improvement Model (SIM) Center staff at Iowa State University undertook the creation of a model for developing curriculum.

At about the same time, national professional subject-area associations and various states began identifying new standards for the various content areas. They described what is important for K-12 students to learn as they prepare for life and work in the twenty-first century. It became obvious that the curriculum development process should address the alignment of local curricula with new state standards.

During the last twenty years, curriculum alignment activities have increased among school organizations that want to improve the efficiency and effectiveness of the instructional and assessment programs. The need to eliminate gaps and/or duplication in the teaching and learning processes is requiring instructional leaders to look even more closely at the skills and concepts of what is to be taught in their schools.

Since the arrival of the federal No Child Left Behind (NCLB) legislation in 2002, curriculum alignment activities have taken on a renewed sense of urgency. As such, the SIM team, having significant experience developing standards-based, aligned curricula and assessments, has streamlined a process to assist instructional leaders with these endeavors.

Major Considerations

When developing curricula and assessments, there are three important considerations that should be understood prior to their development. First, the actual written curriculum documents need to give direction, focus, and accountability in the learning environment. These must be updated or newly created on a scheduled basis by a team of curriculum writers.

Second, the learner outcomes that define what students are expected to learn by the time they graduate must be aligned with the state's content standards. Most school organizations have not yet effectively incorporated these standards into their curricula; in fact, many school organizations lack a written curriculum or any written plan that guides instruction.

Third, the quality-control principle of the alignment of written, taught, and tested curriculum must be applied. This principle indicates the critical role of instructional leaders as curricula and assessments are being developed and implemented. English and Larson (1996) contend that a lack of curriculum alignment may provoke lower achievement because teachers teach content that is not part of the curriculum documents; subsequently, students are not taught what is assessed.

Process Leads to Products

Developing curricula with matching assessments is an intellectually rigorous task that entails following a sophisticated and technical process. A model is needed to assist curriculum writers as they proceed with the task.

A Model for Developing Curriculum

The model for curriculum development, "Process Leads to Products," was created and refined during a five-year, field-based research study involving five school organizations. This study used student achievement as a dependent variable, determining the relationship between the implementation of the newly developed curricula and student learning results. Manatt and Stow (1986) describe this research study and its findings, which were generally positive. The SIM team further refined the process-to-products methodology over the years as new insights were gleaned from the literature and experience.

The process is a set of structured activities used by content-specific committees of teachers and their instructional leaders. The products are the standards-based curricula that become the infrastructure of content areas and their accompanying criterion-referenced assessments. Components of the curriculum development process, which is often referred to as the framework, include the following:

1. A philosophy statement: a set of beliefs about a specific content area

2. Strands or definitions: major themes in the content area

3. Program goals: statements for each strand that express the general intent for learning toward which students work

4. Scope and sequence grids: display the scope of the skills/concepts and the sequence that indicates who (the grade level/course) teaches what (skills/concepts) to what extent (introduce, expand, mastery, mastery expanded, and mastery maintained); as the skills/concepts are defined, subskills/subconcepts are identified

5. Unit plans: include (a) what will be learned? (learner outcomes or exit behaviors), (b) how will you know the students learned the skill/concept? (criterion-referenced assessment techniques both traditional and nontraditional), and (c) how will you teach the skills/concepts? (teacher/student activities along with instructional tools)

The writing process and characteristics of technical writing are used to develop each component of the framework. The writing process—prewriting, drafting, revising, editing, and publishing—ensures that the committees that develop the curricula give careful thought to each component and its relationship to other components. Technical writing emphasizes rules for the format and content of each component, ensuring consistency and clarity.

The curriculum documents serve as communications tools. Components of the curriculum are written in the order listed, a process of moving from general to specific. As each component is written, it remains "tentative" while the subsequent components are developed and may be revised. This helps to ensure consistency among the components. After the developmental process is completed from the philosophy through learner outcomes, a curriculum document is ready to be published as a whole.

What Students Will Learn

Following "tentative" closure on philosophy, strands, and program goals, teachers must think carefully about the skills/concepts or what is to be taught/learned. The skills/concepts within a program goal are identified and sequenced across grade levels and courses prior to writing the learner outcomes. Subskills or subconcepts are identified to be used as the focus when writing learner outcomes. A learner outcome is written using one subskill or subconcept as the focus for the learner outcome.

The learner outcomes have three identifiable parts: condition of learning (the situation in which the students will learn and be assessed), observable behavior (a single action verb), and criterion measure (the level of expectation). Each learner outcome is written for a specific level of Bloom's Taxonomy that is appropriate for the level of learning. Learner outcomes must be stated explicitly so they have only one meaning.

As teachers on a content-area committee draft the learner outcome, they refer to the scope and sequence, list of subskills or subconcepts, state content standards, and specifications of any norm-referenced test used by the school organization. These drafts are revised, based on specific feedback, using the format and content rules for writing learner outcomes.

Assessing What Students Have Learned

After the written curriculum is developed, a set of criterion-referenced assessments is written to measure student learning. These become, in essence, the tested curriculum.

There are two types of assessments: traditional (e.g., multiple-choice items) and nontraditional (e.g., product, process, performance, personal communication). Multiple-choice items are written first in this process because they can be used to assess all levels of Bloom's Taxonomy from knowledge through evaluation, increase diagnostic capabilities, and can be used to assess a broad sample of learner outcomes within a short period of time.

Technical writing rules are also used to write multiple-choice items. Rules that guide this process include writing a stem as a direct question and four foils (response options) with one correct answer and three distracters (options that are plausible but wrong). The foils must avoid negative words, clues, absolutes, and phrases such as "none of the above" and "not enough information." When writing multiple-choice items for learner outcomes at the application, analysis, synthesis, and levels of thinking, the "condition of learning" becomes particularly important because a prompt or display (such as graphs or scenarios) must be created for these items. The prompt or display gives the situation, background, or context the learner needs when answering the test question.

Writing assessments that meet the criteria of well-written items is an intellectually rigorous task. Begin by writing the stem, then create a prompt (if one is needed). The next step is to write the correct answer. Finally, brainstorm three plausible distracters. Think about why these distracters have been chosen, because they become the diagnostic elements of an item. In some cases, there may be more than one correct answer, but only one of them can be used in a multiple-choice question.

When the learner outcomes require that students use the skills and concepts "in depth," nontraditional assessments, which require the learner to actually do something, are developed. A nontraditional technique will assess several learner outcomes. It includes an exercise or scenario task that is created in a meaningful context and elicits the desired performance. The task frames the challenge for students, is content specific, parallels a real-world situation, has a purpose, and engages students in thoughtful application of the learning that is found in a combination of learner outcomes. The criteria (or the essential qualities that will be measured) need to be embedded in the task as it is being written. A critical element of a nontraditional technique is a rubric, a powerful tool used to judge the behaviors exhibited by the student. It clearly establishes the standards, expectations, and levels of quality of the work. A common-sense approach to the assessment of criterion-referenced learning is to use a combination of both traditional and nontraditional techniques. In this way, a more complete picture of student performance is available for data-driven decisions.

Now, the standards-based curricula and criterion-referenced measures, which have been approved by the board of education, become the foundation for the teaching and learning process. This user-friendly set of materials states affirmatively: Of all that could be taught/learned, these are what are important for this school organization. Without such a plan, student learning is left to chance and worthwhile learning will be achieved only by accident or default, not by intentional design.

Guidelines for Instructional Leaders

A recent study (Ruebling et al. 2004) indicated that if improvements are to be made in student learning results, school leaders need to make curriculum and assessment development, implementation, and monitoring a higher priority. These researchers found that school leaders routinely maintain a "hands-off" approach with respect to curriculum development activities, relying entirely on teachers and not personally supervising the implementation of curriculum and assessments.

The Role of Instructional Leaders

Instructional leaders must be able to articulate to their staff a clear rationale for the curricula and the requirements of aligning the written, taught, and tested curricula. There are four important leadership tasks regarding curricula, within the role of being an instructional leader, that focus on the academic success for all students.

1. Active involvement in development of the curriculum.
    According to Marzano, one of the critical roles of leadership is to provide teachers and students with a "guaranteed and viable curriculum" (2003, 173). Therefore, instructional leaders must understand and be involved in the curriculum development process. This involvement helps them demonstrate to teachers the importance of the curriculum documents. Only when instructional leaders are actively involved in curriculum development will the implementation of the newly developed curricula have a high priority.

2. Development of strong teacher teams to implement the newly developed standards-based curricula and assessments.
    Instructional leaders need to place an emphasis on team building. Lambert (2003) stated that leaders provide professional development opportunities for teams. Effective teaching teams must have shared goals, shared accountability for student learning as measured by the assessments, and have diverse teaching and problem-solving skills. Possibilities could include collegial conversations, coaching episodes, or shared decision-making groups, Middle and high schools' leaders can provide time for teachers to be involved in these possibilities during block planning and/or departmental meetings. The leaders should monitor these meetings as suggested by Schmoker, who believes that they should "evaluate meetings for effectiveness and results-orientation" (2001, 42) to determine if they are on target.

3. Support of the comprehensive assessment program: the leaders must support the comprehensive data-driven assessment program.
    Data from the assessment program drives improvement. Teams of teachers need to review student achievement data, study the results, identify areas of strength and areas for growth, and develop plans to improve the teaching and learning process. Carr and Harris suggest using these results as a "data source for action planning" (2001, 62). Instructional leaders must ensure that teachers use the data to plan an effective and improved instructional program.

4. Management of learning through monitoring the implementation of curriculum

Conclusion

Monitoring the implementation of the newly developed curriculum is a must. The instructional leader must monitor lesson plans and have regular conversations with both individual teachers and teams of teachers about teaching and the progress of students. More specific, instructional leaders need to discuss with teachers and teams how they plan instruction, select activities and materials, and prepare assessments that are aligned with the curricula. Leaders need to observe teachers as they are teaching and provide feedback about what is recorded during the observation of the teaching and learning processes. When leaders know grade level and course content as defined in the curriculum documents, they can quickly assess if the teacher is focusing on the essential learning requirements. The data from these processes will provide implications for changes in the teaching during the next review cycle.

Once the products of the process—the standards-based curricula and assessments—are published, school organizations need to do the following:

1. conduct staff development sessions that address four issues: content knowledge required to teach the new curricula, curriculum guide components, use

of the curriculum guide for planning instruction, and components of the comprehensive data-driven assessment plan;

2. focus on learning results and hold teachers and leaders accountable;
3. review assessment data and use them for the benefit of the learners and the improvement of teaching;
4. require and review lesson plans that are based on the written curriculum;
5. define a formal system for revising the curricula;
6. develop a plan to communicate results to all stakeholders: staff, students, board, parents, and community.

To improve the academic success for all students, educators must indeed change how they think and behave.

References

Carr, J. F., and D. E. Harris. 2001. *Succeeding with standards: Linking curriculum, assessment, and action planning.* Alexandria, VA: Association for Supervision and Curriculum Development.

English, F. W., and R. L. Larson. 1996. *Curriculum management for educational and social service organizations.* 2nd ed. Springfield, IL: Charles C. Thomas Publishers.

Lambert, L. 2003. *Leadership capacity for lasting school improvement.* Alexandria, VA: Association for Supervision and Curriculum Development.

Manatt, R. P. 1987. *Lessons from a comprehensive appraisal project.* Ames: Iowa State University.

Manatt, R. P., and S. B. Stow. 1986. *Developing and testing a model for measuring and reporting educational outcomes of K-12 schools, a technical report.* Ames: Iowa State University.

Marzano, R. 2003. *What works in schools: Translating research into action.* Alexandria, VA: Association for Supervision and Curriculum Development.

Ruebling, C. E., S. B. Stow, F. A. Kayona, and N. A. Clarke. 2004. Instructional leadership: An essential ingredient for improving student learning. *Educational Forum* (68) 3: 243–53.

Schmoker, M. 2001. *The results fieldbook: Practical strategies from dramatically improved schools.* Alexandria, VA: Association for Supervision and Curriculum Development.

Stow, S. B. 2000. *A comprehensive approach to the development of a standards-based curriculum which includes assessments.* Ames: Iowa State University.

NANCY A. CLARKE and **SHIRLEY STOW** are education consultants at Iowa State University in Ames. **CHARLES RUEBLING** is an educational consultant and the founder of the Center for School Redesign. **FRANCES KAYONA** is an educational leadership and community psychology professor at St. Cloud State University in St. Paul, Minnesota.

Assessing Problem-Solving Thought

ANNETTE RICKS LEITZE AND SUE TINSLEY MAU

Recent reform efforts that are based on the *Curriculum and Evaluation Standards for School Mathematics* (NCTM 1989) call for an increase in problem solving as part of the mathematics curriculum for students at all levels. Teachers can use problem-solving activities for multiple purposes, such as developing critical-thinking skills, data-organization skills, communication skills, and a risk-taking attitude, as well as making connections among mathematical topics. Regardless of the curriculum goal, teachers face many challenges in finding suitable activities and then assessing the work that students do on these activities. Neither task is easy.

Given the multiple purposes of problem solving, the process of engaging in such an activity is clearly more complex than simply performing routine exercises. Assessment techniques must fully account for the complexity of the task. To do so, we believe that it is advisable for teachers to plan the assessment technique before they engage the students in the problem-solving activity. In this article, we address, in detail, one method of assessment—an analytic scoring rubric—of a particular mathematical problem-solving activity.

Selecting Phases in the Problem-Solving Process

Our particular problem-solving activity, the TV Tally problem, is shown in Figure 1. The first step in developing an assessment plan is to solve the problem. Without solving the problem yourself, you have no knowledge of the crucial elements of the problem and of the problem-solving process.

Once you have arrived at a solution to the problem, you are able to move to the second step, "identify[ing] those phases of the problem-solving process that are of interest" (Charles, Lester, and O'Daffer 1987, 30). According to these authors, problem-solving activities involve seven important thinking skills, four of which we include in our assessment plan:

- understand or formulate the question in a problem;
- select or find the data to solve the problem;
- formulate subproblems, and select appropriate solution strategies to pursue; and
- correctly implement the solution strategy or strategies, and solve subproblems.

TV TALLY

Question: About how many hours of television have you watched in your lifetime?

Directions: Record your estimate and explain your reasoning. Include all of your figuring. Use the back of this page if you need more space.

Figure 1 The problem as presented to sixth graders.
Source: *Puddle Questions, Grade 5* [Westley 1994, 81], © 1994 Creative Publications.

We chose these four phases on the basis of our own solution to the problem, taking into consideration various aspects of the problem that could dramatically alter the solution. That is, we believe that these four phases are essential elements in successfully completing our problem-solving activity.

Understand or Formulate the Question in a Problem

Although this skill may seem self-explanatory, a comment is needed. Many students have an ability to give correct numeric answers without ever seeming to understand the problem. Perhaps they "see" through the problem and are unable to articulate their thoughts, or perhaps they "got lucky" and gave a correct answer. In a true problem-solving situation, a student must understand the problem to begin any sensible or reasonable solution strategy. In the "TV Tally" problem, students need to understand what an estimate is and how to formulate that estimate in some reasonable way. As we work through this problem, the need for a true understanding of the question and evidence of such understanding will become more specific.

Select or Find the Data to Solve the Problem

The students who were given this problem-solving task were in the sixth grade. All the problem statements had calendars for the past twelve years attached to them. Although the calendars were readily available, many students did not use them to calculate their life span. For example, many said that they were twelve years old, and they used entire-year calculations rather than consider that they may be twelve years and three months old. To estimate as accurately as possible, students needed to compute hours of partial years of their life span.

Formulate Subproblems, and Select Appropriate Solution Strategies to Pursue

This phase of the problem-solving activity is much like the previous one. Part of determining appropriate subproblems is computing partial years of television watching. Another part of formulating appropriate subproblems is accounting for seasonal adjustments in television viewing (e.g., children play outside longer in the summer), for changes in life events (e.g., illness or family events could force the child to be sedentary and watch more television, perhaps out of boredom), for changes in age (e.g., starting school limits television watching), and so forth.

Correctly Implement the Solution Strategy or Strategies, and Solve Subproblems

Once the students have determined the subproblems and their solution strategies, it is incredibly easy for them to choose the wrong arithmetic procedure or to make an arithmetic mistake. Correctly implementing the solution strategy includes not only paying attention to detail to reduce arithmetic errors but also choosing correct arithmetic processes.

In selecting these phases, we did not include a phase for evaluating the reasonableness of the answer (Charles, Lester, and O'Daffer 1987). Evaluating the reasonableness of the answer is a metacognitive act. It is the equivalent of Pólya's looking-back step (Pólya 1945), and it occurs after the problem-solving activity. This step was purposely eliminated because we had only limited knowledge of the importance that the teacher had placed on the reasonableness of an answer, not to mention a sixth grader's ability to understand such large numbers. Since any assessment technique must be aligned with the instruction in the classroom, we did not include an evaluation of reasonableness as part of the rubric.

Developing a Rubric

Charles, Lester, and O'Daffer (1987) offer several assessment and scoring methods for measuring problem-solving ability. Among these methods are two rubrics that are particularly useful for scoring problem-solving activities: *focused holistic* and *analytic*. A focused holistic scoring rubric assigns one score to the student's entire solution. An analytic scoring rubric assigns a score to each of several phases of the problem solution. The student's entire score is computed by adding the individual scores from each phase of the solution process.

Understand or Formulate the Question in a Problem
0: Complete misunderstanding
2: Part of the problem misunderstood or misinterpreted
4: Complete understanding

Select or Find the Data to Solve the Problem
0: No life-span calculations
2: Age calculated in whole years
4: Partial-year calculations

Formulate Subproblems, and Select Appropriate Solution Strategies to Pursue
0: Does not consider differing patterns during lifetime
2: Accounts for one adjustment
4: Adjusts for age/seasonal viewing/days of the week/ illnesses, and so forth

Correctly Implement the Solution Strategy or Strategies, and Solve Subproblems
0: No correct processes chosen or used
1: Some, but not all, arithmetic processes correct
2: Correct arithmetic processes for all phases of the problem
3: All arithmetic processes and calculations correct

Figure 2 Analytic scoring rubric for the TV Tally problem.

Westley (1994), the source of this problem-solving activity, offered a focused holistic scoring scale. We have used similar rubrics to evaluate other problem-solving activities. After past assessments, we felt uncomfortable with what we had learned because we had insufficient understanding of students' thinking. As a result, for this problem-solving activity we developed an analytic scoring rubric.

We suggest that teachers develop their own analytic scoring rubrics for assessing problem solving. The advantage to developing your own rubric is that it will be well aligned with instruction in your classroom and sensitive to the peculiarities of your specific problem-solving activity. Developing your own rubric is consistent with the NCTM's mandate that "student assessment must be aligned with, and integral to, instruction" (NCTM 1995, 1).

Once the phases of problem solution have been identified, you are ready for the third step: determine the levels of work within each phase. (See Figure 2.) Notice in our example that we have chosen three levels in the first three (i.e., thinking) phases and four levels in the last (i.e., arithmetic) phase. Our experience has shown that using more than three or four levels in a phase increases the difficulty of distinguishing among levels. Since the work in the thinking phases tends to be more internal, we advise using only three levels in those phases. We prefer three levels because analytic scoring rubrics with fewer than three levels in a phase are not sufficiently sensitive to variation and because those rubrics with more than three levels tend to hinder differentiation. However, the work in the arithmetic phase is external and written; it is easier to observe. In the arithmetic phase, variations in work are more readily observed, so the number of levels may be increased to four.

Once you determine the number of levels in each phase, move to the fourth step, which is to assign point values to each level in each phase. We chose to use zero as the lowest point value in each phase because we believe that middle school students need honest feedback. It does students no justice to give them points for no understanding, no calculations, no subproblem formulation, and no correct arithmetic processes. Students whose thinking demonstrates little problem-solving ability do not acquire that ability by being told that they are doing a good job. Giving students points for no work or understanding implies to them that they have done something correctly, when, in fact, they have not.

One option in assigning point values to each level is to assign consecutive whole numbers, such as 0, 1, and 2, in the phases having three levels and 0, 1, 2, and 3 in phases having four levels. Doing so, however, gives greater weight, and hence greater importance, to the arithmetic process phase than to the thinking phases, which, in fact, are more important to the solution process. Since the purpose is to assess problem-solving ability, we believe that greater weight should be given to the thinking phases. As a result, we chose to double the 0, 1, and 2 point values to 0, 2, and 4 as the point values in the three thinking phases. An examination of the rubric we devised reveals that ours is a 15-point rubric, with 12 points, or 80 percent, devoted to problem-solving thinking and only 3 points, or 20 percent, to arithmetic processes. We believe that this point distribution is appropriate for a problem-solving activity.

Scoring Students' Papers

The rubric has been developed, and the problem-solving activity has been completed. As you begin your assessment, you are faced with the task of scoring students' papers. How do you proceed? You must read the entire solution, performing all the processes along with the student. In fact, as some of our examples illustrate, sometimes you may attempt to draw inferences about students' work. Students are not always forthcoming in their explanations of their problem-solving techniques. Because of these minimal explanations from students, it is imperative that you carefully read the student's solution to be able to get a fairly complete picture of what the student was thinking. Once you have a sense of the student's thinking, you can begin to assign points to each phase of the problem solution.

Assessing Students' Understanding of the Question

One of the most difficult phases to score is the first phase, understanding the question. How do you gather evidence that the student understands? Let us consider Nathan's work (Figure 3a). His explanation, along with the calculations, indicates that he has achieved complete understanding. His

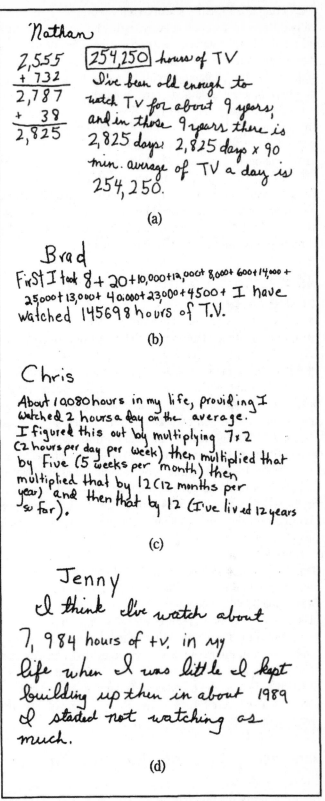

Figure 3 Four students solve the TV Tally problem.

accounting for the number of years he was old enough to watch television, his multiplication process, and his provision for leap years all demonstrate evidence that he understands the complexity of the question.

In comparison, Brad's work (see Figure 3b) is dramatically different. The evidence suggesting his understanding is minimal. First, he gave no written explanation for the numbers he used in the calculations. We *inferred* partial understanding of the problem largely because he added twelve numbers that we assumed corresponded to his age. Additionally, we noted that the first two addends were grossly smaller than the subsequent addends. We inferred that each addend corresponded to his estimate of the number of hours of television that he had watched during each year of his life. Because we *inferred* this correspondence and because Brad gave no solid evidence on the page to explain his thinking, we scored the understanding phase as a 2. That is, we saw insufficient evidence for us to believe that he had either complete misunderstanding or complete understanding.

Assessing Students' Selection of the Data

It is easier to assess the selection of appropriate data than to assess an understanding of the question. Once again, look at Nathan's work in Figure 3a. He did an excellent job of determining the data. Even though he was twelve years old, he reported watching television for nine years, two of which were leap years. From his calculations, we can see that he multiplied 365 by 7 and 366 by 2 then added those products. Although Nathan made an arithmetic mistake in the addition, that error is not an issue in this phase of the assessment. In addition, he took into account partial-year calculations when he added 38 days to his total, since this problem-solving activity was done on 7 February, the thirty-eighth day of the calendar year. We scored Nathan's work in this phase as a 4.

Compare Nathan's selection of data with the selection of data in Chris's work (see Figure 3c). In his work no partial-year calculations were included. Although he presents sufficient detail in the calculations, Chris still calculated his age in whole years only. His score was a 2 in this phase.

In contrast to the two previous examples, consider Jenny's work shown in Figure 3d. She gave no evidence of any life-span calculations. Therefore, we see no evidence of the use of any data in the solution process. Having no evidence of the use of data, we were forced to give Jenny a score of 0 for her selection of data.

Assessing Students' Subproblem Formulation

In this phase of the problem solving, we looked for evidence that the students recognized varying television-watching patterns in their lives. For example, we looked to see whether students adjusted their estimates in some way for the amount of television watched on school days versus nonschool days, summer days versus winter days, or days as an infant versus days as an older child.

Sally made an adjustment to the total by adding some extra hours on days when she was ill (see Figure 4a). We scored this phase of her solution as a 2. Mostly, the other students made no adjustments to their totals, as Tawanna's work demonstrates (see Figure 4b).

Brad's work (see Figure 3b) represents an interesting situation. We disagreed somewhat about whether this phase should be scored as a 4 or as a 2. If we were willing to infer that the addends listed represent numbers of hours during each year of Brad's life, then he has certainly made more than one adjustment for varying television-watching patterns and should be given a score of 4. However, if we are not willing to make such an inference, the subproblem-formulation phase would be scored as a 2 or a 0, depending on our perspective.

Brad's work raises an issue about difficulties in the design of the scoring rubric. As we struggled with, and debated over, how to score the subproblem-formulation phase in his paper, we realized that some modifications to our scoring rubric might be warranted. We mention this difficulty here as something that needs to be dealt with, and later in the article we discuss the issue of what to do in such a circumstance.

One more remark should be made here. The numeric reasonableness of students' accounting for variations is not at issue at this point in the assessment process. We are trying to assess the carefulness of thinking, not the reasonableness of the estimation. It is enough, at this point, that the students have included variations in their television viewing as part of the problem-solving process.

Assessing Students' Correct Implementation

This phase is perhaps the easiest to score. It is certainly the type of scoring with which most teachers are comfortable, and it is the most concrete phase of the problem's solution. Because of the concrete nature of answers and because details of calculations are easily overlooked in this phase, we chose to use four levels of distinction. A student's paper that has no correct arithmetic processes is easily scored. Students' papers showing some, but not all, correct arithmetic processes are more difficult to score. For example, Hsiu-Hsiang (see Figure 4c) has calculated the number of days in twelve years. Then she divided by 6, rather than multiply by 6, because she watches television for six hours a day. Because she uses some, but not all, correct arithmetic processes, we scored her work in this phase as a 1.

Nathan (Figure 3a) has computed the years he has watched television—"about nine years"—and has accounted for two leap years in that time for the partial current year. However, he makes a mistake in addition. Further, he says that he watches television for about 90 minutes each day, and he multiples by 90 rather than convert 90 minutes to 1 ½ hours. Since Nathan has chosen correct arithmetic processes for all phases of the problem, we scored his work as a 2 in this phase.

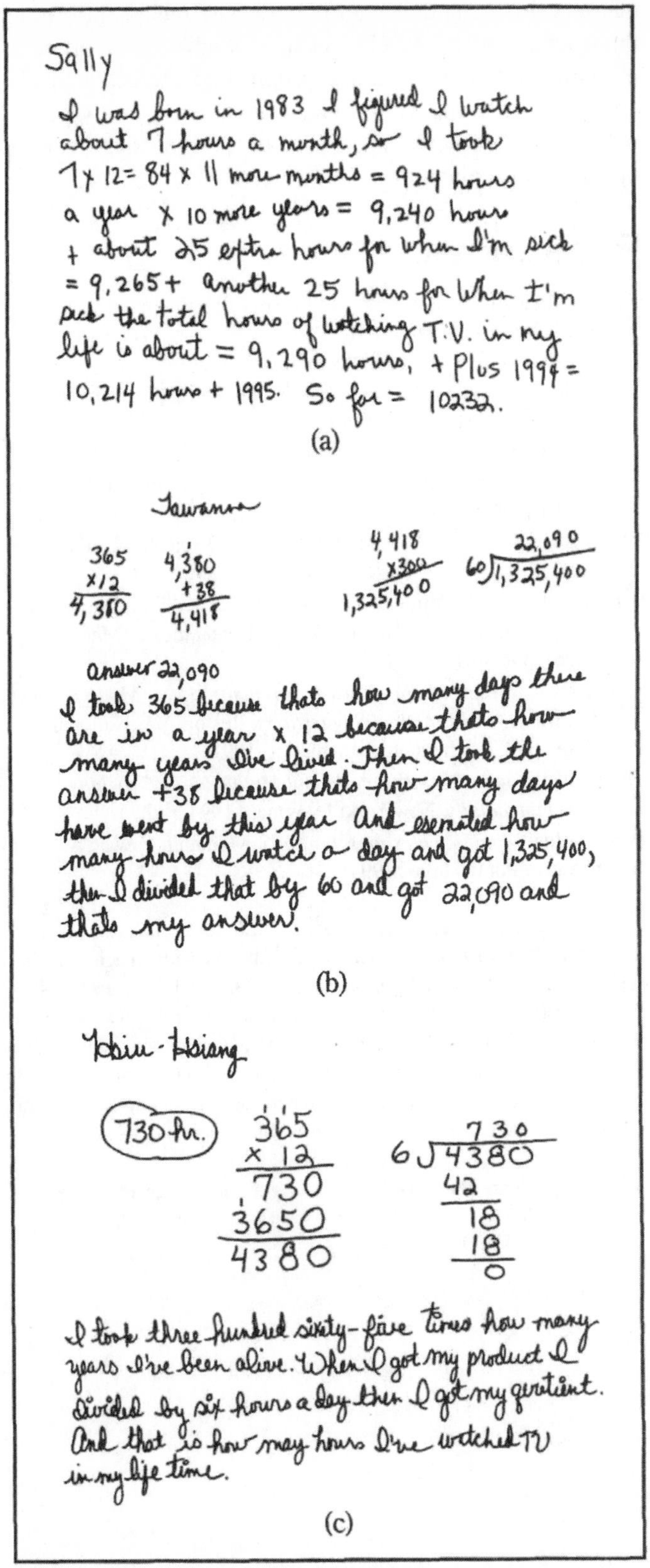

Figure 4 Sally, Tawanna, and Hsiu-Hsiang explore the television question.

for 60 minutes in an hour. Further, each of these arithmetic calculations is correct. We scored Tawanna's work as a 3 in this phase.

An important side note to the discussion of correctly implementing solution strategies is the level of detail of arithmetic calculations and its impact on the solution. It is tempting to say here that because in the formulation-of-subproblems phase, Tawanna has not taken all the pattern variations into account, her final answer is incorrect. Consequently, some teachers may think that her score in the last phase should be lowered. However, we disagree. When scoring the arithmetic part of the solution, we scored according to the calculations that the student deemed necessary. We have already taken into consideration the detail of those calculations in previous phases of the scoring rubric. Deducting points a second time for the same mistake would be inappropriate.

Difficulties in the Assessment Process

As noted previously, part way through the scoring process one student's response caused us to rethink our scoring rubric. At that point we were faced with two options. One option was to modify the rubric and reexamine each student's paper that we had already scored. That option may not be practical, and we are not suggesting that teachers must make such changes. If difficulties arise early in the scoring process, a teacher may be willing to make the change and reexamine every student's paper. Otherwise, a different and more realistic option is to live with the difficulties and change the rubric for the next time, which, in fact, is precisely what we did. We learned from our experience and modified the rubric in preparation for the next time we used this problem-solving activity.

Another difficulty that we encountered was that many students failed to give us adequate written explanation of their thinking. This problem is, in fact, common. Stenmark (1991, 21) notes, "We are likely to discover that students need much more experience with . . . explaining their thinking." This statement implies that we must pay more attention to writing in mathematics, which is consistent with the NCTM *Standards* document (1989) for curriculum. Students will certainly need practice to improve their skills in articulating their thinking.

Final Thoughts about Assessing Problem Solving

Many of us want to be kind as we score and to give points for what we *infer* that our students know rather than for what they have demonstrated on the page. Using a scoring

Tawanna (Figure 4b) has computed the number of years in her life; multiplied by 365 days in a year; added the 38 days for the partial year; multiplied by 300 minutes of television watching a day; and divided by 60, which we assumed stood

51

rubric such as this one demands that we hold our emotional attachment to students in abeyance. We must evaluate the evidence that is on the page. For this exercise to be meaningful for our students, it is imperative that we give them useful feedback. As noted by Schwartz (1996, 397), "praise intended to support children's self-valuing does not necessarily serve the development of academic autonomy, empowering children as thinkers and doers." If the students needed to write more words as an explanation, we need to tell them so. If their calculations were incomplete, if they did not account for varying life patterns, or if they used incorrect arithmetic procedures, as teachers we must articulate these shortcomings to them. Students will not improve their problem-solving abilities if they never receive any feedback that is an honest, clearly explained critique of their work.

It is possible to discuss students' work with them in an honest way that is an attempt to help them improve their problem-solving abilities rather than to point out deficiencies in their thinking. To foster this kind of discussion, a teacher must create an atmosphere of mutual respect and safety for intellectual risk taking. Only then can students move forward in their thinking, confident that the teacher is working with them.

Evaluating problem solving is never easy. It seems that pitfalls appear at every turn, and students do many things that we could not predict and for which we did not account in our rubrics. We recommend that teachers start small. Evaluate one or two problem-solving activities a semester. Score them carefully, and keep notes about the things that were confusing or difficult. Rework your rubric as needed. Then, when parents come to discuss their child's thinking, you will have something to discuss with them—something that is sensitive enough to give true insight into the child's thought process and that can truly measure growth. A good plan of assessment is an invaluable tool for determining many of the things that teachers must do on a routine basis, such as informing the teaching decision, telling students what is important as thinking, and communicating progress to students and parents (Van de Walle 1994). Good assessment rarely occurs with spur-of-the-moment decisions and always requires much advance planning.

References

Charles, Randall, Frank Lester, and Phares O'Daffer. *How to Evaluate Progress in Problem Solving.* Reston, VA.: National Council of Teachers of Mathematics, 1987.

National Council of Teachers of Mathematics (NCTM). *Curriculum and Evaluation Standards for School Mathematics.* Reston, VA: NCTM, 1989.

———. *Assessment Standards for School Mathematics.* Reston, VA: NCTM, 1995.

Pólya, George. *How to Solve It.* Princeton, NJ: Princeton University Press, 1945.

Schwartz, Sydney L. "Hidden Messages in Teacher Talk: Praise and Empowerment." *Teaching Children Mathematics 2* (March 1996): 396–401.

Stenmark, Jean Kerr. *Mathematics Assessment: Myths, Models, Good Questions, and Practical Suggestions.* Reston, VA: National Council of Teachers of Mathematics, 1991.

Van de Walle, John. *Elementary School Mathematics: Teaching Developmentally.* New York: Longman, 1994.

Westley, Joan. *Puddle Questions, Grade 5.* Mountain View, CA: Creative Publications, 1994.

ANNETTE RICKS LEITZE, 00aeleitze @ bsuvc.bsu.edu, teaches mathematics and mathematics education courses at Ball State University, Muncie, IN 47306. Her interests include mathematical problem solving and curriculum integration. **SUE TINSLEY MAU,** smau@iupui.edu, teaches elementary and secondary mathematics methods courses and mathematics content courses for prospective elementary teachers at Indiana University—Purdue University Indianapolis, Indianapolis, IN 46202.

Looking at How Students Reason

Mathematics teachers gain a wealth of information by delving into the thinking behind students' answers, not just when answers are wrong but also when they are correct.

Marilyn Burns

First, a confession: Only during the last 10 to 15 years of my teaching career have I thought deeply about assessing students' understanding and learning progress. As a beginning teacher, I focused on learning to manage my classroom, plan lessons, and hold students' attention. Later, my focus shifted to improving my lessons and expanding my instructional repertoire. During those years, my attention was always firmly on my teaching. Assessment was not one of my concerns. Yes, I gave assignments and quizzes and examined the results, but I did so more to determine grades than to figure out what students were thinking.

Assessment plays a much different role in my teaching today Although I'm no longer a full-time classroom teacher, I still spend time teaching students in elementary classrooms as I try out new instructional ideas. I now approach assessment in an intentional way and incorporate it into every lesson. No longer am I satisfied to simply record students' performance on assignments and quizzes; now, my goal is to find out, as I teach, what the students understand and how they think. I am still interested in honing my lessons, but along with planning the sequence of learning activities, I also prepare to question students about their thinking during class discussions, in individual conversations, and on written assignments. In addition, linking assessment with instruction has become a key issue in the professional development I provide to other teachers.

After teaching a lesson, we need to determine whether the lesson was accessible to all students while still challenging to the more capable; what the students learned and still need to know; how we can improve the lesson to make it more effective; and, if necessary, what other lesson we might offer as a better alternative. This continual evaluation of instructional choices is at the heart of improving our teaching practice.

Uncovering the Way Students Think

In my early teaching years, I was a devotee of *discovery learning,* sometimes called *inquiry learning.* This instructional approach involves designing learning activities that help students discover concepts and make sense of facts and principles for themselves, rather than relying on textbooks or teacher explanations. I implemented this approach by asking the class a carefully prepared sequence of questions, in the style of Socrates. If a student's response was correct, I continued to the next question. If a students response was incorrect, other students would typically raise their hands to disagree, and I'd let a class discussion unfold until someone proposed the correct response. Then I'd continue with the next question. If no students objected to an incorrect response, I'd ask a slightly different question to lead students to the right answer.

Years later, I thought about why the discovery method of instruction seemed flawed. The problem was that when a student gave a correct response, I assumed that both the student who had answered correctly and his or her classmates understood the mathematics behind the problem. I never probed students' level of understanding behind their responses; I just happily continued on my teaching trajectory. As a result, I never really knew what students were thinking or whether their correct answers masked incorrect ideas. I only knew that they had given the answer I sought.

I no longer teach this way. Although I still believe in the value and importance of using questions to present ideas for students to consider, I've broadened my use of both oral and written questions so that I now attempt to probe as well as stimulate students' thinking.

For example, when teaching fractions to a class of 4th graders, I wrote five fractions on the board—$\frac{1}{4}$, $\frac{11}{16}$, $\frac{3}{8}$, $\frac{1}{16}$, and $\frac{3}{4}$—and asked the students to write the fractions in order from smallest to largest. I then added another step by asking them to record their reasons for how they ordered the fractions. After giving the students time to solve the problem, I initiated a whole-class discussion. Robert reported first. He said with confidence, "The smallest fraction is $\frac{1}{16}$." In my early days of teaching, I was accustomed to questioning students when their answers were incorrect, but not when they were correct. Now, however, I asked Robert to explain how he knew that $\frac{1}{16}$ was the smallest fraction. Robert read from his paper, again with confidence,

"Because ¹⁄₁₆ is the lowest number in fractions." The students had previously cut and labeled strips of construction paper to make fraction kits, and ¹⁄₁₆ happened to be the smallest piece in their kits. The fraction kit—a standard tool in my instructional repertoire that I've always found effective for developing students' understanding of fractions—had led Robert to an incorrect generalization.

By questioning Robert's correct response, I was able not only to clear up his misunderstanding but also to improve on the fraction kit lesson to avoid this problem in the future. When I teach this lesson now, I always ask students to consider how we would name pieces that are smaller than ¹⁄₁₆; I talk with them about how we could continue to cut smaller and smaller pieces and find fraction names for even the teeniest sliver.

Incorporating students' reasoning into both written assignments and classroom discussions was a crucial step toward making assessment an integral and ongoing aspect of my classroom instruction. Now it's a staple of my math teaching.

Incorporating students' reasoning into classroom discussions makes assessment an integral aspect of classroom instruction.

Assessment through Students' Written Work

One of the main strategies I use to assess students' learning is incorporating writing in math assignments. There are many ways to present writing assignments that yield as much information as possible about what students are thinking (see Burns, 2004).

Solving math problems often requires making false starts and searching for new approaches.

Ask for more than one strategy. Solving math problems often requires making false starts and searching for new approaches. Students need to develop multiple strategies so that they become flexible in their mathematical thinking and are able to look at mathematical situations from different perspectives. Even when students are performing routine computations, asking them to offer more than one way to arrive at an answer provides insight into their thinking.

Students need to be able to look at mathematical situations from different perspectives.

For example, I worked with one 2nd grade class that had been focusing on basic addition. When they encountered more difficult problems—those involving numbers above 5, such as 9+6 and 7+8—the students' fallback strategy was always counting. Over time, I helped them develop other strategies for addition. One day, to assess their progress, I asked them to add 6+7 and to explain how they could figure out the answer in more than one way. Their work was revealing. Daniel described five methods, including the following method, that showed the progress he had made with the important skill of *decomposing* numbers—taking numbers apart and combining them in different ways:

> You lake 1 from the 6 and 2 from the 7 and then you add 5+5. Then you add on the 1 and the 2 and you get 13.

Ryan, in contrast, was able to offer only two methods, even when I pushed him for more. He wrote,

> (1) You start with the 6 and count on 7 more. (2) You start with the 7 and count on 6.

Although Ryan's work showed that he understood that addition was commutative, it also showed that his addition strategies were limited to counting.

Let students set parameters. A good technique for assessing students' understanding as well as differentiating instruction is to make an assignment adjustable in some way, so that it is accessible and appropriate for a wider range of students. For example, I worked with one 3rd grade class in writing word problems. For several days, the students discussed examples as a group and completed individual assignments. Sometimes I gave a multiplication problem—3 × 4, for example—and asked students to find the answer and also write a word problem around the problem. At other times I gave them a word problem—such as, "How many wheels are there altogether on seven tricycles?"—and asked them to write the related multiplication problem and find the answer. Finally, I gave students the assignment of choosing any multiplication problem, writing a word problem for it, and finding the answer in at least two ways.

Having the students choose their own problems allowed them to decide on the parameters that were comfortable for them. Carrie chose 5 × 2 and wrote a problem about how many mittens five children had. Thomas chose 102 × 4 and wrote a problem about the number of wheels on 102 cars. Each student's choice gave me information about their numerical comfort as well as their skill with multiplication.

Assess the same concept or skill in different ways. I've often found that a student's beginning understanding, although fragile, can provide a useful building block or connection to more robust learning. Sometimes a familiar context can help a student think about a numerically challenging problem. Using flexible assessment approaches enables us to build on students' strengths and interests and help them move on from there.

In a 4th grade class, I watched Josh, who was fascinated by trucks, overcome his confusion about dividing 96 by 8 when I asked him to figure out how many toy 8-wheeler trucks he could make if he had 96 toy wheels. Although his numerical skills were weak, he was able to make progress by drawing trucks and examining the pattern of how many wheels he needed for two trucks, then three trucks, and so on.

Take occasional class inventories. Compiling an inventory for a set of papers can provide a sense of the class's progress and thus inform decisions about how to differentiate instruction. For example, after asking a class of 275th graders to circle the larger fraction—⅔ or ¾—and explain their reasoning, I reviewed their papers and listed the strategies they used. Their strategies included drawing pictures (either circles or rectangles); changing to fractions with common denominators (⁸⁄₁₂ and ⁹⁄₁₂); seeing which fraction was closer to 1 (⅔ is ⅓ away, but ¾ is only ¼ away); and relating the fractions to money (⅔ of $1.00 is about 66 cents, whereas ¾ of $1.00 is 75 cents). Four of the students were unable to compare the two fractions correctly. I now had direction for future lessons that would provide interventions for the struggling students and give all the students opportunities to learn different strategies from one another.

Assessment through Classroom Discussion

Incorporating assessment into classroom discussion serves two goals: It provides insights into students' thinking, and it ensures that no student is invisible in the class, but that all are participating and working to understand and learn. Here are some strategies to get the most out of class discussions.

Ask students to explain their answers, whether or not the answers are correct. When I follow up on both correct and incorrect answers by asking students to explain their reasoning, their responses often surprise me. Some students arrive at correct answers in unexpected ways. For example, when comparing ⅘ and ¾, Brandon changed the fractions so that they had common numerators—¹²⁄₁₅ and ¹²⁄₁₆ He knew that 16ths were smaller than 15ths, so ¹²⁄₁₅ or ⅘, had to be larger! Students may also surprise us by using incorrect reasoning to arrive at the correct answer. Lindsay, a 3rd grader, used $7 \times 3 = 21$ to conclude that $8 \times 4 = 32$. "Each number is just one bigger," she said, and went on to explain that 1 more than 7 is 8, 1 more than 3 is 4, and 1 more than each of the digits in 21 makes the number 32. Although Lindsay's method worked for this problem, it doesn't work for all problems!

Ask students to share their solution strategies with the group. After a student responds to a question that I pose and explains his or her reasoning, I ask the group, "Who has a different way to solve the problem?" or "Who has another way to think about this?" I make sure to provide sufficient wait time to encourage students to share ideas. In addition to providing insights into students' thinking and understanding, this method also reinforces the idea that there are different ways to think about problems and lets the students know that I value their individual approaches.

Call on students who don't volunteer. For many years, I called only on students who had the confidence to offer their ideas. For students who were less confident, I relied on their written work. I didn't want to intrude on shy students and put them under additional stress. I've since changed this practice, partly because of the insights I gained from the excellent professional resource *Classroom Discussions* (Chapin, O'Connor, & Anderson, 2003). I now tell students that it's important for me to learn about how each of them thinks and, for that reason, I need to hear from all of them. I reassure them, however, that if I call on them and they don't know the answer, they should just let me know. I tell them, "It's important for me to know when a student isn't able to explain so I can think about what kind of support to give." I'm always careful to check in with the student later to determine what kind of intervention I need to provide.

Use small-group work. This technique is especially useful for drawing out students who are reticent about talking in front of the whole class. After posing a problem, I'll often say "Turn and talk with your partner" or "Talk with your group about this." Then I eavesdrop, paying especially close attention to the students who don't typically talk in class discussions.

Ask students to restate others' ideas. This is another strategy I learned from *Classroom Discussions*. After a student offers an idea or answer, I call on someone else with the prompt, "Explain what Claudia said in your own words." If the student can't do this, I prompt him or her to ask Claudia to explain again. If the student still isn't able to restate Claudia's idea, I ask another student to try, reminding the first student to listen carefully and see whether this alternate explanation helps. After a student shares, I ask Claudia, "Does that describe your idea?" Depending on my professional judgment about the student and the situation, I may also return to the first student and ask him or her to try again.

Improving Mathematics Teaching

According to the National Council of Teachers of Mathematics (2000),

> To ensure deep, high-quality learning for all students, assessment and instruction must be integrated so that assessment becomes a routine part of the ongoing classroom activity rather than an interruption. Such assessment also provides the information teachers need to make appropriate instructional decisions.

Making assessment an integral part of daily mathematics instruction is a challenge. It requires planning specific ways to use assignments and discussions to discover what students do and do not understand. It also requires teachers to be prepared to deal with students' responses. Merely spotting when students are incorrect is relatively easy compared with understanding the reasons behind their errors. The latter demands careful attention and a deep knowledge of the mathematics concepts and principles that students are learning.

> ## By building and using a wide repertoire of assessment strategies, we can get to know more about our students than we ever thought possible.

But the benefits are worth the effort. By building and using a wide repertoire of assessment strategies, we can get to know more about our students than we ever thought possible. The insights we gain by making assessment a regular part of instruction enable us to meet the needs of the students who are eager for more challenges and to provide intervention for those who are struggling.

References

Burns, M. (2004). Writing in math. *Educational Leadership, 62*(2), 30–33.

Chapin, S. H., O'Connor, C., & Anderson, N. C. (2003). *Classroom discussions: Using math talk to help students learn.* Sausalito, CA: Math Solutions Publications.

National Council of Teachers of Mathematics. (2000). *Principles and standards for school mathematics.* Reston, VA: Author. Available: http://standards.nctm.org

MARILYN BURNS is Founder of Math Solutions Professional Development, Sausalito, California; 800-868-9092; mburns@mathsolutions.com.

Engineering Successful Inclusion in Standards-Based Urban Classrooms

This article reflects the following *This We Believe* characteristics: High expectations for every member of the learning community—Students and teachers engaged in active learning—Multiple learning and teaching approaches that respond to student diversity

Deborah L. Voltz et al.

Meet Amelia Taylor, a sixth grade language arts teacher in an urban middle school. Her classes, like those of her colleagues, contain a diverse mix of students, including those who have been identified as gifted and talented, those who are English language learners, as well as those who have disabilities. Derrick is a student with learning disabilities in Ms. Taylor's class. He enjoys science, art, and sports. Derrick has strong visual/spatial and kinesthetic skills, is creative, outspoken, and enjoys interacting with his peers. On assessment measures, Derrick's literacy skills are at a beginning fourth grade level. Coupled with his academic and developmental record, we know that this young adolescent is easily distracted, has a low tolerance for frustration, and avoids taking intellectual risks. In the spring, like the rest of his classmates, Derrick will take a state assessment designed to measure student performance against established standards for sixth graders. Considering these standards and Derrick's present capabilities, Ms. Taylor is feeling ambivalent about the whole idea of inclusion. If not for the support of Ms. Noble, the special educator who co-teaches with Ms. Taylor during Derrick's language arts class, Ms. Taylor would be ready to give up on Derrick and concede defeat now—before the state assessment is ever given.

With the passage of the No Child Left Behind legislation, there has been increasing emphasis on the use of large-scale tests to monitor students' progress toward meeting educational standards and to hold schools accountable for this progress. While the standards movement is felt across education as a whole, it is often felt with particular force in urban districts, where accountability test scores typically lag behind state and national averages and the resources to assist in closing these gaps are generally scarce (Council of Great City Schools, 2005). Additionally, from the middle school perspective, Lounsbury and Vars (2003) contended:

> Human beings differ in many ways, and these differences are magnified during the middle school years. Individuals go through the massive physical, social, emotional, and intellectual changes of puberty at different times and at different rates. . . . Yet young people dealing with these most profound changes are now confronted by demands that they all measure up to some adult-determined "standards." They, their teachers, and their schools are punished if students do not attain a certain score on a paper-and-pencil test, which may or may not be aligned with the standards. Little or no allowances are made for differences in social background, innate academic ability, handicapping conditions, or even students' command of the English language. When applied strictly, high-stakes testing dooms numbers of students to failure even before they take part in an assessment (p. 10).

At the same time, as efforts abound to have all students reach the same goals, other educational reforms, such as inclusion, are creating increasingly diverse populations of students in general education classrooms. Not only must general education students meet these rigorous goals, but most special education learners will be held to the same goals as well. State and national mandates to meet specific grade level standards for all students place tremendous pressure on both general and special education teachers. As stated by Roach, Salisbury, and McGregor (2002), general education teachers are likely to view inclusion and standards-based reform as "competing rather than complementary agendas" (p. 452).

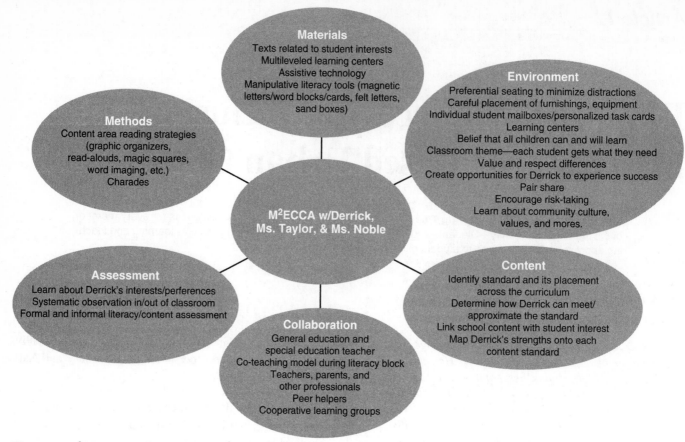

Figure 1 M²ECCA for including Derrick with Ms. Taylor and Ms. Noble

Eighty-two percent of public school teachers teach in classrooms that include students with disabilities (National Center for Education Statistics, 2004). Yet some research has suggested that many teachers feel ill-prepared to implement standards-based reform in heterogeneous learning environments. In a national survey of 400 general education teachers, less than half (37%) reported that they felt well-prepared to teach students with disabilities according to their states' content standards (Goldstein, 2004). Evidence also indicates that accountability assessments may encourage the reluctance of general education teachers and administrators to embrace the inclusion of students with disabilities for fear that the scores of these students will depress school or class scores (Defur, 2002; McDermott & McDermott, 2002). Increased referral rates to special education also have been associated with standardized test-driven accountability systems (Defur, 2002; Parrish, 2000). Consequently, given the apparent tension between the increasing standardization of educational goals and the increasing diversity of the student population, efforts should be made to assist teachers in reconciling and successfully implementing these critical themes in urban middle school education.

The framework featured in Figure 1 (M²ECCA) was designed to address this dilemma. It is grounded in four instructional approaches that address the needs of diverse learners: multicultural education (Banks, 2001), universal design (Orkwis, 1999), sheltered instruction (Echevarria, Vogt, & Short, 2004), and differentiated instruction (Tomlinson, 1999). The M²ECCA framework describes how these four approaches inform the methods, materials, environment, content, collaboration, and assessment required for success in diverse, standards-based classrooms. It provides a structure that helps teachers analyze their instructional approach to facilitate the progression of diverse learners along an established continuum of skills and abilities.

The M²ECCA framework has been field-tested in an urban school district in the South. More than 50 teachers serving students with disabilities in inclusive settings were participants. In this project, participating teachers were asked to complete survey instruments related to teaching in inclusive, standards-based classrooms both before and after the training. They also were asked to revise lesson plans by applying the M²ECCA framework, teach these revised lessons, and then reflect on student learning outcomes. Participating teachers reported that the M²ECCA framework enhanced their ability to design lessons that met the educational needs of their diverse students. Student work samples taken from lessons taught were evaluated based on mastery of standards targeted in the lesson. These student work samples, as well as teacher reflections on lessons taught, supported these teachers' reported growth in the area of teaching in inclusive, standards-based classrooms.

The balance of this article will focus on the application of the M²ECCA framework. Throughout, we will describe what happened with one student, Derrick, as two of his teachers, Ms. Taylor and Ms. Noble, used the M²ECCA framework to guide their instructional practices.

Applying the M²ECCA Framework
Methods of Instruction

In inclusive classrooms, the method of instruction is a critical consideration in implementing standards-based reform. How we decide to teach is important for all learners, but particularly for those with disabilities, those who may be culturally different, or those who vary in other educationally relevant ways from typical students (Hardin & Hardin, 2002). Let us again consider Derrick. We know that Derrick is a sports enthusiast, so by incorporating sports-related content into instruction, Ms. Noble and Ms. Taylor increased the likelihood of his making a deeper connection with their instruction. For example, in teaching the skills of comparing and contrasting, two or more sports teams were used as the elements contrasted. Likewise, we know that Derrick has strong kinesthetic skills, so one of the ways he learns best is through activities such as playing charades with his vocabulary words or acting out segments of a storyline. By observing Derrick, his teachers surmised that he enjoyed interacting with peers, so they allowed him to work with his peers to engage in instructional activities. They understood that these personal interactions had a good chance to improve his learning experience. In other words, when teachers tap into students' strengths, interests, and cognitive styles, the likelihood of engineering successful standards-based, inclusive classrooms increases.

While standards themselves give some guidance as to what is taught, they are silent with respect to issues of methodology. Standards provide a vision of where we should be going instructionally, but determining the best route to get there is largely up to teachers. It is important to remember, however, that the best route varies based on individual student differences.

Materials of Instruction

Instructional materials go hand in hand with instructional methods and also are critical elements in designing inclusive, standards-based classrooms. For example, using supplementary reading materials such as *Sports Illustrated* helped to hook Derrick, given his high interest in sports.

Assistive technology is an additional area that must be considered. Many textbooks are offered in a variety of formats: standard, reduced reading level, large print, audiotape, and digitized (e-text) on a CD. The digitized format provides additional visual and auditory options. Derrick enjoyed loading the CD text into a computer, and with Ms. Noble's assistance, changed the background and font color to meet his learning needs and preferences. By manipulating the screenreading software, Derrick was able to have the text read aloud. Screenreading software also offers a variety of other supports such as highlighting word by word or line by line as the text is read. Additional assistive technologies such as voice recognition software, supported Derrick's writing. Through use of this software, he was able to dictate his work. His use of talking word processors provided him with critical auditory feedback while he entered information. The word prediction software provided visual and auditory spelling support. By using teacher observation and assessment to construct his learning profile, both teachers were able to make wise decisions about which materials would be the most effective with Derrick.

Environment of the Classroom

The physical, organizational, and social environments of the classroom are additional instructional planning considerations. Furnishings, equipment, and materials used efficiently contribute to differentiating instruction. For example, an individual student mailbox was used with Derrick to distribute personalized task cards that focused on his individual need. Erecting learning or interest centers around topics or themes of study also served as a means of individualizing instruction for Derrick.

In terms of the social environment, it is important to get learners to understand that "fair" does not mean that everybody gets exactly the same thing, but rather that everybody gets what they need. So when Derrick's task card differed from those of some of his classmates, these differences were perceived as natural and normal. It is important to establish that individual differences should be valued as a way for us to learn from each other and a way to make our world a more interesting place to be.

It is important to get learners to understand that "fair" does not mean that everybody gets exactly the same thing, but rather what they need.

Behavior management strategies also are important to consider. In Derrick's case, Ms. Taylor knew that he was easily distracted, so she assigned him to sit in an area that minimized distractions. Additionally, because Derrick had a low tolerance for frustration and often responded with aggression, Ms. Taylor used activities that tapped into Derrick's strengths and interests to minimize his frustration. Proactive management strategies such as these helped to reduce Derrick's inappropriate behaviors. On the other hand, eliminating all sources of frustration for Derrick would be impossible and would not prepare him well for life. This suggests that teaching alternate strategies for responding to frustration also would be critical for Derrick.

Finally, it is important to note that behavior is culturally influenced (Neal, McCray, Webb-Johnson & Bridgest, 2003; Townsend, 2000). For example, in some cultures, it is not uncommon or viewed as disrespectful for speakers to engage in overlapping verbalizations; that is to have more than one person speaking at a time. In other cultures, this practice is seen as rude. Likewise, in some cultures, a higher level of physical activity and verbal discourse may be a natural accompaniment to cognitive activity. For example, in Derrick's household, there is a great deal of activity, punctuated by lots of talking, where individuals are engaged in multiple activities. Their behavior differs considerably from families where there may be a greater compartmentalization of activities, doing only one thing at a time. These factors also must be considered in designing responsive educational environments.

Content of Instruction

With the needs of typical students in mind, most standards-based curricula provide a broad view of what students should know and be able to do. What is often missing, however, are the skills that students with disabilities need to mitigate or circumvent the special challenges they face. This is probably more evident in the case of students with low-incidence disabilities such as hearing or visual impairments. For example, curriculum for students who are blind often includes Braille instruction and orientation and mobility training, in addition to the standard curriculum. Even for students with high-incidence disabilities, it is important to teach some skills that may not be an explicit part of a standards-based curriculum. Consider Derrick who needed content focused on anger management, or the self-regulation of behaviors. Some students also require focused instruction on learning strategies designed to facilitate the organization, retention, and/or application of information. Generally, this content is not included in traditional standards-based curricula, which underscores the need to view standards as a general guide to what students should know and be able to do—not as

the sole determiner of everything that needs to be taught, particularly in the case of students with disabilities.

In a similar vein, standards provide general parameters for the content of instruction, but do not provide much guidance with respect to the specific focus areas or subskill areas needed to attain the standards with a given student. Let us consider Derrick's scenario. Ms. Taylor knew the standards dictated that he should be able to "use a wide range of strategies and skills, including retelling information, using general context clues, and making inferences to identify the main idea, to comprehend sixth-grade reading materials" (Alabama State Department of Education, 2003, p. 6). However, Ms. Taylor first needed to glean as much specific information as possible about what Derrick now is and is not able to do with respect to this standard to move Derrick forward. For example, does Derrick effectively integrate visual, phonemic, and contextual cues when reading? Can Derrick comprehend sixth grade reading material when it is read aloud to him? Is word recognition his primary barrier, or is there a more pervasive problem of understanding language, or is the challenge equally balanced between the two? After raising and answering questions such as these, Ms. Taylor identified more specifically what should be emphasized in the content of instruction for Derrick. From previous assessments, Ms. Taylor was aware that, independently, Derrick's literacy skills were at a beginning fourth grade level. However, through additional assessments, she discovered that Derrick comprehended and analyzed sixth grade level material, if it was read aloud to him. Ms. Taylor concluded that problems with word recognition, decoding, and knowledge of structural analysis were the primary barriers to his success with the standard in question. During targeted lessons, she decided to emphasize these areas in the content of instruction for Derrick. Ms. Taylor was able to use assistive technology such as screenreaders, thereby providing Derrick with the necessary reading assistance that allowed him to continue to use grade level, content-rich reading materials as he further developed his vocabulary and comprehension skills.

Collaboration

Collaboration among general and special educators is the cornerstone of successful inclusive classrooms. These educators share the responsibility of teaching students with disabilities and, as such, should routinely engage in sharing information about student assessment, behavior, and progress. These educators should work together as a team in planning the student's individual education program (IEP) and in collaboratively addressing challenges that may threaten the student's success. In many cases, this will involve collaboratively planning and teaching lessons as well as collaboratively evaluating student progress.

In co-teaching situations, the roles of general and special education teachers vary based on the situation. In some instances, both general and special education teachers may equally participate in planning and delivering instruction. In other instances, the general education teacher may take the lead, while the special education teacher supports instruction through teaching academic survival skills, by preteaching prerequisite skills, or by post-teaching or reviewing content originally presented by the general education teacher. It is critical that the teachers involved negotiate these roles prior to beginning the co-teaching process to develop a shared understanding as well as mutual acceptance of these roles. Professional development related to co-teaching also must be provided to prepare teachers to successfully co-teach.

Collaborative roles such as co-teaching, sharing student progress, and collaborative problem-solving also require contextual supports, including specific time built into the school day for this partnership to occur. To provide for this time, some schools have used strategies such as including a special education teacher on each instructional team and providing common planning time for the team. Other schools have used substitute teachers, paraprofessionals, or building administrators to rotate from class to class during the instructional day to allow general education teachers the opportunity to meet with special education teachers. Since it is typically used only once or twice per grading period, this strategy obviously provides for more limited interaction. Even so, it does provide a way to have some protected time when teachers can co-plan blocks of instruction.

Parents also are integral players in the education of students with disabilities, particularly with respect to the development of standards-based IEPs and participation in collaborative problem solving around instructional challenges that may emerge. Hence, collaborative efforts should embrace parents as partners in the education of their children. Strategies such as conducting joint parent conferences or home visits that include both general and special education teachers help to send parents the message that school professionals are working together as a team in the education of their children.

When working with parents, it is important to tailor parental involvement to the strengths and needs of parents, much in the same ways as instruction is tailored to the strengths and needs of students. Practices that support this kind of collaboration include initial conversations with individual parents to set goals for what they would

like the product of their collaboration with educators to be. With such a strategy, the form that parental involvement takes naturally will vary to some extent from parent to parent. However, more substantive partnerships can be developed with parents when they can clearly see that their goals and ideas are acknowledged and acted upon by educators.

Assessment

Assessment both begins and ends the M^{2}ECCA process in inclusive standards-based classrooms. Assessment is used to inform instruction, monitor student progress, and guide program evaluation. It helps us to answer important questions such as: What does the student already know relative to a given standard? How does the student learn best? It also helps us to measure the effectiveness of our instruction. Again, consider Derrick. Ms. Taylor and Ms. Noble planned a short unit focused on using context clues. As a part of the unit, they conducted a fairly simple pre-assessment to determine where Derrick and his classmates were relative to this skill. At the conclusion of the unit, they administered a simple post-assessment to gauge the effectiveness of the unit.

Another major purpose of assessment is program evaluation. In the special education context, assessment is used to evaluate progress toward accomplishing IEP goals and objectives. In the context of standards-based reform, accountability assessments are typically used to determine which students or schools are meeting established standards. For students with disabilities, some accommodations are often allowed in these assessments, in accordance with the IEP. These accommodations maximize the effectiveness of assessment used to evaluate student learning by reducing the extent to which the residual effects of disabilities inappropriately influence students' ability to show what they know. For example, Derrick's IEP included provisions such as extended time for reading assessments. For assessments in other areas, test items were read aloud to him to minimize the extent to which his difficulties in reading interfered with his ability to show what he knew in math, science, or other areas. School districts typically use three key guidelines in determining the appropriateness of testing accommodations: (a) whether the accommodation is related to the student's disability; (b) whether the accommodation is noted in the IEP and used in everyday instruction (not just for high-stakes assessments); and (c) whether the accommodation significantly alters the construct being measured. For example, with respect to this last criterion, it would be unlikely that a district would allow a reading assessment to be read aloud to a student, since that accommodation would alter what was being measured by the reading assessment. Instead of measuring the student's ability to read, the assessment actually would be measuring listening comprehension, if it were read aloud to the student.

Putting It All Together

Since Derrick was not Ms. Taylor's only student, she had to integrate his needs with those of the rest of the class. In the aforementioned unit on using context clues to examine how this happened, Ms. Taylor and Ms. Noble co-taught the literacy block. They used informal assessments to determine more about what each student did and did not know relative to established standards. They also collected information regarding how each student learned best by conducting student observations and talking with students, parents, and former teachers. Using this information, they developed learning profiles for each student. These profiles allowed them to cluster students for skill instruction. For example, they knew that eleven students in the class, other than Derrick, also needed instruction in using context clues. The remaining students, however, did not. So Ms. Noble worked with those students on context clues, while Ms. Taylor worked with the balance of the class on other skill areas.

Ms. Noble integrated a variety of instructional strategies during the unit. For example, in collaborative groups, she allowed students to physically plug in cards containing missing words in a cloze activity. In another activity, she allowed students to draw in an image representing missing words in sentences. Using various strategies such as these, Ms. Noble was able to tap into some of the ways her students learned best. For example, with these activities, Derrick was able to capitalize on his visual/spatial and kinesthetic strengths as well as his predisposition to work with others.

After these lessons, center time provided additional opportunities for reinforcement of skills and was used as a strategy to further differentiate instruction. For example, although eleven students needed the lessons on context clues, those eleven students did not all read at the same grade level. Skill reinforcement materials used in the center were further differentiated by reading level. Additional supports, such as screenreaders, were provided for students who needed them. Ms. Noble also worked with smaller subgroups of students who needed more direct instruction with other decoding skills, in addition to the use of context clues. The content of the reading materials also varied based on the students' interests. Since Derrick enjoyed sports, his reading materials frequently featured this content. This allowed him to benefit from his vast background knowledge in this area. Figure 1 presents a graphic representation of M^{2}ECCA framework applied to Derrick's scenario.

In the above application, each of the elements of the M^{2}ECCA framework can be seen. Methods and materials have been considered through the use of tactile/kinesthetic and visual/spatial activities as well as reading materials to tap into student interests. Aspects of the environment have been considered through the use of the physical arrangement (e.g., learning centers) as well as the classroom ethos that supports differentiated assignments. While standards guide the content, individual student needs have been considered in the planning of short lessons and follow-up activities. Collaboration is evident in the co-planning and co-teaching that undergirds this unit. Finally, assessment both begins and ends the process with the development of the learning profiles and the implementation of the unit assessment. Although M^{2}ECCA helps to focus attention on individual student needs, it is also feasible to implement in a diverse, regular classroom setting. The M^{2}ECCA framework provides a structure for teachers to collaboratively examine critical aspects of instruction to enhance learning outcomes for all students.

References

Alabama State Department of Education. (2003). Alabama course of study. Montgomery, AL: Author.

Banks, J. A. (2001). Cultural diversity and education: Foundations, curriculum, and teaching. Boston: Allyn & Bacon.

Council of Great City Schools. (2005). Beating the odds V: A city-by-city analysis of student performance and achievement gap on state assessment results from the 2003–2004 school year. Washington, DC: Author.

Defur, S. H. (2002). Education reform, high-stakes assessment, and students with disabilities: One state's approach. Remedial and Special Education, 23, 203–211.

Echevarria, J., Vogt, M., & Short, D. J. (2004). Making content comprehensible for English learners: The SIOP model (2nd ed.). Boston: Pearson.

Goldstein, L. (2004, January 8). Highly qualified? Teaching students with disabilities to high standards will depend on the skills of their teachers. In Special Education in an Era of Standards: Count Me In. Education Week, p. 62.

Hardin, B., & Hardin, M. (2002). Into the mainstream: Practical strategies for teaching in inclusive environments. The Clearing House, 75, 175–178.

Lounsbury, J. H., & Vars, G. F. (2003). The future of middle level education: Optimistic and pessimistic views. Middle School Journal, 35(2), 6–14.

McDermott, T. K., & McDermott, D. F. (2002). High-stakes testing for students with special needs. Phi Delta Kappan, 83, 504–505, 544.

National Center for Education Statistics. (2004). The condition of education. Washington, DC: U.S. Department of Education.

Neal, L. I., McCray, A. D., Webb-Johnson, G., & Bridgest, S. T. (2003). The effects of African American movement styles on teachers' perceptions and reactions. Journal of Special Education, 37, 49–57.

Parrish, T. (2000, November). *Disparities in the identification, funding, and provision of special education.* Paper presented at The Civil Rights Project. Cambridge, MA: Harvard University.

Orkwis, R. (1999). *Curriculum access and universal design for learning.* Arlington, VA: ERIC Clearinghouse on Disabilities and Gifted Education.

Roach, V., Salisbury, C., & McGregor, G. (2002). Applications of a policy framework to evaluate and promote large-scale change. *Exceptional Children, 68,* 451–464.

Tomlinson, C. A. (1999). *The differentiated classroom: Responding to the needs of all learners.* Alexandria, VA: Association for Supervision and Curriculum Development.

Townsend, B. L. (2000). The disproportionate discipline of African American learners: Reducing school suspensions and expulsions. *Exceptional Children, 66,* 381–391.

DEBORAH L. VOLTZ is the director of the Center for Urban Education at the University of Alabama at Birmingham. E-mail: voltz@uab.edu. **MICHELE JEAN SIMS** is an associate professor of curriculum and instruction at the University of Alabama at Birmingham. E-mail: mjsims@uab.edu. **BETTY NELSON** is an associate professor of leadership, special education, and foundations at the University of Alabama at Birmingham. E-mail: benelson@uab.edu. **CARMELITA BIVENS** is the special education coordinator for the Bessemer Schools, Bessemer, Alabama. E-mail: cbivens@bessk12.org.

UNIT 3

Monitor Student Learning

Unit Selections

Key Points to Consider

- What practices enable the linking of assessment data and assessment items?
- What are the evidences that conducting formative assessment informs and improves student achievement?
- How can the education community design formative assessments that will provide evidence of student learning using a standards-based curriculum?
- What are advantages and disadvantages to a national assessment policy that mandates the formative assessment teachers must administer?
- What are the differences in the two progress monitoring models (curriculum-based measurement [CBM], and mastery measurement model)? Identify the best classroom practice for using each model.
- Generate a list of pre-assessment strategies that are performance-based rather than supply and selection types.
- After reading, *Seven Practices for Effective Learning,* Jay McTighe and Ken O'Connor, discuss the implications of the student learning curve on grading practices.
- Define the four types of assessment: diagnostic, placement, formative, and summative assessment. State the purposes and characteristics of the four different types of assessment.
- Define the terms curriculum-based measurement, (CBM), mastery measurement model, and response to intervention (RTI). Compare and contrast the two measurement models, and identify the purposes and characteristics.
- Define the term response to intervention (RTI) and identifying why it is an important topic, how the model is being used to "improve" teaching and learning.
- Define feedback responses, evaluative listening, and interpretive listening.
- Compare and contrast the two progress monitoring models (curriculum-based measurement (CBM) and mastery measurement model). Identify the best classroom practice for using each model.
- Analyze the different methods of listening interpretatively and evaluatively.
- After reading, *Seven Practices for Effective Learning,* Jay McTighe and Ken O'Connor, generate a list of pre-assessment strategies that are performance-based rather than supply and selection types.
- Practice writing feedback responses on student work.
- Analyze student work, using one of the example protocols, located on the website, Looking at Student Work, http://www.lasw.org/.
- After reading, *Seven Practices for Effective Learning,* Jay McTighe and Ken O'Connor, use the seven recommended practices as questions and reflect upon a personal assessment practice.

Student Website
www.mhcls.com

Internet References

National Center for Postsecondary Improvement
http://www.stanford.edu/group/ncpi/unspecified/assessment_ states/stateReports.html

Improving America's Schools: A Newsletter on Issues in School Reform
http://www.ed.gov/pubs/IASA/newsletters/assess/index.html

Organisation for Economic Co-operation and Development/ The Programme for International Student Assessment (PISA)
http://www.pisa.oecd.org/pages/0,3417,en_32252351_32235907_ 1_1_1_1_1,00.html

Teacher Vision
http://www.teachervision.fen.com/special-education/ resource/5350.html

School Improvement in Maryland
http://mdk12.org/index.html

Delaware Science Comprehensive Assessment Program
http://www.scienceassessment.org/

Kathy Schrock's Guide for Educators
http://school.discoveryeducation.com/schrockguide/assess.html

4 Teachers Family of Tools
http://www.4teachers.org/tools/

Looking at Student Work
http://www.lasw.org/

Monitoring student learning is a dynamic and ongoing practice that occurs throughout the teaching and learning process. Research studies indicate that teachers who collect information about student progress and encourage students to self-assess typically have higher achievement results. What does 'monitoring student learning' involve? Activities pursued by the teacher and student for the purposes of making decisions, record keeping, and reporting. For example, students use the information to make decisions about their learning and demonstrate how they use their self-regulatory skills. Educators perform tasks related to collecting assessment information and data results for the purpose of documenting student progress and the effectiveness of instruction.

Two monitoring tools that can help teachers to collect performance data are the Student Progress Monitoring model, also known as Curriculum-Based Measurement, and the Mastery Measurement Approach (Safer & Fleishman, 2005). Both practices are concerned with using information or data results to identify students' strengths and instructional needs, to plan and adjust instruction, record and document academic progress, to provide feedback, and communicate with students, families, administrators, and other educators. The primary difference between the two models is the data collection process.

Student Progress Monitoring

Student Progress Monitoring (SPM) is a method for determining how well students are progressing weekly on curriculum goals. Teachers identify instructional goals from the curriculum for the year. They design assessments to align with the goals, then administer the assessments weekly to reveal whether students are on target for reaching the annual yearly goals. Data results are graphed regularly, providing visual evidence of student progress, the rate and pace at which students are learning, and the effectiveness of instruction. By comparing an expected rate of learning to the actual rate of learning, teachers make weekly decisions about the effectiveness of the instruction. Information about this method can be found on the Internet at the National Center on Student Progress Monitoring, http://www.studentprogress.org/.

Mastery Measurement Approach

The Mastery Measurement Approach is a method based on mastery learning. The premise of mastery learning is that all students can achieve, given ample time to learn and quality instruction. Planning instruction for mastery learning, the teacher identifies the objectives (small learning units) from the content and performance standards, administers a pre-assessment, uses the information to plan the lesson, administers formative assessments throughout the lesson, and often, a summative assessment. During the process, the teacher adjusts the instruction when students are unable to demonstrate what they know and can do at the expected level of mastery.

Planning for mastery learning, the teacher typically creates the assessments, plans the instructional procedures, and provides feedback responses. Effective instruction and an efficient

© STOCK4B

assessment system are at the core of this approach. Students participating in mastery learning spend a substantial amount of time studying, including homework. An important premise of mastery learning is that individual differences in learning decrease after a while because the amount of time and type of instruction vary depending upon each student's needs.

Two articles that focus on the characteristics and implementation of these monitoring processes are included. In the first article, important features of the curriculum-based measurement model are described. The second article presents general information about both models; comparing their differences and recommending ways to implement the process to ensure student success.

Monitoring Student Learning

From the beginning to the end of the instruction, teachers monitor student learning. They are interested in knowing whether the instruction is effective in promoting student learning and if not, ways to change the lesson. Teachers are concerned that they are employing effective instructional strategies and providing adequate time so all students can learn. Responsibility for student learning shifted to the instructional aspect of teaching when Carroll and Bloom proposed that all students have the potential to learn when given these three conditions: an opportunity, quality instruction, and sufficient time.

Understanding the role of instruction, there are general questions that teachers seek to answer. Prior to proceeding with instruction, teachers want to know, "What are the students' prerequisite skills and prior knowledge about the topic or content?" A probe or a pre-assessment activity informally administered at the beginning of the instruction provides the answer. Another question that a teacher needs to know is "What is a student's level of mastery of the standard or learning outcome?" This is a different question than the first one. While the first question is inquiring about "what students know about the topic," the second question focuses on a student's placement in the sequence of instruction. Placement assessments are useful in determining the starting point of the instruction or determining an assignment in a particular class.

During instruction, teachers are primarily concerned with the flow of instruction and how easy it is for students to acquire the knowledge and skills being taught. Teachers seek answers to these types of questions: "Which learning tasks are students performing satisfactorily?", "Which learning tasks need to be adjusted?", "Which students are having severe problems and need an intervention or remedial strategy?" or "Which students would benefit cognitively by moving at a more rapid pace?" Assessments used to monitor student learning are called formative or diagnostic assessments. Formative assessments are used to monitor specific learning outcomes for a specific instructional unit. The usefulness of the formative assessment is to identify students' learning strengths and needs. Information is used to make decisions such as: "Is there a need to adjust instruction?", "What type of informative feedback will reinforce good learning and study habits?", and "What corrective prescriptive statements will help the student to improve his or her learning?" If a student persistently struggles with a particular skill, then a diagnostic assessment may reveal the students' learning difficulties. Assessments commonly identified as diagnostic assessments reveal learning problems students have with specific learning tasks. These types of assessments focus on errors a student makes because of his or her inadequate knowledge of vocabulary, a poor grasp of certain skills, or the inability to apply principles or rules to solve problems. Often, teachers administer many different types of formative assessments so students have

an opportunity to demonstrate what they know and can do in many different ways (Gronlund, 1998). At the end of instruction, the teacher is concerned with the degree of mastery the student has achieved. Teachers are interested in knowing answers to these questions: "Which students have mastered the learning outcomes to a degree that they can proceed to the next level of instruction?", "What grade should be assigned to each student?", and "What data should be reported to students, families, school administrators, and other educators?" Summative assessment activities typically provide information for these groups of questions. A **summative assessment** is comprehensive and often occurs at a good place in the instruction that can measure mastery of a particular set of learning goals.

Planning a variety of ways to collect evidence of student learning is beneficial for the teacher and student. Issues that influence assessment results are student learning styles and cultural backgrounds. Some students suffer from assessment anxiety. It is important to remember that there are many ways to demonstrate what one knows and can do. Also, students learn and develop cognitively at different rates and times. Administering multiple assessments allows the teacher to compare the results of different assessments. When inconsistent results appear, the teacher can examine other assessment tasks to seek explanations for the discrepancies before making a decision.

The articles in this unit primarily focus on assessments given during the instruction, commonly referred to as formative assessment, and assessments administered at the end of the instruction or summative assessments. Formative assessments are activities focused on ways to monitor student learning, detect learning errors, and provide feedback to student and teachers. Conversely, summative assessments can provide evidence of students' accomplishments. They are often useful for assigning grades. In the first article, the author discusses differences between formative and summative assessments and their common characteristics. The second article is the seminal article that advanced the discussion of formative assessment and achievement, *Inside the Black Box: Raising Standards Through Classroom Assessment* by Paul Black and Dylan Wiliam.

There are two articles about instructional strategies. The first article discusses assessments for learning and presents five broad strategies for all teachers. Then the authors of the second article propose seven assessment and grading practices. The authors elaborate on each part of the set of strategies providing a caveat that there are ranges of techniques for each strategy. Homework as an important assessment method is included in the unit of articles. The advantages of using homework as an assessment strategy are explored.

The Best Value in Formative Assessment

Ready-made benchmark tests cannot substitute for day-to-day formative assessment conducted by assessment-literate teachers.

STEPHEN CHAPPUIS AND JAN CHAPPUIS

Recently a school leader asked us to provide an example of a good test item on a formative assessment and then show how that item would be different when used on a summative test. He wanted to explain to his staff the difference between formative and summative assessment. His end goal was for teachers to develop assessments to measure how well students were mastering the content standards that would appear on the state accountability test before the test was given in the spring.

His question reflects the confusion many educators have about formative and summative assessment. This confusion isn't surprising: Definitions of formative assessment abound, resulting in multiple and sometimes conflicting understandings. And in part because of these varying definitions and views, practices labeled as formative assessment in schools today vary widely.

One result of No Child Left Behind has been a surge in student testing—much of it voluntary, going well beyond what federal law or state assessment systems require. Many schools and districts administer tests with names like *benchmark, short-cycle,* and *interim assessments* to predict student performance on high-stakes tests and to identify students needing additional help. This increasingly popular level of testing has contributed to the widening scope of what is called formative assessment.

Testing companies in the K–12 education market, seeking to support the trend toward more testing, sometimes advertise products as "formative assessments." This adds to the confusion by encouraging the idea that it's the test itself that's formative (Chappuis, 2005).

In reality, this level of testing is often little more than a series of minisummative tests, not always tightly aligned to what was taught in the classroom. There is nothing inherently formative in such tests—they may or may not be used to make changes in teaching that will lead to greater student learning.

The Difference between Summative and Formative

What is formative assessment, then? First, it's not a product. That was the central misunderstanding of the administrator who asked for an example of a good formative test item. Even though assessments will continue to be labeled *formative* or *summative,* how the results are used is what determines whether the assessment is formative or summative.

To begin, let's look at summative assessment. In general, its results are used to make some sort of judgment, such as to determine what grade a student will receive on a classroom assignment, measure program effectiveness, or determine whether a school has made adequate yearly progress. Summative assessment, sometimes referred to as assessment *of* learning, typically documents how much learning has occurred at a point in time; its purpose is to measure the level of student, school, or program success.

Formative assessment is an ongoing, dynamic process that involves far more than frequent testing.

Formative assessment, on the other hand, delivers information *during* the instructional process, *before* the summative assessment. Both the teacher and the student use formative assessment results to make decisions about what actions to take to promote further learning. It is an ongoing, dynamic process that involves far more than frequent testing, and measurement of student learning is just one of its components.

Summative Assessment Used in Formative Ways

Almost any assessment instrument can be used for summative or formative purposes, but some, by design, are better suited to summative use and others to formative use. For example, state assessments, although they may also have some limited formative use, are designed to provide accountability data and to compare schools and districts. Because their primary purpose is summative, the results may not be communicated in ways that teachers and students can easily interpret and work with.

Further, the results are often delivered months after the administration of the tests. For these reasons, such state tests usually do not function well in a formative way: They can't contribute much information to guide day-to-day instruction or help determine the next learning steps of individual students.

Benchmark assessments, either purchased by the district from commercial vendors or developed locally, are generally meant to measure progress toward state or district content standards and to predict future performance on large-scale summative tests. A common misconception is that this level of assessment is automatically formative. Although such assessments are sometimes intended for formative use—that is, to guide further instruction for groups or individual students—teachers' and administrators' lack of understanding of how to use the results can derail this intention. The assessments will produce no formative benefits if teachers administer them, report the results, and then continue with instruction as previously planned—as can easily happen when teachers are expected to cover a hefty amount of content in a given time.

Teachers also select or develop their own summative assessments—those that count for a grade. Compared with state and district tests, these classroom assessments can more readily be adapted to formative use because their results are more immediately available and their learning targets have been more recently taught. When teachers know what specific learning target each question or task on their test measures, they can use the results to select and reteach portions of the curriculum that students haven't yet mastered. Carefully designed common assessments can be used this way as well.

Students, too, can use summative test results to make decisions about further study. If the assessment items are explicitly matched to the intended learning targets, teachers can guide students in examining their right and wrong answers in order to answer questions such as these:

- What are my strengths relative to the standards?
- What have I seen myself improve at?
- Where are my areas of weakness?
- Where didn't I perform as desired, and how might I make those answers better?
- What do these results mean for the next steps in my learning, and how should I prepare for that improvement?

For students to make maximum use of these questions to guide further study, however, teachers must plan and allow time for students to learn the knowledge and skills they missed on the summative assessment and to retake the assessment. Lack of time for such learning is one of the biggest hindrances to formatively using summative classroom assessments.

Assessment *for* Learning

When teachers assess student learning for purely formative purposes, there is no final mark on the paper and no summative grade in the grade book. Rather, assessment serves as practice for students, just like a meaningful homework assignment does. This is formative assessment at its most valuable. Called assessment *for* learning, it supports learning in two ways:

- Teachers can adapt instruction on the basis of evidence, making changes and improvements that will yield immediate benefits to student learning.
- Students can use evidence of their current progress to actively manage and adjust their own learning. (Stiggins, Arter, Chappuis, & Chappuis, 2006)

Assessment for learning can take many different forms in the classroom. It consists of anything teachers do to help students answer three questions (Atkin, Black, & Coffey, 2001):

Where Am I Going?

- Give students a list of the learning targets they are responsible for mastering, written in student-friendly language.
- Show students anonymous strong and weak examples of the kind of product or performance they are expected to create and have them use a scoring guide to determine which one is better and why.

Where Am I Now?

- Administer a nongraded quiz part-way through the learning, to help both teacher and students understand who needs to work on what.
- Highlight phrases on a scoring guide reflecting specific strengths and areas for improvement and staple it to student work.
- Have students identify their own strengths and areas for improvement using a scoring guide.
- Have students keep a list of learning targets for the course and periodically check off the ones they have mastered.

How Can I Close the Gap?

- Give students feedback and have them use it to set goals.
- Have students graph or describe their progress on specific learning targets.
- Ask students to comment on their progress: What changes have they noticed? What is easy that used to be hard? What insights into themselves as learners have they discovered?

When students use feedback from the teacher to learn how to self-assess and set goals, they increase ownership of their own success. In this type of assessment environment, teachers and students collaborate in an ongoing process using assessment information to improve rather than judge learning. It all hinges on the assessment's ability to provide timely, understandable, and descriptive feedback to teachers and students.

Feedback: The Key Difference

Feedback in an assessment *for* learning context occurs while there is still time to take action. It functions as a global positioning system, offering descriptive information about the work, product, or performance relative to the intended learning goals. It avoids marks or comments that judge the level of achievement or imply that the learning journey is over.

Effective descriptive feedback focuses on the intended learning, identifies specific strengths, points to areas needing improvement, suggests a route of action students can take to close the gap between where they are now and where they need to be, takes into account the amount of corrective feedback the learner can act on at one time, and models the kind of thinking students will engage in when they self-assess. These are a few examples of descriptive feedback:

- You have interpreted the bars on this graph correctly, but you need to make sure the marks on the *x* and *y* axes are placed at equal intervals.
- What you have written is a hypothesis because it is a proposed explanation. You can improve it by writing it as an "if . . . then . . ." statement.
- The good stories we have been reading have a beginning, a middle, and an end. I see that your story has a beginning and a middle, just like those good stories do. Can you draw and write an ending?
- You have described the similarities between _____ and _____ clearly in this paper, and you have identified key differences. Work on illustrating those differences with concrete examples from the text.

In contrast, the feedback from a summative assessment—whether given in the classroom or in a larger context—tells teachers and students who made it to the learning destination and who didn't. The assessment's coded, evaluative feedback—*B+, 84%, Meets Standards, Great Job, Proficient,* and so on—does not identify individual student strengths and areas needing improvement. It does not offer specific information for course correction.

Advantages of Formative Classroom Assessment

Although all formative assessment practices have the potential to increase student learning, assessment for learning in the classroom offers a number of distinct benefits:

- The timeliness of results enables teachers to adjust instruction quickly, while learning is in progress.
- The students who are assessed are the ones who benefit from the adjustments.
- The students can use the results to adjust and improve their own learning.

When we try to teacher-proof the assessment process by providing a steady diet of ready-made external tests, we lose these advantages. Such tests cannot substitute for the day-to-day level of formative assessment that only assessment-literate teachers are able to conduct. The greatest value in formative assessment lies in teachers and students making use of results to improve real-time teaching and learning at every turn.

The greatest value in formative assessment lies in teachers and students making use of results to improve real-time teaching and learning at every turn.

References

Atkin, J. M., Black, P., & Coffey, J. (2001). *Classroom assessment and the national science standards.* Washington, DC: National Academies Press.

Chappuis, S. (2005). Is formative assessment losing its meaning? *Education Week, 24*(44), 38.

Stiggins, R., Arter, J., Chappuis, J., & Chappuis, S. (2006). *Classroom assessment for student learning: Doing it right—using it well.* Portland, OR: Educational Testing Service.

STEPHEN CHAPPUIS (schappuis@ets.org) and JAN CHAPPUIS (jchappuis @ets.org) work with the ETS Assessment Training Institute in Portland, Oregon (www.ets.org/ati).

Learning to Love Assessment

From judging performance to guiding students to shaping instruction to informing learning, coming to grips with informative assessment is one insightful journey.

Carol Ann Tomlinson

When I was a young teacher—young both in years and in understanding of the profession I had entered—I nonetheless went about my work as though I comprehended its various elements. I immediately set out to arrange furniture, put up bulletin boards, make lesson plans, assign homework, give tests, compute grades, and distribute report cards as though I knew what I was doing.

I had not set out to be a teacher, and so I had not really studied education in any meaningful way. I had not student taught. Had I done those things, however, I am not convinced that my evolution as a teacher would have been remarkably different. In either case, my long apprenticeship as a student (Lortie, 1975) would likely have dominated any more recent knowledge I might have acquired about what it means to be a teacher. I simply "played school" in the same way that young children "play house"—by mimicking what we think the adults around us do.

The one element I knew I was unprepared to confront was classroom management. Consequently, that's the element that garnered most of my attention during my early teaching years. The element to which I gave least attention was assessment. In truth, I didn't even know the word *assessment* for a good number of years. I simply knew I was supposed to give tests and grades. I didn't much like tests in those years. It was difficult for me to move beyond their judgmental aspect. They made kids nervous. They made me nervous. With no understanding of the role of assessment in a dynamic and success-oriented classroom, I initially ignored assessment when I could and did it when I had to.

Now, more than three decades into the teaching career I never intended to have, it's difficult for me to remember exactly when I had the legion of insights that have contributed to my growth as an educator. I do know, however, that those insights are the milestones that mark my evolution from seeing teaching as a job to seeing teaching as a science-informed art that has become a passion.

Following are 10 understandings about classroom assessment that sometimes gradually and sometimes suddenly illuminated my work. I am not finished with the insights yet because I am not finished with my work as a teacher or learner. I present the understandings in something like the order they unfolded in my thinking.

The formulation of one insight generally prepared the way for the next. Now, of course, they are seamless, interconnected, and interdependent. But they did not come to me that way. Over time and taken together, the understandings make me an advocate of *informative assessment*—a concept that initially played no conscious role in my work as a teacher.

Understanding 1. Informative assessment isn't just about tests.

Initially I thought about assessment as test giving. Over time, I became aware of students who did poorly on tests but who showed other evidence of learning. They solved problems well, contributed to discussions, generated rich ideas, drew sketches to illustrate, and role-played. When they wanted to communicate, they always found a way. I began to realize that when I gave students multiple ways to express learning or gave them a say in how they could show what they knew, more students were engaged. More to the point, more students were learning.

Although I still had a shallow sense of the possibilities of assessment, I did at least begin to try in multiple ways to let kids show what they knew. I used more authentic products as well as tests to gain a sense of student understanding. I began to realize that when one form of assessment was ineffective for a student, it did not necessarily indicate a lack of student success but could, in fact, represent a poor fit between the student and the method through which I was trying to make the student communicate. I studied students to see what forms of assessment worked for them and to be sure I never settled for a single assessment as an adequate representation of what a student knew.

Understanding 2. Informative assessment really isn't about the grade book.

At about the same time that Understanding 1 emerged in my thinking, I began to sense that filling a grade book was both less interesting and less useful than trying to figure out what individual students knew, understood, or could do. My thinking was shifting from assessment as judging students to assessment as guiding students. I was beginning to think about student accomplishment more than about student ranking (Wiggins, 1993).

Giving students feedback seemed to be more productive than giving them grades. If I carefully and consistently gave them feedback about their work, I felt more like a teacher than a warden. I felt more respectful of the students and their possibilities (Wiggins, 1993). I began to understand the difference between teaching for success and "gotcha" teaching and to sense the crucial role of informative assessment in the former.

Understanding 3. Informative assessment isn't always formal.

I also became conscious of the fact that some of the most valuable insights I gleaned about students came from moments or events that I'd never associated with assessment. When I read in a student's journal that his parents were divorcing, I understood why he was disengaged in class. I got a clear picture of one student's misunderstanding when I walked around as students worked and saw a diagram she made to represent how she understood the concept we were discussing. I could figure out how to help a student be more successful in small groups when I took the time to study systematically, but from a distance, what he did to make groups grow impatient with him.

Assessment, then, was more than "tests plus other formats." Informative assessment could occur any time I went in search of information about a student. In fact, it could occur when I was not actively searching but was merely conscious of what was happening around me.

I began to talk in more purposeful ways with students as they entered and left the classroom. I began to carry around a clipboard on which I took notes about students. I developed a filing system that enabled me to easily store and retrieve information about students as individuals and learners. I was more focused in moving around the room to spot-check student work in progress for particular proficiencies. I began to sense that virtually all student products and interactions can serve as informative assessment because I, as a teacher, have the power to use them that way.

Understanding 4. Informative assessment isn't separate from the curriculum.

Early in my teaching, I made lesson plans. Later on, I made unit plans. In neither time frame did I see assessment as a part of the curriculum design process. As is the case with many teachers, I planned what I would teach, taught it, and then created assessments. The assessments were largely derived from what had transpired during a segment of lessons and ultimately what had transpired during a unit of study. It was a while before I understood what Wiggins and McTighe (1998) call *backward design*.

That evolution came in three stages for me. First, I began to understand the imperative of laying out precisely what mattered most for students to know and be able to do—but also what they should understand—as a result of our work together. Then I began to discover that many of my lessons had been only loosely coupled to learning goals. I'd sometimes (often?) been teaching in response to what my students liked rather than in response to crucial learning goals. I understood the need to make certain that my teaching was a consistent match for what students needed to know, understand, and be able to do at the end of a unit. Finally, I began to realize that if I wanted to teach for success, my assessments had to be absolutely aligned with the

knowledge, understanding, and skill I'd designated as essential learning outcomes. There was a glimmer of recognition in my work that assessment was a part of—not apart from—curriculum design.

Understanding 5. Informative assessment isn't about "after."

I came to understand that assessments that came at the end of a unit—although important manifestations of student knowledge, understanding, and skill—were less useful to me as a teacher than were assessments that occurred during a unit of study. By the time I gave and graded a final assessment, we were already moving on to a new topic or unit. There was only a limited amount I could do at that stage with information that revealed to me that some students fell short of mastering essential outcomes—or that others had likely been bored senseless by instruction that focused on outcomes they had mastered long before the unit had begun. When I studied student work in the course of a unit, however, I could do many things to support or extend student learning. I began to be a devotee of *formative assessment*, although I did not know that term for many years.

It took time before I understood the crucial role of preassessment or diagnostic assessment in teaching. Likely the insight was the product of the embarrassment of realizing that a student had no idea what I was talking about because he or she lacked vocabulary I assumed every 7th grader knew or of having a student answer a question in class early in a unit that made it clear he already knew more about the topic at hand than I was planning to teach. At that point, I began to check early in the year to see whether students could read the textbook, how well they could produce expository writing, what their spelling level was, and so on. I began systematically to use preassessments before a unit started to see where students stood in regard to prerequisite and upcoming knowledge, understanding, and skills.

Understanding 6. Informative assessment isn't an end in itself.

I slowly came to realize that the most useful assessment practices would shape how I taught. I began to explore and appreciate two potent principles of informative assessment. First, the greatest power of assessment information lies in its capacity to help me see how to be a better teacher. If I know what students are and are not grasping at a given moment in a sequence of study, I know how to plan our time better. I know when to reteach, when to move ahead, and when to explain or demonstrate something in another way. Informative assessment is not an end in itself, but the beginning of better instruction.

Understanding 7. Informative assessment isn't separate from instruction.

A second and related understanding hovered around my sense that assessment should teach me how to be a better teacher. Whether I liked it or not, informative assessment always demonstrated to me that my students' knowledge, understanding, and skill were emerging along different time continuums and at different depths. It became excruciatingly clear that my brilliant teaching was not equally brilliant for everyone in my classes. In other words, informative assessment helped me solidify a need for differentiation. As Lorna Earl (2003) notes, if teachers know a precise learning destination and consistently check to see where students are relative to that destination, differentiation isn't just an option; it's the logical next step in teaching. Informative assessment made it clear—at first, painfully so—that if I meant for every student to succeed, I was going to have to teach with both singular and group needs in mind.

If I meant for every student to succeed, I was going to have to teach with both singular and group needs in mind.

Understanding 8. Informative assessment isn't just about student readiness.

Initially, my emergent sense of the power of assessment to improve my teaching focused on student readiness. At the time, I was teaching in a school with a bimodal population—lots of students were three or more years behind grade level or three or more years above grade level, with almost no students in between. Addressing that expansive gap in student readiness was a daily challenge. I was coming to realize the role of informative assessment in ensuring that students worked as often as possible at appropriate levels of challenge (Earl, 2003).

Only later was I aware of the potential role of assessment in determining what students cared about and how they learned. When I could attach what I was teaching to what students cared about, they learned more readily and more durably. When I could give them options about how to learn and express what they knew, learning improved. I realized I could pursue insights about student interests and preferred modes of learning, just as I had about their readiness needs.

I began to use surveys to determine student interests, hunt for clues about their individual and shared passions, and take notes on who learned better alone and who learned better in small groups. I began to ask students to write to me about which instructional approaches were working for them and which were not. I was coming to understand that learning is multidimensional and that assessment could help me understand learners as multidimensional as well.

Understanding 9. Informative assessment isn't just about finding weaknesses.

As my sense of the elasticity of assessment developed, so did my sense of the wisdom of using assessment to accentuate student positives rather than negatives. With readiness-based assessments, I had most often been on the hunt for what students didn't know, couldn't do, or didn't understand. Using assessment to focus on student interests and learning preferences illustrated for me the power of emphasizing what works for students.

When I saw "positive space" in students and reflected that to them, the results were stunningly different from when I reported on their "negative space." It gave students something to build on—a sense of possibility. I began to spend at least as much time gathering assessment information on what students *could* do as on what they couldn't. That, in turn, helped me develop a

conviction that each student in my classes brought strengths to our work and that it was my job to bring those strengths to the surface so that all of us could benefit.

Understanding 10. Informative assessment isn't just for the teacher.

Up to this point, much of my thinking was about the teacher—about me, my class, my work, my growth. The first nine understandings about assessment were, in fact, crucial to my development. But it was the 10th understanding that revolutionized what happened in the classrooms I shared with my students. I finally began to grasp that teaching requires a plural pronoun. The best teaching is never so much about *me* as about *us*. I began to see my students as full partners in their success.

Informative assessment is not an end in itself, but the beginning of better instruction.

My sense of the role of assessment necessarily shifted. I was a better teacher—but more to the point, my students were better learners—when assessment helped all of us push learning forward (Earl, 2003). When students clearly understood our learning objectives, knew precisely what success would look like, understood how each assignment contributed to their success, could articulate the role of assessment in ensuring their success, and understood that their work correlated with their needs, they developed a sense of self-efficacy that was powerful in their lives as learners. Over time, as I developed, my students got better at self-monitoring, self-managing, and self-modifying (Costa & Kallick, 2004). They developed an internal locus of control that caused them to work hard rather than to rely on luck or the teacher's good will (Stiggins, 2000).

Assessing Wisely

Lorna Earl (2003) distinguishes between assessment *of* learning, assessment *for* learning, and assessment *as* learning. In many ways, my growth as a teacher slowly and imperfectly followed that progression. I began by seeing assessment as judging performance, then as informing teaching, and finally as informing learning. In reality, all those perspectives play a role in effective teaching. The key is where we place the emphasis.

Certainly a teacher and his or her students need to know who reaches (and exceeds) important learning targets—thus summative assessment, or assessment *of* learning, has a place in teaching. Robust learning generally requires robust teaching, and both diagnostic and formative assessments, or assessments *for* learning, are catalysts for better teaching. In the end, however, when assessment is seen *as* learning—for students as well as for teachers—it becomes most informative and generative for students and teachers alike.

References

Costa, A., & Kallick, B. (2004). *Assessment strategies for self-directed learning*. Thousand Oaks, CA: Corwin.

Earl, L. (2003). Assessment as learning: Using classroom assessment to maximize student learning. Thousand Oaks, CA: Corwin.

Lortie, D. (1975). *Schoolteacher: A sociological study*. Chicago: University of Chicago Press.

Stiggins, R. (2000). *Student-involved classroom assessment* (3rd ed.). Upper Saddle River, NJ: Prentice-Hall.

Wiggins, G. (1993). Assessing student performance: Exploring the purpose and limits of testing. San Francisco: Jossey-Bass.

Wiggins, G., & McTighe, J. (1998). *Understanding by design*. Alexandria, VA: Association for Supervision and Curriculum Development.

CAROL ANN TOMLINSON is Professor of Educational Leadership, Foundation, and Policy at the University of Virginia in Charlottesville; cat3y@virginia.edu.

From *Educational Leadership*, December 2008, pp. 8-13. Copyright © 2008 by ASCD. Reprinted by permission. The Association for Supervision and Curriculum Development is a worldwide community of educators advocating sound policies and sharing best practices to achieve the success of each learner. To learn more, visit ASCD at www.ascd.org.

Classroom Assessment

Minute by Minute, Day by Day

In classrooms that use assessment to support learning, teachers continually adapt instruction to meet student needs.

SIOBHAN LEAHY ET AL.

There is intuitive appeal in using assessment to support instruction; assessment *for* learning rather than assessment *of* learning. We have to test our students for many reasons. Obviously, such testing should be useful in guiding teaching. Many schools formally test students at the end of a marking period—that is, every 6 to 10 weeks—but the information from such tests is hard to use, for two reasons.

First, only a small amount of testing time can be allotted to each standard or skill covered in the marking period. Consequently, the test is better for monitoring overall levels of achievement than for diagnosing specific weaknesses.

Second, the information arrives too late to be useful. We can use the results to make broad adjustments to curriculum, such as reteaching or spending more time on a unit, or identifying teachers who appear to be especially successful at teaching particular units. But if educators are serious about using assessment to improve instruction, then we need more fine-grained assessments, and we need to use the information they yield to modify instruction as we teach.

Changing Gears

What we need is a shift from *quality control* in learning to *quality assurance*. Traditional approaches to instruction and assessment involve teaching some given material, and then, at the end of teaching, working out who has and hasn't learned it—akin to a quality control approach in manufacturing. In contrast, assessment *for* learning involves adjusting teaching as needed while the learning is still taking place—a quality assurance approach. Quality assurance also involves a shift of attention from teaching to learning. The emphasis is on what the students are getting out of the process rather than on what teachers are putting into it, reminiscent of the old joke that schools are places where children go to watch teachers work.

In a classroom that uses assessment to support learning, the divide between instruction and assessment blurs. Everything students do—such as conversing in groups, completing seat-work, answering and asking questions, working on projects, handing in homework assignments, even sitting silently and looking confused—is a potential source of information about how much they understand. The teacher who consciously uses assessment to support learning takes in this information, analyzes it, and makes instructional decisions that address the understandings and misunderstandings that these assessments reveal. The amount of information can be overwhelming—one teacher likened it to "negotiating a swiftly flowing river"—so a key part of using assessment for learning is figuring out how to hone in on a manageable range of alternatives.

In a classroom that uses assessment to support learning, the divide between instruction and assessment blurs.

Research indicates that using assessment for learning improves student achievement. About seven years ago, Paul Black and one of us, Dylan Wiliam, found that students taught by teachers who used assessment for learning achieved in six or seven months what would otherwise have taken a year (1998). More important, these improvements appeared to be consistent across countries (including Canada, England, Israel, Portugal, and the United States), as well as across age brackets and content areas. We also found, after working with teachers in England, that these gains in achievement could be sustained over extended periods of time. The gains even held up when we measured student achievement with externally mandated standardized tests (see Wiliam, Lee, Harrison, & Black, 2004).

Using this research and these ideas as a starting point, we and other colleagues at Educational Testing Service (ETS) have been working for the last two years with elementary, middle, and high school teachers in Arizona, Delaware, Maryland, Massachusetts, New Jersey, New Mexico, and Pennsylvania. We have deepened our understanding of how assessment for learning can work in U.S. classrooms, and we have learned from teachers about the challenges of integrating assessment into classroom instruction.

Our Work with Teachers

In 2003 and 2004, we explored a number of ways of introducing teachers to the key ideas of assessment for learning. In one model, we held a three-day workshop during the summer in which we introduced teachers to the main ideas of assessment for learning and the research that shows that it works. We then shared specific techniques that teachers could use in their classrooms to bring assessment to life. During the subsequent school year, we met monthly with these teachers, both to learn from them what really worked in their classrooms and to offer suggestions about ways in which they might develop their practice. We also observed their classroom practices to gauge the extent to which they were implementing assessment-for-learning techniques and to determine the effects that these techniques were having on student learning. In other models, we spaced out the three days of the summer institute over several months (for example, one day in March, one in April, and one in May) so that teachers could try out some of the techniques in their classes between meetings.

As we expected, different teachers found different techniques useful; what worked for some did not work for others. This confirmed for us that there could be no one-size-fits-all package. However, we did find a set of five broad strategies to be equally powerful for teachers of all content areas and at all grade levels:

- Clarifying and sharing learning intentions and criteria for success.
- Engineering effective classroom discussions, questions, and learning tasks.
- Providing feedback that moves learners forward.
- Activating students as the owners of their own learning.
- Activating students as instructional resources for one another.

We think of these strategies as nonnegotiable in that they define the territory of assessment for learning. More important, we know from the research and from our work with teachers that these strategies are desirable things to do in any classroom.

However, the way in which a teacher might implement one of these strategies with a particular class or at a particular time requires careful thought. A self-assessment technique that works for students learning math in the middle grades may not work in a 2nd grade writing lesson. Moreover, what works for one 7th grade pre-algebra class may not work for the 7th grade pre-algebra class down the hall because of differences in the students or teachers.

Given this variability, it is important to offer teachers a range of techniques for each strategy, making them responsible for deciding which techniques they will use and allowing them time and freedom to customize these techniques to meet the needs of their students.

Teachers have tried out, adapted, and invented dozens of techniques, reporting on the results in meetings and interviews (to date, we have cataloged more than 50 techniques, and we expect the list to expand to more than 100 in the coming year). Many of these techniques require only subtle changes in practice, yet research on the underlying strategies suggests that they have a high "gearing"—meaning that these small changes in practice can leverage large gains in student learning (see Black & Wiliam, 1998; Wiliam, 2005). Further, the teaching practices that support these strategies are low-tech, low-cost, and usually feasible for individual teachers to implement. In this way, they differ dramatically from large-scale interventions, such as class size reduction or curriculum overhauls. We offer here a brief sampling of techniques for implementing each of the five assessment-for-learning strategies.

Clarify and Share Intentions and Criteria

Low achievement is often the result of students failing to understand what teachers require of them (Black & Wiliam, 1998). Many teachers address this issue by posting the state standard or learning objective in a prominent place at the start of the lesson, but such an approach is rarely successful because the standards are not written in student-friendly language.

Teachers in our various projects have explored many ways of making their learning objectives and their criteria for success transparent to students. One common method involves circulating work samples, such as lab reports, that a previous year's class completed, in view of prompting a discussion about quality. Students decide which reports are good and analyze what's good about the good ones and what's lacking in the weaker ones. Teachers have also found that by choosing the samples carefully, they can tune the task to the capabilities of the class. Initially, a teacher might choose four or five samples at very different quality levels to get students to focus on broad criteria for quality As students grow more skilled, however, teachers can challenge them with a number of samples of similar quality to force the students to become more critical and reflective.

Engineer Effective Classroom Discussion

Many teachers spend a considerable proportion of their instructional time in whole-class discussion or question-and-answer sessions, but these sessions tend to rehearse existing knowledge rather than create new knowledge for students. Moreover, teachers generally listen for the "correct" answer instead of listening for what they can learn about the students' thinking; as Davis (1997) says, they listen *evaluatively* rather than *interpretively*. The teachers with whom we have worked have tried to address this issue by asking students questions that either prompt students to think or provide teachers with information that they can use to adjust instruction to meet learning needs.

As a result of this focus, teachers have become aware of the need to carefully plan the questions that they use in class. Many of our teachers now spend more time planning instruction than grading student work, a practice that emphasizes the shift from quality control to quality assurance. By thinking more carefully about the questions they ask in class, teachers can check on students' understanding while the students are still in the class rather than after they have left, as is the case with grading.

Some questions are designed as "range-finding" questions to reveal what students know at the beginning of an instructional sequence. For example, a high school biology teacher might ask the class how much water taken up by the roots of a corn plant is lost through transpiration. Many students believe that transpiration is "bad" and that plants try to minimize the amount of water lost in this process, whereas, in fact, the "lost" water plays an important role in transporting nutrients around the plant.

A middle school mathematics teacher might ask students to indicate how many fractions they can find between $\frac{1}{6}$ and $\frac{1}{7}$. Some students will think there aren't any; others may suggest an answer that, although in some way understandable, is an incorrect use of mathematical notation, such as 1 over 6½. The important feature of such range-finding items is that they can help a teacher judge where to begin instruction.

Of course, teachers can use the same item in a number of ways, depending on the context. They could use the question about fractions at the end of a sequence of instruction on equivalent fractions to see whether students have grasped the main idea. A middle school science teacher might ask students at the end of a laboratory experiment, "What was the dependent variable in today's lab?" A social studies teacher, at the end of a project on World War II, might ask students to state their views about which year the war began and give reasons supporting their choice.

Teachers can also use questions to check on student understanding before continuing the lesson. We call this a "hinge point" in the lesson because the lesson can go in different directions, depending on student responses. By explicitly integrating these hinge points into instruction, teachers can make their teaching more responsive to their students' needs in real time.

However, no matter how good the hinge-point question, the traditional model of classroom questioning presents two additional problems. The first is lack of engagement. If the classroom rule dictates that students raise their hands to answer questions, then students can disengage from the classroom by keeping their hands down. For this reason, many of our teachers have instituted the idea of "no hands up, except to ask a question." The teacher can either decide whom to call on to answer a question or use some randomizing device, such as a beaker of Popsicle sticks with the students' names written on them. This way, all students know that they need to stay engaged because the teacher could call on any one of them. One teacher we worked with reported that her students love the fairness of this approach and that her shyer students are showing greater confidence as a result of being invited to participate in this way. Other teachers have said that some students think it's unfair that they don't get a chance to show off when they know the answer.

The second problem with traditional questioning is that the teacher gets to hear only one student's thinking. To gauge the understanding of the whole class, the teacher needs to get responses from all the students in real time. One way to do this is to have all students write their answers on individual dry-erase boards, which they hold up at the teacher's request. The teacher can then scan responses for novel solutions as well as misconceptions. This technique would be particularly helpful with the fraction question we cited.

Another approach is to give each student a set of four cards labeled *A*, *B*, *C*, and *D*, and ask the question in multiple-choice format. If the question is well designed, the teacher can quickly judge the different levels of understanding in the class. If all students answer correctly, the teacher can move on. If no one answers correctly, the teacher might choose to reteach the concept. If some students answer correctly and some answer incorrectly, the teacher can use that knowledge to engineer a whole-class discussion on the concept or match up the students for peer teaching. Hinge-point questions provide a window into students' thinking and, at the same time, give the teacher some ideas about how to take the students' learning forward.

Provide Feedback That Moves Learners Forward

After the lesson, of course, comes grading. The problem with giving a student a grade and a supportive comment is that these practices don't cause further learning. Before they began thinking about assessment for learning, none of the teachers with whom we worked believed that their students spent as long considering teacher feedback as it had taken the teachers to provide that feedback. Indeed, the research shows that when students receive a grade and a comment, they ignore the comment (see Butler, 1988). The first thing they look at is the grade, and the second thing they look at is their neighbors grade.

To be effective, feedback needs to cause thinking. Grades don't do that. Scores don't do that. And comments like "Good job" don't do that either. What *does* cause thinking is a comment that addresses what the student needs to do to improve, linked to rubrics where appropriate. Of course, it's difficult to give insightful comments when the assignment asked for 20 calculations or 20 historical dates, but even in these cases, feedback can cause thinking. For example, one approach that many of our teachers have found productive is to say to a student, "Five of these 20 answers are incorrect. Find them and fix them!"

Some of our teachers worried about the extra time needed to provide useful feedback. But once students engaged in self-assessment and peer assessment, the teachers were able to be more selective about which elements of student work they looked at, and they could focus on giving feedback that peers were unable to provide.

To be effective, feedback needs to cause thinking. Grades don't do that. Scores don't do that. And comments like "Good job" don't do that either.

Teachers also worried about the reactions of administrators and parents. Some teachers needed waivers from principals to vary school policy (for example, to give comments rather than grades on interim assessments). Most principals were happy to permit these changes once teachers explained their reasons. Parents were also supportive. Some even said they found comments more useful than grades because the comments provided them with guidance on how to help their children.

Activate Students as Owners of Their Learning

Developing assessment for learning in one's classroom involves altering the implicit contract between teacher and students by creating shared responsibility for learning. One simple technique is to distribute green and red "traffic light" cards, which students "flash" to indicate their level of understanding (green = understand, red = don't understand). A teacher who uses this technique with her 9th grade algebra classes told us that one day she moved on too quickly, without scanning the students' cards. A student picked up her own card as well as her neighbors' cards, waved them in the air, and pointed at them wildly, with the red side facing the teacher. The teacher considered this ample proof that this student was taking ownership of her learning.

Students also take ownership of their learning when they assess their own work, using agreed-on criteria for success. Teachers can provide students with a rubric written in student-friendly language, or the class can develop the rubric with the teacher's guidance (for examples, see Black, Harrison, Lee, Marshall, & Wiliam, 2003). The teachers we have worked with report that students' self-assessments are generally accurate, and students say that assessing their own work helped them understand the material in a new way.

Activate Students as Instructional Resources for One Another

Getting students started with self-assessment can be challenging. Many teachers provide students with rubrics but find that the students seem unable to use the rubrics to focus and improve their work. For many students, using a rubric to assess their own work is just too difficult. But as most teachers know, students from kindergarten to 12th grade are much better at spotting errors in other students' work than in their own work. For that reason, peer assessment and feedback can be an important part of effective instruction. Students who get feedback are not the only beneficiaries. Students who give feedback also benefit, sometimes more than the recipients. As they assess the work of a peer, they are forced to engage in understanding the rubric, but in the context of someone else's work, which is less emotionally charged. Also, students often communicate more effectively with one another than the teacher does, and the recipients of the feedback tend to be more engaged when the feedback comes from a peer. When the teacher gives feedback, students often just "sit there and take it" until the ordeal is over.

Peer assessment and feedback among students can be an important part of effective instruction.

Using peer and self-assessment techniques frees up teacher time to plan better instruction or work more intensively with small groups of students. It's also a highly effective teaching strategy. One cautionary note is in order, however. In our view, students should not be giving another student a grade that will be reported to parents or administrators. Peer assessment should be focused on improvement, not on grading.

Using Evidence of Learning to Adapt Instruction

One final strategy binds the others together: Assessment information should be used to adapt instruction to meet student needs.

As teachers listen to student responses to a hinge-point question or note the prevalence of red or green cards, they can make on-the-fly decisions to review material or to pair up those who understand the concept with those who don't for some peer tutoring. Using the evidence they have elicited, teachers can make instructional decisions that they otherwise could not have made.

At the end of the lesson, many of the teachers with whom we work use "exit passes." Students are given index cards and must turn in their responses to a question posed by the teacher before they can leave the classroom. Sometimes this will be a "big idea" question, to check on the students' grasp of the content of the lesson. At other times, it will be a range-finding question, to help the teacher judge where to begin the next day's instruction.

Teachers using assessment for learning continually look for ways in which they can generate evidence of student learning, and they use this evidence to adapt their instruction to better meet their students' learning needs. They share the responsibility for learning with the learners; students know that they are responsible for alerting the teacher when they do not understand. Teachers design their instruction to yield evidence about student achievement; for example, they carefully craft hinge-point questions to create "moments of contingency" in which the direction of the instruction will depend on student responses. Teachers provide feedback that engages students, make time in class for students to work on improvement, and activate students as instructional resources for one another.

All this sounds like a lot of work, but according to our teachers, it doesn't take any more time than the practices they used to engage in. And these techniques are far more effective. Teachers tell us that they are enjoying their teaching more.

Supporting Teacher Change

None of these ideas is new, and a large and growing research base shows that implementing them yields substantial improvement in student learning. So why are these strategies and techniques not practiced more widely? the answer is that knowing about these techniques and strategies is one thing; figuring out how to make them work in your own classroom is something else.

That's why we're currently developing a set of tools and workshops to support teachers in developing a deep and practical understanding of assessment for learning, primarily through the vehicle of school-based teacher learning communities. After we introduce teachers to the basic principles of assessment for learning, we encourage them to try out two or three techniques in their own classrooms and to meet with other colleagues regularly—ideally every month—to discuss their experiences and see what the other teachers are doing (see Black, Harrison, Lee, Marshall, & Wiliam, 2003, 2004). Teachers are accountable because they know they will have to share their experiences with their colleagues. However, each teacher is also in control of what he or she tries out. Over time, the teacher learning community develops a shared language enables teachers to talk to one another about what they are doing. Teachers build individual and collective skill and confidence in assessment for learning. Colleagues help them decide when it is time to move on to the next challenge as well as point out potential pitfalls.

In many ways, the teacher learning community approach is similar to the larger assessment-for-learning approach. Both focus on where learners are now, where they want to go, and how we can help them get there.

References

Black, P., Harrison, C., Lee, C., Marshall, B., & Wiliam, D. (2003). *Assessment for learning: Putting it into practice.* Buckingham, UK: Open University Press.

Black, P., Harrison, C., Lee, C., Marshall, B., & Wiliam, D. (2004). Working inside the black box: Assessment for learning in the classroom. *Phi Delta Kappan, 86*(1), 8–21.

Black, P., & Wiliam, D. (1998). Inside the black box: Raising standards through classroom assessment. *Phi Delta Kappan, 80*(2), 139–147.

Butler, R. (1988). Enhancing and undermining intrinsic motivation. *British Journal of Educational Psychology, 58,* 1–14.

Davis, B. (1997). Listening for differences: An evolving conception of mathematics teaching. *Journal for Research in Mathematics Education, 28*(3), 355–376.

Wiliam, D. (2005). Keeping learning on track: Formative assessment and the regulation of learning. In M. Coupland, J. Anderson, & T. Spencer (Eds.), *Making mathematics vital: Proceedings of the twentieth biennial conference of the Australian Association of Mathematics Teachers* (pp. 26–40). Adelaide, Australia: Australian Association of Mathematics Teachers.

Wiliam, D., Lee, C., Harrison, C., & Black, P. J. (2004). Teachers developing assessment for learning: Impact on student achievement. *Assessment in Education: Principles, Policy & Practice, 11*(1), 49–65.

SIOBHAN LEAHY, CHRISTINE LYON, MARNIE THOMPSON, and DYLAN WILIAM (dwiliam@ets.org) work in the Learning and Teaching Research Center, Educational Testing Service, Rosedale Rd., Princeton, NJ 08541.

Seven Practices for Effective Learning

Teachers in all content areas can use these seven assessment and grading practices to enhance learning and teaching.

Jay McTighe and Ken O'Connor

Classroom assessment and grading practices have the potential not only to measure and report learning but also to promote it. Indeed, recent research has documented the benefits of regular use of diagnostic and formative assessments as feedback for learning (Black, Harrison, Lee, Marshall, & Wiliam, 2004). Like successful athletic coaches, the best teachers recognize the importance of ongoing assessments and continual adjustments on the part of both teacher and student as the means to achieve maximum performance. Unlike the external standardized tests that feature so prominently on the school landscape these days, well-designed classroom assessment and grading practices can provide the kind of specific, personalized, and timely information needed to guide both learning and teaching.

Classroom assessments fall into three categories, each serving a different purpose, *Summative* assessments summarize what students have learned at the conclusion of an instructional segment. These assessments tend to be evaluative, and teachers typically encapsulate and report assessment results as a score or a grade. Familiar examples of summative assessments include tests, performance tasks, final exams, culminating projects, and work portfolios. Evaluative assessments command the attention of students and parents because their results typically "count" and appear on report cards and transcripts. But by themselves, summative assessments are insufficient tools for maximizing learning. Waiting until the end of a teaching period to find out how well students have learned is simply too late.

Teachers should set up authentic contexts for assessment.

Two other classroom assessment categories—diagnostic and formative—provide fuel for the teaching and learning engine by offering descriptive feedback along the way. *Diagnostic* assessments—sometimes known as *pre-assessments*—typically precede instruction. Teachers use them to check students' prior knowledge and skill levels, identify student misconceptions,

profile learners' interests, and reveal learning-style preferences. Diagnostic assessments provide information to assist teacher planning and guide differentiated instruction. Examples of diagnostic assessments include prior knowledge and skill checks and interest or learning preference surveys. Because pre-assessments serve diagnostic purposes, teachers normally don't grade the results.

Formative assessments occur concurrently with instruction. These ongoing assessments provide specific feedback to teachers and students for the purpose of guiding teaching to improve learning. Formative assessments include both formal and informal methods, such as ungraded quizzes, oral questioning, teacher observations, draft work, think-alouds, student-constructed concept maps, learning logs, and portfolio reviews. Although teachers may record the results of formative assessments, we shouldn't factor these results into summative evaluation and grading.

Keeping these three categories of classroom assessment in mind, let us consider seven specific assessment and grading practices that can enhance teaching and learning.

Practice 1: Use Summative Assessments to Frame Meaningful Performance Goals

On the first day of a three-week unit on nutrition, a middle school teacher describes to students the two summative assessments that she will use. One assessment is a multiple-choice test examining student knowledge of various nutrition facts and such basic skills as analyzing nutrition labels. The second assessment is an authentic performance task in which each student designs a menu plan for an upcoming two-day trip to an outdoor education facility. The menu plan must provide well-balanced and nutritious meals and snacks.

The current emphasis on established content standards has focused teaching on designated knowledge and skills. To avoid the danger of viewing the standards and benchmarks as inert content to "cover," educators should frame the standards and benchmarks in terms of desired performances and ensure that the performances are as authentic as possible. Teachers should then present the summative performance assessment tasks to students at the beginning of a new unit or course.

This practice has three virtues. First, the summative assessments clarify the targeted standards and benchmarks for teachers and learners. In standards-based education, the rubber meets the road with assessments because they define the evidence that will determine whether or not students have learned the content standards and benchmarks. The nutrition vignette is illustrative: By knowing what the culminating assessments will be, students are better able to focus on what the teachers expect them to learn (information about healthy eating) and on what they will be expected to do with that knowledge (develop a nutritious meal plan).

Second, the performance assessment tasks yield evidence that reveals understanding, When we call for authentic application, we do not mean recall of basic facts or mechanical plug-ins of a memorized formula. Rather, we want students to transfer knowledge—to use what they know in a new situation, Teachers should set up realistic, authentic contexts for assessment that enable students to apply their learning thoughtfully and flexibly, thereby demonstrating their understanding of the content standards.

Third, presenting the authentic performance tasks at the beginning of a new unit or course provides a meaningful learning goal for students. Consider a sports analogy. Coaches routinely conduct practice drills that both develop basic skills and purposefully point toward performance in the game. Too often, classroom instruction and assessment overemphasize decontextualized drills and provide too few opportunities for students to actually "play the game." How many soccer players would practice comer kicks or run exhausting wind sprints if they weren't preparing for the upcoming game? How many competitive swimmers would log endless laps if there were no future swim meets? Authentic performance tasks provide a worthy goal and help learners see a reason for their learning.

Practice 2: Show Criteria and Models in Advance

A high school language arts teacher distributes a summary of the summative performance task that students will complete during the unit on research, including the rubric for judging the performance's quality. In addition, she shows examples of student work products collected from previous years (with student names removed) to illustrate criteria and performance levels. Throughout the unit, the teacher uses the student examples and the criteria in the rubric to help students better understand the nature of high-quality work and to support her teaching of research skills and report writing.

A second assessment practice that supports learning involves presenting evaluative criteria and models of work that illustrate different levels of quality. Unlike selected-response or short-answer tests, authentic performance assessments are typically open-ended and do not yield a single, correct answer or solution process. Consequently, teachers cannot score student responses using an answer key or a Scantron machine. They need to evaluate products and performances on the basis of explicitly defined performance criteria.

The best teachers recognize the importance on ongoing assessments as the means to achieve maximum performance.

A rubric is a widely used evaluation tool consisting of criteria, a measurement scale (a 4-point scale, for example), and descriptions of the characteristics for each score point. Well-developed rubrics communicate the important dimensions, or elements of quality, in a product or performance and guide educators in evaluating student work. When a department or

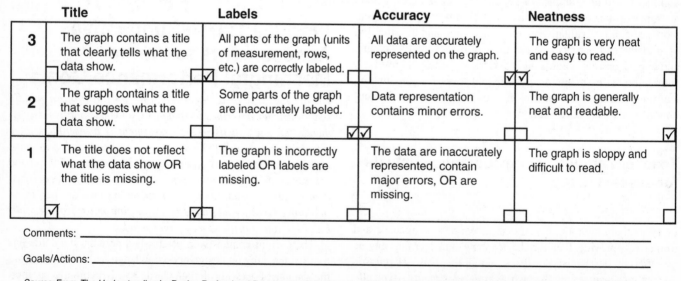

	Title	Labels	Accuracy	Neatness
3	The graph contains a title that clearly tells what the data show.	All parts of the graph (units of measurement, rows, etc.) are correctly labeled. ☑	All data are accurately represented on the graph.	The graph is very neat and easy to read. ☑☑
2	The graph contains a title that suggests what the data show.	Some parts of the graph are inaccurately labeled.	Data representation contains minor errors. ☑☑	The graph is generally neat and readable. ☑
1	The title does not reflect what the data show OR the title is missing. ☑	The graph is incorrectly labeled OR labels are missing. ☑	The data are inaccurately represented, contain major errors, OR are missing.	The graph is sloppy and difficult to read.

Comments: _____

Goals/Actions: _____

Source: From *The Understanding by Design Professional Development Workbook* (p. 183), by J. McTighe and G. Wiggins, 2004, Alexandria, VA: ASCD.

Figure 1 Analytic rubric for graphic display of data.

grade-level team—or better yet, an entire school or district—uses common rubrics, evaluation results are more consistent because the performance criteria don't vary from teacher to teacher or from school to school.

Rubrics also benefit students. When students know the criteria in advance of their performance, they have clear goals for their work. Because well-defined criteria provide a clear description of quality performance, students don't need to guess what is most important or how teachers will judge their work.

Providing a rubric to students in advance of the assessment is a necessary, but often insufficient, condition to support their learning. Although experienced teachers have a clear conception of what they mean by "quality work," students don't necessarily have the same understanding. Learners are more likely to understand feedback and evaluations when teachers show several examples that display both excellent and weak work. These models help translate the rubric's abstract language into more specific, concrete, and understandable terms.

Some teachers express concern that students will simply copy or imitate the example. A related worry is that showing an excellent model (sometimes known as an exemplar) will stultify student creativity. We have found that providing multiple models helps avoid these potential problems. When students see several exemplars showing how different students achieved high-level performance in unique ways, they are less likely to follow a cookie-cutter approach. In addition, when students study and compare examples ranging in quality—from very strong to very weak—they are better able to internalize the differences. The models enable students to more accurately self-assess and improve their work before turning it in to the teacher.

Practice 3: Assess Before Teaching

Before beginning instruction on the five senses, a kindergarten teacher asks each student to draw a picture of the body parts related to the various senses and show what each part does. She models the process by drawing an eye on the chalkboard. "The eye helps us see things around us," she points out. As students draw, the teacher circulates around the room, stopping to ask clarifying questions ("I see you've drawn a nose. What does the nose help us do?"). On the basis of what she learns about her students from this diagnostic pre-test, she divides the class into two groups for differentiated instruction. At the conclusion of the unit, the teacher asks students to do another drawing, which she collects and compares with their original pre-test as evidence of their learning.

Diagnostic assessment is as important to teaching as a physical exam is to prescribing an appropriate medical regimen. At the outset of any unit of study, certain students are likely to have already mastered some of the skills that the teacher is about to introduce, and others may already understand key concepts. Some students are likely to be deficient in prerequisite skills or harbor misconceptions. Armed with this diagnostic information, a teacher gains greater insight into *what to teach*, by knowing what skill gaps to address or by

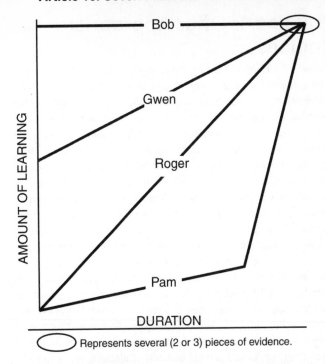

Represents several (2 or 3) pieces of evidence.

Figure 2   Student Learning Curves   Four students master a given learning goal by the end of an instructional segment but have vastly different learning curves.

skipping material previously mastered; into *how to teach*, by using grouping options and initiating activities based on preferred learning styles and interests; and into *how to connect* the content to students' interests and talents.

With performance assessments, the juice must be worth the squeeze.

Teachers can use a variety of practical pre-assessment strategies, including pre-tests of content knowledge, skills checks, concept maps, drawings, and K-W-L (*K*now-*W*ant to learn-*L*earn) charts. Powerful pre-assessment has the potential to address a worrisome phenomenon reported in a growing body of literature (Bransford, Brown, & Cocking, 1999; Gardner, 1991): A sizeable number of students come into school with misconceptions about subject matter (thinking that a heavier object will drop faster than a lighter one, for example) and about themselves as learners (assuming that they can't and never will be able to draw, for example). If teachers don't identify and confront these misconceptions, they will persist even in the face of good teaching. To uncover existing misconceptions, teachers can use a short, nongraded true-false diagnostic quiz that includes several potential misconceptions related to the targeted learning. Student responses will signal any prevailing misconceptions, which the teacher can then address through instruction. In the future, the growing availability of portable, electronic student-response systems will enable educators to obtain this information instantaneously.

Practice 4: Offer Appropriate Choices

As part of a culminating assessment for a major unit on their state's history and geography, a class of 4th graders must contribute to a classroom museum display. The displays are designed to provide answers to the unit's essential question: How do geography, climate, and natural resources influence lifestyle, economy, and culture? Parents and students from other classrooms will view the display. Students have some choice about the specific products they will develop, which enables them to work to their strengths. Regardless of students' chosen products, the teacher uses a common rubric to evaluate every project. The resulting class museum contains a wide variety of unique and informative products that demonstrate learning.

Responsiveness in assessment is as important as it is in teaching. Students differ not only in how they prefer to take in and process information but also in how they best demonstrate their learning. Some students need to "do"; others thrive on oral explanations. Some students excel at creating visual representations; others are adept at writing. To make valid inferences about learning, teachers need to allow students to work to their strengths. A standardized approach to classroom assessment may be efficient, but it is not fair because any chosen format will favor some students and penalize others.

Assessment becomes responsive when students are given appropriate options for demonstrating knowledge, skills, and understanding. Allow choices—but always with the intent of collecting needed and appropriate evidence based on goals. In the example of the 4th grade museum display project, the teacher wants students to demonstrate their understanding of the relationship between geography and economy. This could be accomplished through a newspaper article, a concept web, a PowerPoint presentation, a comparison chart, or a simulated radio interview with an expert. Learners often put forth greater effort and produce higher-quality work when given such a variety of choices. The teacher will judge these products using a three-trait rubric that focuses on accuracy of content, clarity and thoroughness of explanation, and overall product quality.

Teachers need to allow students to work to their strengths.

We offer three cautions. First, teachers need to collect appropriate evidence of learning on the basis of goals rather than simply offer a "cool" menu of assessment choices. If a content standard calls for proficiency in written or oral presentations, it would be inappropriate to provide performance options other than those involving writing or speaking, except in the case of students for whom such goals are clearly inappropriate (a newly arrived English language learner, for example). Second, the options must be worth the time and energy required. It would be inefficient to have students develop an elaborate three-dimensional display or an animated PowerPoint presentation

for content that a multiple-choice quiz could easily assess. In the folksy words of a teacher friend, "With performance assessments, the juice must be worth the squeeze." Third, teachers have only so much time and energy, so they must be judicious in determining when it is important to offer product and performance options. They need to strike a healthy balance between a single assessment path and a plethora of choices.

Practice 5: Provide Feedback Early and Often

Middle school students are learning watercolor painting techniques. The art teacher models proper technique for mixing and applying the colors, and the students begin working. As they paint, the teacher provides feedback both to individual students and to the class as a whole. She targets common mistakes, such as using too much paint and not enough water, a practice that reduces the desired transparency effect. Benefiting from continual feedback from the teacher, students experiment with the medium on small sheets of paper. The next class provides additional opportunities to apply various watercolor techniques to achieve such effects as color blending and soft edges. The class culminates in an informal peer feedback session. Skill development and refinement result from the combined effects of direct instruction, modeling, and opportunities to practice guided by ongoing feedback.

It is often said that feedback is the breakfast of champions. All kinds of learning, whether on the practice field or in the classroom, require feedback based on formative assessments. Ironically, the quality feedback necessary to enhance learning is limited or nonexistent in many classrooms.

To serve learning, feedback must meet four criteria: It must be timely, specific, understandable to the receiver, and formed to allow for self-adjustment on the student's part (Wiggins, 1998). First, feedback on strengths and weaknesses needs to be prompt for the learner to improve. Waiting three weeks to find out how you did on a test will not help your learning.

In addition, specificity is key to helping students understand both their strengths and the areas in which they can improve. Too many educators consider grades and scores as feedback when, in fact, they fail the specificity test. Pinning a letter (*B*-) or a number (82%) on a student's work is no more helpful than such comments as "Nice job" or "You can do better." Although good grades and positive remarks may feel good, they do not advance learning.

Specific feedback sounds different, as in this example:

Your research paper is generally well organized and contains a great deal of information on your topic. You used multiple sources and documented them correctly. However, your paper lacks a clear conclusion, and you never really answered your basic research question.

Sometimes the language in a rubric is lost on a student. Exactly what does "well organized" or "sophisticated reasoning" mean? "Kid language" rubrics can make feedback clearer and more comprehensible. For instance, instead of saying, "Document your reasoning process," a teacher might say,

"Show your work in a step-by-step manner so the reader can see what you were thinking."

Here's a simple, straightforward test for a feedback system: Can learners tell *specifically* from the given feedback what they have done well and what they could do next time to improve? If not, then the feedback is not specific or understandable enough for the learner.

Finally, the learner needs opportunities to act on the feedback—to refine, revise, practice, and retry. Writers rarely compose a perfect manuscript on the first try, which is why the writing process stresses cycles of drafting, feedback, and revision as the route to excellence. Not surprisingly, the best feedback often surfaces in the performance-based subjects—such as art, music, and physical education—and in extracurricular activities, such as band and athletics. Indeed, the essence of coaching involves ongoing assessment and feedback.

Practice 6: Encourage Self-Assessment and Goal Setting

Before turning in their science lab reports, students review their work against a list of explicit criteria. On the basis of their self-assessments, a number of students make revisions to improve their reports before handing them in. Their teacher observes that the overall quality of the lab reports has improved.

The most effective learners set personal learning goals, employ proven strategies, and self-assess their work. Teachers help cultivate such habits of mind by modeling self-assessment and goal setting and by expecting students to apply these habits regularly.

Rubrics can help students become more effective at honest self-appraisal and productive self-improvement. In the rubric in Figure 1, students verify that they have met a specific criterion—for a title, for example—by placing a check in the lower left-hand square of the applicable box. The teacher then uses the square on the right side for his or her evaluation. Ideally, the two judgments should match. If not, the discrepancy raises an opportunity to discuss the criteria, expectations, and performance standards. Over time, teacher and student judgments tend to align. In fact, it is not unusual for students to be harder on themselves than the teacher is.

The rubric also includes space for feedback comments and student goals and action steps. Consequently the rubric moves from being simply an evaluation tool for "pinning a number" on students to a practical and robust vehicle for feedback, self-assessment, and goal setting.

Initially, the teacher models how to self-assess, set goals, and plan improvements by asking such prompting questions as,

- What aspect of your work was most effective?
- What aspect of your work was least effective?
- What specific action or actions will improve your performance?
- What will you do differently next time?

Questions like these help focus student reflection and planning. Over time, students assume greater responsibility for enacting these processes independently.

Educators who provide regular opportunities for learners to self-assess and set goals often report a change in the classroom culture. As one teacher put it,

My students have shifted from asking, "What did I get?" or "What are you going to give me?" to becoming increasingly capable of knowing how they are doing and what they need to do to improve.

Authentic performance tasks help learners see a reason for their learning.

Practice 7: Allow New Evidence of Achievement to Replace Old Evidence

A driver education student fails his driving test the first time, but he immediately books an appointment to retake the test one week later. He passes on his second attempt because he successfully demonstrates the requisite knowledge and skills. The driving examiner does not average the first performance with the second, nor does the new license indicate that the driver "passed on the second attempt."

This vignette reveals an important principle in classroom assessment, grading, and reporting: New evidence of achievement should replace old evidence. Classroom assessments and grading should focus on *how well*—not on *when*—the student mastered the designated knowledge and skill.

Consider the learning curves of four students in terms of a specified learning goal (see Figure 2). Bob already possesses the targeted knowledge and skill and doesn't need instruction for this particular goal. Gwen arrives with substantial knowledge and skill but has room to improve. Roger and Pam are true novices who demonstrate a high level of achievement by the *end* of the instructional segment as a result of effective teaching and diligent learning. If their school's grading system truly documented learning, all these students would receive the same grade because they all achieved the desired results over time. Roger and Pam would receive lower grades than Bob and Gwen, however, if the teacher factored their earlier performances into the final evaluation. This practice, which is typical of the grading approach used in many classrooms, would misrepresent Roger and Pam's ultimate success because it does not give appropriate recognition to the real—or most current—level of achievement.

Two concerns may arise when teachers provide students with multiple opportunities to demonstrate their learning. Students may not take the first attempt seriously once they realize they'll have a second chance. In addition, teachers often become overwhelmed by the logistical challenges of providing multiple opportunities. To make this approach effective, teachers need to require their students to provide some evidence of the corrective action they will take—such as engaging in peer coaching, revising their report, or practicing the needed skill in a given way—before embarking on their "second chance."

As students work to achieve clearly defined learning goals and produce evidence of their achievement, they need to know that teachers will not penalize them for either their lack of knowledge at the beginning of a course of study or their initial attempts at skill mastery. Allowing new evidence to replace old conveys an important message to students—that teachers care about their successful learning, not merely their grades.

Motivated to Learn

The assessment strategies that we have described address three factors that influence student motivation to learn (Marzano, 1992). Students are more likely to put forth the required effort when there is

- *Task clarity*—when they clearly understand the learning goal and know how teachers will evaluate their learning (Practices 1 and 2).
- *Relevance*—when they think the learning goals and assessments are meaningful and worth learning (Practice 1).
- *Potential for success*—when they believe they can successfully learn and meet the evaluative expectations (Practices 3–7).

By using these seven assessment and grading practices, all teachers can enhance learning in their classrooms.

References

Black, P., Harrison, C., Lee, C., Marshall, B., & Wiliam, D. (2004). Working inside the black box: Assessment for learning in the classroom. *Phi Delta Kappan, 86*(1), 8–21.

Bransford, J. D., Brown, A. L., & Cocking, R. R. (Eds.). (1999). *How people learn: Brain, mind, experience, and school.* Washington, DC: National Research Council.

Gardner, H. (1991). *The unschooled mind.* New York: BasicBooks.

Marzano, R. (1992). *A different kind of classroom: Teaching with dimensions of learning.* Alexandria, VA: ASCD.

Wiggins, G. (1998). *Educative assessment: Designing assessments to inform and improve student performance.* San Francisco: Jossey-Bass.

JAY MCTIGHE (jmctigh@aol.com) is coauthor of *The Understanding by Design* series (ASCD, 1998, 1999, 2000, 2004, 2005). KEN O'CONNOR is author of *How to Grade for Learning: Linking Grades to Standards* (Corwin, 2002).

Homework: A Few Practice Arrows

Used correctly, homework tells teachers where students are now and how to better direct them toward their learning goals.

Susan Christopher

Formative assessment has become one of the most powerful items in my teacher toolbox. By using the information I gain through formative assessments, I can adjust activities and lessons to maximize student learning and minimize unnecessary repetition. I can find out what to reteach and how to differentiate to best meet student needs.

Formative assessments also provide an avenue for the middle school students in my Spanish classes to get feedback and ideas on how to improve. Formative assessments enable students to work with what they are learning—to play with it, try it on, and show what they can do without being judged or graded.

What Is Formative Assessment?

Assessments tend to fall into one of two categories: formative and summative. The use of these terms has become muddled, with many teachers using them almost interchangeably. Stiggins, Arter, Chappuis, and Chappuis (2004) refer to the two types of assessment as assessment *for* learning (formative) and assessment *of* learning (summative). Assessment *for* learning happens while students are still in the learning process. These assessments help teachers diagnose student needs, provide feedback, and show students how to improve. In contrast, assessment *of* learning happens after the learning process has ended. These assessments, which include unit exams, projects, and standardized tests, give us a snapshot of what a student has learned at a given point in time. The focus is on assigning a grade to indicate student achievement.

Homework as Rehearsal

One of the most valuable formative assessments a teacher can use is homework. To help students and parents understand my expectations for homework, I equate it with practice in a sports or music setting. Top-level athletes need to practice regularly to be successful. Athletes are not given their final evaluation on the practice field, but at the important game or race. Students need homework as practice so that they can perform well on their summative assessments.

When homework is used as a formative assessment, students have multiple opportunities to practice, get feedback from the teacher, and improve. Homework becomes a safe place to try out new skills without penalty, just as athletes and musicians try out their skills on the practice field or in rehearsals. Effective homework is the rehearsal before the final event.

Effective homework is the rehearsal before the final event.

Because the role of homework has changed in my classroom, so has the way I evaluate it. I no longer count homework when computing student grades. I still collect and comment on students' homework (although not all of it), and I still report to parents whether or nor their child is completing homework assignments, but I set the weight of homework to zero. Surprisingly, the number of students actually completing and turning in assignments has increased since I stopped counting homework for points and started using it solely for practice.

Eliminating the homework grade has also caused students' overall grades to more accurately reflect their performance. In classes where total points are used to determine final grades, homework points often outweigh points for other assessments. If students complete homework assignments and accumulate lots of points, their grade can be distorted toward the high end, even if they *cannot* perform successfully on assessments. Likewise, if students do not complete homework assignments, their grade can be distorted toward the low end, even if they *can* perform successfully on assessments. The power of the homework zero can far outweigh what students demonstrate on other assessments and cause them to give up on learning (O'Connor, 2002).

Grading Practices

In addition to changing the role of homework in the grades I give, I have changed my entire grading practice. I have switched from assessment *categories*—homework, class participation, projects, tests, quizzes, and so on—to a standards-based reporting format. I report my grades based on the major skills that I want students to know and be able to do: understand written and spoken Spanish, write and speak comprehensibly, and accurately use the vocabulary and grammar structures we've learned. I grade student projects, performance assessments, and summative assessments according to these standards, and I no longer put a total percentage grade on assessments. Instead, I put a grade for each standard being assessed so that one test or project often has several different grades, each indicating progress toward a different standard.

For example, on a recent project, students received five grades, one for each of the following: ability to communicate ideas, accuracy of grammar structures, correct word choice, inclusion of all required information, and visual appeal.

I also include a "process" portion for grades (only 10 percent) that includes points for such activities as completing rough drafts, following directions, working with others on projects, and so on. Because I keep this process portion of the grade to a low percentage, student grades are still based primarily on achievement of the standards I have set for them and not on behaviors such as participation and homework completion. Teachers in any subject area can identify the main skills that they expect students to know and be able to do and set up their grading accordingly.

Clearer Communication

Since I started using standards-based grades, I have found that the feedback I give to both students and parents is more meaningful and focused. For example, a quiz or test grade of 85 percent does not indicate what portions of the quiz the student scored well in and what areas the student needs to improve. The score itself is meaningless. By recording grades according to standards, I can *see* which students need to work on listening or reading comprehension, forming verbs, spelling vocabulary words, or making themselves understood when writing or speaking.

These grades also give students information that helps them move closer to the standards. Just by reporting their grades in a standards-based format, I am able to provide parents with more detailed information about their child's progress. Grades that directly report achievement toward a standard measured by specific criteria are meaningful to all stakeholders—students, teachers, and parents.

The Case for Formative Assessment

If we want students to show us what they know and can do as part of a summative assessment, we must provide them with plenty of opportunities to show us what they know along the way. Formative assessment fulfills this role. We can't expect students to hit a target without having them shoot some practice arrows. Formative assessments are the arrows that students shoot along the way in the learning process. Some miss the target completely, others get close, and others score a bull's-eye. By looking at what students do as they shoot their practice arrows, we can keep them motivated to practice, offer encouragement and correction, and help all students hit the mark.

References

O'Connor, K. (2002). *How to grade for learning: Linking grades to standards.* Glenview, IL: Pearson Education.

Stiggins, R., Arter, J., Chappuis, J., & Chappuis, S. (2004). *Classroom assessment for learning. Doing it right—Using it well.* Portland, OR: Assessment Training Institute.

Susan Christopher teaches Spanish at Wydown Middle School in Clayton, Missouri; susan_christopher@clayton.k12.mo.us.

Using Curriculum-Based Measurement to Improve Achievement

A data-driven method provides the most reliable indicator of student progress in basic academic areas.

SUZANNE CLARKE

Response to intervention (RTI) is on the radar screen of most principals these days—finding out what it is, how it can improve teaching and learning, and what needs to be done to implement it effectively. One critical component of RTI that will require particular attention from principals is student progress monitoring, which is required in every tier of RTI. The most commonly used and well-researched method of monitoring progress is curriculum-based measurement (CBM).

Nearly 30 years of empirical evidence tells us that CBM provides a valid and reliable indicator of student progress in basic academic areas, especially reading, math, and writing, and that it can have a positive impact on student achievement (Foegen, Jiban, & Deno, 2007; McMaster & Espin, 2007). Yet CBM was not commonly used by teachers, particularly in general education classrooms (Hosp & Hosp, 2003; Ardoin et al., 2004), until the advent of RTI.

Research has shown that the data gathered from CBM can be used in numerous educational decisions, such as screening, eligibility for special education, and re-integration. More recently, researchers have been examining the effectiveness of CBM in other areas as well, such as predicting performance on high-stakes tests and measuring growth in content areas (Deno, 2003). Mellard and Johnson (2008) discuss the use of CBM from an RTI perspective:

> Within an RTI model, the types of decisions that a system of progress monitoring can inform include whether a student is making adequate progress in the general classroom, whether a student requires a more intensive level of intervention, and whether a student has responded successfully to an intervention and, therefore, can be returned to the general classroom.

What Is CBM?

"CBM is a scientifically validated form of student progress monitoring that incorporates standard methods for test development, administration, scoring, and data utilization" (Stecker & Lembke, 2005). It was developed so that teachers would have measurement and evaluation procedures that they could "use routinely to make decisions about whether and when to modify a student's instructional program" (Deno, 1985).

In contrast to standardized achievement tests, which do not provide immediate feedback, CBM tests are given frequently to track student progress toward annual goals, monitor the effectiveness of interventions, and make instructional changes as needed throughout the year. As Wright (n.d.) points out, "much of the power of CBM . . . seems to lie in its ability to predict in a short time whether an intervention is working or needs to be altered." In an RTI context, CBM can help identify students in need of interventions, decide which level of intervention is most appropriate, and determine if an intervention is successful (Mellard & Johnson, 2008).

Unlike classroom assessments that test mastery of a single skill, each CBM test samples the year-long curriculum and, therefore, measures small student gains toward long-term goals (Stecker, Fuchs, & Fuchs, 2005; Deno, Fuchs, Marston, & Shin, 2001). For example, a third-grade teacher typically tests students on their mastery of multiplication immediately after completing that unit. However, the math CBM would include problems that test each skill that students are expected to master by the end of third grade (e.g., addition, subtraction, multiplication, and division problems). In this way, CBM provides educators with an overall indicator of student competence and progress in the curriculum.

In addition to being an assessment tool that allows educators to frequently measure student progress in the year-long curriculum, there are some additional benefits of CBM:

- It can provide documentation of student progress for accountability purposes, including adequate yearly progress and individualized education programs;
- It can facilitate communication about student progress with parents and other professionals;
- It may result in fewer special education referrals;

- It allows teachers to compare students against other students in the classroom, rather than against national norms; and
- It allows schools and districts to develop local norms that can then guide teachers when interpreting data (National Center on Student Progress Monitoring, n.d.; Holland-Coviello, n.d.).

How Does CBM Work?

One of the key aspects of CBM is that the "mechanics"—how the test is administered, the directions given to students, the procedures for scoring—are standardized (Deno & Fuchs, 1987). Standardization is important because it ensures that the data are valid and reliable indicators of a student's proficiency, allows for individual and group data to be compared across time, and facilitates the development of local norms (Deno, 2003; Wright, n.d.).

CBM probes, or tests, are easy and quick to administer, and are generally given once or twice per week. Each test is different but of equivalent difficulty. "Because CBM converts student academic behaviors into numbers (e.g., number of words read correctly per minute), teachers can easily chart the resulting data over time" (Wright, n.d.) and see when instructional changes need to be made. For example, the oral reading fluency probe has students read aloud from a passage for one minute as the teacher follows along, marking words that are read incorrectly. The number of words read correctly is recorded and graphed. It takes approximately five minutes to administer, score, and graph the result.

On a CBM graph, baseline data indicate a student's initial level of proficiency and a goal line is drawn to connect the baseline data to the desired year-end proficiency level. Following each CBM test, the teacher plots the student's score on the graph to determine whether the student is scoring above or below the goal line, and uses a predetermined rule to decide if instruction needs to be modified. Using the four-point rule, for example, the teacher looks at the four most recent of the first six data points. If all four are above the goal line, the teacher raises the goal; if all four fall below the goal line, an instructional change may need to be implemented (Stecker, Fuchs, & Fuchs, 1999).

Researchers have proposed several decision rules, in addition to the four-point rule, that educators can use to determine if a teaching change is needed. It is critical that one rule is chosen and then applied consistently across time and among all students being monitored.

Teacher Support and Training

Studies have shown that teachers who use CBM to monitor progress, adjust instruction, and determine the effectiveness of interventions have higher rates of student achievement and learning than those who do not use CBM (Bowman, 2003; Mellard & Johnson, 2008; Hosp & Hosp, 2003). As a principal, what factors do you need to consider and address to help prepare and support teachers in the use of CBM?

One research review that examined the effect of CBM on the achievement of students with learning disabilities concluded the following:

- Progress monitoring alone will not have a significant impact on student achievement. Teachers must modify their instruction based on what the data indicate.
- The use of data-based decision rules is important and they should be used by teachers to make necessary instructional changes.
- Computer applications that collect, store, manage, and analyze data make using CBM more efficient and contribute to teacher satisfaction.
- Ongoing teacher support, including a system that provides teachers with instructional recommendations, may be needed (Stecker, Fuchs, & Fuchs, 2005).

While CBM is designed to be time-efficient for teachers, it is important to note that time is cited as the biggest barrier to its implementation. Teachers need time for training and practice in all aspects of CBM, such as how to administer the various probes, how to set annual performance goals, and how to analyze graphs.

Actually using the data to make instructional changes may be one of the most difficult steps for teachers. Wesson (1991) suggests that as districts train teachers to use CBM, they should encourage them to meet regularly with one another, rather than with outside experts, to discuss what they are finding.

A "seamless and flexible system of progress monitoring" (Wallace, Espin, McMaster, Deno, & Foegen, 2007) remains a goal of researchers. In the meantime, three decades of study have produced a significant research base of reliable and valid CBM measures that schools can use to monitor student progress and support RTI implementation.

References

Ardoin, S. P., Witt, J. C., Suldo, S. M., Connell, J. E., Koenig, J. L., Resetar, J. L., et al. (2004). Examining the incremental benefits of administering a maze and three versus one curriculum-based measurement reading probes when conducting universal screening. *School Psychology Review, 33*(2), 218–233.

Bowman, L. J. (2003). *Secondary educators promoting student success: Curriculum-based measurement.* Retrieved February 7, 2008, from http://coe.ksu.edu/esl/lasestrellas/presentations/Lisa_CBM.ppt.

Deno, S. L. (1985). Curriculum-based measurement: The emerging alternative. *Exceptional Children, 52*(3), 219–232.

Deno, S. L. (2003). Developments in curriculum-based measurement. *The Journal of Special Education, 37*(3), 184–192.

Deno, S. L., & Fuchs, L. S. (1987). Developing curriculum-based measurement systems for data-based special education problem solving. *Focus on Exceptional Children, 19*(8), 1–16.

Deno, S. L., Fuchs, L. S., Marston, D., & Shin, J. (2001). Using curriculum-based measurement to establish growth standards for students with learning disabilities. *School Psychology Review, 30*(4), 507–524.

Foegen, A., Jiban, C., & Deno, S. (2007). Progress monitoring measures in mathematics. *The Journal of Special Education, 41*(2), 121–139.

Holland-Coviello, R. (n.d.). *Using curriculum-based measurement (CBM) for student progress monitoring.* Retrieved August 26, 2008, from www.studentprogress.org/player/playershell.swf.

Hosp, M. K., & Hosp, J. L. (2003). Curriculum-based measurement for reading, spelling, and math: How to do it and why. *Preventing School Failure, 48*(1), 10–17.

McMaster, K., & Espin, C. (2007). Technical features of curriculum-based measurement in writing: A literature review. *The Journal of Special Education, 41*(2), 68–84.

Mellard, D. F., & Johnson, E. (2008). *RTI: A practitioner's guide to implementing response to intervention.* Thousand Oaks, CA: Corwin Press and Alexandria, VA: National Association of Elementary School Principals.

National Center on Student Progress Monitoring. (n.d.). *Common questions for progress monitoring.* Retrieved August 26, 2008, from www.studentprogress.org/progresmon.asp#2.

Stecker, P. M., Fuchs, L. S., & Fuchs, D. (1999). *Using curriculum-based measurement for assessing reading progress and for making instruction decisions.* Retrieved February 25, 2008, from www.onlineacademy.org/modules/a300/lesson/lesson_3/xpages/a300c3_40200.html.

Stecker, P. M., Fuchs, L. S., & Fuchs, D. (2005). Using curriculum-based measurement to improve student achievement: Review of research. *Psychology in the Schools, 42*(8), 795–819.

Stecker, P. M., & Lembke, E. S. (2005). *Advanced applications of CBM in reading: Instructional decision-making strategies manual.* Washington, DC: National Center on Student Progress Monitoring.

Wallace, T., Espin, C. A., McMaster, K., Deno, S. L., & Foegen, A. (2007). CBM progress monitoring within a standards-based system. *The Journal of Special Education, 41*(2), 66–67.

Wesson, C. L. (1991). Curriculum-based measurement and two models of follow-up consultation. *Exceptional Children, 57*(3), 246–256.

Wright, J. (n.d.). *Curriculum-based measurement: A manual for teachers.* Retrieved February 5, 2008, from www.jimwrightonline.com/pdfdocs/cbaManual.pdf.

Suzanne Clarke is an issues analyst at Educational Research Service. Her e-mail address is sclarke@ers.org.

Research Matters/How Student Progress Monitoring Improves Instruction

NANCY SAFER AND STEVE FLEISCHMAN

In today's education climate, school success is defined as ensuring achievement for every student. To reach this goal, educators need tools to help them identify students who are at risk academically and adjust instructional strategies to better meet these students' needs. Student progress monitoring is a practice that helps teachers use student performance data to continually evaluate the effectiveness of their teaching and make more informed instructional decisions.

To implement student progress monitoring, the teacher determines a student's current performance level on skills that the student will be learning that school year, identifies achievement goals that the student needs to reach by the end of the year, and establishes the rate of progress the student must make to meet those goals. The teacher then measures the student's academic progress regularly (weekly, biweekly, or monthly) using *probes*—brief, easily administered measures. Each of the probes samples the entire range of skills that the student must learn by the end of the year, rather than just the particular skills a teacher may be teaching that week or month.

This is the key difference between student progress monitoring and mastery measurement approaches, such as teacher-made unit tests. Mastery measurement tells teachers whether the student has learned the particular skills covered in a unit, but not whether the student is learning at a pace that will allow him or her to meet annual learning goals. By regularly measuring all skills to be learned, teachers can graph changes in the number of correct words per minute (reading) or correct digits (math) and compare a student's progress to the rate of improvement needed to meet end-of-year goals. If the rate at which a particular student is learning seems insufficient, the teacher can adjust instruction.

To track student progress, the teacher graphs a line between the student's initial level of performance on a specific skill and the end-of-year goal. Then, the teacher plots the level of performance as each probe is administered. After noting the pattern of progress, the teacher can adjust instruction to improve student learning. If the student's performance falls below the line, the teacher may use more intense instruction (in small groups or one-on-one), reteach the material, or provide additional opportunities for the student to practice certain skills.

Although schools can develop the probes themselves, developing enough equivalent, alternate probes for frequent measurement at each grade level is daunting for many schools. Therefore, they often turn to commercially available products, most of which are computer-based and can automatically graph the progress of individual students. Available products range in cost from under $200 to several thousand dollars. Information about resources and tools recently reviewed by the National Center for Student Progress Monitoring can be found at www.studentprogress.org.

What We Know

Research has demonstrated that when teachers use student progress monitoring, students learn more, teacher decision making improves, and students become more aware of their own performance. A significant body of research conducted over the past 30 years has shown this method to be a reliable and valid predictor of subsequent performance on a variety of outcome measures, and thus useful for a wide range of instructional decisions (Deno, 2003; Fuchs, Deno, & Mirkin, 1984; Good & Jefferson, 1998).

Although student progress monitoring (then called curriculum-based measurement) was initially developed to assess the growth in basic skills of special education students, specific research has validated the predictive use of this method in early literacy programs (Good, Simmons, & Kameenui, 2001) and in the identification of general education students at risk for academic failure (Deno, 2003). In addition, some evidence shows the reliability and validity of student progress monitoring procedures in evaluating the progress of English language learners (Baker & Good, 1995).

Fuchs and Fuchs (2002) conducted an analysis of research on student progress monitoring that considered only experimental, controlled studies. These researchers concluded that

> When teachers use systematic progress monitoring to track their students' progress in reading, mathematics, or spelling, they are better able to identify students in

need of additional or different forms of instruction, they design stronger instructional programs, and their students achieve better. (p. 1)

What You Can Do

Student progress monitoring fits well into the routine of the classroom. The probes can be administered quickly, and the results are immediately understandable and easy to communicate. In some classrooms, students graph their own progress and find it motivating to "make the line go up." The following example shows how a 3rd grade teacher might use student progress monitoring.

During the first week of school, Ms. Cole includes as part of her initial probe of all students in her class an oral passage-reading test. She selects several 3rd grade-level reading passages and has each student read aloud for one minute while she notes any errors. She uses this assessment to identify any students at risk of scoring below grade level in oral reading fluency on the state end-of-year reading test. In reviewing the scores, Ms. Cole sees that six students have low scores, placing them at risk.

Ms. Cole determines each of these student's current reading rate (correct words per minute) as well as the level that student must attain by the end of the year to demonstrate grade-level reading fluency, and graphs a line indicating the necessary rate of growth. Using different but equivalent-level passages, Ms. Cole then administers a one-minute probe to each student each week, graphs the number of correct words the student reads per minute, and compares that score with the goal line.

After six weeks, Ms. Cole sees that the rate of growth for two students is relatively flat, indicating that the reading instruction she is providing for them is not effectively moving them toward their end-of-year goal. Ms. Cole decides to provide 15 minutes of additional reading instruction focusing on particular reading skills to those students each day, and to monitor their progress twice weekly.

After three more weeks, Ms. Cole sees that the growth rate of one student has improved significantly. She discontinues the extra reading instruction but continues to monitor the progress of that student weekly. The second student still shows relatively flat progress, so Ms. Cole refers the student to the school reading specialist, who provides remedial services and continues to monitor the student's progress twice weekly.

Educators Take Note

Deno (2003) points out that because this process was originally designed for use in individualized special education,

The most effective uses of CBM in the formative evaluation of individual student programs almost certainly occur in settings where individual (special) education teachers have the time and skills to respond to the charted progress of individual students. (p. 190)

Researchers are now finding that schools can also use student progress monitoring effectively to support regular education students and special education students in inclusive classrooms. As Fuchs and Fuchs (1998) found, using student progress monitoring with larger groups requires extra effort. But many teachers will find this strategy worth the effort because it provides a powerful tool that can help them adjust instruction to ensure that all students reach high standards.

References

Baker, S. K., & Good, R. H. (1995). Curriculum-based measurement of English reading with bilingual Hispanic students: A validation study with second-grade students. *School Psychology Review, 24,* 561–578.

Deno, S. L. (2003). Developments in curriculum-based measurement. *Journal of Special Education, 37,* 184–192.

Fuchs, L. S., Deno, S., & Mirkin, P. (1984). Effects of frequent curriculum-based measurement and evaluation on pedagogy, student achievement, and student awareness of learning. *American Educational Research Journal, 21,* 449–460.

Fuchs, L. S., & Fuchs, D. (1998). Treatment validity: A unifying concept for reconceptualizing the identification of learning disabilities. *Learning Disabilities Research & Practice, 13,* 204–219.

Fuchs, L. S., & Fuchs, D. (2002). *What is scientifically-based research on progress monitoring?* (Technical report). Nashville, TN: Vanderbilt University.

Good, R., & Jefferson, G. (1998). Contemporary perspectives on curriculum-based measurement validity. In M. R. Shinn (Ed.), *Advanced applications of curriculum-based measurement* (pp. 61–88). New York: Guilford Press.

Good, R. H., Simmons, D. C., & Kameenui, E. J. (2001). The importance and decision-making utility of a continuum of fluency-based indicators of foundational reading skills for third-grade high stakes outcomes. *Scientific Studies of Reading, 5,* 257–288.

NANCY SAFER is a Managing Research Scientist at the American Institutes for Research (AIR), where she serves as Co-Principal Investigator of the National Center on Student Progress Monitoring and Codirector of the K–8 Access Center. She is the former Executive Director of the Council for Exceptional Children. **STEVE FLEISCHMAN,** series editor of this column, is a Principal Research Scientist at AIR; editorair@air.org.

UNIT 4
Performance Assessments

Unit Selections

Key Points to Consider

- What philosophical perspective must a teacher acquire to implement performance assessment strategies?

- What are some problems that teachers encounter when scoring performance assessment activities?

- Identify how authentic or alternative (performance) assessments guide instructional decisions.

- Identify learning outcomes that can be measured with a rubric (performance assessments).

- Identify performance indicators that can be used to construct a rating scale for an area you plan to teach.

- Define holistic and analytic rubrics.

- Identify the characteristics for holistic rubrics and analytical rubrics.

- Define authentic assessments, alternative assessments, performance-based assessments, and direct assessments. Identify purposes and characteristics of each type.

- Compare and contrast two different types of rubrics.

- Design a holistic and analytic rubric for a performance assessment.

- Use the web-based rubric application and create a rubric for an assessment activity.

Student Website
www.mhcls.com

Internet References

Trends in Assessment Research
  http://pareonline.net/
Performance Assessment
  http://performanceassessment.org/consortium/index.html
Alternative Assessments
North Central Regional Educational Laboratory
  http://www.ncrel.org/sdrs/areas/issues/methods/assment/as8lk30.htm
Rubistar
  http://rubistar.4teachers.org/index.php
Authentic Assessment Tool Box
  http://jonathan.mueller.faculty.noctrl.edu/toolbox/standards.htm
New Horizons for Learning
  http://www.newhorizons.org/strategies/assess/front_assess.htm

In the 1990s, the standards movement, advances in cognitive science, and a shift in perspectives about what learning is initiated discussions about different ways to assess student learning. Professional educators called for a type of assessment model that was closer to measuring how students understand and apply knowledge. Terms such as authentic assessments, alternative assessments, performance-based assessments, and direct assessments emerged. Although there are different perspectives about these terms, generally, authentic classroom experiences emphasize real-world tasks, alternative assessments imply something other than a paper-pencil task, and performance-based assessments require the actual doing of a task.

Performance assessments focus on process and progress in development and learning (Wortham, 2005). It is beneficial for teachers to know how students develop cognitively as well as how they use their mental processes to solve problems and think creatively. In essence, they provide a basis for the teacher to evaluate both the effectiveness of the procedure (e.g., the process of collecting data or creating a brochure) and the product (e.g., an essay, painting, or the results of an experiment).

Some educators advocate that a major advantage of using performance assessments is its seamless alignment with the cognitive component of a standard that requires high-level thinking (i.e., creative thinking, critical thinking, analysis, synthesis, and evaluation). In some cases, research has indicated the cognitive and affective benefits of performance assessments. However, teachers are sometimes hesitant to implement this type of assessment because they are unsure about the objectivity of rating or evaluating the "performance."

A complex assessment activity requires a multi-dimensional scoring guide. Choosing the most appropriate format requires the educator to consider these questions: "What concept, skill, or knowledge needs to be assessed?" or "At what level should students be performing?" Other considerations might include: "What knowledge is being assessed: reasoning, critical thinking, creative thinking, or evaluative thinking?", "What process is being evaluated?", or "What should the product look like: characteristics, elements, or components?" By answering these questions, the educator decides whether a checklist, anecdotal record, rating scale, graphic organizer, or rubric would be the best performance-based evaluation method.

Creating a scoring guide such as a rubric or checklist can be an arduous task to some teachers. However, the process of creating the guide delineates exactly the type of performance expected. This approach often gives the teacher a clearer understanding of the appropriate instructional method and strategies to use for teaching. The scoring guide states the

© Image Source/Alamy

expectations and description of the performance. Overall, performance assessments complement traditional types of assessments because the evaluation method focuses one's attention upon student progress and accomplishments.

In an instructional setting, performance assessments range from paper-pencil activities to a "real-life situation." Examples or samples of student work are often collected to document academic growth or to show developmental progress of a particular task. The collection of student work is placed in a portfolio. For example, a portfolio may contain writing samples, journal entries, book reports, laboratory reports, paintings, or work from computer programs. Having proof of a student's accomplishment provides concrete evidence of the level of mastery, plus it shows the developmental process. Portfolios are useful examples to show families during a conference.

The articles chosen for this unit focus on topics about using rubrics, encouraging teachers to use alternative assessment methods, creating different types of rubrics, and using e-portfolios. In the first article, the benefits for using rubrics as an instructional strategy and for grading are discussed. The second article provides a systematic process for creating holistic and analytic rubrics. This article is wonderful for beginning educators. The author discusses a process enabling educators to create both types of rubrics.

Using alternative assessment methods in the classroom is the focus of the third article. The authors provide a guide for professional development. The fourth article discusses the advantages of electronic portfolios. Electronic portfolios can be an easy way to store and share student work.

Teaching with Rubrics
The Good, the Bad, and the Ugly

Heidi Goodrich Andrade

In earlier articles on instructional rubrics, I reported on my work as a researcher interested in how rubrics might (or might not) support academic achievement (Andrade 2000, 2001; Goodrich 1997). This article is a reflection on my use of instructional rubrics as a teacher. Although the two perspectives are complementary, my recent experiences as an assistant professor have taught me a lot about teaching with rubrics. I have found that whether they are good, bad, or even ugly depends on how they are created and how they are used.

A Brief Review of the Basics

A rubric is an assessment tool that lists the criteria for a piece of work or what counts (for example, purpose, organization, details, voice, and mechanics often are what count in a written essay) and articulates gradations of quality for each criterion, from excellent to poor (Goodrich 1997; Popham 1997). The example in table 1 is a rubric that I cocreated with students and a colleague for an undergraduate course on educational psychology. We used it for an assignment that required students to create a fifteen-minute role-play of instruction they designed, drawing on the theories of learning and human development introduced in the course.

The gradations of quality in this rubric, from A to D/F, are what distinguish this or any rubric from a checklist that lists only the criteria for an assignment. Although checklists can be useful assessment tools (I use several of them), they cannot do what rubrics can do, which is to describe desirable qualities as well as common pitfalls in student work. Such descriptions tend to be quite informative for students, thereby helping them think, learn, and produce high quality work (Andrade 2000).

At the most basic level, then, a rubric lists criteria and levels of quality. What makes a rubric an instructional rubric? The ways in which it is used in the classroom. A rubric used exclusively by a teacher to assign grades is a scoring rubric. A rubric that is cocreated with students; handed out; used to facilitate peer assessment, self-assessment, and teacher

feedback; and only then used to assign grades is an instructional rubric. It is not just about evaluation anymore; it is about teaching. Teaching with rubrics is where it gets good.

The Good

Whether we teach elementary school or graduate students, rubrics orient us toward our goals as teachers. We use them to clarify our learning goals, design instruction that addresses those goals, communicate the goals to students, guide our feedback on students' progress toward the goals, and judge final products in terms of the degree to which the goals were met. Like many teachers, I use rubrics before, during, and after I deliver instruction, and the benefits are numerous.

Instructional rubrics help me clarify my expectations and focus my instruction. To begin the process of creating a unit or a course, I list my goals for students, choose or create a project that will help them learn and demonstrate their learning, and draft a rubric for the project. By working backwards in this way, I can design daily lesson plans and choose reading assignments that focus on developing the concepts and skills that students need to do well on the project.

Instructional rubrics help my students understand the goal of an assignment and focus their efforts. I often cocreate a rubric with students by discussing strong and weak examples of student work with them, asking them to brainstorm criteria for their own work, and using the resulting list to write a draft rubric for their comment (see Andrade 2000; Goodrich 1997). As a result, I never hear a student complain that she "didn't know what I wanted."

Instructional rubrics help me give more informative feedback to my students without spending every evening and weekend on this task. We all know that feedback is profoundly educative. Research has shown that feedback can improve learning, especially when it gives students specific information about the strengths and weaknesses of their work (Black and Wiliam 1998). The problem is that giving focused feedback is wildly time consuming. A good rubric

Table 1 Learning Vignettes (LV) Performance Rubric for Educational Psychology Course

	A	B	C	D/F
Instructional objectives	Communicates objectives to audience verbally and in writing and shows how they connect to the assessment of the project. Objectives reflect the generativity of the topic and include ≥ 1 high-level thinking goal(s) (critique, meta-cognition, analyze, interpret, solve complex problems, apply, etc.).	Communicates objectives verbally and in writing but does not connect them to assessment. Objectives only tend to reflect the generativity of the topic and include one high-level thinking goal for students.	Communicates learning objectives to audience by simply saying them or writing a list. Objectives do not reflect the generativity of the topic and/or do not include high-level thinking objectives.	Does not communicate learning objectives effectively and/or objectives do not reflect the generativity of topic and/or does not include high-level thinking objectives.
Instructional theories and techniques	Uses a wide variety of techniques that promote the learning objectives, e.g., modeling, metacognition/thinking skills, attention to misconceptions and motivation, student interaction, wait time, the theory of multiple intelligences (MI), constructivism, ongoing feedback, transfer, reflection on prior knowledge, positive reinforcement, teacher expectations, etc.	Uses a variety of techniques. Most are appropriate for the learning objectives of the lesson. Some may not be well matched with objectives, but none are blatantly inappropriate.	Uses a few teaching techniques. The appropriateness of one or more may be unclear, seem "crammed in," or random.	Uses only one or two approaches to instruction. The approaches used may be limited to "traditional" techniques such as memorization or lecture.
Active engagement	All or most of the instruction involves active engagement on the part of students. The teacher(s) act(s) as a monitor and resource.	Most of the instruction involves active engagement. Lecture and seat work, if used, require thoughtful participation by students.	Lots of teacher talk. Some active engagement is used, but the bulk of the instruction does not rely on it.	Instruction rarely or never actively engages students in learning, e.g., it relies on lecture, worksheets, etc. The teacher acts as director.
Adaptations for atypical students	Student's behavior reflects the case profile. Seamless attention to atypical student. The instruction focuses on the student's needs, uses a variety of appropriate strategies for meeting those needs, and creates a supportive environment that fosters self-worth. Is consistent with laws, policies, and procedures.	Student's behavior tends to reflect the case profile. LV focuses on individual needs, uses some appropriate strategies but over-looks others. Some elements of a supportive learning environment are evident, but others are missing.	Student's behavior does not reflect case profile. The teacher may create a dependency on the part of the student. There is recognition of student's needs but the interventions either do not fill it or single the student out by focusing too much on her/him.	Deals only with typical development or uses only inappropriate strategies, e.g., punishment is the only strategy used with an ADHD student.
Developmental appropriateness	At least one attempt is made to explicitly promote development by addressing common milestones in cognitive, linguistic, personal, social, and/or moral development. All activities and concepts are age appropriate.	All activities and concepts are age appropriate.	Most activities and concepts are age appropriate, but there is one example of a content or a teaching technique that is either too simple or too sophisticated.	Several activities or concepts are not age appropriate.
Presentation	Organized and interesting. Actors know their lines and are professionally dressed. Costumes, scenery, humor, and narration are used effectively. Performance is fifteen minutes long.	Professional. May over-rely on telling instead of showing how techniques are used. Actors talked too fast and/or too quietly.	Some parts were out of character, unpolished, and/or unprofessional. The LV was choppy and/or blah. Went over fifteen-minute time limit.	Inappropriate dress and/or language. No clear attempt to engage audience. Actors read from notes.

allows me to provide individualized, constructive critique in a manageable time frame. I will admit that I still spend a lot of time giving my students written and verbal feedback in addition to a marked-up rubric; I think that it is important. But if I were to simply circle boxes on a rubric and give it back with an assignment, I would still be providing more feedback about the strengths and weaknesses of the work than if I had just assigned a letter grade, and it would not take me any longer.

Rubric-referenced peer- and self-assessment are required for each major assignment in my class, so students get ongoing feedback from a variety of sources. Self-assessment is done simply by circling the text on the rubric that best describes a student's own work and attaching the marked-up rubric to the assignment before handing it in. Peer-assessment is usually done by giving rubric-referenced verbal feedback in class. Neither the self- nor the peer-assessments count toward final grades. As a result, students come to see assessment as a "source of insight and help instead of its being the occasion for meting out rewards and punishments" (Shepard 2000, 10), and they tend to use the feedback to improve on their assignments.

Instructional rubrics allow me to assign more challenging work than I otherwise could. If I had assigned the "learning vignettes" instructional design project (see the rubric in table 1) to my students without a rubric and the accompanying feedback, they likely would have balked or created grasping, unfocused projects. I might have concluded that they were not up to the challenge and lowered my standards. Quite the opposite is true: My students amaze me every time, and my expectations continue to rise.

Instructional rubrics keep me fair and unbiased in my grading. I will admit that I struggle with the temptation to assign grades based in part on irrelevant things such as effort or fondness—but not much. Rubrics keep me honest.

The Bad

Rubrics are not entirely self-explanatory. Students need help in understanding rubrics and their use. When I once handed out a rubric that we had cocreated in class and assumed that students knew what to do with it because we had cocreated it, I was in for a surprise. The more motivated students anguished over what to do with it, and the less motivated filed it in their notebooks and promptly forgot about it. Most of them had never seen a rubric before, so I needed to explain it and give them a bit of practice with it by doing a mock critique as a class.

Similarly, rubrics are not a replacement for good instruction. Even a fabulous rubric does not change the fact that students need models, feedback, and opportunities to ask questions, think, revise, and so on. Anyone can download a rubric from the Web, but using it to support good instruction is another matter. (See http://www.thinkinggear.com/tools/ for an example of how the Web can support the happy marriage of rubrics and instruction.)

Students are not always good at peer-and self-assessment at first, even with a rubric in hand. At their worst, peer assessments can be cruel or disorienting, and self-assessment can be misguided or delusional. Students become good at both, however, once they are convinced of their value and have had some practice (Falchikov 1986). Knowing they can use the feedback they get from their peers and themselves to revise for a better grade helps, as does being held accountable for their assessments by having to sign off on them and hand them in.

Instructional rubrics are not just scoring tools. As I noted earlier, rubrics can serve the purposes of teaching and learning as well as evaluation. Rubrics used only to assign final grades represent not only a missed opportunity to teach but also a regrettable instance of the teacher-as-sole-judge-of-quality model that puts our students in a position of mindlessness and powerlessness.

The Ugly

Issues of validity, reliability, and fairness apply to rubrics, too. We need to worry more about the quality of the rubrics that we use. I have seen some very idiosyncratic rubrics in my day, and this is where it gets ugly. "Alternative" or "authentic" assessments are not exempt from the demands of validity, reliability, and equity (Moskal and Leydens 2000). Reliability and validity are concerned with the consistency and accuracy of the judgments we make about students and their work (Payne 2003). At a minimum, an instructional rubric must be aligned with reasonable and respectable standards and with the curriculum being taught in order to be valid. It must pass a test of reliability by resulting in similar ratings when used by different people. Issues of equity must be addressed by checking to see if the ratings that students receive have too much to do with gender, race, ethnicity, or socioeconomic status.

These concerns do not require us to perform complex statistical analyses but, rather, that we simply worry enough about them to subject our rubrics to critique. Rubrics improve when we compare them to published standards, show them to another teacher, or ask a colleague to coscore some student work. Payne (2003) suggests that "sitting and listening to students critique assessments can be the best source of information about how good evaluations really are" (433), and I agree. These things just take time, guts, and a concern about quality. As teachers, we have plenty of guts and concern for quality; we just need to make time for validity, reliability, and equity. By attending to these important issues, the good of instructional rubrics can far outweigh the bad.

References

Andrade, H. G. 2000. Using rubrics to promote thinking and learning. *Educational Leadership* 57 (5): 13–18.

———. 2001. The effects of instructional rubrics on learning to write. *Current Issues in Education* 4 (4), http://cie.ed.asu.edu/volume4/number4.

Black, P., and Wiliam, D. 1998. Inside the black box: Raising standards through classroom assessment. *Phi Delta Kappan* 80 (2): 139–48.

Falchikov, N. 1986. Product comparisons and process benefits of collaborative peer group and self assessments. *Assessment and Evaluation in Higher Education* 11 (2): 146–66.

Goodrich, H. 1997. Understanding rubrics. *Educational Leadership* 54 (4): 14–17.

Moskal, B., and J. Leydens. 2000. Scoring rubric development: Validity and reliability. *Practical Assessment, Research and Evaluation* 7 (10), http://ericae.net/pare/getvn.asp?v=7&n=10.

Payne, D. A. 2003. *Applied educational assessment.* 2nd ed. Belmont, CA: Wadsworth/Thomson Learning.

Popham, J. W. 1997. What's wrong—and what's right—with rubrics. *Educational Leadership* 55 (2): 72–75.

Shepard, L. 2000. The role of assessment in a learning culture. *Educational Researcher* 29 (7): 4–14.

HEIDI GOODRICH ANDRADE is an assistant professor in the Division of Educational Psychology and Methodology at the University at Albany.

Designing Scoring Rubrics for Your Classroom

CRAIG A. MERTLER

Rubrics are rating scales—as opposed to checklists–that are used with performance assessments. They are formally defined as scoring guides, consisting of specific pre-established performance criteria, used in evaluating student work on performance assessments. Rubrics are typically the specific form of scoring instrument used when evaluating student performances or products resulting from a performance task.

There are two types of rubrics: holistic and analytic (see Figure 1). A **holistic rubric** requires the teacher to score the overall process or product as a whole, without judging the component parts separately (Nitko, 2001). In contrast, with an **analytic rubric,** the teacher scores separate, individual parts of the product or performance first, then sums the individual scores to obtain a total score (Moskal, 2000; Nitko, 2001).

Holistic rubrics are customarily utilized when errors in some part of the process can be tolerated provided the overall quality is high (Chase, 1999). Nitko (2001) further states that use of holistic rubrics is probably more appropriate when performance tasks require students to create some sort of response and where there is no definitive correct answer. The focus of a score reported using a holistic rubric is on the overall quality, proficiency, or understanding of the specific content and skills—it involves assessment on a unidimensional level (Mertler, 2001). Use of holistic rubrics can result in a somewhat quicker scoring process than use of analytic rubrics (Nitko, 2001). This is basically due to the fact that the teacher is required to read through or otherwise examine the student product or performance only once, in order to get an "overall" sense of what the student was able to accomplish (Mertler, 2001). Since assessment of the overall performance is the key, holistic rubrics are also typically, though not exclusively, used when the purpose of the performance assessment is summative in nature. At most, only limited feedback is provided to the student as a result of scoring performance tasks in this manner. A template for holistic scoring rubrics is presented in Table 1.

Analytic rubrics are usually preferred when a fairly focused type of response is required (Nitko, 2001); that is, for performance tasks in which there may be one or two acceptable responses and creativity is not an essential feature of the students' responses.

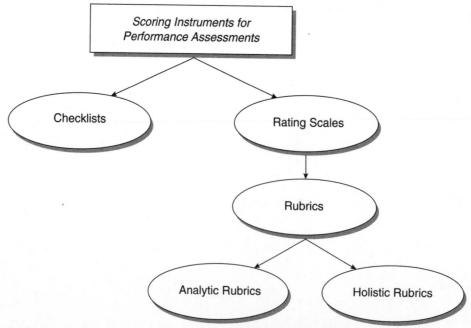

Figure 1   Types of scoring instruments for performance assessments.

Table 1   Template for Holistic Rubrics

Score	Description
5	Demonstrates complete understanding of the problem. All requirements of task are included in response.
4	Demonstrates considerable understanding of the problem. All requirements of task are included.
3	Demonstrates partial understanding of the problem. Most requirements of task are included.
2	Demonstrates little understanding of the problem. Many requirements of task are missing.
1	Demonstrates no understanding of the problem.
0	No response/task not attempted.

Furthermore, analytic rubrics result initially in several scores, followed by a summed total score—their use represents assessment on a multidimensional level (Mertler, 2001). As previously mentioned, the use of analytic rubrics can cause the scoring process to be substantially slower, mainly because assessing several different skills or characteristics individually requires a teacher to examine the product several times. Both their construction and use can be quite time-consuming. A general rule of thumb is that an individual's work should be examined a separate time for each of the specific performance tasks or scoring criteria (Mertler, 2001). However, the advantage to the use of analytic rubrics is quite substantial. The degree of feedback offered to students—and to teachers—is significant. Students receive specific feedback on their performance with respect to each of the individual scoring criteria—something that does not happen when using holistic rubrics (Nitko, 2001). It is possible to then create a "profile" of specific student strengths and weaknesses (Mertler, 2001). A template for analytic scoring rubrics is presented in Table 2.

Prior to designing a specific rubric, a teacher must decide whether the performance or product will be scored holistically or analytically (Airasian, 2000 & 2001). Regardless of which type of rubric is selected, specific performance criteria and observable indicators must be identified as an initial step to development. The decision regarding the use of a holistic or analytic approach to scoring has several possible implications. The most important of these is that teachers must consider first how they intend to use the results. If an overall, summative score is desired, a holistic scoring approach would be more desirable. In contrast, if formative feedback is the goal, an analytic scoring rubric should be used. It is important to note that one type of rubric is not inherently better than the other—you must find a format that works best for your purposes (Montgomery, 2001). Other implications include the time requirements, the nature of the task itself, and the specific performance criteria being observed.

As you saw demonstrated in the templates (Tables 1 and 2), the various levels of student performance can be defined using either quantitative (i.e., numerical) or qualitative (i.e., descriptive) labels. In some instances, teachers might want to utilize both quantitative and qualitative labels. If a rubric contains four levels of proficiency or understanding on a continuum, quantitative labels would typically range from "1" to "4." When using qualitative labels, teachers have

much more flexibility, and can be more creative. A common type of qualitative scale might include the following labels: master, expert, apprentice, and novice. Nearly any type of qualitative scale will suffice, provided it "fits" with the task.

One potentially frustrating aspect of scoring student work with rubrics is the issue of somehow converting them to "grades." It is not a good idea to think of rubrics in terms of percentages (Trice, 2000). For example, if a rubric has six levels (or "points"), a score of 3 should not be equated to 50% (an "F" in most letter grading systems). The process of converting rubric scores to grades or categories is more a process of logic than it is a mathematical one. Trice (2000) suggests that in a rubric scoring system, there are typically more scores at the average and above average categories (i.e., equating to grades of "C" or better) than there are below average categories. For instance, if a rubric consisted of nine score categories, the equivalent grades and categories might look like Table 3.

When converting rubric scores to grades (typical at the secondary level) or descriptive feedback (typical at the elementary level), it is important to remember that there is not necessarily one correct way to accomplish this. The bottom line for classroom teachers is that they must find a system of conversion that works for them and fits comfortably into their individual system of reporting student performance.

Steps in the Design of Scoring Rubrics

A step-by-step process for designing scoring rubrics for classroom use is presented below. Information for these procedures was compiled from various sources (Airasian, 2000 & 2001; Mertler, 2001; Montgomery, 2001; Nitko, 2001; Tombari & Borich, 1999). The steps will be summarized and discussed, followed by presentations of two sample scoring rubrics.

Step 1: *Re-examine the learning objectives to be addressed by the task.* This allows you to match your scoring guide with your objectives and actual instruction.

Step 2: *Identify specific observable attributes that you want to see (as well as those you don't want to see) your students demonstrate in their product, process, or performance.* Specify the characteristics, skills, or behaviors that you will be looking for, as well as common mistakes you do not want to see.

Step 3: *Brainstorm characteristics that describe each attribute.* Identify ways to describe above average, average, and below average performance for each observable attribute identified in Step 2.

Step 4a: *For holistic rubrics, write thorough narrative descriptions for excellent work and poor work incorporating <u>each attribute</u> into the description.* Describe the highest and lowest levels of performance combining the descriptors for all attributes.

Step 4b: *For analytic rubrics, write thorough narrative descriptions for excellent work and poor work for <u>each individual attribute.</u>* Describe the highest and lowest levels of performance using the descriptors for each attribute separately.

Step 5a: *For holistic rubrics, complete the rubric by describing other levels on the continuum that ranges from excellent to poor work <u>for the collective attributes.</u>* Write descriptions for all intermediate levels of performance.

Table 2 Template for Analytic Rubrics

	Beginning 1	Developing 2	Accomplished 3	Exemplary 4	Score
Criteria #1	Description reflecting beginning level of performance	Description reflecting movement toward mastery level of performance	Description reflecting achievement of mastery level of performance	Description reflecting highest level of performance	
Criteria #2	Description reflecting beginning level of performance	Description reflecting movement toward mastery level of performance	Description reflecting achievement of mastery level of performance	Description reflecting highest level of performance	
Criteria #3	Description reflecting beginning level of performance	Description reflecting movement toward mastery level of performance	Description reflecting achievement of mastery level of performance	Description reflecting highest level of performance	
Criteria #4	Description reflecting beginning level of performance	Description reflecting movement toward mastery level of performance	Description reflecting achievement of mastery level of performance	Description reflecting highest level of performance	

Table 3 Sample Grades and Categories

Rubric Score	Grade	Category
8	A+	Excellent
7	A	Excellent
6	B+	Good
5	B	Good
4	C+	Fair
3	C	Fair
2	U	Unsatisfactory
1	U	Unsatisfactory
0	U	Unsatisfactory

Step 5b: *For analytic rubrics, complete the rubric by describing other levels on the continuum that ranges from excellent to poor work <u>for each attribute.</u>* Write descriptions for all intermediate levels of performance for each attribute separately.

Step 6: *Collect samples of student work that exemplify each level.* These will help you score in the future by serving as benchmarks.

Step 7: *Revise the rubric, as necessary.* Be prepared to reflect on the effectiveness of the rubric and revise it prior to its next implementation.

These steps involved in the design of rubrics have been summarized in Figure 2.

Two Examples

Two sample scoring rubrics corresponding to specific performance assessment tasks are presented next. Brief discussions precede the actual rubrics. For illustrative purposes, a holistic rubric is presented for the first task and an analytic rubric for the second. It should be noted that either a holistic or an analytic rubric could have been designed for either task.

Example 1: Subject—Mathematics Grade Level(s)—Upper Elementary

Mr. Harris, a fourth-grade teacher, is planning a unit on the topic of data analysis, focusing primarily on the skills of estimation and interpretation of graphs. Specifically, at the end of this unit, he wants to be able to assess his students' mastery of the following instructional objectives:

- Students will properly interpret a bar graph.
- Students will accurately estimate values from within a bar graph. (step 1)

Since the purpose of his performance task is summative in nature—the results will be incorporated into the students' grades—he decides to develop a holistic rubric. He identifies the following four attributes on which to focus his rubric: estimation, mathematical computation, conclusions, and communication of explanations (steps 2 & 3). Finally, he begins drafting descriptions of the various levels of performance for the observable attributes (steps 4 & 5). The final rubric for his task appears in Table 4.

Example 2: Subjects—Social Studies; Probability & Statistics Grade Level(s)—9–12

Mrs. Wolfe is a high school American government teacher. She is beginning a unit on the electoral process and knows from past years that her students sometimes have difficulty with the concepts of sampling and election polling. She decides to give her students a performance assessment so they can demonstrate their levels of understanding of these concepts. The main idea that she wants to focus on is that samples (surveys) can accurately predict the viewpoints of an entire population. Specifically, she wants to be able to assess her students on the following instructional objectives:

- Students will collect data using appropriate methods.
- Students will accurately analyze and summarize their data.
- Students will effectively communicate their results. (step 1)

Since the purpose of this performance task is formative in nature, she decides to develop an analytic rubric focusing on the following

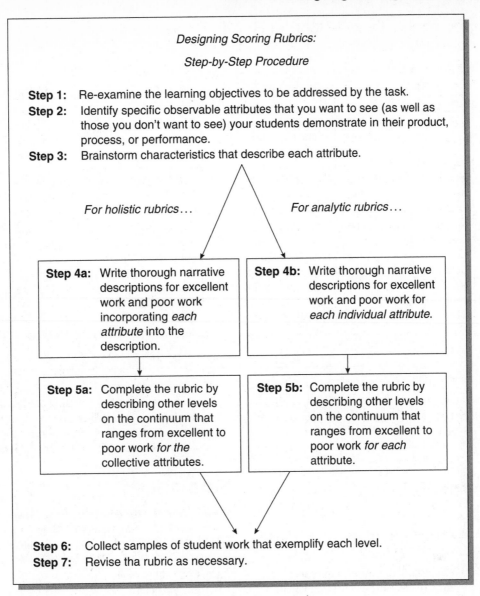

Designing Scoring Rubrics:

Step-by-Step Procedure

Step 1: Re-examine the learning objectives to be addressed by the task.

Step 2: Identify specific observable attributes that you want to see (as well as those you don't want to see) your students demonstrate in their product, process, or performance.

Step 3: Brainstorm characteristics that describe each attribute.

For holistic rubrics...   *For analytic rubrics...*

Step 4a: Write thorough narrative descriptions for excellent work and poor work incorporating *each attribute* into the description.

Step 4b: Write thorough narrative descriptions for excellent work and poor work for *each individual attribute.*

Step 5a: Complete the rubric by describing other levels on the continuum that ranges from excellent to poor work *for the collective attributes.*

Step 5b: Complete the rubric by describing other levels on the continuum that ranges from excellent to poor work *for each attribute.*

Step 6: Collect samples of student work that exemplify each level.

Step 7: Revise tha rubric as necessary.

Figure 2   Designing scoring rubrics: step-by-step procedures.

Table 4   Math Performance Task—Scoring Rubric Data Analysis

Name _____   Date _____

Score	Description
4	Makes accurate estimations. Uses appropriate mathematical operations with no mistakes. Draws logical conclusions supported by graph. Sound explanations of thinking.
3	Makes good estimations. Uses appropriate mathematical operations with few mistakes. Draws logical conclusions supported by graph. Good explanations of thinking.
2	Attempts estimations, although many inaccurate. Uses inappropriate mathematical operations, but with no mistakes. Draws conclusions not supported by graph. Offers little explanation.
1	Makes inaccurate estimations. Uses inappropriate mathematical operations. Draws no conclusions related to graph. Offers no explanations of thinking.
0	No response/task not attempted.

Table 5   Performance Task—Scoring Rubric Population Sampling

Name _____   Date _____

	Beginning 1	Developing 2	Accomplished 3	Exemplary 4	Score
Sampling Technique	Inappropriate sampling technique used	Appropriate technique used to select sample; major errors in execution	Appropriate technique used to select sample; minor errors in execution	Appropriate technique used to select sample; no errors in procedures	
Survey/ Interview Questions	Inappropriate questions asked to gather needed information	Few pertinent questions asked; data on sample is inadequate	Most pertinent questions asked; data on sample is adequate	All pertinent questions asked; data on sample is complete	
Statistical Analyses	No attempt at summarizing collected data	Attempts analysis of data, but inappropriate procedures	Proper analytical procedures used, but analysis incomplete	All proper analytical procedures used to summarize data	
Communication of Results	Communication of results is incomplete, unorganized, and difficult to follow	Communicates some important information; not organized well enough to support decision	Communicates most of important information; shows support for decision	Communication of results is very thorough; shows insight into how data predicted outcome	

Total Score = _____

attributes: sampling technique, data collection, statistical analyses, and communication of results (steps 2 & 3). She drafts descriptions of the various levels of performance for the observable attributes (steps 4 & 5). The final rubric for this task appears in Table 5.

Resources for Rubrics on the Web

The following is just a partial list of some Web resources for information about and samples of scoring rubrics.

- "Scoring Rubrics: What, When, & How?" (http://pareonline .net/getvn.asp?v=7&n=3). This article appears in Practical Assessment, Research, & Evaluation and is authored by Barbara M. Moskal. The article discusses what rubrics are, and distinguishes between holistic and analytic types. Examples and additional resources are provided.

- "Performance Assessment-Scoring" (http://www.pgcps .pg.k12.md.us/~elc/scoringtasks.html). Staff in the Prince George's County (MD) Public Schools have developed a series of pages that provide descriptions of the steps involved in the design of performance tasks. This particular page provides several rubric samples.

- "Rubrics from the Staff Room for Ontario Teachers" (http://www.quadro.net/~ecoxon/Reporting/rubrics.htm). This site is a collection of literally hundreds of teacher-developed rubrics for scoring performance tasks. The rubrics are categorized by subject area and type of task. This is a fantastic resource—check it out!

- "Rubistar Rubric Generator" (http://rubistar.4teachers.org/)

- "Teacher Rubric Maker" (http://www.teach-nology.com/ web_tools/rubrics/) These two sites house Web-based rubric

generators for teachers. Teachers can customize their own rubrics based on templates on each site. In both cases, rubric templates are organized by subject area and/or type of performance task. These are wonderful resources for teachers!

References

Airasian, P. W. (2000). *Assessment in the classroom: A concise approach* (2nd ed.). Boston: McGraw-Hill.

Airasian, P. W. (2001). *Classroom assessment: Concepts and applications* (4th ed.). Boston: McGraw-Hill.

Chase, C. I. (1999). *Contemporary assessment for educators.* New York: Longman.

Mertler, C. A. (2001). Using performance assessment in your classroom. Unpublished manuscript, Bowling Green State University.

Montgomery, K. (2001). *Authentic assessment: A guide for elementary teachers.* New York: Longman.

Moskal, B. M. (2000). Scoring rubrics: what, when, and how?. *Practical Assessment, Research, &Evaluation,* 7(3). Available online: http://pareonline.net/getvn.asp?v=7&n=3.

Nitko, A. J. (2001). *Educational assessment of students* (3rd ed.). Upper Saddle River, NJ: Merrill.

Tombari, M. & Borich, G. (1999). *Authentic assessment in the classroom: Applications and practice.* Upper Saddle River, NJ: Merrill.

Trice, A. D. (2000). *A handbook of classroom assessment.* New York: Longman.

MERTLER, CRAIG A. (2001). Designing scoring rubrics for your classroom. *Practical Assessment, Research & Evaluation,* 7(25). Retrieved January 20, 2009 from, http://PAREonline.net/getvn.asp?v=7 & n=25.

A Teacher's Guide to Alternative Assessment
Taking the First Steps

CAROL A. CORCORAN, ELIZABETH L. DERSHIMER, AND MERCEDES S. TICHENOR

In a fifth grade classroom, students are bent over their graphic calculators rapidly writing observations while the teacher watches. The task is to hypothesize at what point and why the graph flattens as they grasp the calculator's probe with their hand. These children are learning by experimenting with the material to be learned. When it is time to assess these and other skills learned during the unit, the teacher could assess using traditional paper and pencil tests. Instead, the teacher chooses an alternative technique. The students are called individually to eight different stations where they meet with junior interns who have worked with the students throughout the semester. The interns then assess the students in an alternative fashion. For example, three small cars are set on incline planes covered by different surface materials. The student predicts which car will complete the run first and why. Then the student releases the cars down the incline planes to confirm the prediction. The student relates the law of motion that applies to the car demonstration. The intern (which also could be a parent helper, teaching assistant, or even the teacher) uses a rubric with prepared questions to discuss each concept with the student. This type of assessment allows the assessor to determine the depth of student understanding. It also allows students who do know the concept but perhaps struggle with reading or writing to demonstrate their science knowledge.

Classroom-based assessment is the collection and evaluation of evidence of student learning, focusing on indicators of meaningful and valuable student progress (Shepard 1989; Valencia 1990; Farr 1992). This type of assessment includes alternative forms of testing, such as performance tasks, which allow students to communicate or display mastery in different forms. According to Herman, Aschbacher, and Winters (1992), common characteristics for such assessments include (1) asking students to perform, create, produce, or do something; (2) tapping higher-level thinking and problem-solving skills; (3) using tasks that represent meaningful instructional activities; (4) involving real world applications; and (5) using human judgment to do the scoring.

Herman (1992) contends that effective student assessment is grounded in theories of learning and cognition and builds on the skills students need to be successful in the future. Moreover, a quality assessment program uses classroom-based data to inform teaching and to help students become more self-monitoring and self-regulating (Daniels and Bizar 1998). Both students and teachers must continuously take risks and evaluate themselves, and teachers must always develop new instructional assessment roles (Routman 1991; Herman, Aschbacher, and Winters 1992).

Although many educators agree on the importance of using a variety of authentic assessment techniques in the classroom, implementing them is difficult. In other words, many teachers may be unsure of how to combine quality assessment with daily practice. In this article, we describe an assessment ladder that provides a framework for classroom teachers to reflect on their use of traditional versus alternative, or authentic, assessment techniques. Furthermore, we provide suggestions on how teachers can progress up the assessment ladder to incorporate more authentic ways of assessing student learning in their classrooms.

The Assessment Ladder

Developing willingness and the ability to use alternative assessment is a step-by-step process. We compare this process to climbing up a ladder. Teachers take hold of the ladder when, although they currently are not using alternative assessments, they express a desire to explore their uses. As teachers climb toward full implementation of alternative assessment practices, they pass through three levels on this ladder. Table 1 provides sample strategies for each level of the assessment ladder as described in the following sections.

First Steps: Level I

The teacher who uses one or two alternative assessment strategies as a summative measure (grade book) at least once each grading period is on Level I. At this level, the most commonly

Table 1 Sample Strategies
for Various Levels

Level I	Level II	Level III
Rubrics	Journals entries	Self-choice of medium
Portfolios	"I learned" statements	"I can teach"
Checklists	Learning illustrations	
	Self-assessments	

used assessments are rubrics, portfolios, and checklists. These types of assessment are often used in kindergarten or early primary grades. Their use decreases proportionally as students move to the middle grades (Trepanier-Street, McNair, and Donegan 2001). In other words, as students become more competent readers and writers, the assessment strategies often reflect only paper and pencil tasks. However, authentic assessment techniques are effective with all students, even those with weaker writing skills. For example, teachers can use checklists during observations to determine if students complete certain processes or display particular behaviors. Teachers can also use rubrics to evaluate student writing samples or math problems (Kuhs et al. 2001).

Moving Up: Level II

At this level, the teacher uses Level I measures more than once during a grading period. The teacher begins to try a variety of alternative assessments during the grading period and is willing to allow several of the formative assessment strategies to serve as summative measures. Journal entries, especially if the entry information is tied to teaching and learning objectives, give the teacher insight into students' cognitive progress and reveal their attitudes toward content. Journal entries are especially helpful in assessing disjunctive concepts, such as rights and responsibilities. For example, an open-ended journal response to the following hypothetical situation can help a teacher assess the student's grasp of these concepts: "We have been studying our free speech rights in class. James is running for 7th grade class president and you are helping him write a campaign speech. Give him some advice about his rights and responsibilities as he prepares his speech."

Another formative assessment tool that can be used as a summative measure is the "I learned . . ." statements that students write at the end of a lesson. The teacher can ask students to list five things they learned from the lesson. As a formative assessment, the teacher can evaluate the major concepts the students learned during the lesson, as well as identify any gaps or alternative understanding in students' learning. "I learned . . ." statements can also be used as a summative evaluation and entered into the grade book as a quiz grade.

Many other alternative or authentic assessment techniques can be used with students who struggle with language. Labeling a map, conducting a science experiment, or illustrating supporting details of a story are but a few crosscurriculum ways

middle school students can show what they have learned with minimal writing. Furthermore, illustrated learning is especially helpful for teachers of English for Speakers of Other Languages (ESOL) students. It allows teachers to evaluate these students' content knowledge without relying solely on their ability to use the target language.

Although interviews are a time consuming alternative assessment strategy, they are well worth considering. Again, this is a strategy that can be used both as a formative or summative assessment. Individual interviews or conferences with a student allow teachers to evaluate the depth of a student's knowledge. Students can be required to assemble supporting documentation in preparation for the conference. This activity increases both critical and creative thinking strategies.

Other formative assessment strategies—such as self-reporting, record keeping, or spot check techniques—are common ways to assess student progress (Ellis 2002). For example, in a mathematics class, the teacher might ask students to critique their progress while working on a measurement project. Self-reporting would give the students the opportunity to analyze the strengths and weaknesses of their own work. Such reports might also point out ideas that are unclear. Then the teacher, or possibly other students, can provide additional information and support to refocus the learning. Record keeping, another metacognitive strategy, requires that students keep detailed notes about completed assignments. Each record includes the date, assignment, grade, summary notes, and so on. Both of these strategies assess learning during instruction and help students progress in their understanding of their own thinking. Students may also participate in self-evaluation through activity checklists. Checklists help develop student ownership of and responsibility for assignments. The teachers can then turn the checklists into grade sheets. Grade sheets may be weighted differently, and the final grades depend on a total number of points earned by the student. These techniques can provide a much more accurate picture of the knowledge and skills students have learned than traditional paper and pencil formats.

Nearing the Top: Level III

Educators at this level use Levels I and II strategies on a regular basis in their classrooms and allow flexibility in their standard assessments. For example, the teacher might give students the option of crossing out five of the twenty-five short answer questions on a test and inserting five similar questions about material they learned while studying for the test but was not included on the exam. A willingness to substitute what a student perceives as important in a unit of study is an important indicator that a teacher has progressed to Level III.

One of the most difficult assessment changes for teachers to implement is a willingness to encourage students to choose any medium through which to demonstrate their knowledge and understanding of concepts or objectives. For example, if the student learning objective is to describe the process of how a bill becomes a law, the teacher allows the students to choose how they will demonstrate they know this material. In responding

Table 2 Self-Check Guide

Putting up the ladder—Ground floor	• I plan interesting hands-on activities for students but still use traditional paper and pencil tasks to assess learning. • I do not use alternative assessments in my classroom. • I am interested in learning about alternative assessment techniques.
First steps—Level I	• I use one or more alternative assessment strategies as a summative measure at least once each grading period.
Moving up—Level II	• I use Level I measures in my classroom. • I use a variety of formative assessments at least four times during a grading period. • I use some formative assessment strategies in a summative format.
Nearing the top—Level III	• I use the measures listed in Levels I and II. • I encourage students to choose any medium to demonstrate their understanding of concepts and objectives. • I am open to increasing my knowledge of alternative assessment techniques.

to such an assignment, for example, students can develop a rap song and perform it for the class. The rap must touch on all the points the teacher included on a rubric established for alternative assessment presentations. In another example, the learning goal is to demonstrate knowledge of facts, findings, theories, important events, and/or noted scientists studied in life science during this reporting period. Students might decide to develop a game using a Trivial Pursuit format including four categories in the life sciences. Alternative demonstrations of content mastery can result in Jeopardy-like games, vocabulary and concepts incorporated in a video play, a collage, or book reports.

The "I can teach" strategy also is an excellent alternative assessment strategy for middle school students. Using this strategy, the teacher assigns an individual student or a small group of students a topic or teaching objective. They must research and organize the information in preparation to teach the class (Ellis 2002). The teacher offers guidance and a rubric throughout the process.

Teachers who include alternative assessments in their teaching are rewarded with creative student projects that honor a range of intelligences. In addition, students are more enthusiastic about course content and more willing to actively participate in assessing their own learning. Middle school students, in particular, are at the developmental age where they can think both critically and creatively. These students like to work in groups and want to be considered in control of their lives. Encouraging Level III assessments gives these students opportunities to make choices and demonstrate that control.

Teachers who are at Level III continue to experiment with ways to assess what their students know and are able to do. They continue to expand their knowledge of alternative assessment strategies and are willing to help other teachers climb the alternative assessment ladder to make their classroom environments places where students succeed.

Conclusion

Where are you on the assessment ladder? Are you taking your first steps, beginning the climb, or nearing the top? Where do you want to be? As you begin thinking about climbing the ladder, it is important to remember that authentic assessment is integral to the teaching process. It must be continually incorporated into lesson planning. Although many teachers are creative in planning learning activities, they forget to be creative in their assessment of learning. Through integrating teaching and assessment, teachers give children opportunities to demonstrate their learning in more authentic and realistic ways. For example, when one student asks another student to move forward on the teeter-totter—shouting, "Move up, you're heavier and I need to be further from the fulcrum than you. Remember in science when we—" at that point, the teacher has proof that the student fully understands the simple mechanics studied in class.

Table 2 provides a self-check guide for teachers. Educators can use this guide to monitor their progress and focus on opportunities to enrich the repertoire of tools and skills they use to assess student learning. Although taking the first step on the ladder may be overwhelming, uncomfortable, or even scary, it is definitely a step worth taking.

References

Daniels, H., and M. Bizar. 1998. *Methods that matter: Six structures for best practice classrooms.* York, ME: Stenhouse Publishers.

Ellis, A. 2002. *Teaching and learning elementary social studies.* Boston: Allyn and Bacon.

Farr, R. 1992. Putting it all together: Solving the reading assessment puzzle. *The Reading Teacher* 46 (1): 26–37.

Herman, J. L. 1992. What research tells us about good assessment. *Educational Leadership* 49 (8): 74–78.

Herman, J. L., P. R. Aschbacher, and L. Winters. 1992. *A practical guide to alternative assessment.* Alexandria, VA: Association for Supervision and Curriculum Development.

Kuhs, T., R. Johnson, S. Agruso, and D. Monrad. 2001. *Put to the test: Tools and techniques for classroom assessment.* Portsmouth, NH: Heinemann.

Routman, R. 1991. *Invitations: Changing as teachers and learners K–12.* Portsmouth, NH: Heinemann.

Shepard, L. A. 1989. Why we need better assessments. *Educational Leadership* 46 (7): 4–9.

Trepanier-Street, M., S. McNair, and M. Donegan. 2001. The views of teachers on assessment: A comparison of lower and upper elementary teachers. *Journal of Research in Childhood Education* 15 (2): 234–41.

Valencia, S. W. 1990. Alternative assessment: Separating the wheat from the chaff. *The Reading Teacher* 44 (1): 60–61.

CAROL A. CORCORAN, ELIZABETH L. DERSHIMER, AND MERCEDES S. TICHENOR are all associate professors in the Department of Teacher Education at Stetson University in DeLand, Florida.

From *The Clearing House,* May/June 2004. Reprinted by permission of the Helen Dwight Reid Educational Foundation. Published by Heldref Publications, 1319 Eighteenth St., NW, Washington, DC 20036-1802. Copyright © 2004. www.heldref.org

Digital-Age Assessment
E-Portfolios Are the Wave of the Future

HARRY GROVER TUTTLE

Effective 21st century assessment reaches beyond traditional testing to look at the broader accomplishments of learners. Assembling an *e-portfolio,* or electronic portfolio, is an excellent method for assessing students' progress toward school, state, or national academic standards, as well as 21st century skills. An electronic portfolio is a purposefully limited collection of student selected work over time that documents progress toward meeting the standards. Work may be collected over a semester, a year, or even several years, passing from one grade level and teacher to the next. E-portfolios reflect more in-depth, more comprehensive, and better thought-out evidence of student learning than on-demand tests. For instance, a student's three-hour state benchmark essay offers the feedback of a 5/6 score, while an e-portfolio allows students to document the many aspects of their essay writing improvement over the course of a year.

Getting Started

Educators can begin by showing the students sample e-portfolios so they understand the overall format and the richness of artifacts—digitally produced homework, class-work, and projects—that can be put into it. A common e-portfolio format includes a title page; a standards' grid; a space for each individual standard with accompanying artifacts and information on how each artifact addresses the standard; an area for the student's overall reflection on the standard; and a teacher formative feedback section for each standard. Within the e-portfolio, the evidence of student learning may be in diverse formats such as Web pages, e-movies, visuals, audio recordings, and text. Elementary students might explain the biology standard through e-movies of plant experiments and explain their cultural art to another class via a recorded videoconference. Middle school students might demonstrate their understanding of community by posting interviews to a Web site, or for P.E., display their understanding of lifelong fitness through a spreadsheet of their wellness activities. High school students might document their comprehension of negative numbers through digital pictures or record a radio show where they role-play the parts of authors discussing common book themes for a humanities class.

Storing Artifacts

Students need to be able to store all their digital artifacts in one location such as on the network, on a flash drive, or on their class laptop. The ideal scenario is to store them in multiple locations and archived on a CD or DVD. Some teachers have students store their artifacts within a digital folder labeled for the standard such as 1Understand. Others have students save each artifact with the number for the standard such as 3Comparetwopoems.doc. Students spend more time in thinking about the artifacts and less time in trying to figure out what the file contains if the artifact file name is very descriptive.

The Process

Another advantage to e-portfolios is that they encourage self-guided learning. Students take the lead in selecting appropriate artifacts for a given standard and explaining how these exemplify the standard's requirements. Next, they write a reflection, learning that it is not the rewording of the standard nor a description of the learning experience, but rather a statement of what they did not know beforehand, what they learned during the creation process, and what they have yet to learn.

Tools

Educators can select from many possible tools to create e-portfolios. Some use commercial software specifically designed for e-portfolios such as LiveText, Grady Profile, Scholastic Electronic Portfolio, and Sunburst Learner Profile; others use non-commercial software such as Open Source Portfolio. Another avenue is to create e-portfolios from generic software such as word processors, an Adobe Acrobat PDF file, Web pages, multimedia tools, or blogging. Students feel most comfortable with these generic e-portfolio software programs when the instructor provides a high degree of structure through a template.

Assembling the Portfolio

Using the template as a guide, students choose which of their artifacts will go in the final e-portfolio. Because they already know how to word process, they will find it easy to add all the germane parts of their projects into one long document, For example, science students open up a word processed lab report which they've saved, copy the part that illustrates a particular standard, and then paste that portion of the report into the appropriate location under the Standards section of the template. In addition, they may put in any other already created digital artifacts such as images, movies, or sound. The only new work they have to do for the e-portfolio is to write their reflections for each standard.

Blog E-Portfolios

Many word processed e-portfolios are predominantly text-based with a few images, and these can be saved as PDFs to maintain all of the e-portfolio's formatting, such as alignment and font size. In a blog e-portfolio, students create an individual blog entry and give it a name, such as Standard 2. Students enter the e-portfolio parts in reverse order so that the title page is the most recent entry and, therefore, at the top of the blog listing. The reviewer can click on the listing of previous blog entries to see each component. Artifacts can be in the form of text, image, video, or other digital content. Teachers provide a template that each student can copy into the blog since the teacher cannot format each student's blog.

Powerpoint E-Portfolios

For students already comfortable creating multimedia presentations, assembling a PowerPoint e-portfolio is not difficult. Each slide may reflect one component of a standard and therefore a single standard may comprise five or more slides. Students can link pages together to help reviewers navigate. However, PowerPoint is not a good vehicle for long text passages such as an essay. When students use Web pages, they create a page for each standard or a page for each part of the standard. They can link from standard to the supporting artifacts so that the reviewer can easily navigate the e-portfolio.

Ten Tips
Creating an Electronic Portfolio

1. State and explain the specific standards and the subparts of each standard that will be evaluated in the e-portfolio.
2. Tell how the e-portfolio will be assessed and by whom. Share the assessment rubric with students and let them know whether the teacher, a team, or a group of experts will assess the e-portfolio.
3. Model several e-portfolios for the students so they understand the e-portfolio's purpose and general format.
4. Provide a detailed e-portfolio template for the students so they understand what is required for each part of the e-portfolio.
5. Label each class assignment, homework assignment, and project with the appropriate standard; therefore, the students can quickly identify all of the possible artifacts for a particular standard.
6. Provide network and other storage for the students' digital artifacts to facilitate frequent archiving.
7. Model how to select an artifact for the e-portfolio based on how well the artifact reflects the standard.
8. Model a reflection on a standard so that students show their growth in the standard.
9. Include regularly scheduled e-portfolio days in which the students archive artifacts, decide which artifacts best support the standards, assemble their e-portfolios, write their reflections, and, possibly, present it. Some teachers schedule e-portfolio days every 5 weeks, and others do it every 10 weeks.
10. Have an e-portfolio review and provide each student with an assessment of the e-portfolio.

EDUCATOR FEEDBACK IN E-PORTFOLIOS

English Standard	Teacher Rating/6	Teacher Comment
1. Understanding and Information		
A report based on a graph	5	You understood the graph and could apply it to the problem. Use more details from the graph to prove point.
An analysis of a speech	5	Bob, you showed that you can listen and get the main idea from a speech. You did miss the difference between what she has actually done and what she says she will do.
2. Personal Response		
A poem	6	Your poem has a central metaphor. The tone, sound patterns, and images all support that metaphor.
A short story	6	Bob, your story started strong and kept my interest. Your twist ending added to your story's message.

An e-portfolio should include areas where educators can rate student progress and provide helpful feedback.

CLEAR AND ORGANIZED

Title Page

Standards Chart

Standard 1

- Artifact 1 and how it meets the standard
- Artifact 2 and how it meets the standard
- Artifact 3 and how it meets the standard
- Reflections

Standard 2

- Artifact 1 and how it meets the standard
- Artifact 2 and how it meets the standard
- Artifact 3 and how it meets the standard
- Reflection

Teacher Formative Feedback

Educators need to provide a clear e-portfolio template that students can use to easily organize their artifacts and reflections.

The Downside

A disadvantage of these generic software e-portfolios, however, is that there is no management aspect—a teacher cannot compare how well all students have done on a certain standard without manually checking each e-portfolio. Therefore, program evaluation becomes very time-consuming. Also, these student e-portfolios are not cumulative from year to year, so teachers cannot see a growth on the standards over several years in a single e-portfolio. In addition, students who do not understand the mechanics of resizing photographs and other images for their e-portfolios can create files that are too memory intensive for transfer. Furthermore, generic software, unlike many other e-portfolio packages, does not contain an archival space for the students' artifacts.

21st Century Skills

E-portfolios support 21st century skills in a variety of ways. Self-assessment becomes a regular part of learning as students frequently select or re-evaluate which of their work is the best evidence of their skills and strive to create even better evidence in their future assignments. Formative assessment also plays a key role through regular teacher feedback. He or she might comment that a student did a great in-depth explanation on a part of the standard but still needs to address the whole standard in a more comprehensive fashion. Or a teacher may note that the student's critical contrast of two literary works would have been more analytical if the student had contrasted the theme for both novels in the same paragraph.

As we continue to move more deeply into the digital age and increasingly ask students to create and innovate, the e-portfolio is likely to all but replace high stakes and other traditional testing as a method of authentic evaluation.

HARRY GROVER TUTTLE is an educator-in-residence at Syracuse University.

From *Tech & Learning,* February 2007, pp. 22–24. Copyright © 2007 by Tech & Learning. Reprinted by permission.

UNIT 5

Data Driven Decisions

Unit Selections

Key Points to Consider

- How can examining data results promote motivation in the classroom?

- How should teachers determine which assessment activities should be used for evidence of student progress?

- What counts as evidence of meeting learning outcomes?

- What evidence do teachers have that the data results are reliable and valid?

- Is data the only evidence of student learning?

- How can teachers help students overcome their defensiveness when discussing their misconceptions and errors?

- Define the terms: data driven decisions and data-driven instruction.

- Analyze a set of standards for level of mastery and then discuss individual's different perspectives on the topic, "What is rigor?" and "Can common standards of rigor be established within and across grades and disciplines?"

- Choose an assessment and analyze the student data for instructional purposes.

Student Website

www.mhcls.com

Internet References

PDA for Learning
   http://www.ed.gov/about/offices/list/os/technology/plan/2004/site/stories/edlite-Chicago2.html
Assessment and Accountability Comprehensive Center
   http://www.aacompcenter.org/cs/aacc/print/htdocs/aacc/home.htm
WestEd
   http://www.wested.org/cs/we/print/docs/we/home.htm
United States Department of Education: My Child's Academic Success, No Child Left Behind: A Parent's Guide
   http://www.ed.gov/parents/academic/involve/nclbguide/parentsguide.html

The phrase 'data driven decision-making' describes the practice of collecting, analyzing, and interpreting various types of assessment information to guide decisions about school improvement and student performance. Educational assessment data is playing a greater role in the decision-making process. For example, schools require teachers to collect data to identify which students can demonstrate proficiency on state standards and gather data to monitor students' progress as part of their classroom instruction. In many states, data monitoring practices require teachers to provide information on a daily basis. Aggregating data for accountability and analyzing data for monitoring student achievement is an integral component of a school's culture as teachers compile data results as well as track student performance.

The *No Child Left Behind Act of 2001* requires that standardized assessment data be reported publicly for every child to determine whether all children are meeting state standards for a specific grade level and subject matter. To meet this demand, schools must identify student achievement data they need to collect to determine if students are making progress toward the attainment of their yearly progress goals. To support this process, teachers collect data as a way of monitoring student progress toward the attainment of the goals as well as to determine the effectiveness of instruction. Data collection is an ongoing and continuous process.

As a part of this process, data analyze sessions are an integral part of the school culture. Educators are beginning to understand that data driven decision-making is not a fad, but a true commitment to continual improvement of student learning. Research has shown that effective teachers who use data regularly to guide their decisions can have a positive impact on student achievement. In fact, the effectiveness of the instruction can be determined immediately. Collecting informal or formal data about student learning helps shape the instruction as well as determining its effectiveness.

Statistical data is often the information used to substantiate educators' and policyholders' decisions. Examining student work or talking to students to gain an understanding of how they reason and organize their knowledge is also a viable way to collect and record data results. Both ways of collecting and analyzing assessment information are important for planning effective instruction.

Shared Decision-Making

Shared decision-making and collaboration about student learning, assessment practices, and curriculum are changing the school culture. Teachers must be willing to work in teams to discuss and share data results, then set goals. They must know what the data results reveal and be ready to openly discuss challenging instructional and learning issues. Collaboration is necessary because schools must work together to achieve common goals in the context of increased accountability.

Data results are being accepted as indicators of effective teaching. Evolving concepts about learning and studies of how evidence of learning is actually used to show student thinking,

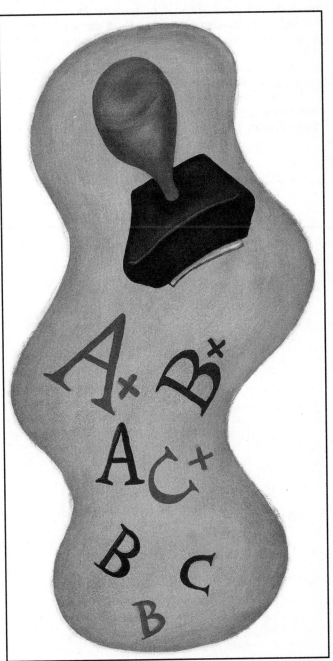

© SW Productions/Getty Images

to inform teaching and instructional practices, and to document student progress or lack thereof, are pushing our ideas about assessment practices and expanding the discussion about the concept of validity and reliability.

The articles in the unit focus on data collection, analyses, and ways to interpret data results. The first article presents information about ways to use data to differentiate instruction. The authors discuss different strategies for collecting data for three different purposes.

Teachers asking the right questions is the central foci of the second article. Two important questions, "Who is succeeding?" and "What are their areas of strength and weaknesses?" can be answered with an improvement plan that establishes priorities and goals.

According to Paul Bambrick-Santoyo, "High-quality assessments do not guarantee student achievement; neither does the analysis of assessment results." He discusses that the key to student success is defining the way to measure standards. The article presents information about different ways a group of teachers at the same grade level chose to interpret a standard and create an assessment item.

The third article provides assessment terms that every educator needs to know. The article presents three major sources of assessment data: external data, school-wide or district-wide benchmark data, and classroom data. Finally, the article presents information about the different ways data results can be used in schools.

The data analysis framework for designing instruction is described in the fourth article. As a student assessment tool, there are guiding questions to assist team members in analyzing data, discussing the patterns and relationships within those data, and constructing interpretations that they can then translate into goals and action steps to improve reading and writing achievement.

The last article in the unit discusses how examining student data by questioning can mobilize a staff, promote data literacy, and help increase student achievement. Questions are presented along with a framework for building data literacy.

Using Data to Differentiate Instruction

In an age of standards, using assessment data to differentiate instruction is essential.

Kay Brimijoin, Ede Marquissee, and Carol Ann Tomlinson

At Redlands Elementary School, Ms. Martez's 5th graders are studying the math concept of greatest common factor.[1] Following an interactive lesson, students participate in a self-assessment procedure that Ms. Martez has created. Using a car wind-shield metaphor, she asks,

> How many [of you] are clear as glass about how greatest common factor works? How many have bugs on your windshield? How many have windshields covered with mud? (Brimijoin, 2002)

On the basis of their spontaneous self-assessment of "glass, bugs, and mud" and their earlier work on greatest common factor, Ms. Martez assigns students to three follow-up activities. With only a few exceptions, the students' self-assessment matches what Ms. Martez had determined from her pre-assessment.

Because the group of students who are as "clear as glass" understands and can apply greatest common factor at both the conceptual and skill levels, she has these students use a Euclidean algorithm to find the greatest common factor in a series of exercises. A group of "buggy" students—who understand the basic concept of greatest common factor, but still need to build their confidence through application—play a greatest common factor game that Ms. Martez has created. And she sends the "muddy" group to sort factors in a giant Venn diagram constructed of two hula-hoops. This oversized graphic organizer provides a kinesthetic and interpersonal learning experience for those who need additional practice to master the basic concept and skills.

During this time, Ms. Martez offers support and answers questions using a red-yellow-green cup system to prioritize student requests for assistance. A student sets a red cup on his or her desk to say "I can't go on without help." A yellow cup means that the student has questions but isn't completely blocked, and a green cup means that the student understands what he or she is doing. Two students tell Ms. Martez they are "really buggy *and* muddy," and she immediately announces the opening of a "math clinic" where she works on intensive, explicit instruction.

Because Ms. Martez had devoted time at the beginning of the year to talk with her students about the importance of gathering assessment data directly from them, students engage in their tasks smoothly and do not question groupings or complain about assignments. She had modeled the windshield strategy and together she and her class had created a generic rubric for each degree of understanding. Teaching students this self-assessment technique helped accustom them to instruction differentiated by readiness and structures that support student-centered learning (Tomlinson, 1999).

Three-Dimensional Data Collection

For Ms. Martez, informal and formal data about student learning not only shape instruction but also determine its effectiveness. She uses multiple methods of data collection and views the process as dynamic and continuous. She sees her role as data collector in three dimensions: to determine students' prior understanding and achievement, to track their responses to moderate challenges, and to measure their outcomes against expected performance goals (Brimijoin, 2002; Bruner, 1963; Tomlinson, 1995).

Informal and formal data about student learning not only shape instruction but also determine its effectiveness.

Pre-Assessment

Ms. Martez uses a wide array of pre-assessments when teaching new content. During a math lesson introducing basic algebra concepts, for instance, she asks students,

> What do you suppose it means to think algebraically? Take out your math logs and write, even if you write that you don't know.

Oral questioning, written journal prompts, objective tests, webbing, K-W-L (What do you *know?* What do you still *want* to know? What did you *learn?*) charts, group discussions, and brainstorming sessions provide rich data about students' existing schema, including critical misconceptions (Bransford, Brown, & Cocking, 2000).

Moderate Challenges

Ms. Martez believes that because students differ in their grasp of key concepts, she must modify her instruction to help them build knowledge, refine skills, and apply understandings on increasingly sophisticated tasks (Wiggins & McTighe, 1998). Assessment helps her modify instruction so that each student is appropriately challenged. She uses paper-and-pencil or performance-based formative assessments, including objective tests or quizzes, quick-writes, essays, and open-ended problems, varying the type according to the content being studied. She also develops a clear sense of what the culminating assessment will be when she first lays out the lesson or unit.

Ms. Martez gives her students "task cards," which specify the steps in a learning process or experience. These cards include a set of directions for a task in order to facilitate independent learning and nurture autonomy. For example, each of Ms. Martez's learning groups had task cards with step-by-step directions to guide them through their assignments on greatest common factor. The task cards also frequently include rubrics that spell out performance expectations on assignments.

At the end of a lesson, students write in their journal a one-line description or an answer to a question about what they have learned in the lesson. Their responses are "exit tickets" for formative or ongoing assessment to help the teacher evaluate the effectiveness of a lesson design and keep instruction focused on key learning goals and individual needs.

Standards Testing

Teaching in a grade that requires state standardized assessments forces Ms. Martez to reconcile her "gotta get it covered and memorized by testing time" mentality and her belief in concept-centered differentiated instruction. She confesses to feeling conflicted about working wholeheartedly in two seemingly contradictory worlds of teaching and learning.

Three weeks before state standards testing, Ms. Martez asks students to go through their math books and select topics that they have mastered and those that need more work. She reflects on the results and decides to set up centers on such topics as fractions, place value, geometry, and statistics, cycling students through centers related to their areas of need, and assigning "experts" to assist their peers.

Using Assessment to Target Learner Needs

Ms. Martez uses questioning and observing to differentiate instruction and ensure that her instruction is a good match for the varied needs of her students (Brimijoin, 2002). She adjusts questions or performance tasks to be more structured for those

who are struggling with a concept and more abstract for those who have mastered the concept. Rather than seeing assessment as an end-of-lesson or end-of-unit phenomenon, Ms. Martez incorporates it at the beginning, at the end, and everywhere in between.

> **Rather than seeing assessment as an end-of-lesson or end-of-unit phenomenon, Ms. Martez incorporates it at the beginning, at the end, and everywhere in between.**

Ms. Martez invests much time and energy in mapping the "start and finish" by first constructing a big picture of assessment results that students bring with them. By the 5th grade at Redlands Elementary, students have one set of state standards test scores from 3rd grade and one set of nationally standardized scores from 4th grade. Ms. Martez enters all these scores on a spreadsheet. During individual conferences, Ms. Martez guides students in setting target goals for their progress and areas of emphasis for her instruction. At the end of the year, she enters all 5th grade scores from state standardized tests and calculates the percentage gains for each student and for the class overall.

At the end of this past year, 74 percent of her students passed the reading assessment, an overall gain of 27 percentage points over their 3rd grade test results; 58 percent passed math, a gain of 5 percentage points; 58 percent passed social studies, a gain of 24 percentage points; and 74 percent passed the science assessment, a gain of 32 percentage points (Brimijoin, 2002). Ms. Martez attributes the improvement in test score results chiefly to her use of pre-assessment, self-assessment, and ongoing assessment to differentiate instruction for individual learning needs:

> The facts stuck because they were scaffolded into existing information, taught at the students' readiness levels, hooked in with interests, and nailed down with instruction targeted to the students' strongest learning styles. . . . Differentiation works in a standardized testing world. . . . We can't afford not to do it and expect to meet state standards, especially in low socioeconomic areas like Redlands. (Brimijoin, 2002, p. 263)

Ms. Martez uses the results of test score analysis to reflect on her teaching, comparing her curriculum design and instruction from one year to the next, noting strengths as well as weaknesses, and identifying questions that still need answering in order to refine her practice (Zeichner & Liston, 1996).

The students are also data collectors. They accept responsibility for monitoring their own progress and see that they have a role in shaping instruction. Ms. Martez weaves information gleaned from journal responses with formative quiz and test results. She sees assessment as a powerful tool to be used through the whole process of teaching and learning; one that demands the same kind of evaluation skills that good teachers use for effective management.

Ms. Martez advises other teachers that carefully articulated, continuous assessment that drives curriculum design "maximizes teaching time, streamlines instruction, and facilitates learning for all students." She insists that assessment is not "just another plate added to the 12-piece service," but a means of enhancing student and teacher performance.

Note

1. This article uses pseudonyms for the teacher and school.

References

Bransford, J., Brown, A., & Cocking, R. (Eds.). (2000). *How people learn: Brain, mind, experience, and school.* Washington, DC: National Academy Press.

Brimijoin, K. (2002). *A journey toward expertise in differentiation: A preservice and inservice teacher make their way.* Unpublished doctoral dissertation. University of Virginia, Charlottesville.

Bruner, J. (1963). *The process of education.* New York: Vintage Books.

Tomlinson, C. (1995). *Differentiating instruction for mixed-ability classrooms.* Alexandria, VA: ASCD.

Tomlinson, C. (1999). *The differentiated classroom: Responding to the needs of all learners.* Alexandria, VA: ASCD.

Wiggins, G., & McTighe, J. (1998). *Understanding by design.* Alexandria, VA: ASCD.

Zeichner, K., & Liston, D. (1996). *Reflective teaching: An introduction.* Mahwah, NJ: Lawrence Erlbaum Associates.

KAY BRIMIJOIN is an assistant professor at Sweet Briar College, Sweet Briar, VA 24595; brimijoin@sbc.edu. **EDE MARQUISSEE** teaches 6th grade at Summit Middle School, 4509 Homestead Road, Fort Wayne, IN 46814; emarquissee@sacs.k12.in.us. **CAROL ANN TOMLINSON** is a professor at the Curry School of Education, University of Virginia, Ruffner Hall, Charlottesville, VA 22904; cat3y@virginia.edu.

From *Educational Leadership,* February 2003. Copyright © 2003 by ASCD. Reprinted by permission. The Association for Supervision and Curriculum Development is a worldwide community of educators advocating sound policies and sharing best practices to achieve the success of each learner. To learn more, visit ASCD at www.ascd.org

First Things First
Demystifying Data Analysis

**To improve student achievement results, use data to focus
on a few simple, specific goals.**

MIKE SCHMOKER

I recently sat with a district administrator eager to understand her district's achievement results. Pages of data and statistical breakdowns covered the table. Looking somewhat helpless, she threw up her hands and asked me, "What do I do with all this?"

Many educators could empathize with this administrator. The experts' tendency to complicate the use and analysis of student achievement data often ensures that few educators avail themselves of data's simple, transparent power. The effective use of data depends on simplicity and economy.

First things first: Which data, well analyzed, can help us improve teaching and learning? We should always start by considering the needs of teachers, whose use of data has the most direct impact on student performance. Data can give them the answer to two important questions:

- How many students are succeeding in the subjects I teach?
- Within those subjects, what are the areas of strength or weakness?

The answers to these two questions set the stage for targeted, collaborative efforts that can pay immediate dividends in achievement gains.

Focusing Efforts

Answering the first question enables grade-level or subject-area teams of practitioners to establish high-leverage annual improvement goals—for example, moving the percentage of students passing a math or writing assessment from a baseline of 67 percent in 2003 to 72 percent in 2004. Abundant research and school evidence suggest that setting such goals may be the most significant act in the entire school improvement process, greatly increasing the odds of success (Little, 1987; McGonagill, 1992; Rosenholtz, 1991; Schmoker, 1999, 2001).

If we take pains to keep the goals simple and to avoid setting too many of them, they focus the attention and energies

of everyone involved (Chang, Labovitz, & Rosansky, 1992; Drucker, 1992; Joyce, Wolf, & Calhoun, 1993). Such goals are quite different from the multiple, vague, ambiguous goal statements that populate many school improvement plans.

Turning Weakness into Strength

After the teacher team has set a goal, it can turn to the next important question: Within the identified subject or course, where do we need to direct our collective attention and expertise? In other words, where do the greatest number of students struggle or fail within the larger domains? For example, in English and language arts, students may have scored low in writing essays or in comprehending the main ideas in paragraphs. In mathematics, they may be weak in measurement or in number sense.

Every state or standardized assessment provides data on areas of strength and weakness, at least in certain core subjects. Data from district or school assessments, even gradebooks, can meaningfully supplement the large-scale assessments. After team members identify strengths and weaknesses, they can begin the real work of instructional improvement: the collaborative effort to share, produce, test, and refine lessons and strategies targeted to areas of low performance, where more effective instruction can make the greatest difference for students.

So What's the Problem?

Despite the importance of the two questions previously cited, practitioners can rarely answer them. For years, during which *data* and *goals* have been education by-words, I have asked hundreds of teachers whether they know their goals for that academic year and which of the subjects they teach have the lowest scores. The vast majority of teachers don't know. Even fewer can answer the question: What are the low-scoring areas within a subject or course you teach?

Nor could I. As a middle and high school English teacher, I hadn't the foggiest notion about these data—from state assessments or from my own records. This is the equivalent of a mechanic not knowing which part of the car needs repair.

Why don't most schools provide teachers with data reports that address these two central questions? Perhaps the straightforward improvement scheme described here seems too simple to us, addicted as we are to elaborate, complex programs and plans (Schmoker, 2002; Stigler & Hiebert, 1999).

Over-Analysis and Overload

The most important school improvement processes do not require sophisticated data analysis or special expertise. Teachers themselves can easily learn to conduct the analyses that will have the most significant impact on teaching and achievement.

The most important school improvement processes do not require sophisticated data analysis or special expertise.

The extended, district-level analyses and correlational studies some districts conduct can be fascinating stuff; they can even reveal opportunities for improvement. But they can also divert us from the primary purpose of analyzing data: improving instruction to achieve greater student success. Over-analysis can contribute to overload—the propensity to create long, detailed, "comprehensive" improvement plans and documents that few read or remember. Because we gather so much data and because they reveal so many opportunities for improvement, we set too many goals and launch too many initiatives, overtaxing our teachers and our systems (Fullan, 1996; Fullan & Stiegelbauer, 1991).

Formative Assessment Data and Short-Term Results

A simple template for a focused improvement plan with annual goals for improving students' state assessment scores would go a long way toward solving the overload problem (Schmoker, 2001), and would enable teams of professional educators to establish their own improvement priorities, simply and quickly, for the students they teach and for those in similar grades, courses, or subject areas.

Using the goals that they have established, teachers can meet regularly to improve their lessons and assess their progress using another important source: formative assessment data. Gathered every few weeks or at each grading period, formative data enable the team to gauge levels of success and to adjust their instructional efforts accordingly. Formative, collectively administered assessments allow teams to capture and celebrate short-term results, which are essential to success in any sphere (Collins, 2001; Kouzes & Posner, 1995; Schaffer, 1988). Even conventional classroom assessment data work for us here, but

with a twist. We don't just record these data to assign grades each period; we now look at how many students succeeded on that quiz, that interpretive paragraph, or that applied math assessment, and we ask ourselves why. Teacher teams can now "assess to learn"—to improve their instruction (Stiggins, 2002).

A legion of researchers from education and industry have demonstrated that instructional improvement depends on just such simple, data-driven formats—teams identifying and addressing areas of difficulty and then developing, critiquing, testing, and upgrading efforts in light of ongoing results (Collins, 2001; Darling-Hammond, 1997; DuFour, 2002; Fullan, 2000; Reeves, 2000; Schaffer, 1988; Senge, 1990; Wiggins, 1994). It all starts with the simplest kind of data analysis—with the foundation we have when all teachers know their goals and the specific areas where students most need help.

What about Other Data?

In right measure, other useful data can aid improvement. For instance, data on achievement differences among socioeconomic groups, on students reading below grade level, and on teacher, student, and parent perceptions can all guide improvement.

Instead of overloading teachers, let's give them the data that they need to conduct powerful, focused analyses.

But data analysis shouldn't result in overload and fragmentation; it shouldn't prevent teams of teachers from setting and knowing their own goals and from staying focused on key areas for improvement. Instead of overloading teachers, let's give them the data they need to conduct powerful, focused analyses and to generate a sustained stream of results for students.

References

Chang, Y. S., Labovitz, G., & Rosansky, V. (1992). *Making quality work: A leadership guide for the results-driven manager.* Essex Junction, VT: Omneo.

Collins, J. (2001, October). Good to great. *Fast Company, 51,* 90–104.

Darling-Hammond, L. (1997). *The right to learn: A blueprint for creating schools that work.* New York: Jossey-Bass.

Drucker, P. (1992). *Managing for the future: The 1990s and beyond.* New York: Truman Talley Books.

DuFour, R. (2002). The learning-centered principal. *Educational Leadership, 59*(8), 12–15.

Fullan, M. (1996). Turning systemic thinking on its head. *Phi Delta Kappan, 77*(6), 420–423.

Fullan, M. (2000). The three stories of education reform. *Phi Delta Kappan, 81*(8), 581–584.

Fullan, M., & Stiegelbauer, S. (1991). *The new meaning of educational change.* New York: Teachers College Press.

Joyce, B., Wolf, J., & Calhoun, E. (1993). *The self-renewing school.* Alexandria, VA: ASCD.

Kouzes, J., & Posner, B. (1995). *The leadership challenge.* San Francisco: Jossey-Bass.

Little, J. W. (1987). Teachers as colleagues. In V. Richardson-Koehler (Ed.), *Educator's handbook.* White Plains, NY: Longman.

McGonagill, G. (1992). *Overcoming barriers to educational restructuring: A call for "system literacy."* ERIC, ED 357–512.

Reeves, D. (2000). *Accountability in action.* Denver, CO: Advanced Learning Press.

Rosenholtz, S. J. (1991). *Teacher's workplace: The social organization of schools.* New York: Teachers College Press.

Schaffer, R. H. (1988). *The breakthrough strategy: Using short-term successes to build the high-performing organization.* New York: Harper Business.

Schmoker, M. (1999). *Results: The key to continuous school improvement* (2nd ed). Alexandria, VA: ASCD.

Schmoker, M. (2001). *The results field-book: Practical strategies from dramatically improved schools.* Alexandria, VA: ASCD.

Schmoker, M. (2002). Up and away. *Journal of Staff Development, 23*(2), 10–13.

Senge, P. (1990). *The fifth discipline: The art and practice of the learning organization.* New York: Doubleday.

Stiggins, R. (2002). Assessment crisis: The absence of assessment FOR learning. *Phi Delta Kappan, 83*(10), 758–765.

Stigler, J. W., & Hiebert, J. (1999). *The teaching gap: Best ideas from the world's teachers for improving education in the classroom.* New York: Free Press.

Wiggins, G. (1994). None of the above. *The Executive Educator, 16*(7), 14–18.

MIKE SCHMOKER is an educational speaker and consultant; schmoker@futureone.com. His most recent book is *The RESULTS Fieldbook: Practical Strategies from Dramatically Improved Schools* (ASCD, 2001).

Data in the Driver's Seat

Two New Jersey schools discover the benefits of interim assessments, clearly defined standards, and data-driven instruction.

PAUL BAMBRICK-SANTOYO

Our story starts with two public middle schools in Newark, New Jersey. Both had student populations representative of Newark's Central Ward, where 90 percent of students qualify for free or reduced-price lunch and 85 percent are black. Students in both schools were generally well behaved and academically on task.

Despite the two schools' similar student populations, their 2003 achievement results revealed two very different pictures. One school, Greater Newark Academy, was in a tailspin: Only 7 percent of its 8th grade students had passed the state math test. The second school, North Star Academy, had more respectable results—well above the district average—but it was still behind its suburban New Jersey counterparts.

Over the ensuing four years, each school made massive gains in student achievement, outstripping the district average by at least 30 points on both math and English/language arts assessments and surpassing the statewide average in almost every category. How did these two schools end up with such tremendous student achievement? Therein lies our story.

Beginning in the 2002–03 school year, North Star Academy launched a model of data-driven instruction with interim assessments at the center, and Greater Newark followed suit the next year. In this case, interim assessments are defined as assessments given every 6 to 8 weeks throughout the school year to measure student progress toward meeting standards. Many schools are using interim assessments today, but not all are seeing such strong achievement gains. What separates those schools that use interim assessments effectively from those that do not? Certain key drivers of data-driven instruction made these two schools—and many more like them—so successful.

Assessment: Great Expectations?

Most 7th grade state math standards have a standard similar to this one used in New Jersey: "Understand and use . . . percents in a variety of situations" (State of New Jersey, Department of Education, 2004). With this limited guidance, math teachers are told to teach to mastery, but it's not always clear what mastery should look like. Consider these classroom assessment questions that six different 7th grade math teachers created to measure mastery of this standard:

1. What is 50% of 20?
2. What is 67% of 81?
3. Shawn got 7 correct answers out of 10 possible answers on his science test. What percentage of questions did he answer correctly?
4. J. J. Redick was on pace to set a college basketball record in career free throw percentage. Going into the NCAA tournament in 2004, he had made 97 of 104 free throw attempts. What percentage of free throws had he made?
5. J. J. Redick was on pace to set an NCAA record in career free throw percentage. Going into the NCAA tournament in 2004, he had made 97 of 104 free throw attempts. In the first tournament game, Redick missed his first five free throws. How far did his percentage drop from right before the tournament game to right after missing those free throws?
6. J. J. Redick and Chris Paul were competing for the best free throw percentage. Redick made 94 percent of his first 103 shots, whereas Paul made 47 of 51 shots, (a) Which one had a better shooting percentage? (b) In the next game, Redick made only 2 of 10 shots, and Paul made 7 of 10 shots. What are their new overall shooting percentages? Who is the better shooter? (c) Jason argued that if J. J. and Chris each made their next 10 shots, their shooting percentages would go up the same amount. Is this true? Why or why not? Describe in detail how you arrived at your answers.

Note how the level of difficulty increases with each question. For the first question, a student could understand 50 percent as one-half and determine the answer without actually using percentages. Questions 3–6 could be considered attempts at real-world application or critical thinking, but Question 6 requires far more critical thinking and conceptual understanding than any other question. Despite these drastic differences, every one of the questions is standards based. This leads to the central point about the relationship between standards and interim assessments: Standards are meaningless until you define how you will assess them.

In many schools, teachers define the standards according to their own level of expectation, and those expectations vary radically from one classroom to the next. Thus, different teachers teach to different levels of mastery. We cannot expect every teacher to teach the skills required for complex problems like Question 6 as the standard for learning if that expectation is not explicit and transparent.

To help teachers hold their students to a common standard of rigor, Greater Newark Academy and North Star Academy shared the same interim assessments that North Star originally designed in alignment with New Jersey state tests. In this way, they defined one common level of mastery to which every grade-level teacher should teach. Teachers saw the assessments before teaching their unit so that they could plan their lessons with those expectations in mind. The assessments were administered every eight weeks, and the tests measured every standard that had been taught up to that date. Thus, the first step on the path to high student achievement was established: transparent, common, rigorous assessments.

Analysis: Watching "Poolside"

High-quality assessments do not guarantee student achievement; neither does the analysis of assessment results. For example, imagine a swimming coach trying to analyze the performance of his team. If he picked up the newspaper the day after the meet and read the times of his third-place swimmer, he might decide that she just has to swim faster. Yet if he had watched that swimmer at the meet, he would have noticed that she was the last one off the starting block but the fastest one in the water. At that point, his analysis would be clear: He needs to focus on getting her off the block faster.

School assessment analysis is no different. Looking at state test or interim assessment results in isolation is like reading a newspaper summary of a sports event: You can only draw summative conclusions, and those conclusions might actually be inaccurate. You have to be "poolside" to analyze effectively.

North Star developed a spreadsheet that teachers in both schools used to analyze results on the interim assessments, but the key factor was having teachers go back to the test to look at individual questions. Teachers in the two schools received results on the day after each assessment. They could then examine the data to determine where the students erred. Seeing which distractors students chose on the multiple-choice questions and examining student work on open-ended questions helped teachers recognize what students misunderstood and plan their instruction accordingly.

For example, a 6th grade math teacher thought her students had problems with rates until she analyzed the question more closely. The question was, "How far would Jennifer travel in 2¼ hours if she drove 36 miles per hour?" The teacher analyzed the students' answers and discovered that most chose Answer C: 72 miles, instead of the correct answer of 81 miles. Thus, the students actually understood rates—because they multiplied 2 hours by the 36 miles to get 72—but they didn't know how to multiply by a mixed number (2 ¼ × 36).

Greater Newark and North Star were able to avoid the mistakes of the swim coach by doing item-level, test-in-hand analysis. This enabled teachers to make solid, root-cause analyses, which in turn facilitated far more effective action plans. Being "poolside" made all the difference: Assessments and analysis were now linked.

Action: Taking Data out of the Binder

Even with high-quality interim assessments and effective analysis, student achievement will not improve without targeted follow-through. Most research about highly effective schools focuses on developing an action plan for reteaching particular standards (Symonds, 2003). Following this advice, schools often develop data binders containing analyses and action plans based on the previous round of assessments and keep a copy in the main office or in each classroom.

Yet the key question remains: Where is that information when teachers plan lessons? If a teacher plans lessons on Sunday night and the data binder is in the classroom, then the effect on teaching is greatly diminished. Action plans must be connected to lesson plans, which need to translate to changes in teaching.

Action plans must be connected to lesson plans, which need to translate to changes in teaching.

Teachers at Greater Newark and North Star developed six-week action plans based on interim assessment results, and the most successful teachers had those action plans in hand when planning lessons. A 5th grade literacy teacher, for example, learned that her students could make basic inferences and identify the main idea, but they couldn't keep track of the sequence of events, nor could they identify the evidence in the text that supported their inferences. So the teacher redesigned her guided reading lessons to ask more questions related to these skills, and she created scaffolded guides to teach these skills more efficiently.

Teachers also used the action plans to design targeted tutoring sessions and differentiated small groups. Some teachers actually stapled their action plans to the front of their lesson plans to remind themselves of the connection between their assessment analysis and their teaching. The seamless coherence among assessments, analysis, and action creates the ideal classroom environment for significant gains in student learning.

Buy-In: Chicken or Egg?

Much research has been done about the data-driven culture of high-achieving schools, especially the role of teacher buy-in (Datnow, Park, & Wohlstetter, 2007). Unfortunately, the research has not adequately answered the question of whether that buy-in was a prerequisite for success—a true driver of achievement—or a by-product of a data-driven culture. An example from one of our two schools helps address this question.

When North Star launched its data-driven instruction model in 2003, most teachers were ambivalent about whether using interim assessments would have any effect. Some wondered, Don't we already assess our students and analyze their progress? A few were outright resistant.

Before the first interim assessment, North Star's leaders had teachers predict the performance of their students by labeling each question in one of three ways: *Confident* (students would answer correctly); *Not Sure* (students might or might not answer correctly); or *No Way* (students would not answer correctly). When the results came in, teachers were shocked to see that their students performed far worse than they expected. They implemented the three principles mentioned previously: using the assessments to evaluate the rigor of their teaching, doing test-in-hand analysis, and applying targeted action plans when planning lessons. They also pored over the next assessment in advance, hungry to prove that they could do better. On that next assessment, almost every teacher had students show gains in achievement.

While the school celebrated these improvements, some teachers still resisted the process. One teacher in particular, Ms. J, was adamant that she was not really improving her teaching and was only teaching to the test. At the end of the 2003–04 school year, school leaders compared her results from the previous year with the current year and saw that her students that year had shown much stronger gains in reading and language than did her students for the previous year, before interim assessments were implemented. The teachers and school culture were the same for both cohorts, the only thing that changed was effective implementation of interim assessments. Although Ms. J clearly saw the incredible gains she had made, she still did not fully endorse the process.

Two years later at a faculty meeting, teachers debated shortening one part of the analysis and action plan process. Ms. J stood up and firmly defended keeping the process as it was because of the incredible value it added to her teaching. In two years, this teacher had gone from being the most vocal opponent to being an ardent supporter. The results came first; the buy-in came next. Data-driven instruction does not require teacher buy-in—it creates it.

Data-driven instruction does not require teacher buy-in—it creates it.

Creating Better Schools

Greater Newark Academy and North Star Academy started at two different places when they decided to implement data-driven instruction: One was in danger of sanctions, and the other was considered good but had not made the transition to excellence. Both saw significant gains as a result of the effective implementation of interim assessments, which included a preestablished assessment calendar and a trained leadership team. In essence, they shifted the focus of the schools from what was being taught to what the students were learning.

These two schools are not alone. Over the past three years, more than 500 school leaders have attended workshops that I have delivered through New Leaders for New Schools and for various school systems. Participants then launched interim assessments and data-driven instruction in their schools. From this work have come dramatic student achievement gains in charter and district schools in the San Francisco Bay Area, Chicago, New York, Memphis, Baltimore, and Washington, D.C. With the proper interplay among interim assessments, analysis, action and data-driven culture, schools can be transformed, and a new standard can be set for student learning.

References

Datnow, A., Park, V., Wohlstetter, P. (2007). *Achieving with data: How high-performing school systems use data to improve instruction for elementary students.* Los Angeles: Center on Educational Governance, Rossier School of Education, University of Southern California.

State of New Jersey, Department of Education. (2004). *New Jersey core curriculum content standards for mathematics.* Trenton, NJ: Author. Available: www.state.nj.us/education/cccs/s4_5fmath.htm

Symonds, K. W. (2003). *After the test: How schools are using data to close the achievement gap.* San Francisco: Bay Area School Reform Collaborative.

PAUL BAMBRICK-SANTOYO is Managing Director of North Star Academy Charter School of Newark, New Jersey, and Lead Faculty for Data-Driven Instruction for New Leaders for New Schools; pbambrick@uncommonschools.org.

Testing and Assessment 101

Terms every board member needs to know to understand complex data.

RONALD S. THOMAS

Do data and assessment terms confuse you? Can you tell the difference between a norm- and a criterion-referenced test? What are benchmark data and why are they so important? What are school abilities tests? What is Adequate Yearly Progress (AYP)?

As your curriculum team clicks through these various phrases, are your eyes starting to roll up in the back of your head?

Don't worry; you are not alone. Understanding assessment data is a complex task, but it's one that we can make easier. While this article can't answer all your questions about assessments, it will give you some of the background you need to be an informed board member.

Nature of Assessment Data

Assessment data are observations or facts that must be collected, organized, and analyzed to become useful. The key point to remember is that data are merely numbers or words that do not have meaning in and of themselves.

Data only acquire meaning when educators and board members sift the numbers through their personal experiences and place them within the context of their school or the district as a whole. Because your personal and social filters are different, don't be surprised if your perception varies from the superintendent and school staff's.

At one time, schools lacked sufficient assessment data to make good instructional decisions, but now many are snowed under with information. Organize your data discussions around a series of questions, such as:

- Where do assessment data come from?
- Why do schools collect assessment data?
- What, exactly, is being assessed?
- Against what criteria are assessment results being measured?

Asking each of these questions provides a useful framework to increase your understanding of what you are discussing.

Where Do Assessment Data Come From?

According to Jonathan Supovitz and Valerie Klein, authors of the widely respected *Mapping a Course for Improved Student Learning,* there are three major sources of assessment data: external data, school-wide or district-wide benchmark data, and classroom data.

External assessment data are standardized norm- or criterion-referenced tests that originate and are scored outside the school. Terra Nova, SAT, Stanford 10, and each state's No Child Left Behind (NCLB) test are examples. Results from external assessments can suggest an initial focus for a school's attention, but they are not designed to be frequent enough or to provide specific enough data to give precise instructional guidance for a whole year.

School-wide or district-wide benchmark data are collected frequently and systematically across an entire grade, content area, or course, perhaps over an entire school district, at several predetermined points in the year. These common assessments can provide guidance for instructional adjustments, interventions, and professional development.

Most importantly, if scored and analyzed collaboratively by teachers, discussion about common assessment results can reinforce a culture of inquiry, based on data, among the staff. However, these are often the most under-utilized type of data in a school because teachers don't have the time to analyze them or the training and experience to collaborate.

Classroom assessment data include quizzes, unit tests, essays, performance assessments, and personal communications developed and administered by individual teachers. Supovitz and Klein liken classroom assessment data to having a personal global positioning system (GPS) for each student. Classroom assessments provide the opportunity to provide quick and flexible feedback to each student throughout the year and to make immediate adjustments in instruction.

Each source serves a different purpose, and reports on student achievement from the three often vary significantly in how they portray data. Successful schools use an established system to bring together the results of all three types when making instructional decisions.

Why Do Schools Collect Assessment Data?

There are two important uses for the assessment data that schools collect. One is for educational accountability (or, in other words, to prove to the public that education is doing its job). State and national external assessments are considered the most important for accountability purposes, while classroom assessments are the least important.

The second major use of assessment data is for instructional decision making—data collected explicitly to improve the job that educators are doing. State and national assessments are the least helpful here. Classroom assessments provide the most useful ongoing data that teachers need to impact instruction, while common assessment data help teachers benchmark student progress against peers in other classes or schools.

To have an effect on the NCLB state test (accountability data), benchmark and classroom assessments (instructional improvement data) must measure student performance using the same content, format, and level of rigor. This will not happen automatically. Teachers need carefully designed assistance to align their classroom assessments with the state standards.

What Exactly Is Being Assessed?

There are four general types of external assessments.

General achievement tests assess the wide spectrum of student knowledge and skills. These tests usually take several hours on multiple days to administer. However, the tests can provide data on vocabulary word analysis, listening and reading/reading comprehension, language (such as spelling, capitalization, punctuation usage, and written expression), math (concepts estimation, problem solving, and computation), science, and social studies. Each commercial series—such as the Iowa Tests of Basic Skills, Terra Nova, and the Stanford 10—includes aligned tests for all grade levels.

Special area achievement tests center on one subject area, such as reading or mathematics. Because of this focus, they can provide more detailed information, such as data on phonemic awareness, decoding skills, letter/sound correspondence, word meanings, and fiction and nonfiction reading comprehension. The Gates-MacGinitie Reading Test is a well-known example. Most state NCLB assessments fall into this category because they focus solely on reading and mathematics.

A subcategory of special area achievement tests are diagnostic assessments. While all assessments have some diagnostic value, these tests are specifically designed to highlight the strengths and weaknesses of students in greater detail. The Stanford Diagnostic Reading Test, the Diagnostic Assessment of Reading, and computerized tests such as the STAR Reading and Math Assessments are examples.

The first three types of assessments are all achievement tests because they provide data on the knowledge and skills students can demonstrate. School abilities tests, which measure abstract thinking and reasoning abilities, provide information on students' potential to learn in school.

Tests such as the Cognitive Abilities Test (CogAT) and the Otis-Lennon School Ability Test (OLSAT 8) measure verbal abilities, such as sentence arrangement, verbal classification, and verbal analogies, as well as nonverbal abilities, including figure classification, pattern matrices, and number inference. Results may be correlated with achievement test data to relate students' actual achievement to their ability to perform in school.

Against What Criteria . . .?

Assessments are standards- or criterion-referenced (CRTs), norm-referenced (NRTs), or a combination of both.

On CRTs, student performance is measured against the content standards (the criteria) that all students should know and be able to do. Standards have been written by each state, usually modeled after national standards documents developed in the 1990s. Some state content standards are very precise and concrete, while others are more global and vague. All test results are reported as the percentage of students at the advanced, proficient, and basic levels in relation to the state's content standards.

States also vary in their performance standards, or the percentage of students the state expects to be in the advanced and proficient levels at each school each year up to 2014. Also called the "cut score," this percentage is known as the annual measurable objective (AMO) in reading and math.

Each state has different content standards, a different state test, and a different "cut score." It is, therefore, impossible to compare scores from state to state on their NCLB tests.

AYP is based on the combined school performance for all grades on the state's NCLB tests. AYP is calculated separately for reading and math. A minimum percentage of students must score "proficient" or "advanced" (at or above the AMO) each year for the school to meet AYP.

The percentage needed to meet AYP will increase each year until it gets to 100 percent. In 2014, under the present NCLB law, all students are expected to meet content standards by scoring at the advanced or proficient levels. All subgroups in the school (including all races, special education students, and children living in poverty) must score at or above the annual measurable objective for the school to meet AYP.

Norm-referenced tests (NRTs) compare student performance to that of a similar group of students who took the test when it was normed—the "norm group." This may have been several years before. Results are often expressed as percentiles (the percentage in the norm group that scored lower than students in your school). Many NRT test developers also report standard-based data in relation to major objectives included in the test.

Too many concepts to make much sense? Many school leaders are struggling with the same issues. As we work together to sort out the uses, value, and importance of assessment data, we can be in a better position to use them effectively and capture the power of data-based decision making.

RONALD S. THOMAS (rathomas@towson.edu) is the associate director of the Center for Leadership in Education at Towson University in Towson, Md. He has worked with more than 100 school improvement teams over the past 15 years.

Making Instructional Decisions Based on Data: What, How, and Why

Koulder Mokhtari, Catherine A. Rosemary, and Patricia A. Edwards

One of my weaknesses has always been documenting a student's progress, because I always found it such an overwhelming task. I would assess students, hand in the scores to an administrator, and then file them away. I literally would assess here and there, never use the results, and concentrate on whole-group instruction. Individual needs based on assessment were never taken into consideration. (Calderon [a kindergarten teacher], cited in Reilly, 2007, p. 770).

If you can relate to Calderon's sense of disenchantment with respect to documenting students' progress in your classroom or school and then not using the information, you are not alone. In our teaching experiences over more than two decades, we have often heard comments such as these from many of the PreK–12 teachers, literacy specialists, and principals in classroom and school settings with whom we have worked. We often found and continue to find that, although these educators spend significant amounts of time collecting assessment data, they do not take time or perhaps know how to organize and use data consistently and efficiently in instructional decision making. When asked, most teachers often admit, like Calderon, that documentation of student literacy progress is one of their weaknesses because it can be an overwhelming and time-consuming task. Other teachers say that they simply lack the knowledge and skills to develop a system for assessing and documenting students' progress.

The challenges that go along with data-based decision making are even more apparent in the current context of increased accountability as seen in local, state, and federal policies. At a time when teachers and administrators are pressed to demonstrate students' literacy growth, collecting, organizing, analyzing, and using data for instructional and curriculum improvement is a new way of working for many educators. How should assessment data be examined to improve instruction and curriculum and thereby advance students' reading and writing performance? In this column, we offer a promising framework

that can support school teams (i.e., teachers, literacy coaches, data managers, and principals) in making sense of various types of data for instructional planning. Instruction that is data based and goal driven sets the stage for continuous reading and writing improvement.

Research on the Intersection of Literacy Assessment and Instruction

Literature on the influence of literacy assessment on instruction focuses on the relationship between assessment and instruction rather than on whether one does or should drive the other. In one extensive study aimed at determining how assessment influences instruction within four particular schools, Stephens and her colleagues (Stephens et al., 1995) found that "the salient relationship was not between assessment and instruction per se. Granted, the two were related, but their relationship was moderated by the decision-making model of the district" (p. 494). The implication here is that assessment and instruction issues are embedded within broader power structures within particular schools and that both are influenced greatly by the decision-making model operating within those schools.

Shea, Murray, and Harlin (2005) noted that schoolwide committees or teams typically have a wide-angle view of student achievement: The information they examine often comes from various sources and diverse perspectives. They suggested that schoolwide teams analyze aggregated or disaggregated assessment data focused on curriculum and instruction for whole classrooms, small groups, or individual learners. After reporting students' current level of achievement, they then can make recommendations pertaining to schoolwide, grade-level, or individualized instruction. However, it is important to keep in mind that "as important as these recommendations are, they should not mark the end of a committee's work. At future meetings, members must review progress made as a result of their recommendations and modify them when appropriate" (p. 148). In other words, the systematic use of data to make instructional decisions requires leadership, training, and the development of a culture of data-driven decision making and accountability.

The analytical framework described in the following section was inspired by the *Standards for the Assessment of Reading and Writing* developed and published collaboratively by The National Council of Teachers of English and the International Reading Association Joint Task Force on Assessment (1994). This valuable report provides a set of 11 standards aimed at guiding the decisions schools make about assessing the teaching of reading and writing. These standards express the conviction Joint Task Force members had that involving the entire school community is essential if assessment is truly to foster student and teacher learning. The report offers guidelines for assessment strategies that reflect the complex interactions among teachers, learners, and communities; that ensure fair and equitable treatment of all students; and that foster thoughtful literacy learning and teaching.

Introducing the Data Analysis Framework for Instructional Decision Making

The Data Analysis Framework for Instructional Decision Making is a practical tool that provides school teams with a structure and process for organizing, analyzing, and using multiple sources and types of data for instructional decision making. Three major categories of data that are considered for improving reading and writing instruction include (1) professional development data, (2) classroom data, and (3) reading performance data.

1. Professional development data may consist of evaluation or feedback surveys and coaches' logs of how they spend their time and the types of activities they engage in to assist classroom teachers.

2. Classroom data may consist of teacher surveys of instructional practices, such as U.S. Elementary Reading Instruction (Bauman, Hoffman, Duffy-Hester, & Moon Ro, 2000), and The Language Arts Curriculum Survey (Center for Policy Research, n.d.), which surveys teachers on the time they spend on reading components and the cognitive demand of learning tasks. Informal data on reading instruction may consist of teachers' daily lesson plans or weekly schedules that include instructional time frames, content taught, and organizational grouping (i.e., individual, small-group, or whole-group instruction). Working together, literacy coaches and teachers may use observational data collected from tools such as the Early Language and Literacy Classroom Observation Toolkit (Smith & Dickinson, 2004) and Classroom Environment Profile (Wolfersberger, Reutzel, Sudweeks, & Fawson, 2004). Coaches' documentation of informal observations conducted systematically and regularly (e.g., Bean, 2004, pp. 106–111 may also provide valuable sources of classroom data.

3. Reading performance data, arguably the most important aspect of instructional decision making, may include standardized tests, criterion-referenced tests, informal classroom assessments, and student-work samples.

Taken together, these sources provide a rich data set for school teams to use in setting goals and devising action steps to improve literacy instruction within classrooms, across grade levels, and throughout schools.

Using the Framework

The Data Analysis Framework for Instructional Decision Making consists of guiding questions to assist school literacy team members in analyzing data, discussing the patterns and relationships within those data, and constructing interpretations that they can then translate into goals and action steps to improve reading and writing achievement (see Figure 1).

General procedures that may guide implementation of the Data Analysis Framework for Instructional Decision Making consist of the following five steps:

1. Organize the data set so that members of the literacy team can partner in analyzing different portions of the data set. Partnering allows for more than one set of eyes on the same data and provokes substantive discussion of individual observations.

2. Select a recorder for the team. The recorder takes notes on the team's discussion of the observations during step 4.

3. Partners analyze their data and each person jots down observations on his or her worksheet.

4. After sufficient time for partners to carefully analyze their data, the team "puts it all together" in a discussion of their findings (patterns in data) and interpretations (what the patterns show in terms of strengths and needs) and then devises professional development and school improvement goals and action steps.

5. The team plans when and how they will communicate the formative plan to other school personnel and stakeholders and monitors the implementation of their plan.

The example provided in Figure 2 illustrates the results of a school literacy team's use of the Data Analysis Framework for Instructional Decision Making. The school team example of a Put It All Together is a composite created from authentic samples of a literacy team's work. The literacy team members included the school-based literacy coach, principal, data manager, and grade-level teacher representatives in an elementary school.

Applications

The Data Analysis Framework for Instructional Decision Making may be applied in a variety of preK-12 educational settings. It can be easily modified to include other types of data collected outside of literacy including mathematics, science, or other subject areas. Its team approach allows for different educator groups to collaborate—teachers within and across grade levels and district-wide school improvement teams. The Data Analysis Framework

Professional development data

    1. What patterns do you observe in the professional development data?
    2. How do you explain the patterns you see in the data?

Classroom data

    1. What are some instructional strengths?
    2. What aspects of instruction show a need for improvement?
    3. What content and strategies are emphasized in the instruction?
    4. What content and strategies are not emphasized?
    5. How do you explain the patterns you see in the data?

Student data

    1. What patterns do you observe in the student data at the school level, grade level, and classroom level?
        a. Where is growth demonstrated?
        b. Is the growth equal across grades?
        c. Is the growth equal for all students?
        d. What are specific areas of strength?
        e. What are specific areas that need improvement?

    2. How do you explain the patterns you see in the data?

Put It All Together

    1. What connections can you make between professional development data, classroom data, and student data?
    2. What are the strengths and needs?
    3. What do the patterns mean for you in your role (e.g., literacy coach, principal, data manager, teacher)?
    4. What are the implications for change as you see them in your role?
    5. Overall, based on the analysis and findings, what are the professional development and school improvement goals?
    6. What action steps will you take to meet the goals?
    7. How will you communicate the improvement plan to other school personnel and stakeholders?

Figure 1   Worksheet for school teams using data analysis framework for instructional decision making

Put It All Together

What connections can you make between professional development data, classroom data, and student data?

Our data overall show that the professional development has helped to improve classroom instructional practices, and the student data shows stronger achievement. Coaching logs showed that the coaches are spending a large amount of time providing professional development in five areas (fluency, phonics, phonemic awareness, comprehension, and vocabulary) and not as much time on individual coaching. The teacher surveys showed strong use of research-based strategies presented at professional development, which may be related to higher Early Language and Literacy Classroom Observation (ELLCO) scores in approaches to curriculum integration, reading instruction, and presence of books. ELLCO scores for oral language facilitation are lower than other areas, and students scoring at or above grade level are not making good gains. This suggests a need for differentiated instruction. Our student data showed improvement over two years, and TerraNova results showed growth in two of three grade levels.

What are the strengths and needs?

Strengths:
Better alignment of curriculum to state indicators (based on Language Arts Curriculum Survey). The disaggregated data show growth for students scoring in the at-risk and some-risk categories. Teachers are using data.

Needs:
Improve instruction for students scoring at or above grade level. First-grade scores dropped at third benchmark so we need to look more closely at first-grade instruction.

What do the patterns mean for you in your role (e.g., literacy coach, principal, teacher, data manager)?

Literacy coach:
Based on my coaching log data, I need to spend more time in classrooms, work more with teachers on differentiating instruction, and follow up with teachers after progress monitoring.

(continued)

Figure 2   Example of a school literacy team's "Put It All Together" from the data analysis framework for instructional decision making

Principal:
I need to more frequently observe classroom instruction and provide feedback.

First-grade teacher:
I should identify specific areas of need for students reading below grade-level expectations and work with the coach to differentiate instruction in areas of need.

Data manager:
I need to stress progress monitoring for students reading at or above grade level more often.

What are the implications for change as you see them in your role?

We need to utilize our data to better plan instruction. We need to streamline interventions and make sure to address needs of students reading at or above grade level. Coaches need to spend more time in classrooms and conduct teaching demonstrations.

Overall, based on the analysis and findings, what are the professional development and school improvement goals?

Professional development goals:

1. Continue to analyze and use data
   - include data at beginning of professional development
   - take time to analyze data

2. Increase differentiated instruction
   - work with teachers to plan for small groups and target needs for instruction
   - continue to examine the content of reading instruction using data and identify specifics within the five areas to target—what we want students to know and be able to do
   - assist teachers with ways to monitor student performance and analyze student work

School goals:

1. Improve data use at classroom and school levels
   - schedule grade-level meetings for teachers to analyze data regularly
   - principal follows up with literacy coach on classroom instructional needs
   - principal schedules regular observations of instruction and provides feedback to teachers

2. Align curriculum, instructional resources, and instruction with student needs
   - use intervention specialists more with first grade
   - examine what's working in our intervention model and make changes as needed
   - examine the core reading program to see how it addresses what we need to teach more effectively

How will you communicate the plan to other school personnel and stakeholders?

At the opening-of-school meeting—principal, literacy coaches, and teachers share in a presentation of findings from the data analysis and communicate broad, school goals. Teachers on the school literacy team meet with grade-level colleagues to refine goals and develop two action steps. The grade-level facilitator records specific goals and action steps.

At the follow-up meeting of the school literacy team, the grade-level facilitators share plans and post them in the professional development classroom. All teachers post respective grade-level goals in classrooms in student-centered language. At regular meetings throughout the year, the school literacy team assesses progress in meeting the goals and monitors or adjusts the action steps accordingly.

Figure 2 Continued

for Instructional Decision Making is easily adapted to small or large teams who may modify the questions to suit local purposes and contexts. As with other collaborative processes, the utility of the framework is best judged by those who use it for its intended purpose—to support a systematic and thorough analysis of multiple sources of data to improve student learning and achievement.

References

Baumann, J.F., Hoffman, J.V., Duffy-Hester, A.M., & Ro, J.M. (2000). The First R yesterday and today: U.S. elementary reading instruction practices reported by teachers and administrators. *Reading Research Quarterly, 35,* 338–377.

Bean, R. (2004). *The reading specialist: Leadership for the classroom, school, and community.* New York: Guilford.

Center for Policy Research. (n.d.). *The language arts curriculum survey* (Unpublished document). Madison, WI: University of Wisconsin.

International Reading Association & National Council of Teachers of English. (1994). *Standards for the assessment of reading and writing.* Newark, DE; Urbana, IL: Authors.

Reilly, M.A. (2007). Choice of action: Using data to make instructional decisions in kindergarten. *The Reading Teacher, 60,* 770–776.

Shea, M., Murray, R., & Harlin, R. (2005). *Drowning in data? How to collect, organize, and document student performance.* Portsmouth, NH: Heinemann.

Smith, M., & Dickinson, D. (2002). *Early language and literacy classroom observation toolkit.* Baltimore: Brookes.

Stephens, D., Pearson, P.D., Gilrane, C., Roe, M., Stallman, A., Shelton, J., et al. (1995). Assessment and decision making in schools: A cross-site analysis. *Reading Research Quarterly, 30,* 478–499.

Wolfersberger, M.E., Reutzel, D.R., Sudweeks, R., & Fawson, P.C. (2004). Developing and validating the classroom literacy environment profile (CLEP): A tool for examining the "print richness" of early childhood and elementary classrooms. *Journal of Literacy Research, 36,* 211–272.

KOULDER MOKHTARI teaches at Miami University, Oxford, Ohio, USA; e-mail mokhtak@muohio.edu. CATHERINE A. ROSEMARY teaches at John Carroll University, University Heights, Ohio, USA. PATRICIA A. EDWARDS teaches at Michigan State University, East Lansing, USA.

From *The Reading Teacher,* December 2007/January 2008, pp. 354–359. Copyright © 2008 by International Reading Association. Reprinted by permission. www.reading.org

Answering the Questions That Count

Examining student data through the lens of pressing questions can mobilize staff, promote data literacy, and help raise student achievement.

DAVID RONKA ET AL.

Daily life in districts and schools requires educators to effectively navigate a sea of data: diagnostic and norm-referenced standardized assessment data, reading assessment data, state and local assessment data, in combination with other data related to instructional programs and demographic, attendance, and dropout trends. This new level of applied data use requires district and school administrators, teacher leaders, and classroom teachers to be data literate, that is, able to use multiple types of assessment and other data to inform decisions that lead to higher student achievement.

Despite the increased amounts of data available, many educators still feel ill prepared to analyze and use their school data effectively. They are data rich, but information poor. Our experiences working with data use in schools and districts have led us to define an effective framework for building data literacy. This framework is fueled by an essential-questions approach that organizes data use around a cycle of inquiry and is grounded in three core components of system wide data use: data quality, data capacity, and data culture.

The Essential-Questions Approach

A study on data use in several urban U.S. high schools showed that when school leaders used questions to focus the collaborative examination of data, school staff became more engaged in the process. When important questions drove the dialogue about school effectiveness, school staff quickly learned how to identify and use different types of data to answer those questions (Lachat & Smith, 2004).

Organizing data use around essential questions about student performance is a powerful strategy for building data literacy. Consider the following questions:

- How do student outcomes differ by demographics, programs, and schools?
- To what extent have specific programs, interventions, and services improved outcomes?
- What is the longitudinal progress of a specific cohort of students?
- What are the characteristics of students who achieve proficiency and of those who do not?
- Where are we making the most progress in closing achievement gaps?
- How do absence and mobility affect assessment results?
- How do student grades correlate with state assessment results and other measures?

Organizing data use around essential questions about student performance is a powerful strategy for building data literacy.

Asking questions such as these enables administrators and teachers to focus on what is most important, identify the data they need to address their questions, and use the questions as a lens for data analysis and interpretation. To avoid the common tendency to get lost in a long list of questions, district or school staff should, in general, identify no more than five or six crucial questions that get at the heart of what they need to know.

School staff should identify five or six crucial questions that get at the heart of what they need to know.

The essential-questions approach provides the fuel that drives collaborative analysis. But to use data purposefully and in a sustained way over time, schools and districts have to address three interrelated components of systemwide data use.

The essential-questions approach provides the fuel that drives collaborative analysis.

Data Quality

Teachers and administrators need to believe in the completeness and accuracy of the data they are expected to use. Data must be sufficiently disaggregated to address questions of concern, displayed in easy-to-understand formats, and available in a timely manner for instructional planning. The most effective way to ensure these conditions is to use technology that supports data disaggregation, provides data access, and generates useful data displays.

Research has emphasized that data disaggregation is essential to effective data use (Johnson, 2002; Lachat & Williams, 2003). Districts and schools are used to getting assessment data that are broadly disaggregated by gender or race/ethnicity. However, disaggregating assessment data by *combinations* of students' demographic characteristics (that is, race/ethnicity by gender or disability) and by the programs in which students are enrolled (that is, race/ethnicity by specific reading or mathematics programs) enables schools to examine the effectiveness of programs for specific groups of students. In addition, disaggregated data linking attendance, mobility, or course grades to assessment results are helpful when looking at the kinds of factors that may influence student performance.

Data-warehousing applications provide the deep disaggregation necessary for meaningful data use (Mieles & Foley, 2005; Wayman, Cho, & Johnston, 2007; Wayman, Stringfield, & Yakimowski, 2004); and midsize to large districts are increasingly using these applications. Researchers have also noted the importance of technology in creating data access and presenting data in useful formats (Mandinach & Honey, 2008; Rudner & Boston, 2003).

Although many schools we have worked with have some form of data-warehousing technology, training typically focuses on how to use the technology itself rather than on how to make meaning of the data. The essential-questions approach has helped educators recognize the power and potential of going beyond aggregated data to identify the data they need and when they need it and to define multiple ways of disaggregating the data.

What It Looks Like in Practice

Improving students' reading skills was a major issue for three high schools in an urban district in which the majority of students were below grade level in their reading assessment scores. Hispanic students—many of whom were English language learners—constituted more than one-half of the population in all three high schools; the percentage of low-income students ranged from 60 to 85 percent.

As part of a high school reform initiative, 10th grade English language arts teachers and literacy coaches worked with a data coach to define essential questions about students' reading performance. Teachers developed the following questions:

- How did students in each of my 10th grade course sections perform on the 9th grade reading vocabulary and reading comprehension assessment?
- Do some of my course sections have a higher proportion of students below grade level in reading skills?

- What is the variation in students' reading skills within each of my course sections?
- How can I meet the instructional needs of students with varying skill levels in reading?

The teachers' questions indicated that, on the standardized reading assessment, they wanted 9th grade vocabulary and comprehension subskill results disaggregated for each of the 10th grade English language arts course sections so teachers would have a profile of students' reading ability in their current classes.

Attempts to answer the questions revealed several data-quality issues:

- The schools had received aggregate total reading results rather than subskill results.
- Data for the 9th grade assessment were organized by the 9th grade homerooms in which the students took the test rather than by the 10th grade English teachers' classrooms in which the students were now enrolled.
- The high schools had no test results for students who had transferred from another high school in the district.
- The schools did not have a dissemination plan to get data to teachers on a timely schedule.

The district's high school reform initiative provided the stimulus and funds to address these data-quality issues. The district acquired technology services that used a data-warehousing application to disaggregate vocabulary and reading comprehension results by students' current course sections and to provide information about vocabulary subskills, including basic vocabulary, synonyms, words with multiple meanings, and use of context clues. The district's director of information services set up new data-verification procedures to ensure that high schools had complete records on transfer students, including assessment results. With the assistance of the data coach, school principals developed a dissemination plan that identified what data would be available and when, who would get the data, and how staff members might use it.

Addressing data quality and disaggregating data for different course sections meant that the 10th grade teachers could answer their essential questions about students currently in their classes. They learned that most students were below grade level in recognizing synonyms and determining meaning for words with multiple meanings but were at grade level or above in using context clues. This enabled teachers to target instruction to focus on word study and word analysis.

The classroom-level assessment data on students' reading skills also helped the literacy coaches answer the questions they had formulated:

- How much instructional support will teachers need for students below grade level in reading vocabulary and reading comprehension?
- How can I use reading subskill data profiles to analyze teachers' professional development needs?

The literacy coaches helped teachers learn instructional strategies that are particularly relevant to English language learners' needs. These included strategies for building vocabulary, helping students understand text structures, and using anticipation guides, graphic organizers, and think alouds. The focus on data continued beyond the reform initiative, and the disaggregated subskill reports became part of the core set of reports the district provided to these high schools.

The high school reform initiative also involved using data-warehousing technology to follow the progress of three cohorts of students from grade 9 to grade 11 on one particular subskill of the state assessment. All three cohorts showed some increases in the percentage of students achieving proficiency in this subskill and significant decreases in the percentage of students scoring at the lowest level of the assessment. Although these positive results can't be directly attributed to teachers' use of assessment data and targeted reading interventions, this focus most likely contributed to improving student performance.

Data Capacity

It's not enough to have high-quality data. Effective data use will not occur unless schools also address data capacity. Building data capacity means establishing data teams, designating data coaches, creating structured time in the school calendar for collaborative analysis, building staff skills in data analysis and assessment literacy, and displaying data in formats that facilitate inquiry and analysis (Boudett & Steele, 2007; Lachat & Smith, 2004; Love, Stiles, Mundry, & DiRanna, 2008).

It's important to ensure the broad representation that makes collaborative analysis meaningful. At the district level, representation should include leadership in curriculum and instruction, the elementary and secondary levels, special programs, student personnel services, research and assessment, and student information services. School teams should include the principal and other instructional leaders, personnel from the guidance department, and grade-level or subject-area teacher representatives. Schedule time for collaborative analysis at key data points, such as when pertinent assessment or quarterly data on attendance and course grade patterns become available. This enables schools to define an annual schedule of when data teams will do their analysis and improvement planning. Using a data coach as a facilitator is an effective strategy for providing an embedded form of professional development to enhance the data teams' skills and assessment literacy.

What It Looks Like in Practice

Many of the schools and districts we have worked with want to go beyond trend data in their analysis of student progress. One urban district in the northeastern United States specifically focused on building the skills of both district and school data teams to analyze multiple types of assessment data. The district used data-warehousing technology to disaggregate longitudinal data that addressed the teams' questions about the performance of different student subgroups. Their analysis of the data led the teams to define questions about the progress of cohorts of students as they moved from one grade to the next. The team

particularly wanted to focus on whether early elementary students were improving their proficiency levels in vocabulary as measured by the reading assessment that all the elementary schools used.

The team explored the data through the lens of the following essential questions:

- Are our students making sufficient grade-to-grade progress in vocabulary development?
- How many of our lowest-performing students on last year's vocabulary assessment improved their proficiency level on this year's assessment?
- What are the characteristics of students who made progress and of those who did not?
- What percentage of students at grade level on a previous year's assessment declined in their performance?
- Do the data indicate that teachers need more training to improve students' vocabulary skills?

Participants discussed how to visually represent the data in displays that would facilitate analysis. We have found that graphic displays created to address one or more essential questions are the most useful. The display shown in Figure 1, for example, enables viewers to examine the grade 3 performance in vocabulary of students who scored at each of three performance levels in that skill in grade 2.

Data capacity was crucial to this district's process of inquiry. The district leadership established and trained district- and school-level data teams, allotted time to engage in collaborative analysis, and made available meaningful data displays driven by essential questions. Ultimately, educators in this district were able to go beyond the superficial (and often inaccurate) conclusions of trend analysis and identify the specific effects of current programming. This enabled the district to target areas in which additional resources were needed to improve instruction. Responses included having reading coaches focus their work with teachers on modeling intensive reading interventions for low-performing students, providing more direct support in teachers' classrooms for struggling students, and establishing more consistent monitoring procedures to determine the success of interventions.

Data Culture

Achieving purposeful and sustained data use necessitates a culture shift. It requires paying deliberate attention to issues of leadership, policy, accountability, shared beliefs, and collaboration (Boudett & Steele, 2007; Firestone & Gonzalez, 2007). This entails establishing and providing leadership direction to data teams, modeling effective data use, scheduling time for collaborative data-driven conversations, and connecting data analysis to clear action steps. Holcomb (1999) compellingly wrote about the importance of mobilizing broad stakeholder involvement and getting people excited about data use. She refers to this as focusing "people, passion, and proof" on strategically aligning all elements of a school to analyze what is and isn't working to improve student learning.

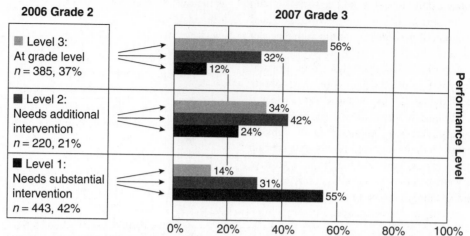

Grade 2 to Grade 3 Progress on Reading Vocabulary Test
N = 1,038

On the vocabulary assessment, 55% of students at Level 1 stayed at this level, and 45% improved; 42% at Level 2 stayed at this level; 34% improved, and 24% declined; 56% at Level 3 stayed at this level, and 44% declined.

Figure 1 Are our students making sufficient Grade-to-Grade progress.

What It Looks Like in Practice

A small rural district had the following questions about the literacy habits and skills of its middle and high school students:

- How do the reading levels of our students compare with those of students across the state?
- How many of our middle and high school students read below grade level?
- Will improving students' reading skills positively affect their performance in core courses and on state and local assessments?
- What are we doing to support accelerated growth in reading for students below grade level?

Our work in this district engaged administrators, teachers, and reading specialists in a data-collection process built on the belief that improving student literacy was everyone's responsibility and that addressing the issue required a commitment to using data for improvement. The data-collection process, which occurred over the course of a few months, brought together student performance data, teacher survey data, and data on school capacity to support literacy. A school-based literacy team facilitated both the data-collection and the data-reporting/data-use processes. When juxtaposed with information about school capacity, the data showed that neither the middle school nor the high school had an effective way to address the needs of the sizeable number of students who read below grade level.

For example, teachers said that many students were unable to analyze what they read, did not like to write, responded to questions with incomplete answers, and had difficulty learning vocabulary. The majority of teachers reported that they did not use several instructional strategies that might address these issues, such as those relating to student choice, student inquiry, the use of technology and varied texts, and student discussion of text materials and what they have learned.

Recommendations included having teachers learn some common instructional strategies targeted to vocabulary development; motivating students to read and write in the content-area classroom through the use of collaborative routines, such as reciprocal teaching and paired reading and summarizing; and teaching students how to think critically when reading and writing. We also recommended that teachers learn a common protocol for looking at student work and that the middle and high school each form a literacy team to support implementation of the literacy improvement initiative.

Other issues emerged during the data-collection process. For example, teachers at the middle school level used three different reading assessments and lacked common protocols for testing. This made it difficult to track student progress. The high school had no system in place to determine the reading proficiency of incoming 9th graders. Despite the clear need, no interventions were available for struggling readers in grades 6–8, and few teachers or administrators in the middle and high schools regularly used existing data about student performance for placement, instructional decision making, or progress monitoring.

In response to our recommendations, the district took several steps that deepened data use at both the district and school levels. The district researched and selected a reading assessment for grades 6–10 that provided subskill reading performance data, including information about vocabulary and nonfiction reading comprehension. This enabled the district to monitor the progress of student cohorts, including those enrolled in intervention classes. At the middle school level, teachers learned protocols for looking at student work and met with students to set reading progress goals. School leaders communicated the expectation that teachers would use the new reading assessment data to determine what types of literacy support needed to occur in content-area classes.

The data-based recommendations led to targeted professional development for the faculty. In the first year, professional development focused on vocabulary-development strategies, instructional strategies to promote engagement and critical thinking in reading and writing, and a common set of instructional strategies to improve reading comprehension. Teachers in some departments began an in-depth look at the literacy demands of their content areas and started to develop common agreements about what they expected students to be able to do.

In the second year, professional development focused on how teachers might promote reading and writing for authentic reasons within and across content areas. A group of teachers began to engage in peer coaching, collecting data on one another's practice and sharing evidence about how specific strategies supported improved teaching and learning. The principal and vice principal conducted literacy walk-throughs to determine the effectiveness of professional development, and teachers received feedback on what was happening in classrooms schoolwide. According to staff, this combination of approaches contributed to gains in student reading achievement at the 6th, 7th, and 8th grade levels for the following two years.

Using data, which teachers and administrators can access online, is now an integral part of the culture in this district. Data use determines professional development needs, intervention requirements, and resource allocation; it focuses discussions about teaching and learning, guides teacher instruction, and monitors progress. Most important, teachers and administrators have a shared belief about its value.

The Data Difference

Schools and districts of all sizes can use the essential-questions approach to become data-driven decision makers focused on improving student learning and achievement. Properly used, data can make a difference in meeting the needs of every student and can be a powerful ally in stimulating positive change and improvement from the central office to the classroom.

References

Boudett, K. P., & Steele, J. L. (Eds.). (2007). *Data wise in action.* Cambridge, MA: Harvard Education Press.

Firestone, W. A., & Gonzalez, R. A. (2007). Culture and processes affecting data use in school districts. In P. A. Moss (Ed.), *Evidence and decision making: The 106th yearbook of the National Society for the Study of Education, Part I* (pp. 132–154). Malden, MA: Blackwell.

Holcomb, E. L. (1999). *Getting excited about data: How to combine people, passion, and proof.* Thousand Oaks, CA: Corwin Press

Johnson, R. (2002). *Using data to close the achievement gap: How to measure equity in our schools* (1st ed.). Thousand Oaks, CA: Corwin Press.

Lachat, M., & Smith, S. (2004). *Data use in urban high schools.* Providence, RI: Education Alliance at Brown University.

Lachat, M., & Williams, M. (2003). Putting student performance data at the center of school reform. In J. DiMartino, J. Clark, & D. Wolk (Eds.), *Personalized learning* (pp. 210–228). Lanham, MD: Scarecrow Press.

Love, N., Stiles, K. E., Mundry, S., & DiRanna, K. (2008). *A data coach's guide to improving learning for all students: Unleashing the power of collaborative inquiry.* Thousand Oaks, CA: Corwin Press.

Mandinach, E. B., & Honey, M. (Eds.). (2008). *Data-driven school improvement: Linking data and learning.* New York: Teachers College Press.

Mieles, T., & Foley, E. (2005). *From data to decisions: Lessons from school districts using data warehousing.* Providence, RI: Annenberg Institute for School Reform at Brown University.

Rudner, L. M., & Boston, C. (2003). Data warehousing: Beyond disaggregation. *Educational Leadership, 60*(5), 62–65.

Wayman, J. C., Cho, V., & Johnston, M. T. (2007). *The data-informed district: A district-wide evaluation of data use in the Natrona County School District.* Austin: University of Texas.

Wayman, J. C., Stringfield, S., & Yakimowski, M. (2004). *Software enabling school improvement through analysis of student data* (Report No. 67). Baltimore: Johns Hopkins University, Center for Research on the Education of Students Placed at Risk.

David Ronka (dronka@pcgus.com) is Executive Director; **Mary Ann Lachat** (mlachat@pcgus.com) is Cofounder and Senior Consultant; **Rachel Slaughter** (rslaughter@pcgus.com) is Senior Associate for Research and Assessment; and **Julie Meltzer** (jmeltzer@pcgus.com) is Senior Advisor for Strategy, Research, and Design at Public Consulting Group's Center for Resource Management, an organization that has worked with states, districts, and schools to improve data use; 200 International Drive, Suite 201, Portsmouth, NH 03801; 603-427-0206.

UNIT 6

Communication, Grading, and Reporting

Unit Selections

Key Points to Consider

- After reading *Feedback that Fits* by Susan Brookhart, discuss these two questions: "How much feedback should be given?" and "Which method is the best way to provide feedback: written or verbal?"

- What is the difference between praise and effective feedback?

- What are some effective ways to communicate student progress and student shortcomings?

- Is it possible that feedback can make students more dependent rather than contributing to independency?

- Does a single measurement represent student learning?

- Do current grading practices hinder or interfere with learning?

- Why and how do we grade?

- How can teachers design reporting systems to truly reflect the measure of students' knowledge?

- Define the term feedback.

- Identify a set of criteria for providing feedback to students.

- Analyze a selection of student work and discuss appropriate feedback statements that will foster cognitive engagement and motivation.

- Compare grading systems from different classrooms and school districts.

- Identify strategies for conducting a parent-teacher conference.

- Plan a mock parent-teacher conference.

- Interview different teachers about their grading practices and write a personal philosophy about grading.

- Examine the guidelines listed in the article, *Partnerships for Learning: Conferencing with Families* by Holly Seplocha and plan a conference schedule.

Student Website

www.mhcls.com

Internet References

GradeConnect
http://www.gradeconnect.com/front/index.php
Engrade
http://www.engrade.com/

Scholastic: Communicating with Parents and Families
http://www2.scholastic.com/browse/parentsHome.jsp
Education World
http://www.education-world.com/a_curr/strategy/strategy046.shtml
National Parent-Teacher Association
http://www.pta.org/

Teachers communicate with a variety of individuals: students, families, other educators, administrators and staff, and public officials. Communicating effectively on matters of student assessment requires teachers to know and use assessment and evaluation terminology appropriately and to articulate issues and decisions. They explain plans and processes for collecting assessment information, the interpretation of data results, and how the results are used to promote student achievement. Student learning is the primary purpose for assessment and evaluation and clear communication helps to facilitate the process.

Communication with Learners

When the purpose of assessment is to promote learning, students want to be informed of their progress. It is natural that a student is interested in knowing "How well did I do?" Conversely, teachers should be eager to provide students with an explanation. Information directed towards helping to guide student learning is known as **feedback.** Educators use the term **feedback** to refer to "the descriptive information given to students that emphasizes their strengths and weaknesses of a performance." The informational nature of feedback appears to be the most critical factor so far as the support of learning is concerned. When learners are given detailed, descriptive, value-free information of what was done well, or how to improve current skills or correct misconceptions, or both, then they can self-adjust.

Effective feedback is at the core of learning. The aim is to keep the student engaged, motivated, and eager to know how to improve. Through teacher explanations, the "Oh, yes, that's right." confirmation/understanding occurs. Educators call this the "Ah, Ah," moment. Once students understand, they are interested in knowing "Is there an easier way?" and "How do I get better?" Other times, a student will struggle and need lots of direction and encouragement. Teachers like to give praise. Hearing the phrase, "Good Job," or "Excellent Work" provides the student with acknowledgment. Yet those simple words do not help the student to improve academically. Feedback information is detailed and value-free knowledge directed towards the successful elements of the task, as well as the errors that need to be corrected, encourages students to analyze their work and think about how they can get better (Grunlund, 1998). When students have a desire to improve, they are motivated to learn. Appropriately given, feedback has motivational and self-assessment implications.

Communication with Families

Families need to be encouraged to be involved as active participants in the assessment process. Research has shown that there is a relationship between student success and family involvement. Children whose parents/guardians assist in their learning by reading to them, helping with homework, supervising their activities, and staying informed and involved in school

© Image Source/Alamy

matters have a tendency to perform better academically than children who are unsupervised or left home alone. Family involvement in education has changed over time: from a perspective of parents as primary educators, to parents as responsible members for their children's success.

Communication and participation are closely related. When school personnel send a message that family involvement is welcome, a reciprocal partnership may form. Families have important information they can share about their children and can provide support with disciplinary problems, while teachers can explain what takes place in the classroom. Keeping families informed is the best way to ensure involvement.

Written messages, phone calls, electronic communication systems, and personal conferences are just a few of the ways schools can remain in contact with families. Today electronic communication technologies make it easy to communicate and collaborate with families and extend the learning community beyond the classroom. For example, school districts can maintain course management systems that enable families to retrieve children's grades, check homework assignments, and keep abreast of important activities and events. Webpages, wikis, and blogs provide generic information and allow families to share ideas and opinions.

Face to face conferences make it possible to share evidence of student learning, to understand families' perspectives about learning, and to plan ways to work cooperatively together. Key components of the face-to-face conference are making parents feel comfortable, encouraging their participation in the schooling of their children, and helping them understand accountability issues. There is a need to establish strong school-family partnerships that value different cultures, different family structures, and different ways of knowing. Educators need to recognize that all children can succeed with mutual support and a commitment to student learning. See this website for more information about parental involvement http://www.ed.gov/parents/academic/involve/nclbguide/parentsguide.html.

Grading and Reporting

Grading and reporting systems serve primarily to communicate student progress. However, grades are useful for making instructional and curriculum decisions. Grading and reporting student progress is one of the most complex tasks that teachers are required to do. There are so many factors that one must consider when establishing a grading practice. Careful thought and planning prior to collecting evidence of student learning will make the task easier. Establishing a systematic method for collecting evidence of student learning and ways to record the information will also streamline the complex task. Communication of student competence relies on a seamless alignment among the instructional goals (standards), the assessment strategies, and the interpretation of the evidence of student learning. If goals are clearly defined in performance terms, the assessment strategy properly chosen, and the evidence correctly interpreted, then reporting becomes a matter of summarizing the data results and communicating the outcomes to the student, families, and administrators. The complexity of the task lies in presenting the information concisely and understandably.

The *No Child Left Behind Act of 2001* requires states and school districts to provide an easy to read, detailed reporting system that informs families whether their children are succeeding and why. States are required to publish data about student achievement disaggregated by race, ethnicity, gender, English language proficiency, migrant status, disabilities status, and low-income status, as well as the teacher's professional qualifications. See this website for more information about assessment and accountability, http://www.ed.gov/policy/elsec/guid/states/index.html.

The articles in this section focus on asking important questions about feedback, communicating with students and parents/guardians, and grading practices. These articles were chosen to help educators learn about these processes as well as to stimulate discussions.

The first article introduces feedback, a method of informing students about their learning. To foster engagement of the reader, the author asks the following questions, "How much feedback should be given?" and "Which method is the best way to provide feedback: written or verbal?"

The next set of articles present information focused on school-family connections. Articles present a variety of information focused on ways to conduct successful conferences, issues to consider prior to having a conference, and alternative ideas for conducting conferences.

The last four articles focus on grading and reporting systems. Three important questions authors pose are "Do current grading practices hinder or interfere with learning?", "Why and how do we grade?", and "How can teachers design reporting systems to truly reflect the measure of students' knowledge?" All three questions emphasize a common concern with practices teachers use for collecting data for grades and the process for reporting student progress.

Feedback That Fits

**To craft teacher feedback that leads to learning,
put yourself in the student's shoes.**

SUSAN M. BROOKHART

From the student's point of view, the ideal "script" for formative assessment reads something like, "Here is how close you are to the knowledge or skills you are trying to develop, and here's what you need to do next." The feedback teachers give students is at the heart of that script. But feedback is only effective when it translates into a clear, positive message that students can hear.

Student Understanding and Control

The power of formative assessment lies in its double-barreled approach, addressing both cognitive and motivational factors. Good formative assessment gives students information they need to understand where they are in their learning (the cognitive factor) and develops students' feelings of control over their learning (the motivational factor).

The power of formative assessment lies in its double-barreled approach, addressing both cognitive and motivational factors.

Precisely because students' feelings of self-efficacy are involved, however, even well-intentioned feedback can be very destructive if the student reads the script in an unintended way ("See, I knew I was stupid!"). Research on feedback shows its Jekyll-and-Hyde character. Not all studies of feedback show positive effects; the nature of the communication matters a great deal.

Recently, researchers have tried to tease out what makes some feedback effective, some ineffective, and some downright harmful (Butler & Winne, 1995; Hattie & Timperley, 2007; Kluger & DeNisi, 1996). Other researchers have described the characteristics of effective feedback (Johnston, 2004; Tunstall & Gipps, 1996). From parsing this research and reflecting on my own experience as an educational consultant working with elementary and secondary teachers on assessment issues, particularly the difference between formative assessment and grading, I have identified what makes for powerful feedback—in terms of how teachers deliver it and the content it contains.

Good feedback contains information that a student can use. That means, first, that the student has to be able to hear and understand it. A student can't hear something that's beyond his comprehension, nor can a student hear something if she's not listening or if she feels like it's useless to listen. The most useful feedback focuses on the qualities of student work or the processes or strategies used to do the work. Feedback that draws students' attention to their self-regulation strategies or their abilities as learners is potent if students hear it in a way that makes them realize they will get results by expending effort and attention.

Following are suggestions for the most effective ways to deliver feedback and the most effective content of feedback. Notice that all these suggestions are based on knowing your students well. There is no magic bullet that will be just right for all students at all times.

Effective Ways to Deliver Feedback
When to Give Feedback

If a student is studying facts or simple concepts—like basic math—he or she needs immediate information about whether an answer is right or wrong—such as the kind of feedback flash cards give. For learning targets that develop over time, like writing or problem solving, wait until you have observed patterns in student work that provide insights into how they are doing the work, which will help you make suggestions about next steps. A general principle for gauging the timing of feedback is to put yourself in the student's place. When would a student want to hear feedback? When he or she is still thinking about the work, of course. Its also a good idea to give feedback as often as is practical, especially for major assignments.

How Much Feedback?

Probably the hardest decision concerns the *amount* of feedback. A natural inclination is to want to "fix" everything you see. That's the teachers-eye view, where the target is perfect achievement of all learning goals. Try to see things from the student's-eye view. On which aspects of the learning target has the student done good work? Which aspects of the learning goals need improvement and should be addressed next? Are any assignments coming up that would make it wiser to emphasize one point over another? Consider also students' developmental level.

What Mode Is Best?

Some kinds of assignments lend themselves better to written feedback (for example, reviewing written work); some to oral feedback (observing as students do math problems); and some to demonstrations (helping a kindergarten student hold a pencil correctly). Some of the best feedback results from conversations with the student. Peter Johnston's (2004) book *Choice Words* discusses how to ask questions that help students help you provide feedback. For example, rather than telling the student all the things you notice about his or her work, start by asking, "What are you noticing about this? Does anything surprise you?" or "Why did you decide to do it this way?"

You should also decide whether individual or group feedback is best. Individual feedback tells a student that you value his or her learning, whereas group feedback provides opportunities for wider reteaching. These choices are not mutually exclusive. For example, say many students used bland or vague terms in a writing assignment. You might choose to give the whole class feedback on their word choices, with examples of how to use precise or vivid words, and follow up with thought-provoking questions for individual students, such as, "What other words could you use instead of *big*?" or "How could you describe this event so someone else would see how terrible it was for you?"

The Best Content for Feedback

Composing feedback is a skill in itself. The choices you make on *what* you say to a student will, of course, have a big influence on how the student interprets your feedback. Again, the main principle is considering the student's perspective.

Composing feedback is a skill in itself.

Focus on Work and Process

Effective feedback describes the students work, comments on the process the student used to do the work, and makes specific suggestions for what to do next. General praise ("Good job!") or personal comments don't help. The student might be pleased you approve, but not sure what was good about the work, and so unable to replicate its quality. Process-focused comments, on the other hand, give suggestions that move the work closer to the target, such as, "Can you rewrite that sentence so it goes better with the one before it?"

Relate Feedback to the Goal

For feedback to drive the formative assessment cycle, it needs to describe where the student is in relation to the learning goal. In so doing, it helps each student decide what his or her next goal should be. Feedback that helps a student see his or her own progress gives you a chance to point out the processes or methods that successful students use. ("I see you checked your work this time. Your computations were all correct, too! See how well that works?") Self-referenced feedback about the work itself ("Did you notice you have all the names capitalized this time?") is helpful for struggling students, who need to understand that they *can* make progress as much as they need to understand how far they are from the ultimate goal.

Try for Description, Not Judgment

Certain students are less likely to pay attention to descriptive feedback if it is accompanied by a formal judgment, like a grade or an evaluative comment. Some students will even hear judgment where you intend description. Unsuccessful learners have sometimes been so frustrated by their school experiences that they might see every attempt to help them as just another declaration that they are "stupid." For these learners, point out improvements over their previous performance, even if those improvements don't amount to overall success on the assignment. Then select one or two small, doable next steps. After the next round of work, give the student feedback on his or her success with those steps, and so on.

Be Positive and Specific

Being positive doesn't mean being artificially happy or saying work is good when it isn't. It means describing how the strengths in a students work match the criteria for good work and how they show what that student is learning. And it means choosing words that communicate respect for the student and the work. Your tone should indicate that you are making helpful suggestions and giving the student a chance to take the initiative. ("This paper needs more detail. You could add more explanation about the benefits of recycling, or you could add more description of what should be done in your neighborhood. Which suggestion do you plan to try first?") If feedback comes across as a lecture or suggestions come across as orders, students will not understand that they are in charge of their own learning.

Feedback should be specific enough that the student knows what to do next, but not so specific that you do the work. Identifying errors or types of errors is a good idea, but correcting every error doesn't leave the student anything to do.

These feedback principles apply to both simple and complex assignments, and to all subjects and grade levels. The following example of ineffective and, especially, effective feedback on a writing assignment reflects these principles in practice.

A Tale of Two Feedback Choices

As part of a unit on how to write effective paragraphs, a 4th grade teacher assigned her students to write a paragraph answering the question, "Do dogs or cats make better pets?" They were asked to have a clear topic sentence, a clear concluding sentence, and at least three supporting details. Figure 1 shows what a student named Anna wrote and what *ineffective* teacher feedback on Anna's paragraph might look like.

To provide feedback, this teacher decided to make written comments on each student's paper and return the papers to students the day after they turned them in. So far, so good. However, the feedback in Figure 1 is all about the mechanics of writing. This doesn't match the learning target for this assignment, which was to structure a paragraph to make a point and to have that point contained in a topic sentence. Because the mechanical corrections are the only comments, the message seems to be that Anna's next step is to fix those errors. However, this teacher has already fixed the errors for her. All Anna has to do is recopy this paragraph. Moreover, there is no guarantee she would understand why some words and punctuation marks were changed. Recopying by rote could result in a "perfect" paragraph with no learning involved!

~~This is why~~ I like dogs better than cats. I think dogs are really playful. They can also be strong to pull you or something. They can come in diff(erent) sizes like a Great Dane or a ~~Wener dog~~ (Dachshund). They can also be in diff(erent) colors. Some are just mut(t)s, others are pedigree. Best of all dogs are cute and cuddly. That is why I like dogs a lot better than cats.

Figure 1 Ineffective Feedback on Anna's Writing Assignment.

The worst part about this feedback, however, is that it doesn't communicate to Anna that she did, in fact, demonstrate the main paragraphing skills that were the learning target. Anna successfully fashioned a topic sentence and a concluding sentence and provided supporting details. She needs to understand that she has accomplished this. Once she knows that, suggestions about how to make her good work even better make sense.

Figure 2 lists *effective* comments a teacher might write on Anna's paper or, preferably (because there is more to say than a teacher might want to write or a 4th grader might want to read), discuss with her in a brief conference. A teacher would probably use a few—but not all—of these comments, depending on circumstances.

Notice that these comments first compare the student's work with the criteria for the assignment, which were aligned with the learning goal. They acknowledge that Anna's paragraph shows that she understands how to produce a topic sentence, supporting details, and a concluding sentence.

The rest of the feedback choices depends on the context. How much time is available to discuss this paper? Which other feedback comments would align with learning targets that have previously been emphasized in class? Which of the possible next steps would be most beneficial for this particular student, given her previous writing? For example, if Anna is a successful writer who likes writing, she probably already knows that describing traits she has observed in her own dog was a good strategy. If she has previously been an unsuccessful writer but has produced a paragraph better than her usual work—because the assignment finally asked a question about which she has

Possible Teacher Comments	What's Best About This Feedback
Your topic sentence and concluding sentence are clear and go together well. You used a lot of details. I count seven different things you like about dogs.	These comments describe achievement in terms of the criteria for the assignment. They show the student that you noticed these specific features and connected them to the criteria for good work.
Your paragraph makes me wonder if you have a dog who is playful, strong, cute, and cuddly. Did you think about your own dog to write your paragraph? When you write about things you know, the writing often sounds real like this.	This comment would be especially useful for a student who had not previously been successful with the writing process. The comment identifies the strategy the student has used for writing and affirms that it was a good one. Note that "the writing often sounds genuine" might be better English, but "real" is probably clearer for this 4th grader.
Your reasons are all about dogs. Readers would already have to know what cats are like. They wouldn't know from your paragraph whether cats are playful, for instance. When you compare two things, write about both of the things you are comparing.	This constructive feedback criticizes a specific feature of the work, explains the reason for the criticism, and suggests what to do about it.
Did you check your spelling? See if you can find two misspelled words. Feedback about making the topic sentence a stronger lead might best be done as a demonstration. In conference, show the student the topic sentence with and without "This is why" and ask which sentence she thinks reads more smoothly and why. Ask whether "This is why" adds anything that the sentence needs. You might point out that these words read better in the concluding sentence.	These comments about style and mechanics do not directly reflect the learning target, which was about paragraphing. However, they concern important writing skills. Their appropriateness would depend on how strongly spelling, style/usage, and word choice figure into the longer-term learning targets.

Figure 2 Examples of Effective Feedback on Anna's Writing Assignment.

something to say—it would be worth communicating to her that you noticed and naming "write about what you know" as a good strategy for future writing.

Feedback Practice Makes Perfect

Feedback choices present themselves continually in teaching. You have opportunities to give feedback as you observe students do their work in class and again as you look at the finished work. Take as many opportunities as you can to give students positive messages about how they are doing relative to the learning targets and what might be useful to do next. Make as many opportunities as you can to talk with your students about their work. As you do, you will develop a repertoire of feedback strategies that work for your subject area and students. The main thing to keep in mind when using any strategy is how students will hear, feel, and understand the feedback.

Make as many opportunities as you can to talk with your students about their work.

References

Butler, D. L., & Winne, P. H. (1995). Feedback and self-regulated learning: A theoretical synthesis. *Review of Educational Research, 65,* 245–281.

Hattie, J., & Timperley, H. (2007). The power of feedback. *Review of Educational Research, 77,* 81–112.

Johnston, R H. (2004). *Choice words. How our language affects children's learning.* Portland, ME: Stenhouse.

Kluger, A. N., & DeNisi, A. (1996). The effects of feedback interventions on performance: A historical review, a metaanalysis, and a preliminary feedback intervention theory. *Psychological Bulletin, 119,* 254–284.

Tunstall, R, & Gipps, C. (1996). Teacher feedback to young children in formative assessment: A typology. *British Educational Research Journal, 22,* 389–404.

Susan M. Brookhart is an educational consultant and Senior Research Associate at the Center for Advancing the Study of Teaching and Learning (CASTL) at Duquesne University in Pittsburgh, Pennsylvania. She is the author of the upcoming (Fall 2008) ASCD book, *How to Give Good Feedback;* susan brookhart@commatbresnan.net.

Developing Teacher-Parent Partnerships across Cultures: Effective Parent Conferences

LuAnn Jordan et al.

The rich cultural diversity of today's special education programs challenges traditional patterns of communication between schools and families. This diversity demands the implementation of communication patterns sensitive to all parents, but particularly to those responding to culture and ability differences. To address these demands, teachers first face the challenge of becoming aware of the personal beliefs, values, and expectations that guide their interactions with others. Second, they need to enhance communication with all families by using culturally responsive interaction practices. This article addresses teachers' challenges in the context of productive teacher-parent conferences because such conferences represent the most common means of family-school communication and offer a building block for teacher-parent partnerships.

Teachers' efforts to engage in culturally sensitive relationships with parents are certainly well intentioned. However, misconceptions are perpetuated by lack of knowledge and experience about culturall.y sensitive interactions (Burstein & Cabello, 1989). A lack of appropriate experience may diminish the effectiveness of interactions, such as those that occur in teacher-parent conferences. However, if the proper groundwork is laid to create a welcoming environment for parents and students, and if appropriate interaction practices are used, educators can encourage a level of parental involvement that will benefit students academically and socially.

Successful parent conferences can lead to positive communication between school and home (Kroth & Edge, 1997). This communication is important in homes from a variety of cultures. In the potentially stressful situation of some parent conferences, such as a conference to share diagnosis of a disability or information about learning or behavior problems, effective conference skills can provide support to families and encourage an atmosphere of collaboration.

This article provides general guidelines for enhancing teacher-parent conferences with parents of diverse cultures.

These guidelines will help teachers minimize misinterpretations and maximize possibilities for partnerships. Examples from a hypothetical conference are used to illustrate points of concern. Suggestions for ensuring that parent conferences become valuable tools for teachers, parents, and students are provided. The family used in the example is a Latino family as this population represents the fastest growing and largest minority group in the nation (Chapa & Valencia, 1993).

The guidelines presented are appropriate for any teacher conference. Moreover, the use of these guidelines is critical when one is building partnerships with families of diverse backgrounds. It is tempting to provide a list of recommendations for distinct ethnic groups (e.g., Asian, Latino, African American), but this approach is detrimental because such a list may contribute to stereotypic perceptions that blur the uniqueness of each family. Furthermore, it is important to address the inter- and intracultural variations that provide richness to each family system. These variations may result from differences in families' level of education, socioeconomic status, years in the United States, language proficiency, pattern of migration, degree of acculturation, geographical location, religious beliefs, and/or occupation (Fish, 1990; Herrera & Wooden, 1988). Thus, in the present article, distinctions among various cultures have not been overlooked. Rather, emphasis has been placed on general culturally responsive guidelines, rather than cultural specifics. The following guidelines are aimed to foster positive teacher-parent relationships, particularly with parents of diverse cultural backgrounds.

Guidelines Using a Variety of Conferencing Styles

Conferences with parents are appropriate and necessary throughout the school year. In general, there are two types of conferences: casual and purposeful. The casual conference provides the opportunity of exchanging information and building rapport in an informal setting. The purposeful conference, on the other hand, is more formal, with a specific goal and in a structured environment. In both types of conferences, it is important for the teacher to be sensitive and respond adequately to diversity among parents and to encourage an accepting climate for interaction.

Casual Conferences

Throughout the year, an ongoing exchange of information occurs between educator and parents. This type of conference is unscheduled and is characterized by informal "chats." Although casual conferences can be conducted at school, they often take place over the telephone or in a public place such as during an accidental meeting in the grocery store.

Through casual conferences, information is shared and participants build rapport on the basis of increased knowledge and understanding of one another. By connecting with parents early, the educator can more successfully engage family involvement. The rapport that develops over time prepares participants for more formal conferences when the need arises.

Casual conferences also serve other agendas, some of which are significant in working with culturally different families. For example, educators have opportunities to learn not only about the child's interests and abilities but also about the family's culture and how it is transmitted to the children in the family (Harry, 1992a). The educator can assess and promote parental and/or family involvement in the schooling process.

Purposeful Conferences

Purposeful conferences are used when the parent and educator have a particular topic, such as academic progress, behavior, or Individualized Education Program (IEP) changes, to discuss. The factor that determines the success of this interaction is the educator's preparation for the conference.

An early introductory contact on the part of the teacher can lay a positive foundation for a more formal interaction later on. Before teachers request parent conferences, they should determine the best avenues for communicating with parents. Multiple methods should be used to ensure communication (e.g., letters, phone calls, informal notes), especially if language differences are a concern. Teachers should also determine which language is best to use in messages and find resources to help them translate communication to and from parents. Regular communication through feedback on student work, newsletters, and invitations to visit the classroom establish a tone of openness in communication that sets the groundwork for formal conferences.

Both parents should be invited to the conference, and other significant members of the extended family may also be included. Some families may have an extended family network whose members may play an important role in the child's development (Hurtado, 1995). Extended family members also represent an important source of family support.

The teacher must allot an adequate amount of time for the conference. Adequate time for meeting permits the teacher and parents to establish common ground. Although unexpected events may interfere with conferences and scheduling, the teacher should do everything possible to keep focused on the student's concerns. The quantity and quality of time devoted to the conference shows the parent how important the issue is to the teacher.

Prepare for the Conference

When team building between parents and professionals occurs, a sense of connection between home and school is created for the child. Unfortunately, many parents may feel vulnerable or uncomfortable around teachers and other education professionals. Thus, they may have concerns about their own relationships with school or staff members in addition to their concern for their child's experiences (Katz, 1994).

To enhance the development of teacher-parent partnerships, educators must first be aware of their own attitudes toward persons from other cultures. This self-awareness is necessary before teachers can communicate effectively with culturally diverse parents (Lynch, 1992). Educators' awareness and appreciation of cultural differences are reflected in their interactions with parents. Just as teachers learn how to design classrooms and implement curricula to reflect and value diversity (Jordan, Peel, & Peel, 1993), so they must acquire skills to effectively interact and communicate with parents of diverse cultures.

Teachers should explore their own preconceived ideas resulting from their own cultural background. Teachers' expectations may affect the success of teacher-parent communication, and the quality of teacher-parents partnerships. Teachers, like most people, relate more easily to those they see as being similar to themselves. Thus, cultural differences between the teacher and parents may affect interactions at both informal and formal levels. Furthermore, many preservice teachers expect to teach students who are much like themselves when they were in school (Kagan, 1992). Our increasingly diverse culture makes this "sameness" situation unlikely and requires teachers to consider several things.

Concept of Family and Family Roles

When teachers are working with parents of diverse cultures and families of students with disabilities, it is important for them to consider their perceptions of family roles within the culture, including the roles of extended family members. Family roles should not be judged based only on personal experience or the perception of a normative group. When this limited perspective is used, diverse families tend to be seen as successful only to the extent to which they adjust to prevailing cultural norms (Reyes-Blanes & Daunic, 1997).

As teachers reflect on their perceptions of family roles, they should view parents as partners in the education of the student with special needs. The parent should be welcomed as a colleague. Only then will the education of the child be seen as a joint endeavor and made more effective—when a collegial relationship between parents and teachers has been established. Parents typically have realistic ideas about their child's abilities and academic and social needs. Therefore, parents' views should figure in decisions regarding child development and program planning (Harry, 1992a; Herrera & Wooden, 1988). Attending to and acting on parents' input involves parents and contributes to enhanced communication. Finally, the educator must acknowledge the role of the parent as the child's primary advocate.

Expectations for Behavior and Academic Performance

Teachers should explore their own ideas about what constitutes appropriate behavior or academic performance. Confusion in family-school communication may result when the teacher's expectations differ from the family's expectations. Students' academic and social behavior may reflect the value the family places on education, the amount and types of the student's household and family responsibilities, the family's expectations for appropriate behavior and academic performance, and the level of parental involvement (Ramey & Ramey, 1994). Teachers need to communicate clearly their expectations for behavior and academic performance to all students and their families.

Cultural Awareness

Once the teacher is aware of personal beliefs, values, and expectations, he or she can engage further in developing cultural competence. A teacher who wishes to build trust with parents of different cultures should learn about their customs and traditions (Harry, Torguson, Katkavich, & Guerrero, 1993). Books and articles can provide general information on cultures. More in-depth information can be gained, however, when the teacher interacts with members of the culture, who serve as cultural informants. People who can provide important cultural information include colleagues (e.g., teacher, paraprofessional, administrator) and community members who belong to the culture.

Plan the Conference Setting
Physical Arrangement

The physical arrangement of the conference area can inhibit or enhance communication and, therefore, should be carefully considered. A comfortable, private area for sitting enhances conversation. For example, small chairs found in classrooms for young children are usually uncomfortable for adults. Schools usually have suitable meeting areas if there are none available in the classroom. Parents and teachers should have a place to sit comfortably

and at eye level with each other without physical barriers between them. This type of setting encourages openness in conversation.

The student's home may also serve as an appropriate setting for a parent conference. Ramey and Ramey (1994) have advocated parent contacts that provide a high level of comfort. Home visits offer a high level of comfort to some parents because the surroundings are familiar. Nevertheless, the teacher should allow the parents to choose the setting for the conference to avoid the parents' perception of the teacher as being nosy or intrusive. Generally, experiences in the home setting are likely to contribute to enhanced communication and greater connection with families. Most families appreciate the interest and effort on the teacher's part and enjoy the opportunity to interact with the teacher outside of school.

Deliver Information Clearly and Constructively

Parent participation in conferences regarding students' evaluation, placement, and development of the IEP is mandated by the Individuals with Disabilities Education Act (IDEA, 1990). Inherent in this parent involvement process, however, are emotional issues that result from the diagnosis of a disability. Often, school personnel are the first to identify the presence of disabilities in students. Educators must take extreme care when communicating with parents about the possible presence of a disability. For example, teachers must be sensitive to parental feelings such as denial, anger, embarrassment, loss, isolation, or blame. Coping with a new diagnosis of disability cannot be oversimplified with distinct emotional "stages"; the coping process is complex and varies among individuals and cultures (Mary, 1990).

Effective communication with parents regarding due process, placement, review, and student achievement is necessary, yet difficult to achieve and maintain. Families need complete, straightforward information regarding their child's disability, preferably provided in the native language. Interpreters may be necessary to enhance the accuracy of the communication based on their knowledge of the culture. Teachers should avoid using the student as interpreter, because this distorts the roles of parent and child.

Families also need full explanations of their rights and due process procedures. Educators must attend to the special information needs of parents of students with disabilities. Moreover, they must be sensitive to special communication needs of parents of diverse cultures as they attempt to keep communication open and helpful. Parents represent a critical source of information about the child's development. Acknowledgment of the parents' knowledge and skill in working with their child leads to parental ownership in solutions and greater assistance with interventions and planning.

Another language barrier to parents may be the language of schools—particularly special education language, which is often full of jargon regarding disabilities and services. This language speeds communication among education professionals, but it is unlikely to carry meaning for anyone else. In a conference situation, therefore, it is incumbent upon the teacher to present information in an appropriate manner. Terminology needs to be relevant and the level of language needs to be free of jargon.

When conferencing with parents, it is wise to use descriptive data regarding student behavior, whether it is academic or social. Any behavior should be described in explicit terms. Data on the number of times a student engages in inappropriate behavior or how long the inappropriate behavior continues helps the teacher describe to the parents what is happening in the classroom.

Communication about disabilities can become complex, not only due to the use of technical language, but also because of one's view of the disability. In some cultures, a child's disability is viewed as a parent's punishment or curse; in other cultures, disability is seen as a challenge, a test of faith or worth, or a natural occurrence (Harry, 1992b). A family's reaction to a disability may be based on tradition, religion, economic level, or prior knowledge and experiences. Teachers who have explored the family's view of disabilities will be able to convey the information in a sensitive manner.

Provide Successful Closure and Plans for Follow-Up

A successful conference closure can make all the difference in what will be accomplished after the meeting. So much can be said during a conference that parents can be overwhelmed and lose sight of their plan of action. The last minutes of the conference should be devoted to summarizing major points and delineating responsibilities. Teachers should check to ensure parents' understanding of critical issues addressed within the conference. A mutually acceptable plan of action should be devised, with parents and teachers aware of their roles (Kroth & Edge, 1997).

Short- and long-term goals should be developed. The action and roles to be taken by the educator, parent, child, and possible other resources should be clarified. An evaluation

---

Student's Background

Student Name: Juan Sanchez

Date of Conference - October 10

Age 10

Grade 5

Location Resource Classroom

Family Data:

Family includes 4 children (including Juan), two parents, and a grandmother. Ms. Sanchez works at the bakery in the local grocery store. Work day is 10:00 AM to 6:00 PM.

Mr. Sanchez works at the local mill and gets home at about 7:00 PM.

Family just moved from another state, difficult transition.

Parents have limited English proficiency, as reported in student records. Home language is Spanish.

Children—Juan 10; Jose 6; Rosa 5; and Miguel 3. All children were born in the U.S.

Juan takes responsibility at home as he cares for younger siblings in the afternoons.

Behavioral Observations:

trouble attending to tasks

possible language problems

arguing constantly

aggressive behavior

Juan speaks mostly English in the classroom; he uses Spanish in social interactions.

General Comments: No previous communication with parents

Parents came to school last year to register the children and later to attend Juan's IEP conference.

Teacher has no background in Spanish.

Figure 1 Background information about Juan Sanchez for the teacher to use in preparation for the conference.

Ms. R.: Mrs. Sanchez? (The woman nods.) Thank you for coming. I'm Ms. Robinson, Juan's teacher. I see Juan told your about the meeting. Have a seat. (They sit across from each other at Ms. Robinson's desk.)

Ms. S.: Nice to meet you. Juan told me he also has a teacher named Mrs. Bundy.

Ms. R.: Mrs. Bundy is Juan's fourth-grade homeroom teacher. Juan is mainsteamed into a regular fourth-grade for math, science, and social studies, because his learning disability is only in reading.

Wasn't that explained to you at his IEP meeting?

Ms. S.: IEP?

Ms. R.: Individual Educational Plan. They should have told you about him being LD then.

Ms. S.: I think I do remember some people talking aobut "LD." There were many important people at that meeting. We had just moved here.

Ms. R.: Well, anyway, we need to talk about what Juan is doing now. I really enjoy teaching Juan, but I'm seeing things now that cannot continue, for Juan's sake as well as the other 15 children I serve.

Ms. S.: Juan doesn't do anything bad at home. I can't believe he has problems here. He needs someone to be firm with him.

Ms. R.: (Mrs. Robinson checks her watch.) I think I am firm with him, he just doesn't listen to me.

Ms. S.: (Her voice rises a bit). Well, exactly what is he doing?

Ms. R.: I'm glad you asked. I have been keeping notes about his behavior. I have them on my desk. (Ms. Robinson starts to look through piles of paper on her desk.) . . . somewhere on my desk.

Intercom interrupts

Secretary: Ms. Robinson, Mr. Jones from Bluefield Elementary is calling.

Ms. R.: What does he want?

Secretary: Just a minute. (There is a pause while the secretary talks to Mr. Jones.)

Ms. Sanchez, meanwhile, becomes agitated. She had to take off time from work to come to school today, and she needed to run errands while she had the time. Nothing has been accomplished. Now the teacher is wasting her time to the intercom!

Secretary: He says he needs to talk to you about the Technology Committee.

Ms. R.: Please tell him I'll call him back as soon as I can. (to Ms. Sanchez) Sorry, now where were we?

Ms. R: Ah yes. Well, I can't seem to find them. I've had such a busy day. (Ms. S. thinks, "If you only knew about my day!") Juan does things that get him into trouble. He argues all the time with other students over little things. He rolls his eyes at me when I ask him to do his work. He has torn up his papers in the last week, and he's carrying some grudge against Tommy, because he hits Tommy whenever I'm not looking. I just don't know what to do with him anymore, and I need your help.

Ms. S.: Well, I don't know why he's acting like that here. He doesn't do that at home. He has a lot of respect for me and his father. Maybe he just doesn't respect you.

Ms. R. Respect is a very general term, Ms. Sanchez, but I certainly have the respect of most of my students. I'm not so much concerned with Juan's respect for me as I am about his behavior.

Ms. R.: We're not getting much accomplished here today, and I really need to pick up my child at day care. Can we reschedule another time?

Mr. S.: That is very hard for me to do, with my work schedule.

Ms. R.: Well see what you can do. In the meantime, you will talk to Juan about his behavior? ("That won't help much," she thinks.)

Ms. S.: (Appearing anxious to leave) OK, I'll talk to him. Let me know if you have any more problems. I'm sorry he's given you so much trouble. ("Yet it doesn't surprise me," she thinks.)

Ms. R.: I'm sorry too. Thank you for coming. (She gathers up her things as she heads for the classroom door, knowing she will be late arriving at the day care.) Good-bye.

Mr. S.: Bye.

As she looks around the classroom. Ms. Sanchez thinks, "No wonder Juan doesn't like it here."

(continued)

Figure 2 Script of conference between parent and teacher regarding Juan's behavior at school.

The arrangement of the conferencing area in our example does little to promote effective communication. Ms. Robinson's desk serves as a physical barrier to conversation. Multiple methods of communication should be used to notify parents of meetings.

Questioning is not a sensitive way to begin a conversation. Here, the teacher should take time to establish rapport with Ms. Sanchez.

Acronyms (IEP) and other forms of professional jargon rarely translate into other languages, and are inappropriate to use in conferencing situations.

This represents a good opportunity to get background information. Past experiences could be crucial in understanding current situations.

Begin with positive statements and keep a constructive approach. The educator must appreciate the relationship between parent and child, and must realize that parents' primary concern is about their child only.

It is important to clarify behavioral and academic expectations while exploring out-of-school behaviors.

People tend to rely on body language to a great extent. When Ms. Robinson checked her watched, she communicated that she felt rushed and wanted to move things along.

Ms. Robinson has used a general complaint as a way to avoid blame. Anecdotal records regarding behavior provide specific information necessary to understanding the problem.

This is an opportunity for Ms. Robinson to read Ms. Sanchez's tone and diffuse the situation.

Student records and anecdotal data should be organized and available. Teacher should be prepared for the meeting.

Measures should be taken to avoid interruptions.

Respect, value, and reinforce parents' time and efforts to become involved in their children's education.

This comment reflects a lack of focus on the conference.

Strong focus on negative behavior and inappropriate use of descriptions. These mostly indicate teacher's judgment rather than objective observations.

Use of slang ("carrying a grudge") could create barriers to understanding, and may cause parents to miss key issues. Moreover, when a teacher tells a parent that she does not know what to do, that prompts a loss of trust from the parents.

The teacher needs to acknowledge the value the parent places on respect, while keeping the child as the focus of the conversation.

The conference has lacked direction from the outset, and now time has run out without anything being accomplished.

The teacher and parents should collaborate to devleop a plan with well-defined responsibilities and goals.

The abruptness of the conference ending prevents closure on any of the areas of concern. Instead of building communication and trust, this conference has probably served to create distrust. Future conferences may be affected by this negative experience for both teacher and parents.

Figure 2 Continued

timeline and method should also be planned. The teacher and parents may decide that appropriate follow-ups will include phone calls, notes, or another conference.

A Teacher-Parent Conference

The following script provides a framework in which effective teacher-parent conferencing guidelines were not applied. This nonexample also helps illustrate the need for culturally responsive interaction practices. Background information on the case is provided in Figure 1. The actual conference script is presented in Figure 2. Comments on best practices have been included along with the script.

Conclusion

The example conference between Ms. Robinson and Ms. Sanchez was lacking in preparation with a vision, interaction that was positive, and conclusions that were meaningful. Mistakes were made throughout the conference that created negative feelings and barriers to communication. The end result was an ineffective conference in which no goals were attained, and an interaction that hindered the possible development of a teacher-parent partnership that might otherwise have been important to the student's life. Better preparation and interaction skill would strengthen school-family relationships and enhance educational planning for the student.

Parental involvement is a sign of successful transition to school (Ramey & Ramey, 1994) and classroom achievement. "The development of positive, respectful, and supportive relations between staff members and parents of diverse backgrounds usually requires a sense of professionalism on the part of the staff that is based on a combination of experience, training, education, and personal values" (Katz, 1994, p. 203). Educators are both challenged and required to involve parents in the educational process of their children. Additional considerations arise when families whose involvement is sought are from diverse cultures. Effective communication becomes a powerful factor in facilitating quality parent involvement experiences.

The use of effective communication skills contributes to positive and productive relationships with parents from any culture. The acquisition and use of culturally sensitive conferencing strategies will help educators structure an atmosphere of mutual respect that enhances family-school partnerships.

References

Burstein, N. D., & Cabello, B. (1989). Preparing teachers to work with culturally diverse students: A teacher education model. *Journal of Teacher Education, 40*(5), 9–16.

Chapa, J., & Valencia, R. R. (1993). Latino population growth, demographic characteristics, and educational stagnation: An examination of recent trends. *Hispanic Journal of Behavioral Sciences, 15,* 165–187.

Fish, M. C. (1990). Family-school conflict: Implications for the family. *Reading, Writing, and Learning Disabilities, 6,* 71–79.

Harry, B. (1992a). An ethnographic study of cross-cultural communication with Puerto Rican-American families in the special education system. *American Educational Research Journal, 29,* 471–494.

Harry, B. (1992b). Making sense of a disability: Low income, Puerto Rican parents' theories of the problem. *Exceptional Children, 59,* 27–40.

Harry, B., Torguson, C., Katkavich, J., & Guerrero, M. (1993). Crossing social class and cultural barriers in working with families. *Teaching Exceptional Children, 26*(1), 48–51.

Herrera, J. F., & Wooden, S. L. (1988). Some thoughts about effective parent-school communication. *Young Children, 43*(6), 78–80.

Hurtado, A. (1995). Variations, combinations, and evolution: Latino families in the United States. In R. Zambrana (Ed.), *Understanding Latino families: Scholarship, policy, and practice* (pp. 40–61). Thousand Oaks, CA: Sage.

Individuals with Disabilities Education Act of 1990, 20 U.S.C. Section 1400 et seq.

Jordan, L., Peel, H. A., & Peel, B. B. (1993). Cultural sensitivity in the young child's learning environment. *The Delta Kappa Gamma Bulletin, 60*(1), 21–25.

Kagan, D. H. (1992). Professional growth among preservice and beginning teachers. *Review of Educational Research, 62,* 129–169.

Katz, L. G. (1994). Perspectives on the quality of early childhood programs. *Phi Delta Kappan, 76,* 200–205.

Kroth, R. L., & Edge, D. (1997). *Strategies for communicating with parents and families of exceptional children.* Denver: Love.

Lynch, E. W. (1992). Developing cross-cultural competence. In E. W. Lynch & M. J. Hanson (Eds.), *Developing cross-cultural competence* (pp. 35–62). Baltimore: Brookes.

Mary, N. L. (1990). Reactions of black, Hispanic, and white mothers to having a child with handicaps. *Mental Retardation, 28*(1), 1–5.

Ramey, S. L., & Ramey, C. T. (1994). The transition to school: Why the first few years matter for a lifetime. *Phi Delta Kappan, 76,* 194–198.

Reyes-Blanes, M. E., & Daunic, A. (1997). Cultural dynamism: An alternative view of cultural diversity. Manuscript submitted for publication.

LuAnn Jordan, PhD, is a research coordinator at the Multidisciplinary Diagnostic and Training Program (MDTP) at the University of Florida. Her current interests include learning disabilities, curriculum-based assessment, and teacher preparation. **Maria E. Reyes-Blanes,** PhD, is an assistant professor in the Department of Special Education and Physical Education at the University of Central Florida. Her current interests include multicultural education, families, and assessment. **Betty B. Peel,** PhD, is an assistant professor in elementary and middle grades education at East Carolina University. **Henry A. Peel,** PhD, is associate vice chancellor for academic administration at ECU. **Holly B. Lane,** PhD, is an assistant scholar in the Department of Special Education at the University of Florida. Her current interests include learning disabilities, reading, and teacher preparation. Address: LuAnn Jordan, MDTP, University of Florida, 1341 Norman Hall, Gainesville, FL 32611.

Partnerships for Learning
Conferencing with Families

HOLLY SEPLOCHA

Conferencing with families is one of a teacher's most important responsibilities. Effective parent-teacher conferences help support young children's learning and development by fostering vital home-school linkages.

Head Start Program Performance Standards, many statewide early childhood education standards, curriculum models, and instruments for determining program quality (*Accreditation Criteria and Procedures* [NAEYC 1998] *and The Early Childhood Environment Rating Scale* [Harms, Clifford, & Cryer 1998]) identify regular parent-teacher conferences as essential ingredients for quality early childhood education.

In NAEYC's position statement on developmentally appropriate practice, the fifth guideline for decisions about developmentally appropriate practice—Establishing reciprocal relationships with families—stresses that program practices are developmentally appropriate when "Teachers and parents share their knowledge of the child and understanding of children's development and learning as part of day-to-day communication and planned conferences. Teachers support families in ways that maximally promote family decision-making capabilities and competence" (Bredekamp & Copple 1997, 22). Effective parent-teacher conferences open the dialogue and offer one vehicle for establishing and strengthening partnerships with families.

While schools and programs vary in the frequency of conferences, all successful and productive parent-teacher conferences share some common features. This article presents a baker's dozen of conferencing tips gleaned from my own experiences as a teacher and as an administrator supporting teachers in building strong partnerships through conferencing.

1. **Offer a flexible conferencing schedule.** With their varying work schedules and other family commitments, not all parents are able to attend a conference during the day or on one designated night. Many parents juggle multiple roles. It helps to offer alternative conferencing times—such as early morning hours, lunch breaks, late afternoons, and early evening hours on different days. Some teachers even meet, say, at the local library on a Saturday to accommodate a parent or guardian who cannot come at other times.

2. **Allow enough time.** Conferences typically run approximately 15–20 minutes. For back-to-back conferences, be sure to schedule some time (about 10 minutes) between each. This will allow for a conference that lasts a little long or a parent who arrives a few minutes late. It also gives you time to jot down any follow-up notes or prepare for the next appointment. If you know you need more time to discuss a special situation, schedule the conference to last longer.

3. **Provide a welcoming atmosphere.** Avoid physical barriers. Don't sit behind your desk, and whenever possible, sit next to rather than across from the parent. Amenities such as adult-size chairs, soft music, and light refreshments help everyone relax. Know the parents' names; check records ahead of time to make sure you have them right. Don't assume that Maria Doe's mother is Mrs. Doe. Nonverbal cues sometimes speak louder than words. Smile, nod, make eye contact, lean forward slightly. Let parents know you're interested and listening.

4. **Be prepared and organized.** Think about which items from the child's portfolio you want to share. Don't overwhelm the family. Select a few work samples that provide evidence of the child's abilities.

5. **Be culturally appropriate.** Effective communication is based on respect for others' values, attitudes, expectations, and culture. Keep in mind that childrearing values and practices are culturally embedded; differences may occur in norms, behaviors, values, role relations (mother/father, grandparent, other family members' roles and responsibilities), and communication patterns. Conferences provide an opportunity to learn more about diverse cultures and family structures and parents' hopes and dreams for their child. Effective teachers develop an appreciation and understanding of issues of diversity and where parents are coming from. Accept differences and avoid stereotyping. No parent wants to be a *bad* parent. Suspend judgment and come to a consensus on goals and values for the child. Remember, parents are the single most important influence and resource in a child's life. Respect families and work toward bridging cultural differences and valuing diversity.

"We": The Most Important Feature of a Parent-Teacher Conference

The foundation for constructive parent-teacher relationships is frequent and open communication and mutual resPect. When you are positively involved in your child's education, your child will flourish. Teachers prepare for conferences by reflecting on each child's interests and progress. Here are some ways you can prepare to actively participate in parent-teacher conferences.

Be willing and ready to share information about your child and family. Families are the most important influence and resource in a child's life. You know your child better than anyone else and have valuable insights to share with the teacher. Advocate for your child. Share things about your child's life at home—personality traits, challenges, habits, friends, hobbies, and talents—that you feel are important for the teacher to know. What kinds of things do you enjoy doing with your child? How do siblings relate to their brother/sister and vice versa? What kind of discipline do you use? What are your dreams for your child? What are your concerns?

Stay focused on your child. You are no longer the shy student who avoided the teacher's gaze. Nor are you the active four-year-old who seemed to always need the teacher's help to stay on task. It is natural for your ideas about teachers and their role to be shaped by your own school experiences, but being aware of these views can help you stay focused on your child and his/her unique temperament, individual needs, and special interests.

Never miss a parent-teacher conference. Use the conference as an opportunity to exchange information with the teacher and discuss ways to work together to enhance your child's education. If your work schedule makes it difficult to meet during regular hours, make this clear to the teacher and try to set up a meeting time that is good for both of you. If you can't visit in person, schedule a telephone call to discuss your child's progress.

Arrive on time. Teachers usually have a tight schedule for conferences—typically 20 minutes per child and family. If you would like additional time to talk, ask for it ahead of time

so you and the teacher can discuss Your ideas, concerns, and suggestions. Be considerate of other parents whose conferences will take place after yours. Remember that the teacher needs a few minutes between conferences to record and reflect on the information shared and to prepare for the next parent.

Remember, children can hear and remember what is said. Young children often get mixed messages when they hear adults talking about them, no matter how positive the conversation may be. Arrange for a caregiver for your child or bring a family member to occupy him or her during the conference. If this is not possible, bring a favorite toy or activity to engage the child in another part of the room. Unless a child is expressly invited to take part, the conference is a time for you and the teacher to discuss your child.

Listen with an open mind. Concentrate on what the teacher is saying instead of what you are going to say next. Ask questions when you don't understand. If you disagree with a strategy, say so and tell the teacher why. Voice your concerns, but be open to suggestions. Stay on the subject: your child's progress.

Be prepared. Think about or write down one or two questions to ask the teacher. It's a good idea to ask the most important question first, in case time runs out. Remember, while teachers have specialized education, they don't have answers for everything. Teaching just isn't that simple.

Keep the conversation focused on what can be done for your child. When there are problems, parents and teachers need to stay calm and work together for the best interest of the child.

Stay involved. Try to visit the center or school frequently, not just for conferences and Back to School Night. Ask the teacher to suggest activities you can do at home to reinforce your child's learning. Look for opportunities to engage yourself in your child's education.

6. **Stay focused on the child.** The purpose of parent-teacher conferences is to share information about the individual child and to share ideas for fostering continued growth. While parents may tell you of other family needs and concerns, it's important to remember that you are not a professional counselor or social worker. You are trained as a teacher of young children and should make referrals to appropriate staff for other issues that arise. If there are no qualified professionals on staff, give the family a list of community resources. You are also not their friend or confidant. Don't allow the conference to lose focus.

7. **Start by describing the child's strengths, interests, or abilities.** Sharing positive examples with parents

typically puts them at ease. You want to establish a connection, and the child is the link. Be specific: share an anecdote of something humorous or interesting that happened last week or today, or show a photo of the child's work or a work sample on display in your room. One teacher I know calls these positive points "glows and grows."

8. **Encourage parents to share ideas and information.** Conferences are a time to build teamwork and collaboration. Listen to what parents have to say about their child. Solicit their ideas. Parents want to be good parents and want the best for their child. Recognize and accept that there are multiple avenues for families to be involved in their child's education. Use the

conference as a way to learn more about the child and the family. Successful partnerships encourage sharing and learning.

9. **Refrain from responding to seemingly hostile or threatening comments.** It's natural for parents to have concerns and even to worry about their child. Their ideas about the kind of role teachers should fill are colored by their own past school experiences. Remember, parenting can be difficult, and many parents have less formal training for their role than you have for yours. If the conference does get out of control, end it tactfully. Schedule another time to meet.

10. **Avoid using jargon and loaded words such as** *immature* **or** *problems.* Terms such as *cognitive development, gross motor skills,* and *phonemic awareness* can be confusing. Use language that can be understood by all, and avoid generalizations and labeling. Instead of saying "Keron has strong classification skills," say, for example, "Keron does well sorting objects by categories such as size and shape."

11. **Share suggestions for at-home activities.** Parents appreciate specific tips for doable activities that can help their child. Recommend simple activities that use readily available household items. Emphasize that everyday tasks like doing laundry and grocery shopping are vehicles for learning. Consider family budgets and available time. Don't expect parents to buy special materials. (And remember, not everyone cooks with a measuring cup.) Don't overwhelm parents with lists of things their child needs to work on. Focus on one or two specific action steps you can work on together.

12. **End the conference on a positive note.** Thank all parents for coming to the conference. Stress partnering and continued open communication, and let families know their support is needed and appreciated. Engage parents in planning the best ways to assist their child. Express confidence in the child's abilities to continue to grow and develop. Save at least one encouraging or positive comment about the child to end the conference.

13. **Take a moment to reflect and document the discussion and plans.** Jot down a few notes about the gist of the conference and any follow-up needed. Assess your own performance. Were you well prepared? Was the atmosphere comfortable and supportive? Did you use time well? Did you begin on a positive note? Did you encourage parents to talk and offer suggestions? How could the conference have been better? What did you learn that will help you foster the child's continued development and learning?

References

Bredekamp, S., & C. Copple, eds. 1997. *Developmentally appropriate practice in early childhood programs.* Rev. ed. Washington, DC: NAEYC. Position statement online: www.naeyc.org/resources/position_statements/daptoc.htm.

Harms, T., R. M. Clifford, & D. Cryer. 1998. *The early childhood environment rating scale.* Rev. ed. New York: Teachers College Press.

NAEYC. 1998. *Accreditation criteria and procedures of the National Association for the Education of Young Children.* Rev. ed. Washington, DC: Author.

HOLLY SEPLOCHA, EdD, is an assistant professor of early childhood education at William Paterson University in Wayne, New Jersey. A former preschool teacher, she has been in the field now for more than 25 years. Having conferenced with hundreds of parents, Holly integrates building family partnerships into her work with teachers.

Student-Led Parent-Teacher Conferences

John A. Borba and Cherise M. Olvera

One way to improve the academic performance of students is to involve them directly in the assessment of their classroom work. In particular, student-led parent-teacher conferences encourage students to participate actively in the evaluation of their academic progress, which motivates students to think about and act on personal initiatives to improve learning. Student-led parent-teacher conferences also enable students to communicate directly with teachers, parents and other adults about their learning experiences.

Gustine Middle School, in Gustine, California, has a population of 373 sixth-, seventh-, and eighth-grade students; teachers there have implemented student-led parent-teacher conferences. Conference conversations are based on each student's portfolio, which includes samples of completed work and written self-reflections. During conference discussions, students take responsibility for their learning. They share their academic and social strengths, weaknesses, and goals for the subsequent grading period. The open dialogue with both parents and teachers during conferences allows each student to gain personal insight as a learner, enhance his or her sense of self, and concentrate on how to improve learning (Hackmann 1997; Picciotto 1996; Shannon 1997).

Prior to 1996, Gustine Middle School annually held two traditional parent-teacher conferences. Staff evaluation of the traditional conference concept raised two concerns: low parent attendance and student indifference. A review of the literature led Gustine Middle School staff to conclude that the absence of students during parent-teacher conferences might be a leading factor responsible for those problems.

Shannon (1997) conducted a study on student-led conferences and found that they caused students to accept greater personal responsibility for learning and enhanced the students' ability to share personal achievements and accomplishments with teachers and parents. Lenski, Riss, and Flickinger (1996) concluded that students were empowered through student-led parent conferences because the conferences provided a forum in which to share and discuss their strengths, weaknesses, progress, and academic and social goals. These findings are consistent with the positive results realized at L'Ouverture Elementary, an inner-city computer magnet school in Wichita, Kansas, that has received several awards for successfully motivating and engaging students in learning. The principal of L'Ouverture, Howard Pitler, identified student-led parent-teacher conferences as one academic activity that contributed to the success of the school (Lumsden 1996).

Hackmann (1996) concluded that student-led conferences generate higher parent attendance rates than traditional parent-teacher conferences. The same conclusion was reached by Little and Allan (1989), who conducted an evaluation of the student-led parent-teacher conference concept at fifteen elementary schools. Hackmann (1995) learned that parent perceptions of the effectiveness of student-led conferences are both positive and negative. However, teacher responses regarding their effectiveness are overwhelmingly positive.

The Gustine Experience

In the fall of the 1996–97 academic year, Gustine Middle School implemented student-led parent-teacher conferences at the seventh-grade level after the first reporting period. Approximately 80 percent of the students attended with their families. The attendance rate of parents of seventh graders was the highest ever experienced at the school. One parent wrote to her daughter after the conference,

> It [the conference] gave us both time out of our busy schedules to sit one-on-one, reviewing and discussing work completed in class. I am now more aware and have a better understanding about things you have been discussing with me at home. Thank you for a job well done.

Another parent reflected on the teacher's role:

> The teachers made themselves readily available to answer questions and give information. All of the teachers came up and introduced themselves. Good work Gustine Middle School staff! I hope this way of presenting the conferences continues.

During the spring conferences in the same academic year, the traditional parent-teacher format was used. The parent attendance rate for the second series of conferences at the seventh-grade level was a little over 10 percent. The success of the student-led parent-teacher conference experiment at the seventh-grade level prompted expansion of the program to the sixth and eighth grades during the subsequent school year.

Hackmann (1997) and Le Countryman and Schroeder (1996) suggested that student-led conferences consist of three phases: (1) preconference preparation, (2) conference, and (3) postconference evaluation. Gustine teachers adopted a six-stage process to encourage wider acceptance and implementation of the concept by teachers in grades 6 and 8. The six-stage process also became a guide for helping students develop portfolios of their work and conduct successful conferences. Many of the ideas incorporated into each stage were adapted from a handbook on student-led conferences developed by Miller (1995). The teachers collaboratively determined the contents and organization of the student portfolios and developed procedures for implementation of student-led parent-teacher conferences. The six stages that define Gustine Middle School's approach are described below:

Stage 1

Gustine teachers chose to have students use three-ring binders to store their completed work and written reflections. The binders consist of eight sections: introduction, English, history, mathematics, science, physical education, exploration, and quarter grades. The introductory section of each binder includes a letter that introduces the student, an autobiographical poem, and a summary of personal reflections. All of the core subject sections begin with a self-reflection on academic gains that the student has made since the end of the last grading period. In addition, each student lists strengths and weaknesses in that subject and provides a brief description of citizenship behavior for the given grading period. The student also sets goals for the next grading period. Each core subject section contains four pieces of work, two selected by the teacher and two selected by the student.

Stage 2

The second stage involves preparation of the portfolios. The students write the introductory letters and autobiographical poems in their English classes. Students use a form developed by Miller (1995) and modified by the Gustine teachers to guide them through the self-reflection process for each core subject.

A letter informing parents of upcoming student-led parent-teacher conferences is sent home with each student. The letter explains to parents that their child will be leading the regularly scheduled spring parent conference by sharing a portfolio of his or her work and progress since the end of the last grading period. The letter further informs parents that teachers will be available to answer questions regarding their child's portfolio and other academic performance and progress issues. The parent letter includes the conference dates and a return slip for requesting a specific day and time.

Stage 3

The teachers refer to stage 3 as "portfolio organization day." Students pick up their portfolio binders in their first-period classes and use time in each class of the day to complete a reflection page and insert four samples of work for that subject. All of the selected work comes from completed assignments that teachers or students have opted to save since the

end of the last grading period. Those materials are typically saved in individual student files in each classroom. At the end of the day, the students return their portfolios to the classrooms where they are stored.

Stage 4

Training is the fourth stage. The teachers at each grade level share storage and training responsibilities on a rotational basis. In 2000, those responsibilities were assigned to the science teachers, who conducted training over a three-day period. Students learned how to lead a conference and practiced the procedure during their regular science classes. On the first day of training, the teacher trainers model conference procedures and activities. The agenda for the first day of training includes the following:

- Procedures for walking into the conference room and taking the portfolio with the correct student identification sticker
- Protocol for greeting conference participants (i.e., welcoming parents and other student guests at the door, shaking their hands, and thanking them for coming to the student-led parent-teacher conferences)
- Information on the room setup for conferencing and the procedure for seating parents and other guests
- Advice on explaining the purpose of the conference to parents
- Tips on presenting and explaining portfolios; the teacher trainers suggest, that the students provide a brief summary of their accomplishments and reflections, address areas where improvement is needed, share descriptions and explanations as to why certain assignments were selected for inclusion in the portfolios, and allow time for parents to make comments and ask questions
- Conference closure; for instance, students are advised to reiterate their academic and social goals, ask parents if they have any additional questions, including those they wish to direct to the teachers, and thank parents and other adult guests for attending their conferences

On day 2 of training, students pair up and practice the conference format with their peers. One student presents while the other actively listens and provides feedback. After fifteen minutes, each pair exchanges roles. Day 3 of training is very exciting for students. On this day members of the community (school board members and city officials) are invited to sit in the place of parents as students present their portfolios. Community members are asked by teachers beforehand to provide positive feedback and words of encouragement.

Stage 5

Stage 5 is the actual conference night. The teachers post their schedules outside the classrooms where the conferences are conducted. The schedule for each grade level allows for five fifteen-minute conferences to occur simultaneously. The room for each grade is arranged so one conference can take place in each corner, with the fifth taking place in the center. The conference areas are spread out to ensure privacy and to allow teachers to circulate, interject themselves as needed, and answer questions for parents.

Stage 6

After each conference, teachers thank parents for coming and invite each to write a letter to his or her child that shares personal feelings and opinions about the conference and/or the child's recent performance and goals for the next reporting period. Stage 6 is dedicated to reviewing and analyzing the parent letters.

After the spring 2000 conferences, parents, teachers, and students were surveyed about their perceptions of the student-led parent-teacher conference concept. Parent comments were very positive about the concept overall. The following generalizations about the conferences were drawn from the comments and are consistent with outcomes reported by Guyton and Fielstein (1989):

- Opportunities for self-reflection improve the ability of students to think about what they have learned, accomplished, or failed to accomplish
- Students become more aware of their strengths and weaknesses
- Students expand their capacities to set personal goals for improvement
- Social skills of students are enhanced when they personally showcase their accomplishments and interact with adults
- Students take personal responsibility for their learning by sharing their accomplishments and shortcomings

A teacher succinctly captured the essence of the student-led parent-teacher conference concept when she stated, "Students get to have several adults listen to just them." Another teacher further elaborated, "The best part of the process is the social skills that are taught and the fact that it prepares students for future experiences such as job interviews."

Three parents indicated that they prefer the traditional conferences, generally agreeing with one parent who wrote, "I prefer the more formal settings with each teacher explaining grades, strengths and weaknesses, class work and homework assignments." However, most parents echoed an observation made in the parent survey: "It was a good way to open up communication between him [child] and us [parents] regarding his goals and achievements." Another parent was more specific: "The benefits are as follows: communication with our child in his classroom setting, through his own words, well prepared portfolio, and with teachers nearby to answer any questions we had."

The ethnic minority parents who responded to the open-ended survey indicated strong support for the student-led approach. One Hispanic parent indicated that the language barrier often made it uncomfortable to attend traditional parent conferences. She also shared that the presence of her child helps to remove language and other sociocultural barriers and facilitates better communication and cooperation between the school and home.

Finally, the results of a survey on the students' opinions showed that a majority perceived the conferences as helpful in facilitating self-reflection, identifying strengths and areas where improvement is needed, and increasing parent involvement at home.

Conclusions

Student-led parent-teacher conferences at Gustine Middle School have proved effective in centering learning evaluation and goal setting directly on the student. The Gustine teachers adapted the conferences to make the concept successful within the unique academic and social parameters of their school. Their well-organized six-stage approach, which includes development of portfolios, selection of completed assignments, self-analysis and reflection, and presentation practice, contributes to the success of the Gustine program. An analysis of student and parent survey results indicates that a majority perceive the concept as a positive learning experience. A parent briefly summarized the benefits of student-led teacher-parent conferences:

- Students take ownership of their learning
- Students share with teachers the burden of explaining to their parents, if necessary, reasons for poor performance and behavior
- All of the child's teachers are available in one area for private conferences, if necessary
- Parent attendance rates are significantly higher
- Students are not left at home wondering exactly what their teachers had to say about them

The principal of Gustine Middle School stated, "These conferences can be emotional for both the students and parents. I have seen parents and students cry and at least for a short period of time become closer." An experience at the spring 2000 conferences demonstrated that the conferences can be poignant for staff members, as well. A male student who was not able to have a parent or relative attend his conference invited the school custodian to fill in. The custodian graciously accepted the invitation. Although it was not obvious to the student, it was a very emotional experience for the custodian and the teachers who were present. This student, who daily must overcome the challenge of an uncaring home environment, capitalized on an opportunity to share his past accomplishments and goals for the future.

The Gustine experience underscores the need for policymakers, educators, and members of the community to pay closer attention to ideas that can have a direct impact on student learning in the classroom and parent involvement in their children's education. Although most current education reforms in the United States are focused on elementary and secondary schools, policymakers are beginning to realize that eleven-, twelve-, and thirteen-year-olds need the same level of attention. As policymakers, educators, and communities begin to focus renewed efforts at reform in the middle schools, we suggest that serious consideration be given to student-led parent-teacher conferences.

References

Guyton, J. M., and L. L. Fielstein. 1989. Student-led parent conferences: A model for teaching responsibility. *Elementary School Guidance and Counseling 24* (2): 169–72.

Hackmann, D. G. 1995. Student-led conferences: Encouraging student-parent academic discussions. Paper presented at the Annual Conference of the National Middle School Association, New Orleans, LA. ERIC, ED 388 449.

_____. 1996. Student-led conferences at the middle level: Promoting student responsibility. *NASSP Bulletin 80* (578): 31–36.

_____. 1997. Student-led conferences at the middle level. University of Oregon Report No. IR EDO-PS-97-19. ERIC, ED 407 171.

Le Countryman, L., and M. Schroeder. 1996. When students lead parent-teacher conferences. *Educational Leadership 53* (7): 64–68.

Lenski, S.D., M. Riss, and G. Flickinger. 1996. Honoring student self-evaluation in the classroom community. *Primary Voices K–6 4* (2): 24–32.

Little, A. W., and J. Allan. 1989. Student led parent-teacher conferences. *Elementary School Guidance and Counseling 23* (3): 210–18.

Lumsden, L 1996. Motivating today's students: The same old stuff just doesn't work. *Portraits of Success 1* (2): 2–9.

Miller, S. E. 1995. *Student led conferences: 1995-97 S.T.A.R.S. middle school version.* Workshop packet. Southridge Middle School.

Picciotto, L. P. 1996. *Student-led parent conferences.* New York: Scholastic.

Shannon, K. C. 1997. Student-led conferences: A twist on tradition. *Schools in the Middle 6* (3): 47–49.

JOHN A. BORBA is an associate professor of education at California State University, Stanislaus, and **CHERISE M. OLVERA** is an administrator at Chatom Elementary School, in Turlock, California.

From *The Clearing House,* July/August 2001. Reprinted by permission of the Helen Dwight Reid Educational Foundation. Published by Heldref Publications, 1319 Eighteenth St., NW, Washington, DC 20036-1802. Copyright © 2001. www.heldref.org

Grades as Valid Measures of Academic Achievement of Classroom Learning

JAMES D. ALLEN

What is the purpose of grades? In this article I present one answer to this question from a perspective that many educators might see as somewhat radical or extreme. The perspective that I take is based on the fundamental educational psychology assessment principle of validity—the validity of what learning is being assessed and the validity of the communication of that assessment to others. I believe most teachers fail to give grades to students that are as valid as they should be. Because grading is something that has been done to each of us during our many years as students, it is hard to change the invalid "grading" schema that has become embedded in our minds. Now, as educators often required to grade students, and because of this embedded schema, we often grade students in invalid ways similar to how we were graded. Inadequate education in valid assessment and grading principles and practices is a reason many teachers continue to perpetuate invalid grading practices with students. Since educational testing and assessment is a major content knowledge area in educational psychology, the issues regarding assessment and grading that I address in this article could well be addressed in an educational psychology course. If our preservice and inservice teachers are going to learn appropriate assessment and grading practices then educational psychologists need to provide the relevant information in their classes.

The most fundamental measurement principle related to meaningful assessment and grading is the principle of validity (Gallagher 1998; Gredler 1999; Linn and Gronlund 2000; Stiggins 2001). Although there are many validity issues involved in classroom assessment that classroom teachers should consider, such as making sure the way they assess students corresponds to the type of academic learning behaviors being assessed (Ormrod 2000), the focus here is on the valid assessment and communication of final class grades as summaries of students' academic achievement of content knowledge of a subject. Validity addresses the accuracy of the assessment and grading procedures used by teachers (Gallagher 1998; Gredler 1999; Linn and Gronlund 2000). Do the assessment procedures and assignment of grades accurately reflect and communicate the academic achievement of the student? Validity is important because the sole purpose of grades is to accurately communicate to others the level of academic achievement that a student

has obtained (Snowman and Biehler 2003). If the grades are not accurate measures of the student's achievement, then they do not communicate the truth about the level of the student's academic achievement. Unfortunately, as stated by Cizek, even as "grades continue to be relied upon to communicate important information about [academic] performance and progress . . . they probably don't" (1996, 104).

Assigning grades to students is such a complex (and sometimes controversial) issue that some educators have proposed their abolition (Kohn 1999; Marzano 2000). Although I find this an interesting proposal, especially if one is trying to establish a classroom learning environment that is student-centered and encourages self-regulation and self-evaluation, the current reality for most teachers is that they are required to assign grades indicating students' academic achievement in the subjects they teach. Therefore, grading should be as valid as possible. Not only is grading a major responsibility of classroom teachers, but it is also a practice with which they are often uncomfortable and that they find difficult (Barnes 1985; Lomax 1996; Thorndike 1997). The sources of the discomfort and difficulty for teachers regarding the grading of students seem to be threefold. First, the student activities that teachers think should constitute "academic achievement" and how to handle ancillary features of achievement such as students' efforts varies tremendously from teacher to teacher. Although ancillary information such as effort and attitude could be part of an overall student report, they should not be part of a grade that represents academic achievement (Tombari and Borich 1999). Second, teachers often seem to be unsettled regarding the communication function of grades, and they often try to communicate multiple pieces of information about students that can not possibly be contained within a single academic mark. This is an issue of making sure the grade is accurate as a valid communication to others. Third, because of the first two issues, many teachers assign grades that are invalid and not built on a solid principle of measurement (Cizek 1996; Marzano 2000). In addition, partially due to their long career as students experiencing invalid grading practices, as well as inadequate preservice and inservice education on assessment and grading, teachers continue to perpetuate invalid grading practices. Let us consider each of these points in greater depth.

Miscommunication and Confusing Purposes of Grades

Although students learn many things in the classroom, the primary objective is for students to learn academic content knowledge of a particular subject. In order for teachers to know if students are achieving this academic knowledge, they generally are required to not only assess students' knowledge in some way, but eventually summarize that assessment into a letter or numerical grade. This is known as "summative" evaluation. Hopefully, teachers are also gathering nongraded "formative" assessments of students to provide feedback to students as they learn, as well as considering how to motivate students to learn and encouraging them to be self-regulated learners. However, generally, teachers have to eventually place a grade on a grade sheet indicating what level of content knowledge a student has achieved in the subject listed. But why do we place a grade on a grade sheet, report card, or transcript? Why do we create a permanent written record of the grade? And why is the grade listed next to a name of an academic course such as English, U.S. History, Algebra, or Educational Psychology?

As illustrated by the title of the 1996 Yearbook of the Association for Supervision and Curriculum Development, Communicating Student Learning to interested parties is an important function of schools and teachers (Guskey 1996). Although there are various means to communicate student learning, currently a single report card grade for each academic subject is the most common and generally accepted system in middle and secondary schools (Bailey and McTighe 1996; Lake and Kafka 1996). Bailey and McTighe argue that as a communication system, "the primary purpose of secondary level grades and reports [is] to communicate student achievement" so that informed decisions can be made about the student's future (1996, 120). Similarly, authors of major texts devoted to classroom assessment suggest that the major reason for assigning grades is to create a public record of a student's academic achievement that can accurately and effectively communicate to others the level of mastery of a subject a student has demonstrated (Airasian 2000; Gallagher 1998; Gredler 1999; Linn and Gronlund 2000; Nitko 2001; Oosterhof 2001; Stiggins 2001). Nitko points out that: "Grades . . . are used by students, parents, other teachers, guidance counselors, school officials, postsecondary educational institutions, and employers. Therefore [teachers] must assign grades with utmost care and maintain their validity" (2001, 365). However, according to Marzano, in contrast to teachers', students', parents', and community members' assumption that grades are valid "measures of student achievement . . . grades are so imprecise that they are almost meaningless" (2000, 1). Due to the wide variability in the criteria used in grading practices from teacher to teacher, the validity of student grades is unknown and they have limited value as guides for planning the academic and career futures of students (Thorndike 1997). Thus, if a single grade on a report card or transcript is to effectively communicate information to all these varied parties, then that single grade has to have some shared and accurate meaning (O'Connor 1995).

This lack of shared meaning seems to be found throughout our education system. A study by Baron (2000) shows that there is lack of coherence in the beliefs about grades held by parents and students and those held by the education community. Even in the same school, teachers often hold very different views about the purpose of grades and fail to communicate with their colleagues about their grading practices (Kain 1996). Grading practices by teachers rarely follow the measurement principles and grading practices recommended in measurement textbooks (Cross and Frary 1996; Frary, Cross, and Weber 1993). New teachers often work independently and are left to figure out their own grading policies, gradually adhering to the school's norms. There is a similar lack of coherence and communication among college teachers (Barnes, Bull, Campbell, and Perry 1998). Friedman and Frisbie (1995, 2000) make a particularly strong argument for making sure that report card grades accurately report information to parents about a student's academic progress and that teachers and administrators share a common understanding of what information a grade should communicate. They suggest that since grades become part of a students' permanent record, the purpose of these grades must be to communicate a valid summary of a student's academic achievement in the subject that is listed next to the grade on the record.

Grading systems used by teachers vary widely and unpredictably and often have low levels of validity due to the inclusion of nonacademic criteria used in the calculation of grades (Allen and Lambating 2001; Brookhart 1994; 2004; Frary, Cross, and Weber 1993; Olson 1989). Teachers have been found to make decisions about grades related to student effort in attempts to be "fair" in their grading practices (Barnes 1985). Studies have found that two out of three teachers believe that effort, student conduct, and attitude should influence final grades of students (Cross and Frary 1996; Frary, Cross, and Weber 1993). It has also been shown that grades are used as a motivational tool as well as to develop good study habits (Oosterhof 2001) and desirable classroom management behaviors (Allen 1983). Grades should not be a hodgepodge of factors such as student's level of effort, innate aptitude, compliance to rules, attendance, social behaviors, attitudes, or other nonachievement measures (Friedman and Frisbie 2000; Ornstein 1994). Although these factors may indirectly influence students' achievement of content knowledge, subjective—and often unknown to the teacher—factors such as these complicate the ability to interpret a grade since these factors may directly conflict with each other and distort the meaning of a grade measuring academic achievement (Cross and Frary 1996; Guskey 1994; Linn and Gronlund 2000; Nitko 2001; Stiggins 2001; Stumpo 1997). Nonacademic factors are often used as criteria for assigning grades because some teachers consider the consequences of grades more important than the value of clear communication of information and the interpretability of the grades (Brookhart 1993). It follows then that instead of the grade being a function of what a student has learned it has become a function of many variables. Simply put, it would appear that grades are often measures of how well a student lives up to the teacher's expectation of what a good student is rather than measuring the student's academic achievement in the subject matter objectives.

A grade can not be a teacher's "merged judgment"[1] of these factors, since as a single letter or numeric mark, the reported grade must communicate a single fact about the student if it is to be a valid or accurate source of information coherently shared between the reporter of the grade and the grade report's audience. How is the reader of a student's single grade on a transcript to know which factors are included and how much each unknown factor was weighed by the grade-giver to determine the grade? Also, since many of these factors such as effort, motivation, and student attitude are subjective measures made by a teacher, their inclusion in a grade related to academic achievement increases the chance for the grade to be biased or unreliable, and thus invalid. The purpose of an academic report is to communicate the level of academic achievement that a student has developed over a course of study. Therefore, the sole purpose of a grade on an academic report, if it is to be a valid source of information, is to communicate the academic achievement of the student. If other factors about the student are deemed important, such as a student's attitude, level of effort, or social behavior, then other appropriate forms of reporting these factors must be made available and used. If a multidimensional view of the student is desired, then a multidimensional system of reporting is required. Using a single grade as a summary of a teacher's "merged judgment" of a student leads to miscommunication, confusion, and a continuation of the lack of coherence among stakeholders about what a grade represents.

Since important decisions are often based on a student's grade, invalid grades may result in dire consequences for the student. Grades can open up or close down important learning opportunities for students (Jasmine 1999). With high grades, students get admitted to colleges and universities of their choice and receive scholarships and tuition assistance, since grades are a major selection criterion in the college admission process. The reverse is also true. It is very difficult for students to get admitted to some schools if their grades are not sufficiently high. Invalid grades that understate the student's knowledge may prevent a student with ability to pursue certain educational or career opportunities. Also, based on principles of attribution and social cognitive theories, if students receive grades lower than ones that accurately depict their true level of academic knowledge, it may lead students to believe they lack the ability to succeed academically and lower their sense of self-efficacy as well as their motivation to learn (Pintrich and Schunk 2002).

Grading and Lack of Professional Training

Cizek argues that the "lack of knowledge and interest in grading translates into a serious information breakdown in education" and that "reforming classroom assessment and grading practices will require educators' commitment to professional development, [and] classroom-relevant training programs" (1996, 103). Cizek's statement implies that an important area that needs to be addressed is the training of teachers in grading practices based on sound measurement principles relevant to their classroom lives.

This lack of knowledge about measurement theory and application to grading practices is a pervasive problem with preservice teacher training at the college level (Goodwin 2001; Schafer 1991; Stiggins 1991, 1999). One of the goals of a teacher education program should be to prepare preservice and in-service teachers to develop effective methods to assess students and to communicate clearly and accurately through their grading practices that assessment to others. However, very few teacher education programs include measurement or assessment courses. Allen and Lambating (2001) found in a random sample of teacher education programs that less than one-third required an assessment course, and many of those that did were courses focused on "informal" assessments, or standardized assessment of students with special needs and not focused on classroom assessment and grading. Fewer than half of the fifty states require specific coursework on assessment for their initial certification of teachers (Lomax 1996; O'Sullivan and Chalnick 1991; Stiggins 1999).

Although assigning grades is probably the most important measurement decision that classroom teachers make, the coverage of grading in assessment textbooks is often not as fully developed as other measurement topics that are less relevant to teachers' day-to-day assessment practices (Airasian 1991; Lomax 1996). According to Stiggins (1999), how the concepts of "reliability" and "validity" are related to classroom grading practices is not addressed in the courses which introduce these terms to our preservice teachers. It is important to look at this issue because validity and reliability are considered the most fundamental principles related to measurement and therefore important to classroom assessment and grading (Gallagher 1998; Gredler 1999; Linn and Gronlund 2000).

Some argue that even when teachers are provided with some measurement instruction, they still use subjective value judgements when assigning grades (Brookhart 1993). Undergraduate teacher education majors, when asked about the criteria that should be used for their own grades, believe that "effort" is more important than amount of academic content learned (Placier 1995). One contributing factor may be that after sixteen years of obtaining grades based on factors other than academic achievement, teachers-in-training have a difficult time accepting theoretical principles that do not match with their personal experience. Many beliefs about school practices are well established before students enter college and often are resistant to change (Britzman 1986, 1991; Ginsberg and Clift 1990; Holt-Reynolds 1992; Pajares 1992; Richardson 1996). They form many of their perspectives about teaching from their years of observing teachers and their teaching practices (Lortie 1975). They have been recipients of hundreds of grades from their K–12 teachers and college professors before taking on the responsibility of assigning grades to their own students. Their perception regarding grades comes from their own long experience as students.

Brookhart (1998) suggests that classroom assessment and grading practices are at the center of effective management of classroom instruction and learning. Through the use of real classroom scenarios, preservice teachers need to be taught assessment strategies in relationship to instruction and not as decontextualized measurement principles. As the past president of the American Educational Research Association, Lorrie Shepard has stated: "The transformation of assessment practices cannot be accomplished in separate tests and measurement courses, but rather should be a central concern in teaching methods courses" (2000, 4). In addition to instruction on how to assess and grade using sound principles of measurement, research suggests that preservice teachers need hands-on experience in grading students and how to work with cooperating teachers who assess and grade in ways different than those learned by the preservice teachers (Barnes 1985; Lomax 1996).

What the literature suggests is that educators at all levels make decisions when assigning grades that are not based on sound principles of validity that ensure the grade is a meaningful communication of a student's level of academic achievement. The literature also suggests that students in teacher education programs may be more influenced by the grading practices they have experienced as students in the past, as well as in their current courses taught by their education professors, than by what they learn about assessment and grading in their courses. Additionally, teachers in the field, as products of teacher education programs, seem to exhibit grading practices that confirm that they have not been influenced by measurement courses (Lambating and Allen 2002). This may be because they did not take any assessment courses, or because their long-held beliefs about grading were left unchallenged and the courses did not focus on assessment and grading issues related to measuring classroom learning.

Educational Implications and Conclusion

Concerns about the validity and reliability of grades for communicating meaningful information about students' academic progress have been raised for a long time (see Starch and Elliot 1912, 1913a, 1913b; Adams 1932). In addition, trying to help teachers to understand the purpose and effective functions of grades in the overall evaluation system has been addressed repeatedly in the literature (Airasian 2000; Brookhart 1993; Cross and Frary 1996; Gredler 1999; Guskey 1996; Linn and Gronlund 2000; Marzano 2000; O'Connor 1995; Stiggins 2001). However, there seems to be little progress being made in this area in actual classroom practice.

Two major thrusts need to occur in reforming grading practices. First, if factors such as effort, attitude, compliance, and behavior are to be noted about a student on a report card, then they should be reported with a separate mark and not figured in as part of a grade for academic achievement of content knowledge. However, as in most situations, if a teacher must summarize and communicate a student's classroom progress in an academic subject through a single report card grade, then there must be a consensus that the grade represents the most accurate statement of the student's academic achievement, and only academic achievement. This is the essence of valid assessment. To include nonacademic criteria, such as the student's effort, compliance, attitude, or behavior, makes the grade impossible to interpret in any meaningful way. Perhaps, a simple way to reach

this consensus is to teach ourselves and those we prepare to be teachers to reflect on the following question: "If I was given a student's transcript with a single letter grade listed next to the subject I teach, what would be the most logical interpretation I could make about what the grade represents about the student's knowledge of that academic subject?" Therefore, that is what I should try to have my grades communicate to whomever will read and interpret them in the future.

In order for teachers to act consistently in assigning valid grades based only on appropriate achievement criteria, a second major initiative needs to be undertaken to help teachers understand how to make good grading decisions. This initiative is best addressed through teacher education programs taking on the challenge to improve the assessment training of their students and improve their own grading practices. This entails several dimensions.

First, students' long-held beliefs about the purpose and use of grades need to be challenged by teacher educators. Students' beliefs and value systems related to grades need to be exposed and examined to help them understand the unscientific basis of their grading beliefs. Second, once these beliefs are exposed, instructors must provide students with the theoretical base for good assessment and grading practices as explicated by measurement experts that would replace students' naive notions of assessment and grading. This could be either through self-contained measurement courses taught in a relevant manner by educational psychologists, or integrated into methods courses through collaboration between educational psychology and teacher-education specialists. It would help if more teacher-education programs required adequate instruction on classroom assessment and grading practices. There also needs to be more effective and meaningful grading practices addressed in-depth in measurement textbooks. Third, teacher education students need to be provided with opportunities to encounter grading activities before they are placed into student teaching, in order to practice applying assessment principles and theory to classroom grading issues. Finally, during student teaching experiences, education majors must be given the opportunity, in conjunction with their cooperating teachers and the support of their college supervisors, to actually develop and implement a valid evaluation and grading plan. Schools of education need to work with school district teachers to help improve the communication system for which grades function. Providing in-service "assessment and grading" workshops for practicing teachers, especially those operating as cooperating teachers, might help to establish a consensus of what is appropriate criteria to use for determining and assigning valid grades to indicate academic achievement.

One way to accomplish many of the above steps is through the use of case studies that focus on assessment and grading dilemmas often faced by real teachers. Discussion of case studies can help students to reflect on and expose their belief systems about grades and grading, and analyze them in relationship to educational psychology assessment principles such as validity. One example is the Sarah Hanover case which focuses on a grading dilemma a teacher must deal with when the question of the validity of a student's grade is raised by the student's parent (Silverman, Welty, and Lyon 1996).

However, the area that may be the most difficult to address is the change in the grading practices that teacher educators use in evaluating students. As long as preservice and in-service teachers take classes from education professors who base grading decisions on more than academic achievement, they will have little reason to either believe what we say or practice what we preach about assessment and grading. As teacher educators, we need to model sound grading practices in our own courses in which grades accurately communicate students' achievement of content knowledge learned in our courses, and not how hard they work or how often they attend our classes.

My intention in this article has been to suggest that by giving serious reflection to the meaning of the educational psychology measurement principle of validity, grading practices can improve and the grades we assign to students as teachers can be more accurate and educationally meaningful. We need to begin to break the cycle of invalid grading practices that prevail throughout the education system, and the only behaviors we as teachers can truly control are our own.

Note

1. The author has borrowed this phrase from an anonymous reviewer.

References

Adams, W. L. 1932. Why teachers say they fail pupils. *Educational Administration and Supervision* 18:594–600.

Airasian, P. W. 1991. Perspectives on measurement instruction. *Educational Measurement: Issues and Practice* 10 (1): 13–16, 26.

———. 2000. *Assessment in the classroom: A concise approach.* 2nd ed. Boston: McGraw-Hill.

Allen, J. D. 1983. Classroom management: Students' perspectives, goals and strategies. Paper presented at the annual meeting of the American Educational Research Association, Montreal, Canada, April.

Allen, J. D., and J. Lambating. 2001. Validity and reliability in assessment and grading: Perspectives of preservice and inservice teachers and teacher education professors. Paper presented at the annual meeting of the American Educational Research Association, Seattle, April.

Bailey, J., and J. McTighe. 1996. Reporting achievement at the secondary level: What and how. In Guskey 1996, 119–40.

Barnes, L. B., K. S. Bull, N. J. Campbell, and K. M. Perry. 1998. Discipline-related differences in teaching and grading philosophies among undergraduate teaching faculty. Paper presented at the annual meeting of the American Educational Research Association, San Diego, April.

Barnes, S. 1985. A study of classroom pupil evaluation: The missing link in teacher education. *Journal of Teacher Education* 36 (4): 46–49.

Baron, P. A. B. 2000. Consequential validity for high school grades: What is the meaning of grades for senders and receivers? Paper presented at the annual meeting of the American Educational Research Association, New Orleans, April.

Britzman, D. P. 1986. Cultural myths in the making of a teacher: Biography and social structure in teacher education. *Harvard Educational Review* 56 (4): 442–56.

———. 1991. *Practice makes practice: A critical study of learning to teach.* New York: State University of New York Press.

Brookhart, S. M. 1993. Teachers' grading practices: Meaning and values. *Journal of Educational Measurement* 30 (2): 123–42.

———. 1994. Teachers' grading: Practice and theory. *Applied Measurement in Education* 7 (4): 279–301.

———. 1998. Teaching about grading and communicating assessment results. Paper presented at the annual meeting of the National Council on Measurement in Education, San Diego, April, 1998.

———. 2004. *Grading.* Upper Saddle River, NJ: Pearson/Merrill/Prentice Hall.

Cizek, G. J. 1996. Grades: The final frontier in assessment reform. *NASSP Bulletin* 80 (584): 103–10.

Cross, L. H., and R. B. Frary. 1996. Hodgepodge grading: Endorsed by students and teachers alike. Paper presented at the annual meeting of the National Council on Measurement in Education, New York, April.

Frary, R. B., L. H. Cross, and L. J. Weber. 1993. Testing and grading practices and opinions of secondary teachers of academic subjects: Implications for instruction in measurement. *Educational Measurement: Issues and Practice* 12 (3): 2330.

Friedman, S. J., and D. A. Frisbie. 1995. The influence of report cards on the validity of grades reported to parents. *Educational and Psychological Measurement* 55 (1): 5–26.

———. 2000. Making report cards measure up. *Education Digest* 65 (5): 45–50.

Gallagher, J. D. 1998. *Classroom assessment for teachers.* Upper Saddle River, NJ: Merrill/Prentice Hall.

Ginsburg, M. B., and R. T. Clift. 1990. The hidden curriculum of preservice teacher education. In *Handbook of research on teacher education*, ed. W. R. Houston, 450–65. New York: Macmillan.

Goodwin, A. L. 2001. The case of one child: Making the shift from personal knowledge to informed practice. Paper presented at the annual meeting of the American Educational Research Association, Seattle, April.

Gredler, M. E. 1999. *Classroom assessment and learning.* New York: Longman.

Guskey, T. R. 1994. Making the grade: What benefits students? *Educational Leadership* 52 (2): 14–20.

———. 1996. *ASCD Yearbook, 1996: Communicating student learning.* Alexandria, VA: Association for Supervision and Curriculum Development.

Holt-Reynolds, D. 1992. Personal history-based beliefs as relevant prior knowledge in coursework: Can we practice what we preach? *American Educational Research Journal* 29 (2): 325–49.

Jasmine, T. 1999. Grade distributions, grading procedures, and students' evaluations of instructors: A justice perspective. *Journal of Psychology* 133 (3): 263–71.

Kain, D. L. 1996. Looking beneath the surface: Teacher collaboration through the lens of grading practices. *Teachers College Record* 97 (4): 569–87.

Kohn, A. 1999. Grading is degrading. *Education Digest* 65 (1): 59–64.

Lake, K., and K. Kafka. 1996. Reporting methods in grades K–8. In Guskey 1996, 90–118.

Lambating, J., and J. D. Allen. 2002. How the multiple functions of grades influence their validity and value as measures of academic achievement. Paper presented at the annual meeting of the American Educational Research Association, New Orleans, April.

Linn, R. L., and N. E. Gronlund. 2000. *Measurement and assessment in teaching*. 8th ed. Englewood Cliffs, NJ: Merrill/Prentice Hall.

Lomax, R. G. 1996. On becoming assessment literate: An initial look at preservice teachers' beliefs and practices. *Teacher Educator* 31 (4): 292–303.

Lortie, D. 1975. *Schoolteacher: A sociological study*. Chicago: University of Chicago Press.

Marzano, R. J. 2000. *Transforming classroom grading*. Alexandria, VA: Association for Supervision and Curriculum Development.

Nitko, A. J. 2001. *Educational assessment of students*. 3rd ed. Upper Saddle River, NJ: Merrill/Prentice Hall.

O'Conner, K. 1995. Guidelines for grading that support learning and student success. *NASSP Bulletin* 79 (571): 91–101.

Olson, G. H. 1989. On the validity of performance grades: The relationship between teacher-assigned grades and standard measures of subject matter acquisition. Paper presented at the annual meeting of the National Council on Measurement in Education, San Francisco, March.

Oosterhof, A. 2001. *Classroom application of educational measurement*. Upper Saddle River, NJ: Prentice Hall.

Ormrod, J. E. 2000. *Educational psychology: Developing learners*. 3rd ed. Upper Saddle River, NJ: Merrill/Prentice Hall.

Ornstein, A. C. 1994. Grading practices and policies: An overview and some suggestions. *NASSP Bulletin* 78 (561): 55–64.

O'Sullivan, R. G., and M. K. Chalnick. 1991. Measurement-related course work requirements for teacher certification and recertification. *Educational Measurement: Issues and Practice* 10 (1): 17–19, 23.

Pajares, M. F. 1992. Teachers' beliefs and educational research: Cleaning up a messy construct. *Review of Educational Research* 62 (3): 307–32.

Pintrich, P. R., and D. H. Schunk. 2002. *Motivation in education*. 2nd ed. Upper Saddle River, NJ: Merrill/Prentice Hall.

Placier, M. 1995. "But I have to have an A": Probing the cultural meanings and ethical dilemmas of grades in teacher education. *Teacher Education Quarterly* 22 (1): 45–63.

Richardson, V. 1996. The role of attitudes and beliefs in learning to teach. In *Handbook of research on teacher education*, 2nd ed., J. Sikula, T. Buttery, and E. Guyton, 102–19. New York: Macmillan.

Schafer, W. D. 1991. Essential assessment skills in professional education of teachers. *Educational Measurement: Issues and Practice* 10 (1): 3–6, 12.

Shepard, L. A. 2000. The role of assessment in a learning culture. *Educational Researcher* 29 (7): 4–14.

Silverman, R., W. M. Welty, and S. Lyon. 1996. *Case studies for teacher problem solving*. 2nd ed. New York: McGraw-Hill.

Snowman, J., and R. F. Biehler. 2003. *Psychology applied to teaching*. 10th ed. Boston: Houghton Mifflin.

Starch, D., and E. C. Elliot. 1912. Reliability of grading of high-school work in English. *School Review* 20:442–57.

———. 1913a. Reliability of grading work in mathematics. *School Review* 21:254–59.

———. 1913b. Reliability of grading work in history. *School Review* 20:676–81.

Stiggins, R. J. 1991. Relevant classroom assessment training for teachers. *Educational Measurement: Issues and Practice* 10 (1): 7–12.

———. 1999. Evaluating classroom assessment training in teacher education programs. *Educational Measurement: Issues and Practice* 18 (1): 23–27.

———. 2001. *Student-involved classroom assessment*. 3rd ed. Upper Saddle River, NJ: Merrill/Prentice Hall.

Stumpo, V. M. 1997. 3-tier grading sharpens student assessment. *Education Digest* 63 (4): 51–54.

Thorndike, R. M. 1997. *Measurement and Evaluation*. 6th ed. Upper Saddle River, NJ: Merrill/Prentice Hall.

Tombari, M., and G. Borich. 1999. *Authentic assessment in the classroom*. Upper Saddle River, NJ: Merrill/Prentice Hall.

JAMES D. ALLEN is a professor of educational psychology in the Department of Educational and School Psychology at the College of Saint Rose in Albany, New York.

From *The Clearing House*, May/June 2005. Reprinted by permission of the Helen Dwight Reid Educational Foundation. Published by Heldref Publications, 1319 Eighteenth St., NW, Washington, DC 20036-1802. Copyright © 2005. www.heldref.org

Grading to Communicate

Grades can only be a shiny distraction—unless we make them a strong message.

TONY WINGER

Throughout my career as an educator, I have experienced frustration with how my traditional classroom grading practices have influenced my students' learning. When I discuss this issue with colleagues, parents, and—most important—students, I find that I am not alone in my frustration. Paradoxically, grades detract from students' motivation to learn. It is time to reconsider our classroom grading practices.

Does Grading Interfere with Learning?

As a young teacher, I found the authority to give grades empowering. The grade was my ace in the hole, providing the leverage needed to entice students to cooperate. But as time passed, it dawned on me that the manner in which I was using grades conflicted with my deeper purposes as an educator. Again and again, students met my passion for a subject with their pragmatic concern for their grade. I wanted my economics students to wrestle with issues of equity or debate the costs and benefits of a minimum wage; they wondered whether the upcoming test would be essay or multiple-choice. I wanted my sociology students to consider the powerful role that group attachments play in personal decisions about religion or romance; they cared more about how many pages they would need to write for the essay.

I wanted my students to wonder, to understand, and ultimately to be changed. Many of them simply wanted a good grade.

I wanted my students to wonder, to understand, and ultimately to be changed. Many of them simply wanted a good grade. And the irony is, they were only responding as other educators and I had conditioned them to respond. We had trained them to see grades as a commodity rather than as a reflection of learning.

Comments from a student panel that my school district organized to investigate grading practices further elucidated the problem. Students reported that they see their schoolwork as a game

they play for grades—a game that at best treats learning as incidental, and at worst distracts students from making meaning. One student referred to this grade game as academic bulimia: Students stuff themselves with information only to regurgitate it for the test, with little opportunity for the thoughtful engagement that would produce deep understanding and growth.

Do Grades Measure What We Value Most?

I recall telling my students, "Work hard and your grade will be fine." Although I did not realize it, the message to students was clear: My unconscious curriculum was one of compliance.

Rather than Principles and Practices of Economics, my class might more accurately have been named Principles and Practices of Being a Good Kid. Some students received good grades and learned little; others learned much and failed. Grades measured students' willingness to cooperate and work hard rather than their understanding of economics or their ability to use that understanding to think more clearly about their world. I was not assessing the learning that I valued most.

Do Grades Provide Accurate Feedback?

When grades are not deliberately connected to learning, they provide little valuable feedback regarding students' academic strengths and weaknesses, and can even be counterproductive. I recently spoke with a frustrated father whose daughter is on the honor roll at her high school. He finds that despite her hard work and high grades, his daughter's writing skills are deficient. He is having a difficult time convincing this honor student that her skills need improvement. Rather than supporting learning, her grades are actually providing misleading information.

A colleague's experience reveals another manifestation of this problem. In the middle of the semester, she asked her language arts students to identify one area in which they hoped to improve during the second half of the course. Instead of identifying a skill, such as writing organization or reading comprehension, most students listed either tests or homework. Rather than identifying gaps in student learning, this teacher's grading practices had focused students' attention on the assessment tools.

Getting to Grading That Works

Three years ago, I became an instructional coach at Heritage High School in Littleton, Colorado, where I had taught for 14 years. As a result of the training I received in this new position, I began to significantly revise my approach to grading, and I now guide other teachers in doing the same. Littleton Public School District has launched a districtwide initiative to address the issue of grading practices. After a year of research and study, including soliciting input from parents and teachers, the board of education has authorized a representative teacher pilot group to explore changing how we grade our students.

The problems my colleagues and I have experienced point to a crucial disconnect between learning and grades. If we expect our grades to promote learning, then we must be sure that our grades assess and report the learning that we believe is most essential. We as educators must become more conscious of our goals: the knowledge we want our students to understand; the skills we want them to refine; the kinds of reasoning we want them to demonstrate; and the connections we hope they will make between abstract concepts and life.

Once we have clarified what knowledge, skills, reasoning, and connections we believe are essential in our classrooms, we can choose components based on this essential learning on which we will base our grades. For example, in a language arts class, the overall grades might he separated into the components of reading comprehension, writing process, writing product, speaking, literary elements, and effort/citizenship. It is important that these grade components align with the state and district standards; some may be drawn primarily from content or skills already identified by such standards. A grade that is separated into distinct components on the basis of key learning becomes a meaningful communication—to students and parents alike—about what students have and have not mastered.

Once I began deliberately defining what I wanted students to learn, a healthier grading system fell into place. In my Introduction to Sociology class for juniors and seniors, I grouped essential academic expectations into four components: conceptual understandings, application, analysis and evaluation, and formal writing.

To assess conceptual understanding, I monitored students' basic grasp of course content. For example, I expected students to be able to identify what sociologist Charles Cooley meant by *the looking glass self* and to explain the difference between a *functionalist* and a *conflict* view of society. The application component assessed students' ability to make personal connections between course concepts and life. The analysis and evaluation component assessed how well students could use sociological concepts to deepen and challenge their understanding of the larger society. The formal writing component assessed students' writing skills.

Nonacademic Factors

Although grades should definitely reflect the quality of students' academic performance, many teachers believe that students' work habits, responsibility, and attitudes—what researcher Robert Marzano (2000) calls nonacademic factors—are also important.

I believe it is essential to report academic and nonacademic factors separately. We can assess a student's ability to turn things in on time and report it as part of a nonacademic grade component. This assessment, however, should not distort feedback regarding that student's ability to understand a concept or write an essay. In the previously cited language arts example, nonacademic factors are recorded under the effort/citizenship grade component. In the grading scheme for my sociology class, I included a nonacademic component called work habits, which was worth 10 percent of the overall class grade. With a disaggregated grading system, I can simultaneously give accurate feedback on students' learning of essential concepts or skills and their performance on nonacademic factors.

In keeping track of students' work in my sociology course, I grouped each course assignment under one of the five components of essential learning, depending on what kind of learning the assignment tapped. For example, because students' journal entries and reflection worksheets prompted them to connect course concepts and life, scores for those assignments counted toward the application component. I counted some assignments under more than one component; a major paper, for instance, might receive an academic grade for ideas and content grouped under analysis and evaluation and a nonacademic grade for work habits, reflecting whether the student writer completed all steps of the process on time.

I based the letter grade for each component on the average score of all assignments grouped under that component. Each component was worth a specified percentage of the overall letter grade, and I computed the overall course grade by combining the grades for the five components according to the predetermined weight of each. I updated each student's scores continually on a student summary form that I maintained online. Each student and parent could see this individual form anytime, and I also printed this report in preparation for parent-teacher conferences.

Sticky Issues
Handling Homework

When assessing homework assignments, it's especially important to distinguish between academic achievement and nonacademic factors. When we base a significant portion of a student's grade on homework, then the aggregate grade may be a more accurate measure of a student's effort than of his or her learning. In the past, students in my classes who completed homework often received good overall grades even when their actual understanding, as measured by tests, was unsatisfactory. Conversely, students who failed to turn in homework often received low or failing grades even when they had excellent understanding of the content. I do assess the quality of homework: A student who does poor work or shows a lack of understanding will get only partial credit. But my experience suggests that even the quality of the work on an assignment that goes home is more an indicator of nonacademic work habits than of academic understanding. And it is obvious that when an assignment is not turned in at all, we can draw no conclusions about the offending student's knowledge or skills.

To resolve this issue, I consider a student's diligence in doing daily homework as a nonacademic grade component and his or her in-class assessments as a measure of learning. When I combine these components into an overall grade, I weigh the work habits portion at 10–20 percent, which acknowledges the importance of nonacademic factors while placing a greater emphasis on academic learning.

Late Work

With regard to work turned in late, I make a distinction between late daily homework assignments and late major projects or papers. If daily homework is recorded only in the nonacademic portion of the grade, it seems acceptable to me that a teacher might not accept or credit late homework. A student who does not turn in all daily assignments but who has mastered the material can still receive a high grade in the academic component if he or she demonstrates strong learning through in-class assessments. Conversely, a student who turns in all of his or her homework but is not learning will receive high marks for the nonacademic portion, but not on academic components.

Major assignments like projects or papers, however, should be handled differently. Because they are important learning opportunities, they should be accepted even when they are late. The difficulty arises in determining how to assign a grade to late work. A common practice for teachers is to simply reduce the grade, but this practice confuses the issue. A lower grade for an essay turned in late does not accurately communicate how well the student has learned and performed. The grade may indicate that the student is a poorer writer than he or she actually is. With a disaggregated grade, however, the teacher can record a low work habits grade to reflect that the student missed the deadline while giving the paper a grade on the academic component that accurately reflects what the student has learned.

In my sociology class, I assigned students three formal papers. Students were required to successfully complete these assignments to pass the class. I assessed three separate components for each paper: an analysis and evaluation grade for content, a work habits grade for fulfilling the steps and turning the paper in on time, and a formal writing grade that reflected waiting skills.

The first semester I tried this approach, it paid high dividends. As I collected our first formal writing assignment, in which students were to observe and document a social pattern, one student sheepishly admitted to not having completed the paper. I reminded him that although he would lose work habits points, he could still get full credit for the academic portions if he turned in a quality paper. He went back to work monitoring social patterns and turned the paper in the next week. In assessing it, I discovered that although his writing was mediocre, his ideas were inspired. This student received three grades for this assignment: an *F* for work habits, an *A* for analysis and evaluation, and a *C* for formal writing. I was able to report the lateness of the student's work without dampening his enthusiasm or distorting the feedback the grade provided. Most important, the student took full advantage of this important learning opportunity: In fact, he went on to pursue sociology at the postsecondary level. Much would have been lost if I bad simply told him to forget the assignment because I do not accept late work.

Extra Credit

If students are allowed to raise their grade through extra-credit work that is independent of essential learning, then that raised grade reinforces the view of grades as a commodity to be earned. When a student asks for an extra-credit assignment to raise his or her grade, I remind the student that the purpose of grades is to assess and promote learning. A low grade simply communicates a learning gap; the way to raise the grade is to learn more. I explain that although I do not believe in extra credit, I do believe in opportunities for further learning. A student who scored low on a formal paper, for example, may seek extra writing help, rewrite the paper, and try for a higher grade. If a student received a low quiz grade, he or she may take the quiz again to demonstrate mastery of the material. This approach helps reinforce the view that grades are a communication tool, not the goal.

Finding a Better Way to Motivate

If we want to keep the focus on learning, we must not depend on grades to motivate our students. In 1945, junior high school teacher Dorothy De Zouche stated, "If I can't give a child a better reason for studying than a grade on a report card, I ought to lock my desk and go home and stay there" (p. 341). Sixty years later, assessment expert Richard Stiggins (2005) declares that "we can succeed as teachers only if we help our students *want* to learn" (p. 199).

As they begin their schooling, young learners are quite inquisitive, eager to read their first chapter book and excited to discover their place in the world. But many students' innate curiosity is stifled by an education system that too often values compliance over creativity, taking tests over testing theories, memorizing over understanding, and high grades over learning.

If educators wish to convince students that we value their understanding, their reasoning, their ideas, and their creativity, we must practice what we preach. By creating meaningful grade components rooted in essential learning, separating out nonacademic factors to ensure that we assess true learning, and sharing our passion for what we teach, we can use grades as a communication tool rather than as the goal.

References

De Zouche, D. (1945). "The wound is mortal": Marks, honors, unsound activities. *Clearing House, 19,* 339–344.

Marzano, R.J. (2000). *Transforming classroom grading.* Alexandria, VA: ASCD.

Stiggins, R. (2005). *Student-involved assessment for learning.* Upper Saddle River, NJ: Pearson/Prentice-Hall.

TONY WINGER is an instructional coach and social studies teacher at Heritage High School, 1401 W. Geddes Ave., Littleton, CO 80120; 303-347-7618: twinger@lps.k12.co.us.

Making the Grade in Middle School

The right grading policies can promote both self-esteem and academic success among middle schoolers.

RUTH DYRNESS AND ALBERT DYRNESS

The middle school years are among the most formidable, as students transition from youth to adulthood. A student's psyche endures the assault of peer pressure, parental pressure, and hormonal dynamics. Self-esteem, consequently, is a significant attribute in developing the strong character necessary to successfully navigate middle school. Because a student's grades can greatly influence how the student feels about his or her ability to learn, teachers and administrators have an imperative to strive to report grades that are an accurate measure of the student's achievement in a subject.

The initial step toward achieving accurate assessment is acknowledging the inherent difficulty. Among other challenges, teachers must separate academic merit from behavior incentives, and develop instruction and assessments that encourage success.

Promoting Self-Esteem

Common sense and a decade of research have shown that a close relationship exists between self-esteem and academic achievement (Shindler 2006). Even those who would downplay the role of self-esteem in student achievement admit that positive self-esteem is a helpful attribute and improves a student's ability to deal with adversity (Baumeister et al. 2005). Implicit in a teacher's charter should be to cultivate and promote self-esteem by teaching students how to be successful.

Some teachers practice a method of teaching in which students are allowed to fail in the hope that they may learn from their mistakes and be motivated to improve. The problem with this approach is that—in order to learn—students actually must fail. Failing for the sake of a motivational lesson could lead to such poor self-esteem that students may lack the will or courage to try again.

An example of this learn-by-failing approach occurs when a teacher requires students to take lecture notes as the sole study resource for an exam. If the notes are insufficient or erroneous, the student will learn this only through a poor exam score; the lesson is that the student needs to take better notes. By reviewing and correcting the notes prior to the exam, a teacher could help students avoid failure and cultivate success. The student's lesson in this case is that good notes result in good scores. If the purpose of the assignment was to learn to take good notes, the notes could be graded and returned prior to the exam.

Appropriate grading of the student's work is as important as the grading policy itself. Grading of exams and assignments is a naturally negative event. The work begins with perfection, and points are deducted for each error until the final score is compiled. Typically, the grader makes comments only on wrong—not right—answers. According to Richard Curwin and Allen Mendler's principal teachings (as cited in Charles 2005), teachers should use a grading system that provides encouraging feedback without damaging the student's willingness to try. Students would be encouraged if a grader commented, "Creative answer, but not quite what I was looking for."

In the liberal arts, ample opportunity exists to give students positive feedback. If criticism is needed, it should come in a "criticism sandwich"—that is, a compliment followed by criticism followed by another compliment (Webber 2005). This grading technique would help to preserve the student's self-esteem while giving a fair assessment of the student's work. Strong, Silver, and Robinson (1995) suggested that convincing students they can succeed is an important element in keeping them engaged and motivated.

In designing an appropriate grading system, middle school teachers have the added burden of dealing with the mental and emotional challenges of adolescence. Considerable research has shown a decline in student motivation as students transition from elementary to middle school (Anderman and Midgley 1998). Middle school students typically need to be motivated to do the work necessary to establish their knowledge of a subject and make it their own. This work can be repetitive, uninteresting, and viewed as having no applicability to their future, leaving teachers with the challenge of motivating students to do the necessary work and to remember to turn it in on time.

Using Grades as a Motivator

A mistake some middle school teachers make is to use grades as a behavioral motivator. Many teachers view grading and behavioral management together as one and the same (Friedman 1998).

Whenever these teachers need to motivate their students, they attach some effect to the student's grade. If the teacher believes that homework is important, credit toward the student's grade is attached to the homework. If behavior is a problem, some teachers will award extra credit toward the student's grade for exemplary behavior and deduct credit as a deterrent to poor behavior.

Using a student's grade as a motivator is not educationally defensible (Friedman 1998). Grades should not be based on a student's behavior, but should remain exclusively a reflection of the student's command of the subject (London 1996). Teachers need to explore other ways to motivate students (Friedman 1998). Brewster and Fager (2000) have assimilated some suggestions to motivate students that do not involve grades:

- ensure that course materials relate to students' lives and highlight ways learning can be applied in real-life situations;

- allow students to have some degree of control over learning;
- assign challenging, but achievable tasks for all students;
- arouse students' curiosity about the topic being studied; and
- design projects that allow students to share new knowledge with others.

Late-Work Policies

Many schools maintain a policy of not accepting late or incomplete work. This practice might limit the amount of grading the teacher or aides would have to perform, but does not provide an opportunity for the teacher to evaluate the student's progress. Further, the practice makes no distinction between a student who does the work but does not turn it in on time and a student who does not do the work at all. When grading on a strict

---

Accurately Assessing Students

Every educator has a duty to provide opportunities for all students to demonstrate their knowledge, whether through exams, projects, or presentations. Through these opportunities, educators can reduce assessment errors—which exist and are generally underestimated (McMillan 2000)—and achieve more accurate student assessment.

Grade Credit

Grade credit should be reserved for assessment activities. Though participation might allow a teacher to evaluate a student, nonparticipation does not provide an opportunity for evaluation. Moreover limited participation cannot be viewed as a lack of understanding and, therefore, cannot be used to negatively affect a student's grade.

Required assignments, such as homework or note taking also should not influence a student's grade. To ensure that students perform these requirements, pass/fail criteria for the course could be applied, without influencing student assessment.

Grading Methodology

Should exams be graded on a strict percentage or a curve? Both systems comprise arbitrary and subjective elements. The difficulty is in separating the true measure from random error.

Grading on a curve provides flexibility for a teacher to prepare exams with problems of varying degrees of difficulty. Random errors tend to shift the mean score of a class, but not the distribution. Therefore, random errors are minimized when grading on a curve. Grading on a curve, however, is a class rank method of grading and may not provide a clear evaluation of the command of the subject. Nonetheless, the method does minimize a number of variables that create uncertainty when grading on a strict percentage basis. These variables include:

- exam difficulty;
- the clarity with which the material is presented;

- the fidelity with which the exams are graded; and
- the degree to which credit for non-exam work is in proportion to the student's demonstrated achievement.

A strict percentage grading policy places the burden on teachers to manage the variables that limit their ability to arrive at an accurate assessment For example,

- Exams must be formulated so that a predetermined method of assessment matches the percentage correct.
- When grading exams, the grader must give partial credit to distinguish between answers that show a partial understanding of the subject and those that demonstrate a complete lack of understanding.
- The exam questions need to be clear and not open to misinterpretation, such as "Which of the following does not . . . ." In evaluating the responses, graders will not be able to distinguish students who lack the knowledge from those who misinterpret the question.
- Even the number of points assigned to each problem and the total number of problems must be carefully considered. Using a T-distribution, the minimum number of problems required to essentially eliminate the difference in the sample and the true population is 30 (Spears 2006).

Student assessment is inherently an exercise in professional judgment (McMillan 2000). The number of points assigned to a given problem can bias the grader's assignment of partial credit. Figure 1 shows the difference in percentage credit given by subtracting a single point from a problem with varying maximum point totals. Giving two points for partial credit on a three-point problem appears fair, but in terms of percentage represents 66 percent or a D letter grade. Measuring on a scale of 0 to 100 has been used since the early 1900s (Moll 1998) and is clearly the most intuitive scale. Giving partial credit so that the percentage correct for a particular problem correlates to

Continued

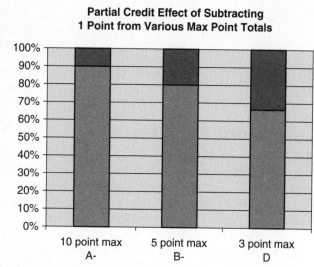

Figure 1 Partial credit.

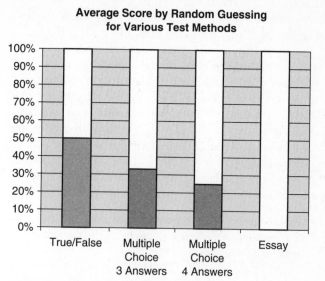

Figure 2 Random guessing.

a specific letter grade is imperative. The grader should ask, "Does this answer translate to an A, B, C, D, or F understanding?"

Exam Design

Exam design is aimed at revealing the student's true knowledge of the subject. A student's comprehension is demonstrated more clearly in an essay format than in a multiple-choice format. According to Criswell and Criswell (2004), more of the student's logic and understanding are revealed using the essay format, where a student must articulate a correct response. Math problems requiring work to be shown are intrinsically analogous to essay questions. In true/false and multiple-choice exams, even random guessing likely will not produce a 0 percent score. Figure 2 shows the average

score that would be produced by guessing at true/false or multiple-choice exams.

Because the minimum practical score of these exam types is different, averaging them lo arrive at a combined grade would be biased. Even more important is that students will learn and study differently depending on the type of exam (McMillan 2000). Studying for multiple-choice exams tends to involve more memorization, while studying for essay exams usually entails a deeper search for understanding.

Some exams are further complicated by the assignment of variable point totals for specific problems. Still other exam questions are cumulative. If the first part of the question is answered incorrectly, answers to the remaining questions inevitably will be wrong. Exam generation is just as important as how the exam is graded in reflecting true knowledge of the material.

percentage, the absence of this distinction degrades the intrinsic meaning of the grading scale.

Late work must be accepted because getting a zero for a late assignment is an incorrect measure of the student's knowledge.

In a strict percentage grading methodology, late work must be accepted because getting a zero for a late assignment is an incorrect measure of the student's knowledge. Because average scores of work that are turned in are generally much higher than zero, including a zero in the grade calculation would create an unintended bias. Using the median instead of the mean would provide a fairer assessment when combining scores with a single zero and would not dramatically affect the overall grade (London 1996).

If a teacher is not going to accept late work, he or she must provide evidence that the work was not turned in on time. Students should initial a log, acknowledging that they did or did not turn in the assignment on the due date. This system avoids potential student claims that the assignment was turned in but lost by the grader.

When grading a project or presentation, the emphasis should be placed on content, not instructions. If a cover sheet is missing, for example, teachers should not deduct enough points that would result in a letter-grade reduction, because the resulting grade is not a true measure of the student's knowledge. Some teachers make the mistake of grading students on their ability to follow directions, giving it equal weight with a student's ability to comprehend the subject. This system makes the student's knowledge assessment intrinsically less accurate.

Some might find the no-credit-for-late-work policy an incentive for students to be more responsible about their assignments. When the student fails to complete the assignment on time, however, no further incentive for completion remains after the due date has expired. In this case, the student does not get an opportunity to learn, and the teacher forfeits an opportunity to evaluate the student. Even as an incentive, this policy falls short, because the consequences of being irresponsible are suffered sometimes weeks after the time of the infraction. The consequence—a lower grade reported once a quarter—is so far removed from the time of the infraction that any intended cause-and-effect relationship is virtually lost.

Not only is the no-credit-for-late-work policy an ineffective motivator, but it also can result in unintended outcomes. For example, the policy can inadvertently encourage truancy in students who are grade-conscious. Schools that use this policy typically allow the absent student to make up the missed work without a penalty. Any time a student completes an assignment at home but forgets to bring it to school, that student must make a choice: Does the student skip class and thereby get an extra day to turn in the assignment, or does the student go to class and get no credit for the late work? Depending on the importance of the assignment to the student's grade, one might find that even well-intentioned students would choose skipping class over the prospect of suffering the lower grade.

Perhaps a better approach would be to offer students the opportunity to turn in late work with a penalty. The penalty should not be a decrease in the student's grade, but instead should require additional work for the benefit of receiving full credit on the original assignment. This gives students an opportunity to repent for being irresponsible and allows them to benefit from being exposed to additional material. The threat of additional work provides the incentive to be more responsible in the future. The amount of work assigned by a teacher is a much more effective motivator than just the prospect of a lower grade by the end of the quarter.

Closing Thoughts

Primarily because of the strong relationship between grades and resulting self-esteem, the obligation of teachers and administrators is to strive to make grades a true reflection of the student's demonstrated knowledge. Grades should represent a measure of students' knowledge of the subject and not be used to coerce a certain behavior.

Grades should represent a measure of students' knowledge of the subject and not be used to coerce a certain behavior.

With initiative and forethought, teachers can, no doubt, devise a system that motivates students to complete and turn in the assigned work. The key is for teachers and administrators to recognize the limits of various grading practices (Moll 1998)

and to embrace the idea that student assessment need not be constructed with inflexible rules. Rather, a grading system is an investigative effort to ascertain the student's true knowledge of a subject and to convert that information into a defined grade.

Accurate assessment can help cultivate the often fragile self-esteem of the middle school student. A well-conceived grading policy will not allow students to feel helpless, but will lead them to conclude that earnest effort will result in academic success.

References

Anderman, L. H., and C. Midgley. 1998. *Motivation and middle school students*. Champaign, IL: ERIC Clearinghouse on Elementary and Early Childhood Education. ERIC ED 421 281.

Baumeister, R. F., J. D. Campbell, J. I. Krueger, and K. D. Vohs. 2005. Exploding the self-esteem myth. *Scientific American* 292(1): 84–91.

Brewster, C., and J. Fager. 2000. *Increasing student engagement and motivation: From time-on-task to homework*. Portland, OR: Northwest Regional Educational Laboratory. Available at: www.nwrel.org/request/oct00/textonly.html.

Charles, C. M. 2005. *Building classroom discipline*, 8th ed. Boston: Pearson Education.

Criswell, J. R., and S. J. Criswell. 2004. Asking essay questions: Answering contemporary needs. *Education* 124(3): 510.

Friedman, S. J. 1998. Grading teachers' grading policies. *NASSP Bulletin* 82(597): 77–83.

London, H. 1996. Do our grading systems contribute to dumbing down? *NASSP Bulletin* 80(580): 117–21.

McMillan, J. H. 2000. Fundamental assessment principles for teachers and school administrators. *Practical Assessment, Research & Evaluation* 7(8). Available at: http://PAREonline.net/getvn.asp?v=7&n=8.

Moll, M. 1998. A brief history of grading. *Teacher: Newsmagazine of the BC Teachers' Federation* 11(3). Available at: www.bctf.ca/publications/NewsmagArticle.aspx?id=13110.

Shindler, J. V. 2006. Creating a psychology of success in the classroom: Enhancing academic achievement by systematically promoting student self-esteem. Available at: www.calstatela.edu/faculty/jshindl/teaching/self-es.htm.

Spears, M. 2006. One-sample inference—Estimation. MATH 419: Intersession 2006 class minutes. Available at: www.harding.edu/mspears/class/math419/Summer2006/minutes.html.

Strong, R., H. F. Silver, and A. Robinson. 1995. Strengthening student engagement: What do students want (and what really motivates them)? *Educational Leadership* 53(1): 8–12.

Webber, C. 2005. Self-esteem. Available at: www.netdoctor.co.uk/sex_relationships/facts/selfesteem.htm.

RUTH DYRNESS has been a paraprofessional for the San Ramon Unified School District for two years. She earned a B.S. in Biology and a Multiple Subject Teaching Credential from California State University, East Bay. **ALBERT DYRNESS** is Vice President of ADVENT Engineering, Division of Professional Education, in San Ramon, CA. He is a former Executive Producer of edutainment software for children at RPJ Multimedia. He earned a BSME at CSU Sacramento and an MSME at MIT.

UNIT 7

Self-Assessment and Motivation

Unit Selections

Key Points to Consider

- What are some concerns teachers have with showing students weak examples of learning tasks?

- Discuss the differences between the two terms: self-assessment and self-evaluation.

- Discuss the traffic light method after reading *Helping Students Understand Assessment*, Jan Chappuis

- Define the terms self-assessment, self-evaluation, self-directed, self-managing, self-monitoring, metacognition, and self-regulation.

- Define the term high-expectations.

- Identify ways to encourage students to establish expectations that are similar to teacher expectations (Discuss how that conversation takes place in a classroom).

- How does a teacher encourage students to internalize high expectations?

- Adopt a checklist to use in one's professional practice (*Launching Self-Directed Learners,* Arthur I. Costa and Bena Kallick)

Student Website
www.mhcls.com

Internet References

ALPS, Active Learning Practice for Schools
http://learnweb.harvard.edu/alps/tfu/info3f.cfm
Looking at Student Work
http://www.lasw.org/
Self-Assessment in Portfolios
http://www.ncrel.org/sdrs/areas/issues/students/learning/lr2port.htm

Assessment and evaluation are often regarded as activities conducted by teachers, principals, and administrators. This philosophy overlooks the direct contribution students can make to the assessment and evaluation process. Students involved in self-assessment learn to reflect, analyze, and set goals. When students self-evaluate, they are judging or rating their work. According to Carl Rodgers (1969), "It is when students take the responsibility for deciding important criteria, determining goals, and stating the extent to which they will achieve those goals, that they truly learn to take responsibility for their learning."

Self-assessment is a set of tasks involving planning, implementing, monitoring, and regulating, and if necessary, modifying learning goals and finally reporting on whether those goals were achieved. Students involved in a self-assessment activity are taking personal responsibility for their learning by identifying what goals they "need to know" and documenting "how well" they succeeded. When students decide "what and how" to learn, they are making choices that are most appropriate for themselves. Eventually, a student understands what learning is.

Self-evaluation is the task of comparing a performance against a set of criteria or expectations. Documenting and reporting achievement gains or lack of an accomplishment is rooted in an individual's perspective of his/her competence level. Enabling students to critique their performance based on a defined set of criteria helps students to develop an understanding about the way they think and learn new knowledge and skills. Being aware of one's capabilities, knowing, or the opportunity to set criteria for evaluation are steps in developing into an autonomous, independent learner.

Often, students are not very proficient at being aware of their performance or accurate in their judgments. Frequently, students need guidance through the initial process. Rating scales and rubrics are performance-based assessments that students can use as guides. Self-evaluation followed by a conference with the teacher can have cognitive and motivational benefits.

Knowing that one is making progress enhances self-efficacy (belief in one's ability) and promotes motivation. Also, allowing students to set goals strengthens their commitment to learn. As students achieve their goals, they have a tendency to set higher expectations due to their belief in their abilities and because they are motivated.

"Why would teachers want to involve students in the assessment process?" Self-assessment is the self-reporting component that enables students to make decisions about learning. Research has shown that when students are given choices, they are more likely to be interested in persevering during difficult tasks, set higher expectations, and seek answers and help from others. When they notice that they are actually performing better, then they feel good about themselves. Confidence in learning builds from knowing that the goal was achieved.

This unit addresses the mutual relationship that exists between the teacher and student in terms of an assessment practice. For assessments to be effective and the information gleaned to be useful, students must understand and share the goals for learning. Two topics in this unit are helping students understand the assessment-evaluation processes and strategies to guide and direct student learning when engaged with peers during self-assessment.

© Jose Luis Pelaez Inc/Blend Images/Corbis

In the first article, the author suggests that formative assessments promote learning when they help students to ask three important questions, "Where am I going?", "Where am I now?", and "How can I close the gap?" These questions can be the basis for reading the other articles because they focus on enabling the learner to self-assess and self-evaluate (Chappuis, 2005, p.39).

Providing students with prompts or a visual chart are useful strategies for encouraging the practice of self-assessment and self-evaluation. In the next two articles, the authors describe the use of rubrics and checklists to guide students' analysis, planning, and monitoring.

In the article, *Launching Self-Directed Learners,* there are several useful instructional-assessment methods for students and teachers. The authors included several teacher-directed metacognitive questions that can be asked to encourage students to reflect on their thinking.

Helping Students Understand Assessment

Formative assessments promote learning when they help students answer three questions: Where am I going? Where am I now? and How can I close the gap?

JAN CHAPPUIS

During the last decade, many schools have begun to emphasize formative assessment. As teachers work to develop short-cycle or common assessments and engage in data-driven decision making, they typically remain in the central decision-making role. This approach reflects the underlying assumption that teachers control learning. Although teachers must create the conditions for learning, however, students ultimately decide whether they feel capable of learning and whether they will do the work. Therefore, students are equally important users of formative assessment information. The research tells us why.

Necessary Components of Formative Assessment

In their 1998 synthesis of research, Black and Wiliam reported that formative assessment produced significant learning gains, with effect sizes between 0.4 and 0.7. They noted, however, that in schools achieving these gains, students were the primary users of formative assessment information. In such schools,

- Formative assessment began with offering students a clear picture of learning targets.
- Students received feedback on their work that helped them understand where they were with respect to the desired learning target.
- Students engaged in self-assessment.
- Formative assessment provided an understanding of specific steps that students could take to improve.

Sadler (1989) had previously reported similar findings. In describing the role of formative assessment in developing expertise, he identified three conditions required for students to improve:

The student comes to hold a concept of quality roughly similar to that held by the teacher, is able to monitor

continuously the quality of what is being produced during the act of production itself, and has a repertoire of alternative moves or strategies from which to draw at any given point. (p. 121)

This research on effective formative assessment suggests that students should be able to answer three basic questions: Where am I going? Where am I now? and How can I close the gap? (adapted from Atkin, Black, & Coffey, 2001). The seven strategies described in the following sections can help ensure systematic student involvement in the formative assessment process (Stiggins, Arter, Chappuis, & Chappuis, 2004).

Where Am I Going?

Students need to know what learning targets they are responsible for mastering, and at what level. Marzano (2005) asserts that students who can identify what they are learning significantly outscore those who cannot.

To make significant achievements, students need to know what learning targets they are responsible for mastering, and at what level.

Strategy 1: Provide a clear and understandable vision of the learning target. Share the learning targets before you begin instruction, in language your students can understand. For example, when introducing a reading comprehension unit calling for inference, you might say, "We are learning to *infer*. This means we are learning to make reasonable guesses on the basis of clues." Or provide students with a written list of learning targets described in student-friendly language, such as,

We are learning about fractions. We are learning to

- Read and write fractions with halves, thirds, fourths, and tenths.
- Read and write mixed numbers (whole numbers plus fractions).
- Change fractions written as tenths into decimals.

When working with more complex content standards that call for performance assessment, such as "Writes clearly and effectively," introduce the language of the scoring guide that the school will use to define quality. To do this, ask students what they think constitutes good writing, and then help them identify where their concept of good writing matches the concepts in the scoring guide. If the scoring guide is above students' reading level, you might want to create a student-friendly version.

Strategy 2: Use examples of strong and weak work. To know where they are going, students must know what excellent performance looks like. Ask students to evaluate anonymous work samples for quality and then to discuss and defend their judgments, using the language of the scoring guide in the case of performance assessments. Such an exercise will help students develop skill in accurate self-assessment.

Teachers often use strong examples, or exemplars, but avoid using weak examples because they worry that students will accidentally emulate them. On the contrary, when students evaluate weak examples that mirror common problems, they become more proficient at identifying their own weaknesses and gain a better understanding of quality. To introduce work samples to students, you might

1. Distribute to students a student-friendly version of the scoring guide you will use to evaluate their final products.
2. Choose one aspect of quality (one trait) to focus on.
3. Show an overhead transparency of a strong anonymous sample, but don't let students know it's a strong example. Have students work independently to score it for the one trait using the student-friendly scoring guide. You may ask students to underline the statements in the scoring guide that they believe describe the work they're examining.
4. After students have settled on a score independently, have them share their scores in small groups, using the language of the scoring guide to explain their reasoning.
5. Ask the class to vote and tally their scores on an overhead transparency. Then ask for volunteers to share their scores and the rationale behind them. Listen for, and encourage, use of the language of the scoring guide.
6. Repeat this process with a weak anonymous sample, focusing on the same trait. Do this several times, alternating between strong and weak papers, until students are able to distinguish between strong and weak work and independently give rationales reflecting the concepts in the scoring guide (Stiggins et al., 2004).

Where Am I Now?

When my daughter was in 3rd grade, she once brought home a math paper with a smiley face, a minus 3, and an *M* at the top. When we asked her what the *M* meant she had learned, she looked at us as though we were trying to trick her and replied, "Math?" When we asked her what that meant she needed to work on, she frowned and ventured, "Math?"

Students gain insight from explaining the learning that their work represents and what they plan to work on next.

Papers marked like this one do not give students the information they need. At best, such marks might tell the student, "I'm doing OK in math," but they will not enable the student to assess his or her own strengths and weaknesses. You can use the following two strategies to help students identify how they are currently performing in relation to the learning and actions that are expected of them.

Strategy 3: Offer regular descriptive feedback. Black and Wiliam (1998) recommend that to improve formative assessment, teachers should reduce *evaluative* feedback—such as "*B+* . Good work!" or "You didn't put enough effort into this"—and increase *descriptive* feedback, such as "You maintained eye contact with your audience throughout your whole presentation" or "Your problem-solving strategy for dividing all the people into equal groups worked well right up to the end, but you need to figure out what to do with the remaining people."

The quality of the feedback, rather than its quantity, determines its effectiveness (Bangert-Downs, Kulik, Kulik, & Morgan, 1991; Sadler, 1989). The most effective feedback identifies success and also offers students a recipe for corrective action (Bloom, 1984; Brown, 1994). Grades and other coded marks—such as $\sqrt{}$ + and 92%—do not tell students what areas they need to improve. Instead, such marks signal that the work on this piece is finished.

Here are some simple actions you can take to provide effective feedback:

- After students have practiced using a scoring guide with anonymous work and they understand the meaning of the phrases in the scoring guide, highlight phrases that describe strengths and weaknesses of their work. If you are working with a multitrait scoring guide, limit feedback to one or two traits at a time.
- Have students *traffic light* their work (Atkin et al., 2001), marking it with a green, yellow, or red dot to indicate the level of help they need. Allow students with green and yellow dots to provide descriptive feedback to one another, while you provide feedback for students with red dots.

Strategy 4: Teach students to self-assess and set goals. In giving students descriptive feedback, you have modeled the kind of

---

My Strengths and Areas to Improve
Trait (s): _____
Name: _____
Name of Paper: _____
Date: _____

My Opinion
My strengths are _____
_____

What I think I need to work on is _____
_____

My Teacher's or Classmate's Opinion
Strengths include _____
_____

Work on _____
_____

My Plan
What I will do now is _____
_____
_____
_____

Next time I'll ask for feedback from _____
_____

Figure 1 Student self-assessment form
Source: From *Classroom Assessment for Student Learning: Doing It Right—Using It Well*, by R. J. Stiggins, J. Arter, J. Chappuis, and S. Chappuis, 2004, Portland, OR: Assessment Training Institute.

thinking you want them to do as self-assessors. As a next step, turn that task over to students and guide them in practicing self-assessment and goal setting. You may find it useful to have students identify the strengths and weaknesses of their work before you offer your own feedback. Have them complete a form like the one in Figure 1 and staple it to their work when they turn it in. Respond with your feedback, either on the form or orally.

To help students align their expectations with yours, ask them to turn in a scoring guide with their work, highlighting in yellow the phrases in the guide that they believe represent the quality of their work. On the same scoring guide, highlight in blue the phrases that you think describe their work, and return the guide to them. Where the highlighted phrases are green (blue over yellow), your feedback matches the student's self-assessment. Any highlighted phrases that remain blue or yellow, however, indicate areas in which the student probably needs to refine his or her vision of quality (Stiggins et al., 2004).

If you are using a selected-response test, you can arrange the items according to the learning targets they assess and give students the list of learning targets correlated to the test item numbers. When they receive their corrected test, students can identify which learning targets they have mastered and which learning targets they need to work on further. They can then develop a plan for how they will improve the targeted areas.

This practice is especially effective if students have the opportunity to retake the test.

How Can I Close the Gap?

The final essential step in making formative assessment work is to keep students in touch with what they can do to close the gap between where they are now and where they need to be.

Strategy 5: Design lessons to focus on one aspect of quality at a time. This strategy breaks learning into more manageable chunks for students. For example, suppose that students are learning to design and conduct scientific investigations, and one part of the scoring guide describes the qualities of a good hypothesis. If students are having trouble formulating hypotheses, they can refer to that portion of the scoring guide as they differentiate between strong and weak examples of hypotheses, practice drafting hypotheses, give one another descriptive feedback on their drafts, and assess their own drafts' strengths and weaknesses.

One of the strongest motivators is the opportunity to look back and see progress.

Strategy 6: Teach students focused revision. Let students practice revising their work before being held accountable by a final grade. You might begin with one of the anonymous, weak work samples that your students have evaluated (see *Strategy 2*). Focusing on just the single aspect of quality that they evaluated, ask students to work in pairs to either revise the sample or create a revision plan describing what the anonymous student needs to do to improve the work. Then ask students to apply the same process to their own work, either revising it to make it better or submitting a revision plan. For example, after assessing their draft hypotheses in science, students could use the scoring guide to write out what they need to do to improve their hypotheses.

Strategy 7: Engage students in self-reflection and let them document and share their learning. We know the power of self-reflection to deepen learning for adults. It also works for students. One of the strongest motivators is the opportunity to look back and see progress.

In a skill-based course, such as physical education, students can fill out a daily form that asks two questions: "What are two important things you learned from today's class?" and "What is one goal you have for tomorrow's class?"

Student portfolios can also promote students' self-reflection. In collecting their work and insights in portfolios, students have the opportunity to reflect on their learning, develop an internal feedback loop, and understand themselves better as learners. To use portfolios in this way, students must clearly understand their learning goals, the steps that they have taken toward reaching those goals, and how far they have come. Involving students in parent-teacher conferences can accomplish the same purpose. Students gain insight from explaining to their parents the learning that their work represents, their strengths as learners, and what they plan to work on next.

Students at the Center

The seven strategies described here are designed to help students better understand their learning goals, recognize their own skill level in relation to the goals, and take responsibility for reaching the goals. By expanding our formative assessment practices to systematically involve students as decision makers, teachers acknowledge the contributions that students make to their own success and give them the opportunity and structure they need to become active partners in improving their learning.

References

Atkin, J. M., Black, P., & Coffey, J. (2001). *Classroom assessment and the National Science Education Standards*. Washington, DC: National Academy Press.

Bangert-Downs, R. L., Kulik, C-L. C., Kulik, J. A., & Morgan, M. T. (1991). The instructional effect of feedback in test-like events. *Review of Education Research, 61*(2), 213–238.

Black, P., & Wiliam, D. (1998). Inside the black box: Raising standards through classroom assessment. *Phi Delta Kappan, 80*(2), 139–148.

Bloom, B. (1984). The search for methods of group instruction as effective as one-to-one tutoring. *Educational Leadership, 41*(8), 4–17.

Brown, A. L. (1994). The advancement of learning. *Educational Researcher, 23*(8), 4–12.

Marzano, R. (2005). *What works in schools* (PowerPoint presentation). Available: www.marzanoandassociates.com/pdf/Short Version.pdf

Sadler, D. R. (1989). Formative assessment and the design of instructional systems. *Instructional Science, 18*, 119–144.

Stiggins, R. J., Arter, J., Chappuis, J., & Chappuis, S. (2004). *Classroom assessment* for *student learning: Doing it right—using it well*. Portland, OR: Assessment Training Institute.

JAN CHAPPUIS is an author and consultant at the Assessment Training Institute, 317 SW Alder St., Ste. 1200, Portland, OR 97204; 503-228-3014; jchappuis@assessmentinst.com.

Self-Assessment through Rubrics

Rubrics can be a powerful self-assessment tool—if teachers disconnect them from grades and give students time and support to revise their work.

HEIDI ANDRADE

A key element of formative assessment is feedback. The trouble is, most teachers have difficulty finding time to give all students the feedback they need when they need it. Fortunately, students themselves can be excellent sources of feedback. Under the right conditions, student self-assessment can provide accurate, useful information to promote learning.

Assessment versus Evaluation

During self-assessment, students reflect on the quality of their work, judge the degree to which it reflects explicitly stated goals or criteria, and revise. Self-assessment is formative—students assess works in progress to find ways to improve their performance. Self-evaluation, in contrast, is summative—it involves students giving themselves a grade. Confusion between the two has led to these misconceptions about self-assessment that make many teachers hesitant to try it: (1) Students will just give themselves As, and (2) They won't revise their work anyway, so there's no point in taking time for self-assessment.

Can these misconceptions be true? Yes, sadly true—*if* the results of a self-assessment are counted toward a grade or students are not given time for and help with revision. If, on the other hand, students understand the value of self-assessment, are taught how to do it, share their teacher's understanding of quality (Sadler, 1989), and have the support needed to improve their work, they can accurately self-assess and effectively revise.

The differences between self-evaluation and self-assessment may seem subtle, but they are powerful in practice.

The differences between self-evaluation and self-assessment may seem subtle, but they are powerful in practice. When my colleagues and I asked students about their attitudes toward self-assessments they had done that did not count toward grades,

the responses were positive (Andrade & Du, 2007). Students commented that self-assessment helped them feel prepared, improved the quality of their work, and gave them a better understanding of what they had achieved. Specific perceived benefits included improved ability to focus on key elements of an assignment, increased effectiveness in identifying strengths and weaknesses in their work, and higher motivation. Said one student,

> Self-assessment . . . just eases your mind about doing your papers and stuff; it doesn't make you so anxious, and you can actually work ahead a little bit.

Yet in another study, when the researchers asked students about self-evaluations they had done that counted for 5 percent of their grades, those students' attitudes were somewhat negative: They voiced concerns about fairness and the possibility of cheating by inflating self-evaluations (Ross, Rolheiser, & Hogaboam-Gray, 1998). Other research (Boud & Falchikov, 1989) has shown that students do tend to inflate self-evaluations when they will count toward formal grades. For these reasons, I subscribe to a purely formative notion of self-assessment as feedback *for* oneself *from* oneself.

Rubrics as Student Self-Assessment Tools

One way to support thoughtful self-assessment is to provide a rubric or create one with students. A rubric is a document that lists criteria and describes varying levels of quality, from excellent to poor, for a specific assignment (Andrade, 2000). Many teachers use rubrics for scoring student work, but rubrics can do much more. In the hands of students, a good rubric can orient learners to the concept of quality as defined by experts in a field, inform self- and peer assessment, and guide revision and improvement. Rubrics can be informative as well as evaluative.

Unfortunately, some rubrics define quality for an assignment too narrowly, leading teachers to worry that rubrics result in cookie-cutter products from students and limited feedback from teachers. If that is the case, the rubric in question is a bad one and should be shredded.

Popham (2006) contrasts a poor rubric description with an effective one. On a rubric to assess students' performance on a writing assignment about donating blood, in which one of the criteria is *organization,* a narrow, overly task-specific description of the highest level of performance might require that the piece "describe the importance of blood giving, the steps in giving blood, the impact of 'Mad Cow' disease, and the reasons people cannot give blood too frequently." A more effective description of the highest level of organization might state that the piece "contains an introduction, a body, and a conclusion. The structure is appropriate for the task: for instance, an order-of-importance, logical, or chronological structure."

When carefully designed, perhaps collaboratively with students, good rubrics can provide students with important guidelines without constraining creativity and can be a boon to self-assessment. The process of rubric-referenced self-assessment involves three basic steps.

Setting Clear Expectations

The expectations for the task or performance should be clearly articulated by either the teacher, the students, or both. Because students become better acquainted with the task at hand when they are involved in thinking about what counts and how quality is defined, I often create all or part of my rubrics in class with students.

For example, in a recent study in English/language arts and social studies classes in grades 3 through 7 (Andrade, Du, & Wang, in press), I began by asking students to analyze an example of a relatively strong persuasive essay. After the class had thoroughly appraised the sample in terms of its strengths and weaknesses (something students tend to be amazingly good at), I asked them to list the qualities of a really good persuasive essay, drawing on their critique of the sample. If a class overlooked a quality that I thought was important, I added it to the list with an explanation. This activity generated a list of qualities—*clearly states the opinion; supports it with facts; makes sense, is convincing; has a good beginning, middle, and ending,* and so on—that provided the basis for the criteria on our rubric.

With my own classes for undergraduate and graduate students, I go on to ask students to combine related qualities into rubric-sized criteria: For instance, *clearly states opinion, supports it with facts, and is convincing* would become part of an *Ideas and Content* criterion. I create the rest of the rubric outside class, sketching out four levels of quality for each criterion. I show the rubric to the students, ask them for their questions and comments, and revise the rubric for clarity as needed. Only after I am confident that students understand and accept the rubric do I ask them to begin an assignment.

Conducting Self-Assessment

Students create rough or first attempts at their assignment, be it a story, word problem, lab report, baseball bat swing, or speech. They monitor their progress on the assignment by comparing their performances to the rubric. In my research on writing,

I have had students in grades 3 through 8 use pencils in various colors to underline key phrases in the rubric, then underline or circle in their drafts the evidence of having met the standard articulated by each phrase. For example, students underlined *clearly states an opinion* in blue on their persuasive essay rubric and then underlined in blue the opinion they had stated in their persuasive essay drafts—if they could find it. If they discovered they had not met the standard, they wrote themselves a reminder to make improvements when they created their final drafts.

This procedure can take one or two class periods. Students working on a persuasive essay can look at global criteria like *ideas and content, organization,* and *voice* on one day and then self-assess more fine-grained criteria like *word choice, sentence fluency,* and *conventions* on another day.

Revising

Students use the feedback from their self-assessments to guide revision. For example, in the colored-pencil activity just described, we used orange pencils to look at sentence beginnings, which were part of the *sentence fluency* criterion. Students circled in orange the first word in each sentence in their essay and then counted up the number of times they used the most common sentence starters. If they had a word or phrase that appeared a lot (in the case of the persuasive essays, it was usually "I" as in "I think . . .") they made a note of this problem. In their next draft, they attempted to change the beginnings of some sentences to increase variety.

The revision step is crucial. Students are savvy, and they will not self-assess thoughtfully unless they know that their efforts can lead to opportunities to actually make improvements.

Self-Assessment Works

Although my students have told me that they thought the self-assessment I required was "a big pain" at first, their attitudes have usually become positive after they try it. They have to try it: I generally will not review or grade a piece of work that is not accompanied by a self-assessment. After experiencing rubric-referenced self-assessment, they tend to value it. In a study of my former undergraduates (Andrade & Du, 2007), students reported that they could self-assess effectively, that they were more likely to self-assess when they knew what their teachers expected, and that their self-assessments were typically followed by serious attempts to revise and improve their work.

The process of student self-assessment through rubrics can be enhanced with peer assessment and teacher feedback, of course. Just the three steps described here, however, have been associated with improvements in elementary and middle school students' writing (Andrade & Boulay, 2003; Andrade, Du, & Wang, 2007). In these and other studies (Ross, Rolheiser, & Hogaboam-Gray, 1999), students improved not just in mechanics, but also in their ability to handle such sophisticated qualities as content, organization, and voice. Further, the improvements in the quality of student writing had practical significance. For instance, when the findings of the 2007 study by Andrade, Du, and Wang were translated into typical classroom grades, the average grade for the group that engaged in rubric-referenced self-assessment was a low *B* whereas the average grade for the comparison group was a high *C*.

Similar results have been found in mathematics. After teaching some teachers but not others to implement self-assessment in their 5th and 6th grade math classes, Ross, Hogaboam-Gray, and Rolheiser (2002) found that students in the treatment group outperformed students in the comparison group. Self-assessment has also been shown to be effective in social studies (Lewbel & Hibbard, 2001); science (White & Frederiksen, 1998); and even on external national examinations (MacDonald & Boud, 2003).

If students produce it, they can assess it; and if they can assess it, they can improve it.

Self-assessment can be useful in any subject. If students produce it, they can assess it; and if they can assess it, they can improve it.

References

Andrade, H. (2000). Using rubrics to promote thinking and learning. *Educational Leadership, 57*(5), 13–18.

Andrade, H., & Boulay, B. (2003). Gender and the role of rubric-referenced self-assessment in learning to write. *Journal of Educational Research, 97*(1), 21–34.

Andrade, H., & Du, Y. (2007). Student responses to criteria-referenced self-assessment. *Assessment and Evaluation in Higher Education, 32*(2), 159–181.

Andrade, H., Du, Y., & Wang, X. (2007, April). *Putting rubrics to the test: A study of the effects of rubric-referenced self-assessment on students' writing.* Paper presented at the annual meeting of the American Educational Research Association, Chicago, IL.

Andrade, H., Du, Y., & Wang, X. (in press). Putting rubrics to the test: The effect of a model, criteria generation, and rubric-referenced self-assessment on elementary school students' writing. *Educational Measurement: Issues and Practice.*

Boud, D., & Falchikov, N. (1989). Quantitative studies of student self-assessment in higher education: A critical analysis of findings. *Higher Education, 18,* 529–549.

Lewbel, S. R., & Hibbard, K. M. (2001). Are standards and true learning compatible? *Principal Leadership (High School Ed.), 1*(5), 16–20.

MacDonald, B., & Boud, D. (2003). The impact of self-assessment on achievement: The effects of self-assessment training on performance in external examinations. *Assessment in Education, 10*(2), 209–220.

Popham, W. J. (2006). *Mastering assessment: A self-service system for educators.* New York: Routledge.

Ross, J. A., Hogaboam-Gray, A., & Rolheiser, C. (2002). Student self-evaluation in grade 5–6 mathematics: Effects on problem-solving achievement. *Educational Assessment, 8*(1), 43–59.

Ross, J. A., Rolheiser, C., & Hogaboam-Gray, A. (1998). Skills-training versus action research in-service: Impact on student attitudes to self-evaluation. *Teaching and Teacher Education, 14*(5), 463–477.

Ross, J. A., Rolheiser, C., & Hogaboam-Gray, A. (1999). Effects of self-evaluation training on narrative writing. *Assessing Writing, 6*(1), 107–132.

Sadler, D. R. (1989). Formative assessment and the design of instructional systems. *Instructional Science, 18,* 119–144.

White, B. Y., & Frederiksen, J. R. (1998). Inquiry, modeling, and metacognition: Making science accessible to all students. *Cognition and Instruction, 16*(1), 3–118.

HEIDI ANDRADE is Assistant Professor of Educational and Counseling Psychology at the University at Albany, State University of New York, 1400 Washington Ave., ED 233, Albany, NY 12222; 518-437-4422; handrade@uamail.albany.edu.

Launching Self-Directed Learners

Through thoughtfully designed instruction, schools can teach students to take charge of their own learning.

Arthur L. Costa and Bena Kallick

Schooling is much like a spaceship launchpad. All the life-support systems remain attached to the command center until the moment of liftoff when the spaceship is suddenly on its own. So, too, are students launched from school into life, internalizing the lessons they have learned in the classroom so they can successfully navigate on their own.

Skillful navigation depends, however, on effective feedback systems. Students need to learn how to guide themselves along the way, monitor their progress toward a specific destination, and make small maneuvers and midcourse corrections. Thus, school becomes the launchpad for a life of self-directed learning.

Defining Self-Directed

What does *self-directed* mean? When confronted with complex and sometimes ambiguous and intellectually demanding tasks, self-directed people exhibit the dispositions and habits of mind required to be self-managing, self-monitoring, and self-modifying (Costa & Garmston, 2001; Costa & Kallick, 2004).

Self-managing. Self-managing people control their first impulse for action and delay premature conclusions. They generally approach tasks by clarifying outcomes and gathering relevant data that will illuminate the problem. They think flexibly and develop alternative strategies to accomplish their goals. Self-managing individuals draw on past knowledge and apply it to new situations. They imagine, create, and innovate (see Costa & Kallick, 2000).

Self-monitoring. Self-monitoring people think about their own thinking, behaviors, biases, and beliefs as well as about the effects that such processes and states of mind have on others and on the environment. They have sufficient self-knowledge to know what works for them. They establish conscious metacognitive strategies to monitor the effectiveness of their plans and help them make any necessary alterations. Self-monitoring people persevere in generating alternative plans of action, and they know how and where to turn when confronted with perplexing situations. They listen to others with understanding and empathy.

Self-modifying. Self-modifying people can change themselves. They reflect on their experiences and evaluate, analyze, and construct meaning. They apply what they have learned to future activities, tasks, and challenges. Such people communicate their conclusions with clarity, precision, and prudence, and they readily admit that they have more to learn. Curious and motivated, they remain open to continuous learning.

> **Self-managing, self-monitoring, and self-modifying capabilities characterize peak performers in all walks of life.**

Self-managing, self-monitoring, and self-modifying capabilities transcend all subject matter commonly taught in school and characterize peak performers in all walks of life. These capabilities make for successful relationships, continuous learning, productive workplaces, and enduring democracies. Education should strive to develop these intellectual dispositions more fully.

Self-Directedness and Self-Assessment

The challenge for educators is to move these expectations from rhetoric to reality by making self-directed learning an explicit outcome for students. Lesson units and learning activities should challenge students to engage in a variety of authentic, rich tasks that require strategic planning, creative approaches, and complex thinking skills (Moulds, 2003-2004). The following scenarios illustrate how students can practice self-directedness and self-assessment in the classroom.

Self-Directed Learners in Secondary School

As part of a project in their U.S. history class, high school students tackle aspects of the upcoming presidential election. They divide into groups on the basis of their interest in a particular

STRATEGIC DISPOSITIONS The team member:	OFTEN	SOMETIMES	NOT YET
• Listens with understanding and empathy • Paraphrases ideas before responding • Clarifies ideas, concepts, or terminology • Poses questions to engage thinking			
• Energizes the group with new ideas • Supports the group when there is frustration • Persists/finds alternatives when the group is stuck			
• Monitors for accuracy and precision • Cross-checks references • Uses spell-checker • Edit with care			

Figure 1 How are we doing? A process checklist for group work.

Source: Adapted from Costa & Kallick, 2000.

candidate and set to work preparing a one-minute TV ad for the campaign. The groups draw on their prior knowledge of the candidates, become aware of their biases, and examine the assumptions underlying campaign rhetoric. Students construct, clarify, and pose questions to guide their investigations, developing a set of process and content goals for their projects. Goals might include listening to one another with understanding and empathy or welcoming multiple perspectives on an issue.

The teacher invites students to monitor their teamwork using a "How Are We Doing?" checklist (see Figure 1). Checklists provide guidelines for applying, monitoring, and evaluating performance on specific indicators of self-directed learning. Students respond to questions that encourage them to develop awareness of their own and others' skills and behaviors, to operate from data rather than from speculation, and to know when to relinquish certain ideas in favor of other, more valid ones (Baker, Costa, & Shalit, 1997).

The teacher poses several metacognitive questions to encourage students to reflect on their thinking: How did you decide to participate in your particular group? What did you learn from your group's "How Are We Doing?" assessment? How will you carry this learning forward to future group work? How did your decisions affect you and others in your group? As you anticipate future team meetings, what commitments might you make to strengthen the group's productivity? The students respond to these questions in writing. One student indicates that although she is learning to think interdependently, she is too shy and sometimes feels that she has nothing to add to the group. She decides to focus on improving her group communication skills.

The teacher asks students to describe whether or not they met their established goals. Team members point out that they are working more and more interdependently, and they explore modifications that will enhance their productivity.

With their first-draft storyboard and script in hand, students devote a class period to thinking interdependently with "critical friends," who may be either inside or outside their group. They reflect on project goals, due dates, strategies, and suggested changes. Partners agree on a specific time to meet again to monitor the process for accuracy and quality. Groups then pair up to present their scripts and share critical feedback about presentation strengths, weaknesses, and possible improvements. Groups also meet with the teacher to clarify work plans, strategies, midcourse adjustments, and criteria for project completion (see Figure 2 for a checklist for educators).

After revising their ads, group members present their projects to a community-based audience. The students ask the audience to complete a checklist that rates how effectively each ad promoted its candidate and illustrated student knowledge of the U.S. election process. This type of evaluation is important because it provides students with critical feedback from adults other than their teachers.

The teacher scores presentations on content accuracy, organization, strength of persuasive images, and appropriate use of conventions.

The teacher scores presentations using a rubric that focuses on content accuracy, organization, strength of persuasive images, and appropriate use of conventions (see Figure 3). Students self-assess using the same rubric, and teacher and students meet to discuss any discrepancies. These discussions have proven powerful in terms of clarifying what the

The following structured opportunities help students become self-directed:

Have students confer with a "critical friend."
- Presenter discusses his or her goals and timeline.
- Responder asks clarifying questions.
- Both parties discuss any possible modifications.
- Partners schedule a meeting to check work for accuracy and quality.

Hold student-teacher conferences. Ask students such questions as
- What is your work plan?
- What difficulties are you having in accomplishing your plan?
- How realistic are your goals given your time frame?
- What part of this project especially intrigues you?
- What strategies have you tried? What strategies might you try?
- How will you know when your work is ready to turn in?

Provide a self-reflection worksheet for new subject matter that has students reflect on the following questions:
- Do I understand why I have to read this material? For a test? For a report?
- What do I already know about this subject?
- What predictions about this material might I make even before I read it?
- Where can I obtain additional information?
- How much time will I need to learn this?
- What are some strategies that I can use to learn this?
- Did I understand what I just read?
- Do I know it well enough to retell it after I have finished reading? Do I know it well enough to answer questions on a test?

Determine whether students are becoming more aware of their own thinking by asking them about the problem-solving process. Have students
- List the steps and explain where they are in the sequence of a problem-solving strategy.
- Trace the pathways they took and any dead ends they encountered.
- Describe what data are lacking and the students' plans for producing those data.

Figure 2 Self-directed learning. A checklist for educators.

standards-based rubric means and how well the work stacks up against the standards.

Following their formal presentations, students rate their group's effectiveness by writing an evaluation in their journals. They consider a number of questions: How did you think about solving the problem of creating a persuasive presentation? What steps did you take? Draw the metacognitive pathways you followed and the dead ends you experienced on the road to solving the problem. What strategies enabled you to persist when you encountered obstacles? What intrigues and wonderments will you continue to ponder long after this project is completed and the election is over?

One student wrote that when various obstacles to his plan surfaced, he wanted to quit and walk away from the group. But he stuck with it and remained confident that his project would turn out fine. Another student, musing on the challenges of the assignment, wondered how presidents could persevere through all the problems they encountered on the job.

Self-Directed Learners in Elementary School

Students in this 6th grade classroom have been keeping a folder of their writing throughout the school year. The teacher suggests that they build a portfolio, which should show improvement on the basis of the standards emphasized during the year. Students look over their work and choose examples that show growth, selecting two pieces from early in the year, two from the middle, and two from the end.

Students actively make choices and reflect on their thinking by responding in writing to a number of questions: Why did you choose this piece? How did you modify your writing using the feedback you received from both your "critical friend" and the teacher? How does your progress as a writer demonstrate your continuous learning? One student noted that she was trying to become more creative in her writing and that she enjoyed making readers laugh.

Assessment will be based on the following criteria:
- Clarity of content and perspective
- Organization
- Presentation: Use of examples and visual aids

Speaker rating (1 = excellent, 4 = limited):

1. Excellent speaker confidently explains the candidate's point of view. The main points are significant and accurate. Speaker provides good examples and clear, creative, and persuasive visual aids.

2. Very good speaker presents the candidate's point of view and is clear and well organized. The speaker provides good examples and effective visual aids.

3. Moderate speaker presents the candidate's point of view. Chosen points are not always the most significant ones. The speaker provides few examples; the visual aids do not necessarily help to make a point. The sequence of the presentation is sometimes confusing.

4. Limited speaker shows a limited understanding of the candidate's point of view. The presentation is difficult to follow, with few examples. Visual aids are limited and difficult to interpret.

Figure 3   How effectively did you present your political candidate?

Students also write a letter to the reader of their portfolios, celebrating their growth as writers during the year. Writing a letter to a particular audience helps students recognize their thinking styles and capabilities as they formalize their perceptions about how they work. Students respond to prompts that ask them to clarify what they are good at in writing, what skills they have difficulty with and where they would like to improve, and what gets them excited about the writing process (see Figure 4). In one such portfolio, a student explained that she learned about microbiology most effectively when she was conducting lab activities and building models. She noted that as a physically active person, she learned best when she could move around the classroom. She also pointed out that her growing understanding of science bolstered her respect for a healthy body and a healthy environment.

An Other-Directed Era

Unfortunately, educators are awash in a sea of too many standards for the number of days in a school year, and they are struggling to find their direction (Marzano & Kendall, 1998). Further, in the current political climate, the key to school success is higher test scores. Externally administered assessments tied to these standards shift the focus of teaching to transmitting test-related information and make it difficult to sustain curriculum and instructional strategies designed for individual meaning making and personal, self-directed learning. Although we may desire to develop students' capacities for self-directedness, we may be helping to mold a generation of other-directed, dependent, externally motivated learners.

Educators must persist in developing self-directed learners in an other-directed education era. We must reclaim a sense of direction based on what we value most and provide education experiences that enable students to become responsible, self-directed, continuous learners.

We must make our good intentions a reality by explicitly addressing what we value through curriculum design, thoughtful instruction, and opportunities for student self-assessment and reflection. Students need the opportunity to look back and reflect on finished work. They also need to learn how to look forward to the next assignment with strategies for improvement. Too often we hear students say, "I already finished that assignment!", as though completing the task—rather than learning from the process—is what matters. When teachers focus on student self-direction, however, the question changes. Students ask themselves, "What have I learned? Who am I becoming?"

Students ask themselves, "What have I learned? Who am I becoming?"

Striving for excellence is a lifelong task, not a singular event meant to satisfy a teacher. We want to see students develop a love of learning and not feel solely dependent on the judgment of others to determine the value of what they are learning. Given many opportunities over time, students will frequently assess themselves and cultivate the strength and humility of continuous learning.

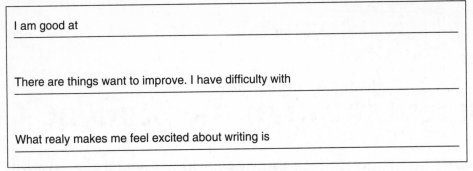

I am good at

There are things want to improve. I have difficulty with

What realy makes me feel excited about writing is

Figure 4　I am celebrating my growth in writing this year.

References

Baker, B., Costa, A., & Shalit, S. (1997). Norms of collaboration: Attaining communicative competence. In A. Costa & R. Liebmann (Eds.), *The process-centered school: Sustaining a Renaissance Community* (pp. 119–142). Thousand Oaks, CA: Corwin.

Costa, A., & Garmston, R. (2001). *Cognitive coaching: A foundation for renaissance schools.* Norwood, MA: Christopher-Gordon.

Costa, A., & Kallick, B. (2000). *Habits of mind: A developmental series.* Alexandria, VA: ASCD.

Costa A., & Kallick, B. (2004). *Assessment strategies for self-directed learning.* Thousand Oaks, CA: Corwin.

Marzano, R. J., & Kendall, J. S. (1998). *Awash in a sea of standards.* Aurora, CO: Mid-continent Research for Education and Learning.

Moulds, P. (2003–2004). Rich tasks. *Educational Leadership, 51*(4), 75–79.

ARTHUR L. COSTA is Professor Emeritus at California State University, Sacramento, California; artcosta@aol.com. **BENA KALLICK** is an education consultant in Westport, Connecticut; bkallick@aol.com. They are coauthors of *Habits of the Mind: A Developmental Series* (ASCD, 2000).

From *Educational Leadership,* September 2004. Copyright © 2004 by ASCD. Reprinted by permission. The Association for Supervision and Curriculum Development is a worldwide community of educators advocating sound policies and sharing best practices to achieve the success of each learner. To learn more, visit ASCD at www.ascd.org

Assessment through the Student's Eyes

Rather than sorting students into winners and losers, assessment for learning can put all students on a winning streak.

RICK STIGGINS

Historically, a major role of assessment has been to detect and highlight differences in student learning in order to rank students according to their achievement. Such assessment experiences have produced winners and losers. Some students succeed early and build on winning streaks to learn more as they grow; others fail early and often, falling farther and farther behind.

As we all know, the mission of schools has changed. Today's schools are less focused on merely sorting students and more focused on helping all students succeed in meeting standards. This evolution in the mission of schools means that we can't let students who have not yet met standards fall into losing streaks, succumb to hopelessness, and stop trying.

> **We can't let students who have not yet met standards fall into losing streaks, succumb to hopelessness, and stop trying.**

Our evolving mission compels us to embrace a new vision of assessment that can tap the wellspring of confidence, motivation, and learning potential that resides within every student. First, we need to tune in to the emotional dynamics of the assessment experience from the point of view of students-both assessment winners and assessment losers. These two groups experience assessment practices in vastly different ways, as shown in "The Assessment Experience." To enable all students to experience the productive emotional dynamics of winning, we need to move from exclusive reliance on assessments that verify learning to the use of assessments that support learning—that is, assessments *for* learning.

Assessment *for* Learning

Assessment for learning turns day-to-day assessment into a teaching and learning process that enhances (instead of merely monitoring) student learning. Extensive research conducted around the world shows that by consistently applying the principles of assessment for learning, we can produce impressive gains in student achievement, especially for struggling learners (Black & Wiliam, 1998).

Assessment for learning begins when teachers share achievement targets with students, presenting those expectations in student-friendly language accompanied by examples of exemplary student work. Then, frequent self-assessments provide students (and teachers) with continual access to descriptive feedback in amounts they can manage effectively without being overwhelmed. Thus, students can chart their trajectory toward the transparent achievement targets their teachers have established.

The students' role is to strive to understand what success looks like, to use feedback from each assessment to discover where they are now in relation to where they want to be, and to determine how to do better the next time. As students become increasingly proficient, they learn to generate their own descriptive feedback and set goals for what comes next on their journey.

Teachers and students are partners in the assessment for learning process. For example, teachers might have students study samples of work that vary in quality and collaborate in creating their own student-friendly version of a performance assessment scoring rubric. Or students might create practice versions of multiple-choice tests that parallel the content of an upcoming final exam, which they can then use to analyze their own strengths and weaknesses and to focus their final preparation for that exam. Students can accumulate evidence of their learning in growth portfolios. They can also become partners with teachers in communicating about their own learning successes by leading their parent/teacher conferences.

Assessment for learning provides both students and teachers with understandable information in a form they can use immediately to improve performance. In this context, students become both self-assessors and consumers of assessment information. As they experience and understand their own improvement over time, learners begin to sense that success is within reach if they

The Assessment Experience

For Students on Winning Streaks	For Students on Losing Streaks
Assessment Results Provide	
Continual evidence of success	Continual evidence of failure
The Student Feels	
Hopeful and optimistic	Hopeless
Empowered to take productive action	Initially panicked, giving way to resignation
The Student Thinks	
It's all good. I'm doing fine.	This hurts. I'm not safe here.
See the trend? I succeed as usual.	I just can't do this . . . again.
I want more success.	I'm confused. I don't like this—help!
School focuses on what I do well.	Why is it always about what I can't do?
I know what to do next.	Nothing I try seems to work.
Feedback helps me.	Feedback is criticism. It hurts.
Public success feels good.	Public failure is embarrassing.
The Student Becomes More Likely To	
Seek challenges.	Seek what's easy.
Seek exciting new ideas.	Avoid new concepts and approaches.
Practice with gusto.	Become confused about what to practice.
Take initiative.	Avoid initiative.
Persist in the face of setbacks.	Give up when things become challenging.
Take risks and stretch—go for it!	Retreat and escape—trying is too dangerous!
These Actions Lead To	
Self-enhancement	Self-defeat, self-destruction
Positive self-fulfilling prophecy	Negative self-fulfilling prophecy
Acceptance of responsibility	Denial of responsibility
Manageable stress	High stress
Feeling that success is its own reward	No feelings of success; no reward
Curiosity, enthusiasm	Boredom, frustration, fear
Continuous adaptation	Inability to adapt
Resilience	Yielding quickly to defeat
Strong foundations for future success	Failure to master prerequisites for future success

keep trying. This process can put them on a winning streak and keep them there.

When we use assessment for learning, assessment becomes far more than merely a one-time event stuck onto the end of an instructional unit. It becomes a series of interlaced experiences that enhance the learning process by keeping students confident and focused on their progress, even in the face of occasional setbacks.

The goal of assessment for learning is not to eliminate failure, but rather to keep failure from becoming chronic and thus inevitable in the mind of the learner. Duke University basketball coach Mike Krzyzewski has pointed out that the key to winning is to avoid losing twice in a row (Kanter, 2004, p. 251). He meant that if you lose once and fix it, you can remain confident. Losing twice, though, can raise questions, crack that confidence, and make recovery more difficult. So

when learners suffer a failure, we must get them back to success as quickly as possible to restore their confidence in their capabilities. This is the emotional dynamic of assessment for learning.

Scenario 1: Set Students up for Success

Here is an example of the use of assessment for learning that builds student confidence from the start. Notice who develops and uses the assessment.

A high school English teacher assigns students to read three novels by the same author and develop a thesis statement about a common theme, consistent character development, or social commentary in the novels. They must then defend that thesis in a term paper with references. To set students up for success, the teacher begins by providing them with a sample of an outstanding paper to read and analyze. The next day, the class discusses what made the sample outstanding.

As their next assignment, the teacher gives students a sample paper of poor quality. Again, they analyze and evaluate its features in some detail. Comparing the two papers, students list essential differences. The class then uses this analysis to collaboratively decide on the keys to a high-quality paper.

After identifying and defining those keys, the students share in the process of transforming them into a rubric—a set of rating scales depicting a continuum of quality for each key. The teacher provides examples of student work to illustrate each level on the quality continuum.

Only after these specific understandings are in place do students draft their papers. Then they exchange drafts, analyzing and evaluating one another's work and providing descriptive feedback on how to improve it, always using the language of the rubric. If students want descriptive feedback from their teacher on any particular dimension of quality, they can request and will receive it. The paper is finished when the student says it is finished. In the end, not every paper is outstanding, but most are of high quality, and each student is confident of that fact before submitting his or her work for final evaluation and grading (Stiggins, in press; Scenario 1 adapted by permission).

Scenario 2: Help Students Turn Failure into Success

Here is an illustration of assessment for learning in mathematics used to help a struggling elementary student find the path to recovery from a chronic sense of failure. Notice how the teacher highlights the meaning of success and turns the responsibility over to the student. In addition, notice how the learner has already begun to internalize the keys to her own success.

Gail is a 5th grader who gets her math test back with "60 percent" marked at the top. She knows this means another *F*. So her losing streak continues, she thinks. She's ready to give up on ever connecting with math.

But then her teacher distributes another paper—a worksheet the students will use to learn from their performance on the math test. What's up with this? The worksheet has several columns. Column one lists the 20 test items by number. Column two lists what math proficiency each item tested. The teacher calls the class's attention to the next two columns: *Right* and *Wrong*. She asks the students to fill in those columns with checks for each item to indicate their performance on the test. Gail checks 12 right and 8 wrong.

The teacher then asks the students to evaluate as honestly as they can why they got each incorrect item wrong and to check column five if they made a simple mistake and column six if they really don't understand what went wrong. Gail discovers that four of her eight incorrect answers were caused by careless mistakes that she knows how to fix. But four were math problems she really doesn't understand how to solve.

Next, the teacher goes through the list of math concepts covered item by item, enabling Gail and her classmates to determine exactly what concepts they don't understand. Gail discovers that all four of her wrong answers that reflect a true lack of understanding arise from the same gap in her problem-solving ability: subtracting 3-digit numbers with regrouping. If she had just avoided those careless mistakes and had also overcome this one gap in understanding, she might have received 100 percent. Imagine that! If she could just do the test over . . .

She can. Because Gail's teacher has mapped out precisely what each item on the test measures, the teacher and students can work in partnership to group the students according to the math concepts they haven't yet mastered. The teacher then provides differentiated instruction to the groups focused on their conceptual misunderstandings. Together the class also plans strategies that everyone can use to avoid simple mistakes. When that work is complete, the teacher gives students a second form of the same math test. When Gail gets the test back with a grade of 100 percent, she jumps from her seat with arms held high. Her winning streak begins (Stiggins, Arter, Chappuis, & Chappuis, 2004; Scenario 2 adapted by permission).

Redefining Our Assessment Future

We know how to deliver professional development that will give practitioners the tools and technologies they need to use assessment effectively in the service of student success. (Stiggins et al., 2004; Stiggins & Chappuis, 2006). Thus far, however, the immense potential of assessment for learning has gone largely untapped because we have failed to deliver the proper tools into the hands of teachers and school leaders. If we are to fulfill our mission of leaving no child behind, we must adjust our vision of excellence in assessment in at least two important ways that will help us balance assessment of and assessment *for* learning.

First, we must expand the criteria by which we evaluate the quality of our assessments at all levels and in all contexts. Traditionally, we have judged quality in terms of the attributes of the resulting scores; these scores must lead to valid and reliable inferences about student achievement. As a result, schools have lavished attention on characteristics of the instruments that produce such scores. In the future, however, we must recognize that assessment is about far more than the test score's dependability—it also must be about the score's effect on the learner. Even the most valid and reliable assessment cannot be regarded as high quality if it causes a student to give up.

Assessment cannot be regarded as high quality if it causes a student to give up.

We must begin to evaluate our assessments in terms of both the quality of the evidence they yield and the effect they have on future learning. High-quality assessments encourage further learning; low-quality assessments hinder learning. Understanding the emotional dynamics of the assessment experience from the student's perspective is crucial to the effective use of assessments to improve schools.

Second, we must abandon the limiting belief that adults represent the most important assessment consumers or data-based decision makers in schools. Students' thoughts and actions regarding assessment results are at least as important as those of adults. The students' emotional reaction to results will determine what they do in response. Whether their score is high or low, students respond productively when they say, "I understand. I know what to do next. I can handle this. I choose to keep trying." From here on, the result will be more learning. The counterproductive response is, "I don't know what this means. I have no idea what to do next. I'm probably too dumb to learn this anyway. I give up." Here, the learning stops.

In standards-driven schools, only one of these responses works, especially for students who have yet to meet standards. Assessment for learning is about eliciting that productive response to assessment results from students every time. It can produce winning streaks for all students.

References

Black, P., & Wiliam, D. (1998). Assessment and classroom learning. *Educational Assessment: Principles, Policy, and Practice, 5*(1), 7–74.

Kanter, R. M. (2004). *Confidence: How winning streaks and losing streaks begin and end.* New York: Crown Business.

Stiggins, R. J. (in press). Conquering the formative assessment frontier. In J. McMillan (Ed.), *Formative assessment: Theory into practice.* New York: Teachers College Press.

Stiggins, R. J., Arter, J. A., Chappuis, J., & Chappuis, S. (2004). *Classroom assessment FOR student learning: Doing it right— using it well.* Portland, OR: ETS Assessment Training Institute.

Stiggins, R. J., & Chappuis, J. (2006). What a difference a word makes: Assessment FOR learning rather than assessment of learning helps students succeed. *Journal of Staff Development, 27*(1), 10–14.

RICK STIGGINS is Founder and Director of the ETS Assessment Training Institute, 317 SW Alder St., Suite 1200, Portland, OR, 97204; 800-480-3060; www.ets.org/ati.

Test-Your-Knowledge Form

We encourage you to photocopy and use this page as a tool to assess how the articles in *Annual Editions* expand on the information in your textbook. By reflecting on the articles you will gain enhanced text information. You can also access this useful form on a product's book support website at *http://www.mhcls.com*.

NAME: _____   DATE: _____

TITLE AND NUMBER OF ARTICLE: _____

BRIEFLY STATE THE MAIN IDEA OF THIS ARTICLE:

_____

LIST THREE IMPORTANT FACTS THAT THE AUTHOR USES TO SUPPORT THE MAIN IDEA:

_____

WHAT INFORMATION OR IDEAS DISCUSSED IN THIS ARTICLE ARE ALSO DISCUSSED IN YOUR TEXTBOOK OR OTHER READINGS THAT YOU HAVE DONE? LIST THE TEXTBOOK CHAPTERS AND PAGE NUMBERS:

_____

LIST ANY EXAMPLES OF BIAS OR FAULTY REASONING THAT YOU FOUND IN THE ARTICLE:

_____

LIST ANY NEW TERMS/CONCEPTS THAT WERE DISCUSSED IN THE ARTICLE, AND WRITE A SHORT DEFINITION:

We Want Your Advice

ANNUAL EDITIONS revisions depend on two major opinion sources: one is our Advisory Board, listed in the front of this volume, which works with us in scanning the thousands of articles published in the public press each year; the other is you—the person actually using the book. Please help us and the users of the next edition by completing the prepaid article rating form on this page and returning it to us. Thank you for your help!

ANNUAL EDITIONS: Assessment and Evaluation 10/11

ARTICLE RATING FORM

Here is an opportunity for you to have direct input into the next revision of this volume.
We would like you to rate each of the articles listed below, using the following scale:

1. **Excellent: should definitely be retained**
2. **Above average: should probably be retained**
3. **Below average: should probably be deleted**
4. **Poor: should definitely be deleted**

Your ratings will play a vital part in the next revision.
Please mail this prepaid form to us as soon as possible.
Thanks for your help!

RATING	ARTICLE
	1. Assessments and Accountability (Condensed version)
	2. Why Has High-Stakes Testing So Easily Slipped into Contemporary American Life?
	3. Assessment around the World
	4. Are Standards Preventing Good Teaching?
	5. Schools, Poverty, and the Achievement Gap
	6. Making Benchmark Testing Work
	7. Mapping the Road to Proficiency
	8. Curriculum Mapping: Building Collaboration and Communication
	9. Developing Standards-Based Curricula and Assessments: Lessons from the Field
	10. Assessing Problem-Solving Thought
	11. Looking at How Students Reason
	12. Engineering Successful Inclusion in Standards-Based Urban Classrooms
	13. The Best Value in Formative Assessment
	14. Learning to Love Assessment
	15. Classroom Assessment: Minute by Minute, Day by Day
	16. Seven Practices for Effective Learning
	17. Homework: A Few Practice Arrows
	18. Using Curriculum-Based Measurement to Improve Achievement
	19. Research Matters/How Student Progress Monitoring Improves Instruction

RATING	ARTICLE
	20. Teaching with Rubrics: The Good, the Bad, and the Ugly
	21. Designing Scoring Rubrics for Your Classroom
	22. A Teacher's Guide to Alternative Assessment: Taking the First Steps
	23. Digital-Age Assessment: E-Portfolios Are the Wave of the Future
	24. Using Data to Differentiate Instruction
	25. First Things First: Demystifying Data Analysis
	26. Data in the Driver's Seat
	27. Testing and Assessment 101
	28. Making Instructional Decisions Based on Data: What, How, and Why
	29. Answering the Questions That Count
	30. Feedback That Fits
	31. Developing Teacher-Parent Partnerships across Cultures: Effective Parent Conferences
	32. Partnerships for Learning: Conferencing with Families
	33. Student-Led Parent-Teacher Conferences
	34. Grades as Valid Measures of Academic Achievement of Classroom Learning
	35. Grading to Communicate
	36. Making the Grade in Middle School
	37. Helping Students Understand Assessment
	38. Self-Assessment through Rubrics
	39. Launching Self-Directed Learners
	40. Assessment through the Student's Eyes

NO POSTAGE
NECESSARY
IF MAILED
IN THE
UNITED STATES

ABOUT YOU

Name

Date

Are you a teacher? ☐ A student? ☐
Your school's name

Department

Address   City   State   Zip

School telephone #

YOUR COMMENTS ARE IMPORTANT TO US!

Please fill in the following information:
For which course did you use this book?

Did you use a text with this ANNUAL EDITION? ☐ yes ☐ no
What was the title of the text?

What are your general reactions to the Annual Editions concept?

Have you read any pertinent articles recently that you think should be included in the next edition? Explain.

Are there any articles that you feel should be replaced in the next edition? Why?

Are there any World Wide Websites that you feel should be included in the next edition? Please annotate.

May we contact you for editorial input? ☐ yes ☐ no
May we quote your comments? ☐ yes ☐ no